Town and country in pre-industrial Spain

Cambridge Studies in Population, Economy and Society in Past Time

Series Editors:

PETER LASLETT, ROGER SCHOFIELD and E. A. WRIGLEY

ESRC Cambridge Group for the History of Population and Social Structure

and DANIEL SCOTT SMITH

University of Illinois at Chicago

Recent work, in social, economic and demographic history has revealed much that was previously obscure about societal stability and change in the past. It has also suggested that crossing the conventional boundaries between these branches of history can be very rewarding.

This series will exemplify the value of interdisciplinary work of this kind, and will include books on topics such as family, kinship and neighbourhood; welfare provision and social control; work and leisure; migration; urban growth; and legal structures and procedures, as well as more familiar matters. It will demonstrate that for example, anthropology and economics have become as close intellectual neighbours to history as have political philosophy or biography.

Town and country in pre-industrial Spain

Cuenca, 1550–1870

DAVID SVEN REHER

*Associate Professor, School of Political
Science and Sociology, Universidad
Complutense de Madrid*

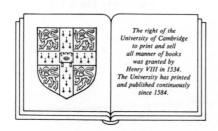

The right of the
University of Cambridge
to print and sell
all manner of books
was granted by
Henry VIII in 1534.
The University has printed
and published continuously
since 1584.

CAMBRIDGE UNIVERSITY PRESS

Cambridge
New York   Port Chester
Melbourne   Sydney

Published by the Press Syndicate of the University of Cambridge
The Pitt Building, Trumpington Street, Cambridge CB2 1RP
40 West 20th Street, New York, NY 10011, USA
10 Stamford Road, Oakleigh, Melbourne 3166, Australia

© Cambridge University Press 1990

First published 1990

Printed in Great Britain at the University Press, Cambridge

British Library cataloguing in publication data
Reher, David Sven
Town and country in pre-industrial Spain: Cuenca
1550–1870. – (Cambridge studies in population
economy and society in past time; 12)
1. Spain. Cuenca. Economic conditions, history.
Demographic aspects
I. Title
330.946'47

Library of Congress cataloguing in publication data
Reher, David Sven
Town and country in pre-industrial Spain: Cuenca 1550–1870
David Sven Reher.
p.   cm. – (Cambridge studies in population, economy, and
society in past time; 12)
Bibliography.
Includes Index.
ISBN 0–521–35292–4
1. Cuenca (Spain) – Population – History.
2. Cuenca (Spain) – Economic conditions.
3. Cuenca (Spain) – History.
I. Title.   II. Series.
HB3620.C84R44   1990
304.6'0946'47 – dc20   89–35676   CIP

ISBN 0 521 35292 4

*This book is dedicated to
my parents Anne and Sven
and to my boys
Antonio and Guillermo*

Contents

Tables

Illustrations

FIGURES

Preface

Research for this book began many years ago during the Fall of 1975. Over the years many of the original postulates underlying the project have changed. At first I was very influenced by the French "Annales" school of historiography, but as the project progressed the work of British and American currents of historical demography and social history became increasingly important to me. Both of these sources of inspiration can be seen in this book. My original ties to the town of Cuenca were purely circumstantial, and were based on its accessibility to Madrid and the existence of adequate archival sources. Now my attitude to the town is anything but indifferent. This book is written in homage to a beautiful, often forgotten and little understood town which centuries ago became trapped in the backwaters of Castilian history and was never again able to free itself.

This project would never have been possible without the help of many people. Antonio Domínguez Ortiz, the premier historian of early modern Spain, guided my steps from the very beginning. Had he not graciously accepted me as a doctoral student in 1974, the present book might never have been finished. People and institutions in Cuenca and in Madrid also gave me much needed support. Dimas Pérez Ramírez, archivist of the Diocesan Archive of Cuenca, and Elena Lázaro Corral and, later, Miguel Jiménez Monteserin, archivists of the Municipal Archive facilitated my work in every possible way. Felipe Ruiz Martín, Jordi Nadal, Vicente Pérez Moreda, Juan Sanz Sampelayo and Julio Molina generously allowed me to use some unpublished results of their own research. Carlos Sanz Blanco, Pedro Luis Iriso and Javier Gavilán shared their technical expertise with me; Manuel Pinedo, Francisco Blanco, Beatriz Nogueras, Carlos Muñoz, Nieves Pombo and Margarita Delgado helped in different aspects of archival research, and Guillermo and Antonio Reher drew up many of the figures and maps in the text. I owe them all a very real debt of thanks.

In the course of this project I have also received considerable institutional support. Two grants greatly facilitated my work. IBM Spain gave on-going funding for the computing aspects of the project, and its employees José Luis Ruiz and Jesús Sánchez Lladó willingly and patiently answered my queries and solved most of the computing problems related to the project. The actual writing of this book was greatly facilitated by a grant received from the Tinker Foundation of New York during the 1987–1988 academic year. During that period, the Universidad Complutense de Madrid gave me academic leave which proved essential for the completion of the project. I have also benefited from prolonged stays with the Cambridge Group for the History of Population in Cambridge, England (during the Summers of 1986 and 1988) and with the Graduate Group in Demography at the University of California at Berkeley (during the 1987–1988 academic year).

Massimo Livi Bacci, Peter Laslett, Dudley Baines, Patrick Galloway, David Ringrose, Vincente Pérez Moreda, Richard Wall, and Robert Lee have read different parts of the manuscript. Their incisive and often pointed critical comments have enabled me to correct many of the weak points of my text. They are responsible for much of what is good in this book. Any mistakes or weaknesses are entirely mine.

1

Towns in historical perspective

Towns were uniquely important for all sectors of pre-industrial societies. For the peasant a town was a foreboding place because it was alien to his rural way of life, the source of power which conditioned his existence and drained away an important part of any surplus he might have via taxes and rents. Yet he needed it in countless ways for his own economic and spiritual survival: it was the market for many of the goods he produced, the center of religious and civil authority where conflicts could be resolved or petitions made, and the place where he could take refuge in times of crises. For the Crown, towns were a vital part of the entire structure of royal authority and taxation; for the nobility, especially after the end of the fifteenth century, they were ideal places to live; for the bourgeois and artisan sectors of society, they were essential to their very existence. Societies in which towns were numerous and large were considered prosperous; societies with few towns were backward; Italy and the Low Countries, on the one hand, and European Russia, on the other, are examples of this.

For students of historical societies, towns, urban areas and urban systems are no less important. They have been considered the hallmark of industrialization and modernization processes, and, more generally, an important stimulus for change. Most authors insist on the fact that towns can only be understood within the context of the society as a whole, and yet high levels of urbanization (especially when not centered on one parasitical city) are often considered key indicators of general economic well-being and modernization.[1] The

---

[1] In *The Structures of Everyday Life* Fernand Braudel stated that urbanization was "the sign of modern man." He did, however, qualify this by insisting that: "these densely populated cities, in part parasites, do not arise of their own volition. They are what society, the economy and politics allow or oblige them to be. They are a yardstick, a means of measurement . . . Above all, a great city should never be judged in itself: it is

1

idea of towns as motors of change has provoked widespread debate among historians. Many authors feel that towns were often mere theaters for economic processes whose origins had little to do with their existence, or at least that towns should be viewed as parts, or manifestations, of social, economic and political systems.[2] Few authors, however, doubt that high levels of urbanization and integrated urban systems have traditionally been the signs of economically healthy societies.[3]

The present study, however, is not primarily concerned with the role played by towns for economic growth in society as a whole. Rather, it is an attempt to understand human behavior patterns in towns. While these patterns have demographic, economic, social, cultural and geographic implications, basically they are all modes of individual and collective human behavior. Urban residents rather than towns themselves will be central to our analysis. Ultimately we will ask whether, from a behavioral standpoint, as Braudel once said, "a town is always a town."[4] Despite its apparent simplicity, the question is a complicated one and, if we are to address it adequately, several different analytical frameworks must be used.

Some years ago, Roger Mols in his monumental *Introduction à la démographie des villes d'Europe du XIVe au XVIIIe siècle* defined towns by their demographic importance (population density and size) and the economic and administrative functions they fulfilled. While, much like most other historians and geographers, he ended up using a threshold size to identify towns (in his case, 4,000 inhabitants), his definition emphasizes the importance of towns as links between the rural world and the rest of society, and between rural areas and other urban centers. The key here is the central function performed by the

---

located within the whole mass of urban systems, both animating them and being in turn determined by them" (1981: vol. 1, pp. 556–557).

[2] The classic analysis of the role played by towns in economic growth is E. A. Wrigley's paper on the importance of London for English society and economy (1967). At a more theoretical level, and to some extent contradicting both Wrigley and Braudel, Philip Abrams (1978: 23) feels that towns played no causal role in economic growth but rather were simply the places in which those processes of growth took place. Numerous other authors have participated in a debate which touches on a wide range of subjects, from the parasitical nature of large towns to the economic significance of entire urban systems. See, for example, Wrigley (1978), Daunton (1978), de Vries (1984), Ringrose (1983), Hoselitz (1953, 1954), Sjoberg (1960), Reisman (1964), Hohenberg and Lees (1985).

[3] Hohenberg and Lees suggest that this may not be entirely true when referring to Mediterranean Europe (1985: 108).

[4] See Braudel (1981: 481). This opinion is vigorously opposed by Abrams (1978: 9, 17, 24–25).

town linking its hinterland to the outside world.[5] Both the rural world and society as a whole end up being essential components of Mols' definition of towns.

The importance of the extra-urban world for an adequate understanding of the make-up and functions of urban societies, and possibly of urban behavior as well, should not be underestimated. Individual towns were tied both to their own hinterlands and to other towns. The relationship of towns to their surrounding countryside was based on more than the mere perception of rural rents, the subjugation of rural areas to urban administrations, the export of urban-produced goods to rural markets and the purchase of rural agricultural products in towns. Urban behaviour patterns were different from those in rural areas, and frequently towns have been considered agents of change for their surrounding areas as well. To what extent are these ideas empirically sound? To what extent was urban behavior different? Were towns in pre-industrial societies motors of change? There are no ready answers to these questions and there is even evidence that the existence of towns may have helped reinforce social and economic structures in rural areas, especially insofar as they provided an escape valve for rural populations.

A more basic question deals with the extent to which people in towns lived apart from their rural roots. Here, once again, the answer is unclear. It is not easy to identify the directionality of influence between the rural and urban worlds. In Braudel's words (1981:486), "the towns urbanized the countryside, but the countryside 'ruralized' the towns too." Braudel was speaking of economic relations; might the same "reciprocity of persepctives" be said to exist for human behavior as well? Probably the influence was mutual, and rural behavior patterns were not entirely dissimilar to those of the inhabitants of towns. Migrants themselves were probably the key agents of many of these links. Their movement from the village to the town, and often back again, ended up being an on-going contribution of rural attitudes to urban life, and perhaps also of urban attitudes and patterns to rural areas. The role of migration and, more generally, of human exchanges between towns and their countryside, loom as essential parts of our entire discussion. The nature of the relations linking urban and rural behavior patterns is an open issue of vital importance if we are to reach

[5] Mols' entire approach to societies is based on the conviction that they are completely integrated systems. "Dès qu'une agglomération remplit vis-à-vis des localités environnantes le rôle du coeur ou du cerveau chez un être vivant, cette agglomération possède une fonction centrale. Ainsi, en toute rigueur, le noyau paroissial ou administratif d'une commune, même rurale, remplit une fonction centrale vis-à-vis des hameaux" (Mols, 1954–1956: vol. 1, pp. xxi-xxii).

an adequate understanding of the role played by towns in early modern societies.

The factors influencing urban behavior were not restricted to local dynamics. Demographers studying more recent periods have considered that regional "cultural" variables played a key explanatory role during the demographic transition in Europe.[6] One of the most remarkable aspects of Spain has been and is the existence of pronounced regional patterns of human behavior, cultural structures, and economic realities. Spanish regional variation seems to be even more pronounced than in most other European nations. The fact that urban populations participated in larger regional cultural patterns would help explain why striking similarities between urban and rural dynamics always seem to crop up when one studies Spain's past. This was unquestionably the case between 1860 and 1930, and was probably also true at earlier dates.[7]

Yet urban behavior cannot be entirely explained either by rural or by regional influences. It is also true that "a town is a town" and life there differed radically from life in rural areas. Population densities were much higher, infections spread more easily, economies were monetary, practically everyone depended on the marketplace for food, and active population structures differed completely from those in the countryside. These were the symbols of urban culture and society and were bound to affect urban patterns of behavior. An understanding of these specifically "urban" aspects of towns is essential if we are to approach the subject in a fruitful way. If behavior was influenced by immediate economic and social factors, then urban patterns were bound to differ from rural ones. We already know that nuptiality and fertility tended to be lower and mortality higher in urban areas, and these may only be the most visible differences. One of the goals of this book is to arrive at a clear empirical understanding of the specificity of urban behavior.

Studying towns and behavior is clearly a question of perspective, or rather, perspectives. Urban patterns must be seen in conjunction with those of their own hinterlands, of their regions and of those common to all urban areas. In this book a number of key issued will be analyzed from these different perspectives. In chapter 2 the basic economic and social structures of towns will be defined and their development

---

[6] This was one of the basic results stemming from the Princeton European Fertility Project. See Coale and Watkins (1986).

[7] For recent work emphasizing the regional diversity of Spain's population history, see Reher (1986, 1989a); Iriso Napal and Reher (1987); Nadal (1988); Pérez Moreda (1988a); Rowland, (1988); Livi Bacci (1988). William Leasure (1963) was one of the first to point out the demographic importance of regional variables in Spain.

traced, and patterns of urbanization will be analyzed.[8] Much of the rest of the book will be dedicated to analyzing aspects of collective and individual urban behavior. Demographic patterns, the relation between economic fluctuations and vital events, human and institutional responses in times of crisis, family and inheritance practices, and migrational patterns will all be discussed. In every case the existing patterns of behavior will be defined as precisely as possible. The extent to which these patterns are specifically urban, or rather reveal rural and/or regional roots, is central to our entire discussion, and I have therefore made abundant use throughout the book of comparative examples taken from both rural areas and towns.

The task, though, is not a simple one because it hinges not only on detecting the similarities, but also on defining the directionality of influence. Did towns influence their surrounding areas, did the rural areas influence towns, or was it perhaps a combination of both? The subject of migrational patterns (rural to urban, urban to rural, and urban to urban) looms as a key issue not only for behavioral patterns in individual towns, but also for the structuring of the entire urban system. Braudel (1981: 489–490) felt that basically it was the poor who migrated to towns from local rural areas, and bourgeois migrants only came from other towns. Was this true? Evidence would suggest that perhaps Braudel over-simplified the social make-up of migrants, their geographical origin, and the direction of their movement.

The rural and the urban worlds were connected in numerous ways. The flow of rents and crops from the countryside to the town, that of manufactured goods, authority and culture from towns to villages, and that of migrants between both worlds were not the only points of contact. Family economies, marriage and job markets, and inheritance patterns often implicated both worlds simultaneously. Times of crisis tended to bring rural and urban areas into often conflictual contact. In this book I argue in favor of a holistic vision of pre-industrial society which includes both town and countryside as socially, economically and culturally interdependent entities.

Ultimately the central theme of this book addresses the question of urban structures and urban behavior patterns, whether or not they were influenced by rural, regional or specifically urban factors. In other words, it is a book about towns and human, economic and social

---

[8] Several valuable studies of Spanish towns have appeared since Bennassar's magnificent monograph on Valladolid was published in 1967. Our understanding of overall urbanization processes, however, has not fared so well. Other than some very general notions, very little is known about pre-1850 urbanization patterns in Spain. Ringrose's study of Madrid (1983) is the only attempt to analyze regional urban systems during the pre-industrial period.

Map 1. The province of Cuenca

behavior in towns. It is also a book about the Castilian town of Cuenca and its inhabitants between the sixteenth and the nineteenth centuries. This micro-analytical perspective will enable me to pinpoint more precisely a number of the mechanisms I have already mentioned and will stimulate more far-reaching discussion of urban areas in general. Taking Cuenca as a case in point, I hope to be able to verify or refute a number of the hypotheses mentioned earlier.

With a population today of just over 40,000 inhabitants and located midway between Madrid and Valencia, Cuenca is one of the smallest capitals in the Spain (Map 1.1). This has not always been the case. Originally the center of one of the *taifa* kingdoms in Al-Andalus, Cuenca was taken from the Muslims by the Christian armies under Alfonso VIII in 1177. In the centuries following its conquest Cuenca's geographical location worked to its economic advantage, and growth affected all sectors of urban society. Situated in the foothills of the Iberian mountain range which separated Castile from Aragon, it was able to control a good part of the transhumance along the Cuenca *cañada* which acquired such importance in Spain between the fourteenth and sixteenth centuries.[9] The result was an economy centered on the wool industry which provided raw material for export as well as for home manufacture.

The importance of the town grew steadily, especially after the latter part of the fourteenth century when the frontier of the Kingdom of Castile had moved definitively to the South and the political, demographic and economic turmoil of the thirteenth and fourteenth centuries had passed. The fifteenth and sixteenth centuries were ones of great prosperity for the town. During this period Cuenca, which had been given ample privileges in its *Fuero* (municipal charter) after the Conquest, increased its political, religious and economic importance in Castile. It was an episcopal see, one of the 18 Castilian towns with a vote in the Cortes, and the home of one of the early tribunals of the Inquisition (1489). It had a royal corregidor as well as a mint. The times of prosperity ended abruptly during the seventeenth century when the town's population diminished and it lost much of its economic importance. Despite a hesitant recovery of some of its earlier vitality during the eighteenth century, Cuenca was never again a significant national or even regional economic force. Throughout this period, however, it never lost its specifically urban nature: it continued to be a source of royal and ecclesiastical power and farming never occupied more than a very small part of its active population.

[9] *Cañadas* were the routes used by the transhumant flocks of medieval Spain. For more on this subject, see Klein (1920) and Iradiel Murugarren (1974).

One of the most characteristic aspects of Cuenca was and is its physical location. For the traveler in early modern Spain, or the peasant from some local village, the approach to the town must have been a very impressive one. Possibly the most prominent of all Spanish hill towns, Cuenca straddles the ridge leading from the valley floor towards the top of the Cerro de San Felipe, some 250 meters above. The town, and the ridge, are flanked by two canyons, two rivers and two hills as high as the Cerro de San Felipe. Cuenca often gives the impression of being perched above two abysses, and at some sections of the upper part of town, the distance between these two canyons is less than 75 meters. From the bottom of the town to the uppermost urbanized district around the castle, there is a gain in altitude of almost 150 meters, making for an incline of almost 15 per cent in the relatively short distance separating the two.

Cuenca has traditionally been a joy to contemplate, but hell to walk around in. This was in the minds of many travelers, both then and now. Antonio Ponz in his famous *Viage de España* (1789) points this out with a certain irony:

... the city of Cuenca is situated on a great hill, between two even taller hills, separated by two chasms made by the Jucar and the Huecar rivers. The walls of the city begin at the very base of the hill, and end at an extraordinarily high altitude. If you want to walk its streets, especially some of them, it is practically necessary to make use of pulleys; and I have been told that sometimes mules have been known to collapse if, after a normal day of work, they have been made to go to the top of the town under a full load. In order to reach the inn where I was staying ... which was not very far up the hill, I proceeded very slowly, not just out of compassion for the horse I was riding but also to keep from falling down on the streets of Cuenca, which seem to be made precisely for that. (Ponz, 1789: vol. 3, Carta primera, pp. 4–5)[10]

The town itself reflects the constraints of its geographical location. As Ponz pointedly stated, walking there was difficult and often dangerous. The laconic annotation in the parish registers that "he slipped on the ice and fell over the cliff" is not infrequent during the winter months. Available space was hard to come by and as the town began to grow during the fifteenth and sixteenth centuries, ingenious solutions were devised. At first, Cuenca descended from the medieval heights of the twelfth and thirteenth centuries in search of the valley floor; but once there, an unhealthy environment and more hills made

[10] There are a number of historical descriptions of Cuenca and most of them make special reference to its impressive geographical location. See, for example, Mártir Rizo (1629: 4–6), Quadrado and Fuente (1978: 243–247), and Doré and Davillier (1862–1873). An interesting description of Cuenca and life during the latter part of the eighteenth century, based on the magnificent view of the town made by Juan de Llanes y Massa, can be found in Jiménez Monteserín (1983).

further expansion difficult. Unlike any other medieval town in Spain and possibly in Europe, space was found by building upwards. The result was a unique distribution of urban space and probably the highest population density of any urban area in Spain. Once again the pen of Antonio Ponz gives us a succinct description of Cuenca:

Some of the houses, which practically hang from the cliffs in Cuenca, are 10 and even 12 stories high, and above the roofs of those you can see the foundations of others in such a way that from outside town you can normally see jackasses peering out of some window which seems to be the living room of one house, but is really the stable of another. (Ponz, 1789: vol. 3, Carta quinta, p. 127)[11]

Ponz was not exaggerating. All around the town, houses were practically perched at the edge of the cliffs, and there is a neighborhood in the vicinity of the parishes of San Martín and Santa Cruz, noted for its "skyscrapers." When seen from the east (from the Cerro del Socorro) these buildings were – and are – up to 10 stories high, while on the other side they are only three or four stories high. In this whole area of town the main entrance to houses always has two stairways, one leading up and the other down.

Cuenca is located between two impressive canyons shaped by two rivers, the Jucar and the Huecar, each of which has had differing importance for the town. To the West, the Jucar river, which originates in the mountains of Cuenca some 75 kms away and drains into the Mediterranean Sea south of Valencia, winds its way beneath the town through a very abrupt canyon. The Huecar, tributary to the Jucar, is little more than a stream, but it has always been by far the more important of the two for the life of the town. One of the springs feeding it was and is the source of potable water for the town and its waters irrigate many of the small farms along its banks which produce many of the vegetables consumed in town. Once it reaches the town itself, its valley opens up towards the flat lands to the south and thus it was also the river which has occasionally flooded the lower areas of town, fed the swampy lands which were only fully drained during the nineteenth century, and where most of the wool was washed. It closes off the entire old town to the south, and then flows into the Jucar. A fair idea of the lay-out of the town can be derived from a close inspection of the eighteenth-century map of Cuenca by Mateo López (Map 1.2).

[11] In 1778 the French traveler Jean François Peyron insisted on the same point: "and then in front of you appears the eagle's nest of the town of Cuenca. I have seldom seen a more picturesque or surprising sight. Imagine a town built in the heights on a naked outcropping of rock, and dominated by still more rugged mountains; and with houses whose doorways, you might say, are on the rooftops of the neighboring houses" Peyron (1783: vol. 2, pp. 132–133).

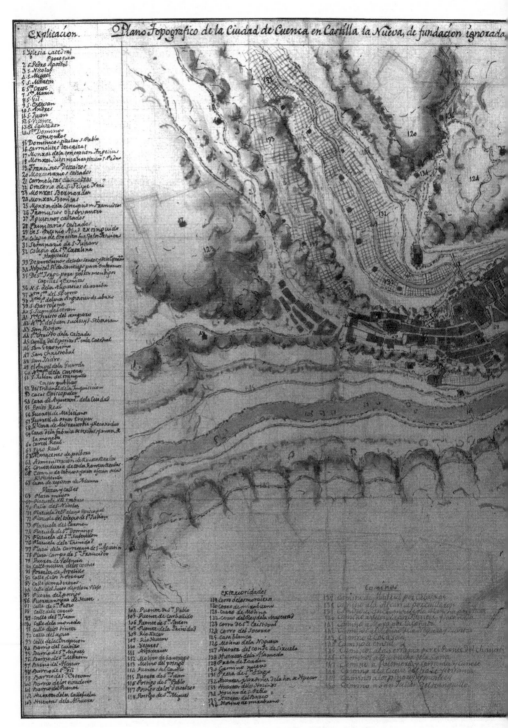

Map 1.2 Cuenca in the eighteenth century

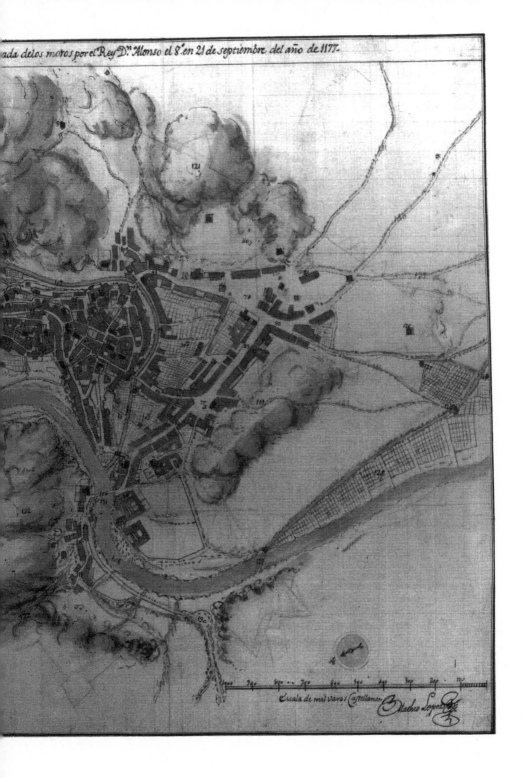

Escala de mil varas Castellanas

Matheo Lopez

One of the architectural symbols of Cuenca, before its destruction towards the end of the nineteenth century, and a source of continued admiration, was a bridge spanning the Huecar river canyon more than 50 meters above the river and some 150 meters long. It was built to connect the main town with the convent of San Pablo on the other side of the canyon. The bridge was commissioned in 1533, took 56 years to build and is said to have cost 63,000 ducats (more than the annual income of many of the most important noble houses in Spain). This bridge was commissioned and financed by Juan del Pozo, canon of the cathedral, who built the convent on the other side of the canyon as well.[12] Not only was the bridge a fitting testimony to the geographic realities of the town, and a tribute to the wealth and ingenuity of Juan del Pozo, it was also a symbol of the importance of the Church for the life of the town. Between the sixteenth and eighteenth centuries the Church was unquestionably the most important institution in town and many of the most ambitious construction and urban renewal projects during that period were financed by it.

Yet the story of Juan del Pozo's bridge is more than just the story of the philanthropic intentions of a cathedral canon, or of the economic importance of the Church. As Peyron noted in 1783, the money was spent with no other purpose in mind than to facilitate access of the faithful to the convent of San Pablo. Canon Pozo's faith, made manifest in the public works he promoted, or on his tombstone in San Pablo ("Here lies the unworthy Canon Juan del Pozo"), was shared by many of his fellow *conquenses*.[13] Popular faith was an ever-present aspect of Cuenca society which should not be forgotten when studying demographic, family or migratory patterns. Though it may not always be reflected in statistics, its presence is undeniable and, at least in Cuenca, any vision of urban society which failed to take account of it would be incomplete.

Ana Martínez and Pedro Bordallo are good examples of this popular faith. As young children in the parish of San Martín, some time around 1530, they had both taken vows of chastity in honor of Our Lady of Perpetual Help, and had promised to climb to her shrine atop the Cerro del Socorro (on the other side of the Huecar canyon) every day of their lives. According to the testimony registered in the year of their death in 1609, each was unaware that the other one had taken the vow and it only became known when the families tried to bring them together in marriage, because of their "equality in virtue, life and

---

[12] For more on Juan del Pozo's bridge, see Quadrado and Fuente (1978: 295–297), Ponz (1789: 115–119), Mártir Rizo (1629: 103–104), and Peyron (1783: vol. 2, p. 133).
[13] This name, pronounced 'konkenses', is given to the inhabitants of Cuenca.

customs." Their life together revolved around their devotion to Our Lady and, on her deathbed, Ana spoke of many near-miraculous experiences involving her and her trips to the shrine on the Cerro de Socorro. She died on 20 November 1609 and Pedro Bordallo died, mad, 19 days later. Religion and the Church were an essential part of the lives of the citizens of Cuenca. Ana Martínez and Pedro Bordallo were quintessential *conquenses*; the popular faith they so eloquently expressed was common to most of Spain. The importance of the Church and of popular religion will appear frequently, albeit indirectly, in the course of this book.

Despite its originality, or perhaps because of it, in many ways Cuenca was a typical example of a medium-size pre-industrial town in Castile or indeed in much of southern Europe. Its urban landscape with high population densities, large buildings, and few open spaces was prototypically urban. Its active population never included more than marginal percentages of population living from agriculture, and they normally resided outside the urbanized part of town itself. Textile workers, various groups of tradesmen, an ample bureaucracy, some nobles, the important religious, economic and numerical presence of the Church, a royal mint, a printing press, a library and book-dealers were all unmistakable signs of its urban nature. There can be little doubt that this beautiful and often vexing town was urban in every way and it provides an excellent opportunity to explore a number of important issues regarding towns and urban populations which were raised earlier and which have been discussed only marginally in much of the historical literature. For the purposes of this study Cuenca will fulfill a double role: as itself and as an example of all urban areas in pre-industrial Spain.

Even though in the course of my research I have made in-depth, often systematic, use of numerous local and national sources, I am well aware that the present book is a foray into unexplored terrain in Spain. Ultimately, it is an impressionistic view of a pre-industrial town and will not provide definitive answers to many of the issues raised in this chapter. I can only hope that it will clarify the debate and open new horizons for future research both in Europe and elsewhere. Though our discussion is firmly rooted in Spain, Castile and Cuenca, the issues raised may well have universal implications, especially if similar patterns can be found in other towns during other periods within other cultural and economic contexts. Whether or not this happens remains to be seen. For the present, I can only hope that this book will encourage people to bring renewed vigor and fresh ideas to the fascinating phenomenon of towns in pre-industrial societies.

2

Growth and decadence of a Castilian hill town

Cuenca is an eloquent example of the tenuous and often ephemeral nature of urban growth and prosperity. During the period under study, it went from a peak of economic and demographic fortune into a centuries-long decadence from which it has yet to emerge. In the sixteenth century Cuenca was a vibrant and dynamic middle-sized Castilian town with a vigorous economy and considerable political influence in royal affairs. It was an essential part of a network of towns in the central part of Spain which gave fifteenth- and sixteenth-century Castile a distinctly urban flavor. By the nineteenth century, Cuenca was a ghost of its former self and had become a sleepy provincial capital whose meagre industrial production was destined almost entirely for the home market. By then there was little or no urban system to be found in a Castile which, apart from Madrid, had become one of the more rural regions of Western Europe. The demise of Cuenca and of urban Castile continues to be one of the perplexing mysteries of Spanish history. The central aim of this chapter is to further understanding of this disaster.

During the sixteenth century the town of Cuenca was riding a wave of prosperity and growth which had begun in the latter part of the fourteenth or early fifteenth century. This prosperity was based on two major sources of wealth: the Church and a prosperous textile industry. By the sixteenth century the bishopric of Cuenca had become one of the richer ones in Spain. Thanks to a multitude of rents, both from its own possessions and from the tithe, the Church controlled more wealth in the town of Cuenca than any other social group. It was a key link between Cuenca and its surrounding hinterland, funneling surpluses of grain and income into town in return for religious and other types of less spiritual goods and services.[1]

Cuenca was also one of the major textile-producing towns in Spain. After its reconquest from the Muslims, it had been able to turn its defensive hilltop location to its economic advantage. This was especially so during the fourteenth and fifteenth centuries, once New Castile ceased to be a war zone and the frontier between Al-Andalus (Muslim Spain) and the Kingdom of Castile finally moved well to the South. Strategically located on one of the major routes of the Mesta, it was a key point where sheep were sheared in the course of their biannual transhumant migration.[2] This was not only a major source of income of the town, but a principal supply of raw material for the local textile industry as well. Ultimately, the pressure of a prosperous textile industry forced the town to grow beyond its original hilltop location of the Middle Ages, and previously undeveloped land between the fortress and the Huecar river was settled during the fifteenth century. As will become clear shortly, the residents of this newly urbanized part of town worked mainly in the textile industry, making use of the wool washed in the river itself. Growth was so important that population spilled over into the marshy plains below and on to the slopes of two adjoining hills, creating the working-class neighbourhoods of San Anton and Tiradores. By the mid-sixteenth century, Cuenca and Segovia were the most important producers of woolen cloth, certainly in Castile and possibly in the entire peninsula. It maintained active connections with other centers in Castile and throughout Europe and northern Africa.[3]

Two centuries later, the late medieval prosperity was little more than a fond and all-too-distant memory. One of the most noteworthy aspects of the urban landscape was the large numbers of abandoned buildings. According to Muñoz y Soliva (1860: 334), in Cuenca in 1721 there were 1,485 abandoned houses "in ruins." The seventeenth century had wreaked havoc on the town's fortunes, and its pride. After the crisis, the eighteenth century was one of recovery, rebuilding and enlightened reform. Spearheaded by members of the Church, like

---

[1] Naturally, the role of the Church in urban society went far beyond the economic implications of its institutional presence. This will become more clear in subsequent chapters of this study.

[2] The Mesta was the guild of transhumant livestock owners which was founded in 1273 by Alfonso X and abolished in 1836. During the fifteenth and sixteenth centuries it was an immensely powerful institution. The classic study of the Mesta was written by Klein (1920).

[3] During the fifteenth and sixteenth centuries Cuenca cloth was sold at the fairs of Medina del Campo and on the international markets of the Levant and in northern Africa (Iradiel Murugarren, 1974: 237–242).

bishop Palafox, and other reformers, numerous attempts were made to rekindle the almost forgotten spirit of old. Some progress was made. Population increased, a mint, a modest paper industry and an important cloth factory, owned by the Cinco Gremios Mayores of Madrid, were all founded.[4] Despite these efforts, Cuenca no longer had any role to play in the economic regeneration taking place in many areas of Spain at that time. Even though it remained a town with a large proportion of artisans, much as had always been the case, industry was geared only to the local market and had few contacts beyond the not-so-distant perimeters of the province itself. As before, the Church continued to be powerful and, together with royal and local public administration, became the dominant force in the urban economy. Certain wealthy families remained, like the Cerdan de Landa family, who did indeed invest in the local economy, but there were certainly not enough of them to make much of a difference, and certainly far fewer than that powerful group of wool merchants and textile manufacturers of the sixteenth century.

The nature of the changing times can be seen in the following, almost anecdotal, example. Every year the cathedral chapter used to lease out the rights to collect the tithe in the different villages within its jurisdiction. In the sixteenth century, most of those bidding were bourgeois entrepreneurs related to the wool industry and speculating with cereal production. During the seventeenth and eighteenth centuries, these bidders were mostly canons of the cathedral itself. The economic essence of urban life in the sixteenth century, based on industrial production and speculative investment, had been replaced by local production and secure rents.

How did this happen? Just how exceptional was Cuenca's experience? These are major questions which must be addressed if we are to understand its long-term development. Our first task will be to trace the basic profile of the collapse: its magnitude, its timing, its effects on the internal structure of the urban population. The general evolution in the town's size and the make-up of its active population will be the point of departure for this inquiry. Whether or not Cuenca's experience was unique is another, still more important issue. Adequately addressing it, however, is only possible if the experience of Cuenca is placed within the larger context of urban Castile and urban Spain. In this way, a discussion of the nature and development of urban Spain becomes essential to this discussion of Cuenca. Here, the results will

[4] For overviews of the economic history of Cuenca during the eighteenth century, see Troitiño Vinuesa (1984: 34–45); Larruga (1787: vol. 19).

be revealing but hardly surprising. Cuenca's fall was part of the widespread economic and demographic demise of almost all of urban Castile. Cuenca, then, was not alone, nor was it fully in control of its own destiny. There were many culprits: royal imperial policy was one, the Castilian bourgeoisie's obsession with secure rents and noble titles, another, over-urbanization during the sixteenth century, yet another. Rural demographic patterns will also emerge as a key element for the understanding of long-term urban development everywhere.

The issue of the decline of Castile has been the subject of on-going debate among students of early modern Spain since the writers of the late sixteenth and early seventeenth centuries.[5] The present chapter will participate in that debate, though it will certainly resolve very little. The empirical information it provides regarding the experience of one town and that of an entire urban system will contribute to defining more precisely the limits of the debate, the extent of decline and of subsequent recovery.

Population development over three centuries

A modest but indispensable beginning for this discussion is to trace the long-term development of the population of Cuenca. In order to do this properly, it is necessary to turn either to existing recounts of total population or to parish registers. Both of these sources have certain advantages and disadvantages.

Listings of inhabitants provide the most direct way to estimate the total population of the town at any given moment. Historical listings do not fulfill what might be considered modern statistical criteria, and great care must be taken in their use and interpretation. During the earlier part of the period under study, listings are infrequent, irregular, and often fail to count certain key elements of the urban population (widows, clergy, nobility, etc.). For Cuenca we have been able to find a good number of them, especially from the eighteenth century

---

[5] The decline of Castile was the central issue tackled in the writings of these reformers (*arbitristas*). For most of them, population was the key to understanding the entire process. See, for example, Sancho de Moncada (1619), Fernández de Navarrete (1626), Caxa de Leruela (1631), Martínez de Mata (1650–1660), Saavedra Fajardo (1640), their precursor Tomás de Mercado (1569), and many others. The best work about the demographic ideas of these thinkers is by Martin Rodríguez (1984). See also Le Flem (1976).

The subject of the decline of Castile continues to provoke widespread debate among historians. For recent attempts at synthesis, see Philips (1987), Elliott (1977), Casey, (1985), Ringrose (1983).

on, though in most cases some adjustments were required.[6] Most, though not all, of the listings are local recounts and are housed in the Archivo Municipal de Cuenca.[7]

One of the principal defects of pre-modern recounts of inhabitants is that generally only household heads were counted. Deciding on a factor for converting the number of household heads (*vecinos*) in to total inhabitants has been discussed by numerous authors, many of whom have proposed varying multiplying factors.[8] In the case of Cuenca, I have adopted a rough and ready approach. There are a number of dates for which I have data on both household heads and total inhbitants (1693, 1724, 1800, 1844). In all of these, the factor is near 4.0. Aware of the relatively unchanging nature of household size in Cuenca, I have decided on a factor of 4 for all listings where only household heads appear.[9]

Another on-going problem with listings of inhabitants is that often they do not include certain urban groups. This has occurred in some of those used in Table 2.1. For example, widows are underestimated in 1591, servants suffer the same fate in 1707, and clergy and servants are missing in 1719. Whenever feasible, adjustments were made, though generally I have kept data manipulation to a minimum.[10] A major

---

[6] Some of the listings used were of relatively poor quality. This is especially true with the 1644 *padrón* which was retained because it is the only recount available between 1591 and 1693. Other listings were of excellent quality, such as the one from 1561 and several of those from the eighteenth and nineteenth centuries.

[7] The listings of 1561, 1571 and 1597 can be found in the Archivo General de Simancas (AGS), Sección Expedientes de Hacienda. Data for 1591 come from the census of that year. 1571 and 1597 figures are also taken from AGS, Expedientes de Hacienda. The data used were first published by Tomás González in 1829. For further information on the 1591 census, see E. García España with A. Molinié-Bertrand (1984–1986); Molinié Bertrand, (1976–1984, 1985). The listing of 1693 is kept in the Municipal Archive of Cuenca and is a copy of another in Simancas. The 1752 data are taken from the Catastro del Marqués de la Ensenada, and can be consulted in the Municipal Archive. Data for 1787 comes form the Census of Floridablanca (1787) and is housed in the Archivo de la Academia de la Historia. At present the Instituto Nacional de Estadística is in the process of publishing this important census in its entirety. Data for 1800 are probably based on the original returns for the Census of Godoy (1797–1800), which can be found, once again, in Cuenca. Data for 1836 are taken from the *Guía del Ministerio de la Gobernación del Reino* (1836: 259). The 1857 and 1860 data are taken from the first modern Spanish censuses of those years. All other population totals come from local listings kept in the Municipal Archive.
  Numerous other recounts of population exist as well but they are generally of inferior quality or pertain to periods for which we already have sufficient data.

[8] Among those articles dedicated specifically to this subject within a Spanish context, see Bustelo Garcia del Real (1973), and Martin Galán (1985). For more general overviews of the source material available for the study of historical demography in Spain, see Martin Galán (1981).

[9] The great stability in mean household size has come to light in two recent studies of the subject in Spain. See, for example, Reher (1988a: 154; 1988b: 64).

[10] A detailed account of these adjustments can be found in Reher (1983: 76–187).

Table 2.1   *Total population data for Cuenca*

Data	Household heads	Estimated total population[a]	Total population	Total population including institutions[b]
1561	3,461	13,888		14,644
1571	3,265	13,060		13,860
1591	3,120	12,480		13,280
1597	3,083	12,332		13,132
1644	1,200	4,800		5,600
1693	1,464		5,651	6,451
1707	1,334		5,315	6,115
1719	1,433	5,732		6,532
1724	1,502		5,940	6,740
1730	1,491	5,964		6,764
1732	1,527	6,108		6,908
1733	1,567	6,268		7,068
1752	1,812	7,248		8,048
1771	1,704	6,816		7,616
1787				7,902
1800	1,780		6,996	7,857
1801	1,884	7,536		8,336
1805	1,544	6,176		6,976
1813	1,220	4,880		5,680
1821	1,665		6,197	6,997
1836	1,679			6,805
1841	1,504			6,037
1844	1,428			5,861
1857				7,610
1860				7,357

[a] Data in this column are derived by multiplying total number of household heads by 4.
[b] Data in this column reflect the presence of an estimated institution of 800 persons.
Notes
See text for further details.

omission in most of the listings is population living in institutions (convents, schools, jails, etc.). In 1787 there were 861 persons living in such institutions (367 in convents, 287 in schools and institutions for children – including the Casa de Niños Expósitos for foundlings – and 207 in other institutions). In 1797 there was a similar number of people. Though the size of these groups was clearly never constant, attempts have been made to adjust other population estimates to include the institutional population.[11] While this procedure is not exact, it should give us a general idea of the total size of the town's population.

The results of this exercise are contained in Table 2.1 and give us the broad outlines of Cuenca's long-term development. Population reached a high point during the second half of the sixteenth century.[12] After 1591 there was a dramatic drop in population. Data from 1644 put population size at less than 40 per cent of its 1591 level. By the end of the century population was still well below half what it was at the end of the sixteenth century. The eighteenth century, on the other hand, was one of moderate growth, and by century's end the population of the town was nearly 22 per cent higher than it was 100 years earlier. The beginning of the nineteenth century coincided with another sharp drop in population which was followed by a period of ups and downs, in which no clear tendency can be seen.

The centuries-long decline of the city is confirmed by the data on population totals. Sixteenth-century levels of population were never again reached throughout the period under study. 1561 levels were reached only towards the end of the nineteenth century, but by then Cuenca's relative position in urban Spain was much weaker than ever before. The turning point in the town's fortunes came some time during the early part of the seventeenth century; and, at least in my view it was not merely a cyclicial oscillation, but rather a permanent change in the town's destiny.

Data like these have a number of inherent weaknesses. Apart from doubts arising regarding the reliability of the estimates themselves, the lack of regular recounts makes a more precise understanding of long-term development simply impossible. Here, parish register material can prove to be a useful complement to irregular estimtes of total population. In Cuenca, there are only records for 7 of the 14 urban parishes. [13] They are all located in the upper part of town and contained approximately 30 per cent of the town's total population. Yearly totals of births, deaths and baptisms, along with nine-year moving averages, can be seen in figures 1.1 and 1.2. With certain constraints,

---

[11] 800 people have been added to each of the listings.

[12] While the population of 1591 is lower than that of 1561 or 1571, there is not enough data to pinpoint the timing of the change in tendency.

[13] These parishes are San Pedro, San Nicolás, Santiago, San Martín, Santa María, Santa Cruz and San Gil. The archives for the other parishes were all lost during the Civil War. Even the existence of these seven registers is in part a matter of luck. Some years ago the parishes were consolidated into one (Santiago) which was the parish of the cathedral itself. At the outbreak of the Civil War, the records were in the home of the parish priest and thus were not found by those people actually involved in anti-clerical violence.

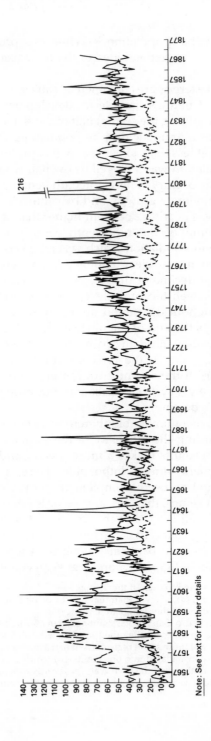

Figure 2.1 Baptisms, marriages and deaths in Cuenca, 1562–1877

Note: See text for further details

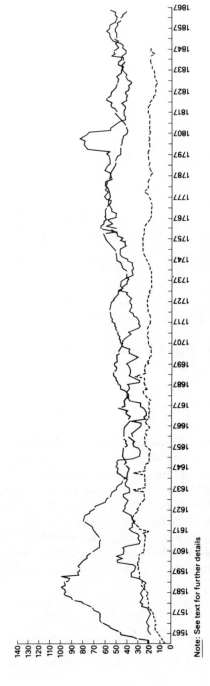

Figure 2.2 Baptisms, marriages and deaths in Cuenca (nine-year moving average)

Note: See text for further details

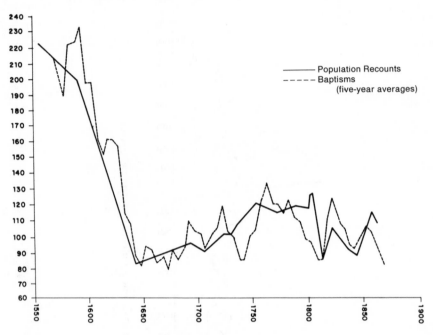

Figure 2.3 Total population of Cuenca (index numbers: 100 = average 1701–1750)

these give a clear picture of the evolution of vital events for a period of nearly three centuries.[14]

A number of aspects of Cuenca's historical development, and of the parish registers themselves, can be derived from the data. One of the most visible is the on-going under-registration of infant and child mortality. This persists until the latter part of the eighteenth century when death registration becomes more or less complete.[15] Once registration becomes adequate, it is also apparent that in normal years there was hardly any advantage of births over deaths. Between 1760 and 1860, for example, deaths outnumbered births in one out of every two years. The surplus of births over deaths was at best limited, and

[14] These constraints pertain mostly to the period before 1620 when not all of the parish registers had begun. Thus the apparent increase in births, deaths and marriages before 1600 is not correct.

[15] As will become apparent in chapter 3, shortcomings in the registration of deaths have severely restricted my ability to estimate mortality levels prior to the nineteenth century. Mortality peaks, however, are clearly visible throughout the entire period.

quite possibly non-existent.[16] Lower fertility and higher mortality in urban areas, as opposed to their rural hinterland, left little room for natural population growth.[17] Any increase in urban population was mainly a function of the intensity of migration, and Cuenca was no exception in this. This point is essential to arguments advanced later in this chapter.

With certain reservations, baptisms can also be considered as a proxy indicator for population size. Naturally this assumes that fertility and nuptiality are constant, and even then baptisms would only indicate the size of the child-bearing generation, and not that of the population as a whole. The assumption of the unchanging nature of vital behavior is clearly not justifiable. However, we should bear in mind that in traditional societies changes in fertility and nuptiality tended to be gradual and were probably less important in determining medium-range birth fluctuations than the size of the child-bearing cohort in society. The great advantage of using baptisms as an indicator of size is that the timing and intensity of great population swings can be monitored fairly closely.[18]

If we observe the long-term evolution of our estimates of population size based on baptisms and on population recounts (Figure 2.3), there is clearly a close correlation between the two series. Both reflect the basic pattern of decline during the first half of the seventeenth century, slow and uncertain recovery until the end of the eighteenth century, sharp decline at the beginning of the nineteenth and modest recovery thereafter. There can be little doubt about this basic pattern in Cuenca.

Looking once again at the trends set out by the series of baptisms, the entire picture comes into sharper focus (Figures 2.1 and 2.2). In the period prior to 1590, the data suggest that population growth had ceased. During the 1590s there was a pronounced decline in population which leveled off during the latter part of the decade. The great plague of 1597–1602, which so devastated other parts of the peninsula, affected population in Cuenca, but only temporarily, and by the beginning of the seventeenth century a certain stability seemed to

---

[16] An excess of deaths over births was a fairly common situation in pre-modern towns. For an eighteenth-century Spanish example of this, see Rodríguez Cancho (1981: 112–120). The first author to cite the chronic excess of deaths over births in towns was John Graunt (1662).

[17] Two recent articles have shown this situation to be the case in nineteenth- and early twentieth-century Spain. See Iriso Napal and Reher (1987); Reher (1989).

[18] Insofar as baptisms reflect the actual size of child-bearing cohorts, they are also quite sensitive to migration patterns.

have been regained.[19] Beginning in 1604 an almost uninterrupted period of decline set in and, with the exception of a brief respite during the 1620s, lasted until mid-century.

During this entire period, there were three major epidemics in the town (1597, 1605–1606, 1647–1648), and a couple of lesser ones. It would be very difficult, however, to argue that mortality crises played a significant role in the decline of the town's population. The frequency and intensity of crises were not especially great during this period, and the decline itself was an almost uninterrupted trend which lasted for at least five decades.[20] A valid explanation for this period of decline must include other variables.

Urban population was lowest between 1647 and 1683, and initiated a gradual recovery thereafter. This recovery was interrupted momentarily during the early part of the eighteenth century, probably because of the War of Spanish Succession, and then again during the 1730 and early 1740s. After a period of consistent growth between 1745 and 1785, Cuenca entered another cycle of consistent population loss which lasted until 1815. A worsening economic situation towards the end of the eighteenth century, the devastating crisis of 1804 followed by the negative effects of the Peninsular War all contributed to this intense, though temporary, period of decline. After a short interlude of growth subsequent to 1815, stagnation once again appeared to set in. This last period, which is quite surprising in a moment of generalized demographic growth in most of the peninsula, was probably related to the loss of much of the wealth of the Church, which for centuries had been the major source of wealth in the town, due to the great disentailment laws of the 1830s.

Economic structures and their development

The analysis and understanding of urban economic structures and their development will shed considerable light on the nature of the town itself and on some of the implications of its prolonged period of decline. The most straightforward way to analyze economic structures is through active population data, which in Cuenca can be gleaned from listings of inhabitants as early as the sixteenth century. The use of these data is subject to certain limitations mainly deriving from the fact that only household heads have occupations, and almost all occu-

---

[19] For the best overview of this epidemic see, Bennassar (1969) and Pérez Moreda (1980: 245–293).
[20] Pérez Moreda (1980: 320–326) also tends to minimize the importance of mortality crisis for the decadence of rural Castile.

Table 2.2   *Active population in Cuenca, 1561–1822*

Sector	1561	1707	1724	1752	1771	1800	1820	1856
Agriculture	9.6	23.8	24.7	29.1	24.6	21.8	28.5	37.6
Industry	58.0	36.8	35.1	29.6	35.1	33.2	26.0	20.1
Services	23.4	20.9	27.6	28.4	27.6	33.3	38.1	35.9
Church	9.0	18.4	12.6	12.9	12.6	11.7	7.4	6.4
Total	100.0	99.9	100.0	100.0	99.9	100.0	100.0	100.0

Note Active population data refer only to household heads.
Sources 1561, Archivo General de Simancas; all other dates correspond to local listings of inhabitants found in the Archivo Municipal de Cuenca. For 1752, 1771, 1800 and 1856 raw data were taken from Troitiño (1984: 91, 295) and reworked for inclusion in this table.

pations refer to males.[21] Women are only included when they have some sort of expressly stated profession.[22] For the present study, the following general categories have been established: agriculture, industry, services and the Church.[23]

Cuenca, like a number of other towns in both Old and New Castile, had a relatively important industrial sector and limited proportions of agriculturally based population residing in town (Table 2.2). In 1561 the agricultural population made up less than 10 per cent of the total active population, though subsequently this proportion rose to between 20 and 30 per cent during most of the period. One of the reasons for this development is the classification itself of day laborers within the agricultural sector. Traditionally in Spain, day laborers were considered to be agricultural laborers though, strictly speaking, they were simple people who worked for a daily wage. This means that within an urban context, day laborers might well have worked in agriculture, in the town itself as unskilled workers, or in both. In the sixteenth century there is little doubt about the matter because a clear distinction was drawn between agricultural day laborers (*jornaleros*)

[21] For this reason, domestic servants are not included in our classifications of active population.
[22] This is relatively infrequent because most female household heads are listed as "widows" or "pauper widows," with no further annotation as to their specific economic activity, if indeed they had any.
[23] Agriculture is mainly made up of farmers and day laborers. Industry includes all types of artisans and industrial workers (when they exist). The services sector represents, by and large, most of the privileged groups in town which are not related to the Church. It includes bureaucrats, nobles, merchants, transport workers and shop-keepers, etc. Finally, the Church includes the clergy itself (priests, canons, etc.), and professions of the laity which depend on the Church (such as sacristans). It excludes the regular clergy.

and urban workers (*trabajadores*). This last category disappears in subsequent listings due mainly to the disappearance of the textile industry, and perhaps partially because of the emergence of a new category which encompasses day laborers in both urban and rural economic activities. By the nineteenth century, this certainly seems to be the case; earlier, it is not clear. With certain reservations, then, we have included day laborers within the agricultural sector.

Despite what has just been said, it would seem that the changes which can be observed between 1561 and 1707 with regard to the importance of agricultural population in town may well have been the consequence at least in part, of an actual ruralization of the urban population. This was due to the fact that the agricultural sector of the urban economy was relatively unaffected by the great decline of the seventeenth century, as opposed to other groups which experienced grave population losses. In other words, the relative weight of the sector increased, but actual numbers remained farily constant; thus, we might call it ruralization by default.[24] The other great increase in agricultural population, which took place during the first half of the nineteenth century, would seem to be mostly an increase in day laborers, this time due almost entierly to the progressive imposition of liberal economic hiring practices which increased the proportions of day laborers in the urban economy. *De facto* ruralization during this period would seem out of the question.

Cuenca was one of the typical industrial towns so often found in Castile. This was never so true as in 1561 when artisans and industrial laborers made up nearly 60 per cent of the active population. During the seventeenth century the weight of this sector diminished sharply both in relative and in absolute terms.[25] Even so, thoughout the period approximately one third of the active population worked in that sector.

Another significant part of the active population worked in the services sector. During the period we are studying, this sector increased in importance and ended up including over one third of the town's active population. This growth, especially evident after the beginning of the eighteenth century, was due primarily to the increase in the number of people working for the royal and local administration. The acceleration of the trend in the nineteenth century merely echoes the process whereby provincial capitals ended up concentrating ever higher proportions of administrative responsibility. It is

[24] There were 217 household heads in this sector in 1561 and 283 in 1724.
[25] The actual number of people employed in the sector diminished by 70 per cent, going from 1,312 workers in 1561 to 403 in 1724.

interesting to note that at no time during the period under study did many nobles choose to reside in the town itself. In the eighteenth century, only about 2 per cent of household heads belonged to the nobility. Cuenca had always been an industrial or a clerical town, but, unlike Valladolid, Seville or even Madrid, never one in which the nobility played a relevant role.

The numerical importance of the Church (not including the regular clergy) was appreciable, hovering throughout much of the period at slightly over 11 per cent of the active population. Only twice did this importance noticeably wane: once, during the sixteenth century, because of the weight of the industrial sector of town, and again, during the nineteenth, due to the effects of the continued liberal onslaught on ecclesiastical institutions and privileges (the abolition of the Inquisition, the tithe and entail, the defrocking of much of the regular clergy, etc.). The numerical presence of the Church was, of course, only a pale reflection of its far greater economic and social significance. It had always been the most important economic institution in Cuenca, though during the fifteenth and sixteenth centuries the weight of the textile industry had tended to obscure this fact. Even though the demise of the town's fortunes must have had negative repercussions for the Church's wealth (especially for the tithe), they were evidently less important than among the secular parts of urban society. Thus its relative economic influence in town increased, and by the eighteenth century it was clearly the major source of urban wealth. In 1752 the Church, both as an institution and in the person of priests and canons, owned 57.7 per cent of all houses in Cuenca, 51.7 per cent of all rental income and 44.9 per cent of all surface area dedicated to housing.[26] The role it played in urban life was so great that the undermining of its economic base of power during the nineteenth century led to yet another period of decadence for the town.[27]

At least two out of every five persons in town either worked for the Church or in the services sector. Cuenca was a town dominated by economic groups which lived from rents rather than produced wealth. Only in 1561 was this markedly different. The demise of industrial activity in Cuenca had made way for a new type of town

[26] The nobility owned 13.1 per cent of houses, 16.7 per cent of income and 18.8 per cent of surface area. Other owners had 29.0 per cent, 31.6 and 36.3 per cent respectively. These data are based on the Catastro del Marqués de la Ensenada (Troitiño, 1984: 60–68).

[27] During the first half of the nineteenth century, the fate of many towns of New and Old Castile where the Church was the preponderant economic force was similar. Toledo and Ávila are examples of this process.

Table 2.3   *Active population in the industrial sector, 1561–1771*

Industry	1561		1707		1724		1771	
	n	%	n	%	n	%	n	%
Wood (lumber and carpentry)	63	4.8	20	5.7	19	4.7	39	8.2
Pottery, ceramics	16	1.2	9	2.6	8	2.0	11	2.3
Construction and decoration	73	5.6	44	12.6	50	12.4	100	21.1
Metallurgy	98	7.5	39	11.2	29	7.2	38	8.0
Leather, shoemaking	109	8.3	84	24.1	68	16.9	89	18.8
Clothing	73	5.6	42	12.1	44	10.9	70	14.8
Textile	646	49.2	80	23.0	148	36.7	94	19.8
Others	234	17.8	30	8.6	37	9.2	33	7.0
Total	1,312	100.0	348	99.9	403	100.0	474	100.0

Sources 1561, Archivo General de Simancas; 1707, 1724 and 1771, Archivo Municipal de Cuenca.

oriented towards ecclesiastical and civil administration, rather than production.

The structure and evolution of the industrial sector in Cuenca loom as the key to the long-term processes of growth and decline. In an effort to provide a clearer understanding of the fundamental process of change, this sector has been broken down into different economic sub-groups whose fortunes can be followed between the sixteenth and the eighteenth centuries (Table 2.3). Cuenca in 1561 was dominated by the textile industry which occupied nearly half of the entire sector and 28.5 per cent of the active population of the entire town. Everything we know about this industry indicates that it was very dynamic, making use of a good part of the wool sheared locally, and with markets in rural parts of the province, other Castilian towns and abroad. Little is known of the organization of the industry itself, though it seems that most of the workers were grouped together in small shops. Protoindustrial activity, based either in town or in surrounding rural areas, was apparently far less important than urban production itself.[28] The economic activities of most other groups seem

[28] The situation was somewhat different in Old Castile where rural production was relatively more important. For more on this subject, see Iradiel Murugarren (1974: 105–118).

to have been oriented almost exclusively toward local production and consumption either in Cuenca or in the immediately surrounding area. By the eighteenth century, the textile industry was no longer the dominant industry in town. Between 1561 and 1707, its relative weight in the town had been halved and its numbers had dwindled by some 88 per cent! In 1613 the reformer Caxa de Leruela estimated that production was only 7 per cent of levels holding in 1600. He may not have been exaggerating.

Many historians have attempted to provide an adequate interpretation for the destruction of the Castilian textile industry.[29] From their accounts, certain common explanations emerge. Ultimately the Castilian bourgeoisie and its textile industry were caught in a vicious circle of ever-dwindling profits. One of the principal causes for this was the rampant inflation of the sixteenth century, itself partially a result of the influx of American treasure (Hamilton, 1934). This left Castilian textiles in a relatively disadvantageous position with respect to foreign manufactures, which tended to be more stylish and were better suited to the trends in upper-class tastes. The result was that non-Castilian manufactures were able to make serious inroads into local markets. Royal policy also played a fundamental role in this process as an ever-increasing demand for revenue, either in the form of new taxes or succulent promises of permanent rents in return for cash donations, tended to decrease profit margins. For a while population growth and a favorable international position, especially in America, helped the industry continue to grow. Yet it was only a matter of time before the textile entrepreneurs ended up turning their backs on the industry and scrambling to invest in landed rents. The mentality of profit and speculation had been replaced by that of rents and security; in the words of Braudel (1972: 2: 725–734), it was the defection of the bourgeoisie. From the standpoint of the textile manufacturers in Cuenca, lack of capital investment by people who now preferred to invest in royal credit or rural rents, together with a diminishing market, were the keys to a depression which had reduced the number of dyer's shops in town from 27 to 2 in a short period of time.[30]

Only artisan industries producing for the home market were left in the town. While the importance of some of them increased considerably during the eighteenth century, the fact remains that none seemed

---

[29] For a good description of the textile industry and its decline in Segovia, see García Sanz (1977: 208–221). For a more general overview, see Domínguez Ortiz (1973c: 133–138).

[30] These reasons were cited in the text drawn up by the weavers to request a restructuring of the *alcabala* tax in 1599. See AGS, Expedientes de Hacienda, 89. This information was graciously facilitated to me by Felipe Ruiz Martín.

to dominate an industrial sector which was no longer important in Cuenca anyway. The economic dynamism of the sector had gone. This reality can also be seen in the data on the commercial revenue of the town. A global estimate of this income, as shown by the *correduría mayor y menor* and the *sisa vieja*, indicate that revenues had reached a high point between 1577 and 1590 but had fallen by over 60 per cent before 1640. Perhaps even more revealing is the fact that despite sustained growth over much of the eighteenth century, by the time the high point of the eighteenth century was reached, between 1781 and 1790, revenues were still 35 per cent below their peak period during the sixteenth century.[31] Cuenca was no longer an economic force to be reckoned with on a national or even a regional level.

These data, however, only give a very approximate idea of overall commercial activity.[32] The revenues mentioned were closely linked to population size and do little to indicate industrial productivity or, when referring to food products, living standards. In order to control for this, I have performed a very simple exercise of dividing the adjusted revenue by the total number of household heads at four different dates. If per capita commercial activity in 1590 was 100, in 1644 it was 75, in 1707 it was 81 and in 1800 it was 91.[33] Depite the fact that the eighteenth century in Cuenca was a period of increasingly vibrant economic activity, by the end of the Ancien Régime, pre-1600 levels of per capita output were still far from being attained.

A pronounced decrease in total population size and in the percentage of active population in industry were the most visible transformations between 1561 and 1724. These changes tended to affect the different areas of town almost equally. Traditionally Cuenca had always been divided into an upper town where services and the clergy predominated, as opposed to a lower one where the industrial and agricultural populations tended to live and work.[34] The basic spatial

---

[31] These data are based on the work of David Ringrose (1983: 282–283, 303–306) and are taken from the Archivo Municipal de Cuenca, legs. 147–154, 582, 1131, 1546, 1549. The data used have been adjusted for inflation based on Hamilton's (1934; 1937) price series for New Castile.

[32] They only show tax revenue derived from certain commercial activities, independent of whether or not they include only, or even fundamentally, the trade of manufactured products.

[33] Naturally this exercise is but a crude approximation because it makes no allowance for the possibility of changing tax structures. These, however, changed slowly in Ancien Régime society and I am fairly sure that the basic pattern would have contined the same.

[34] This is, of course, a simplification of a very complex social reality. In 1561 52.7 per cent of the active population of the upper part of town worked in industry or agriculture, as opposed to 73.8 per cent in the lower part of town. In 1724 these percentages were

distribution of social structures was largely unaffected by the crisis of the seventeenth century and lasted, in fact, until well into the twentieth.

Cuenca, Castile and urban Spain

An understanding of the experience of Cuenca ultimately ends up posing further and more vexing questions. To what extent was Cuenca alone? What role did Cuenca play in Castile's urban system? Was its experience similar to that of other towns in Castile or in Spain? If it was, were there any common denominators which might allow us to understand the process more thoroughly? Generally, Cuenca's collapse would seem to be part of the often mentioned and little understood collapse of urban Castile. Despite the pioneering work of de Vries (1984), Ringrose (1983), and other scholars, very little is known about the empirical parameters of that collapse.[35] At a more general level, perhaps even less is known about the nature of the urban system itself, its size, its development, its economic structures or the geographical distribution of its urban centers.[36] Yet the extent to which Cuenca can be understood without understanding this wider context is certainly questionable at best. Addressing some of these questions will occupy much of the rest of this chapter.

A thorough analysis of Spanish urban systems is beyond the scope of this book. Here my approach to the subject will be intuitive (though certainly not unsystematic) and partial. Unpublished or recently published data will be marshaled in order to show the geographical distribution of towns in Spain, their evolution over time, and their basic economic structures. Later, a close look will be taken at the evolution of some key towns in New Castile and this will be related to rural population fluctuations. The empirical data are sometimes incomplete and their quality not always as high as I might like.[37] Taken as a whole, however, they help offer viable answers to many of the questions posed.

In order to understand the basic distribution of towns in Spain, as well as their patterns of growth, I have used data for 1591, 1787 and

40.2 and 69.4 repectively. For more on the spatial differentials of Cuenca society, see Troitiño (1984: 90–111), Reher (1983: 249–261).
[35] Even de Vries' excellent book, which deals only marginally with Spain, is flawed by faulty data regarding city size in Spain between 1500 and 1800.
[36] On this subject see, Perpiñá Grau (1954), Capel Sáez (1974), Díez Nicolás (1972), Estalella and Gubern (1970), Gómez Mendoza and Luna Rodrigo (1986), and Melón y Ruiz de Gordejuela (1966).
[37] These problems will be pointed out whenever pertinent.

Map 2.1 Historic regions of Spain and important towns mentioned in the text

1857.[38] The data base for 1591 is based on the Censo de Población de Castilla, carried out by Philip II. Since this recount lists only household heads, total population figures have been derived by muliplying the number of heads by 4.5.[39] By and large, doubtful population data have

[38] Most of these data have been recently published by Pilar Correas (1988). The general, though not always consistent, criteria followed by the author in her article was that data were gathered for all towns which had least 5,000 inhabitants in 1857.

[39] There are difficulties inherent in this procedure because some towns have multipliers of more than 4.5, while for others (like Cuenca) it was less. Since it is impossible to ascertain the multipliers for most of the towns in the Census, I have opted for an average one. In any case, all population data in this census are only approximate estimates. Had I decided to estimate total rural population, a lower multiplier would certainly have been used because generally household size in rural areas was lower than in adjacent towns due to the numbers of servants in urban households and to the relative lack of institutional population.

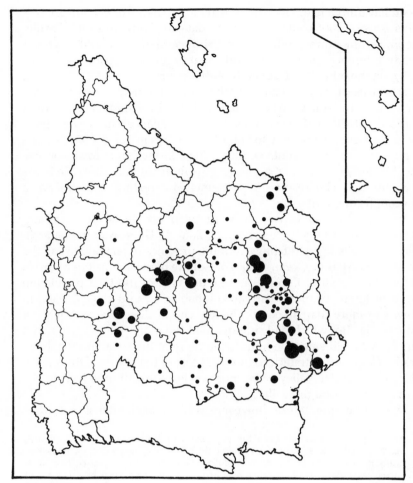

5,000–9,999
10,000–19,999
20,000–49,999
≥ 50,000

Map 2.2 Urban Castile and Andalusia, 1591

been left untouched, since there is no alternate form of estimation.[40] This census only contains accurate data for New and Old Castile, Leon, Estremadura, Andalusia and Murcia. Map 2.1 should serve as a ready reference guide for the principal regions of Spain.[41] Data for 1787, on the other hand, cover the entire peninsula and are taken from the Census of Floridablanca.[42] All material for 1857 comes from the first "modern" census to be carried out in Spain. This data set affords a fair look at the basic structures of the Castilian urban system for a period of 270 years, and for all of urban Spain for the end of the eighteenth and nineteenth century. The distribution of towns by size can be found in Maps 2.2, 2.3 and 2.5; growth rates are shown in Maps 2.4 and 2.6. The results are extremely interesting and deserve a thorough commentary.

In 1591 there were two areas of relatively dense urbanization, separated by a largely de-urbanized zone.[43] There was the Guadal-quivir river valley, stretching from the province of Jaén almost all the way to the Atlantic Ocean. It had one of the highest densities of urban population in all of Europe, as 62.9 per cent of the total population lived in towns of more than 5,000 inhabitants, and 38.9 per cent in towns of more than 10,000.[44] The key city of the entire area was, of course, Seville, which had proudly held the monopoly on trade with the New World since the foundation there of the royal monopoly on trade (Casa de Contratación) in 1504. Most of the towns of this part of the Guadalquivir valley were more or less directly involved in the Indies trade through Seville.

It would be premature, however, to consider the density of urban

[40] An exception to this has been the population of Madrid, which was seriously miscalculated for the 1591 census when only a general estimate of 7,500 household heads is given (García España and Molinié-Bertrand, 1986: 397–401). If we base ourselves on the series of baptisms contained in Carbajo Isla's recent book (1987: 256), it is clear that Madrid's population was between 75,000 and 95,000 inhabitants towards the end of the sixteenth century. I have revised the figures accordingly.

[41] All references to the Canary Islands have been eliminated so as to facilitate our interpretation of the census results.

[42] The original village by village returns for most of the census can be found in the Archive of the Academia de la Historia located in Madrid. The Instituto Nacional de Estadística will shortly be publishing the entire census. Thus far, volumes corresponding to approximately half the country have been published. Local data for Navarre are missing in the census. See García España (1986–1989).

[43] It must be remembered that much of Spain is not included in Map 2.2. Nevertheless, indirect evidence leads us to believe that the two areas of dense urbanization which appear on the map were in fact the most important ones on the peninsula.

[44] Using only country-level data compiled by de Vries (1984: 39), it is clear that no other area in Europe had levels of urbanization similar to those shown by Andalusia. The highest in 1600 was the Netherlands with 24.3 per cent of its population in towns of more than 10,000 inhabitants.

Table 2.4 *Urban population, by region*

Region	Towns > 5,000 No. of towns 1591	1787	1857	Per cent urban 1591	1787	1857	Towns > 10,000 No. of towns 1591	1787	1857	Per cent urban 1591	1787	1857
Andalusia	43	72	136	62.9	53.0	58.4	15	24	49	38.9	34.2	38.0
New Castile	29	24	40	22.7	26.6	35.3	5	2	10	9.6	15.2	23.3
Old Castile/Leon	14	13	19	11.4	6.6	9.5	8	3	9	8.8	2.8	6.7
Estremadura	14	8	30	20.7	13.5	32.4		1	3		2.9	7.3
Valencia/Murcia		35	67		50.1	55.1	1	11	21	2.5	34.3	34.7
Aragon		7	10		13.4	16.0		1	4		6.9	10.8
Basque Country/northern coast		6	19		8.9	21.4		5	8		9.5	15.2
Catalonia		14	30		26.3	31.5		4	18		16.6	27.0
Balearic Islands		7	13		43.0	58.2		2	4		25.0	35.5
Canary Islands		7	7		32.7	26.6		1	3		6.2	16.2
Galicia		2	18		2.2	21.3		2	12		2.2	18.4
Total		195	389		23.8	32.4		56	141		14.7	21.6

Note The totals for Andalusia in 1591 do not include data from the provinces of Almería, Granada or Málaga. Due to the administrative definition of "municipality," data from Galicia are practically impossible to interpret.

population in this region as being solely the consequence of trade with the New World. There are also reasons to believe that this part of Andalusia had traditionally been the most urbanized on the peninsula since at least Muslim and possibly even Roman times. Agricultural productivity in the region was quite high, thus providing ready support for urban populations with or without the existence of the New World. Ultimately, trade with the New World was probably only incidental to the existence itself of this urban system, but a key factor in its sixteenth-century vitality.

The Castilian meseta also had an urban system of its own, though levels of urbanization were not so high as in Andalusia (Table 2.4). This system was characterized by the presence of three large cities (Madrid, Valladolid and Toledo) together with a number of small and medium-sized towns (among them, Cuenca). In Castile, the decade of the 1590s was a period of flux.[45] Earlier, Toledo and Valladolid had been the key centers, but Madrid was in the process of asserting itself thanks to the transfer of the court there by Philip II in 1561. Urban areas of Castile were linked by a network of commercial and administrative ties, which gave them the very real appearance of being a system, as defined by Jan de Vries.[46] In Castile most towns had more or less specific niches: Toledo was the religious capital and an important silk manufacturing center; Valladolid, the home of many noble families and the traditional seat of much of the government in Castile; Burgos controlled commerce to the north and Toledo to the south; Medina del Campo and Medina de Rioseco, galvanized the wool trade and many of the banking interests; Cuenca, Segovia, and Zamora were all industrial centers; Salamanca and Alcalá de Henares were university towns; and Salamanca specialized in the manufacture of leather products.[47] It was a well-integrated system, and many of its

[45] For an overview of population trends in Spain during the late sixteenth and early seventeenth centuries, see Ruiz Martín (1967), Pérez Moreda (1988a: 369–375), Domínguez Ortiz (1973c: 69–87), and Nadal (1984: 28–42; 1988).

[46] Basing his ideas on the work of geographers, de Vries (1984: 82) has attributed the following properties to urban systems: "The elements of the system are cities, and these are dependent on each other ... in an organized complexity. Their interdependence implies that the cities are differentiated – that they vary sufficiently in their specializations and functions not to be faithful replicas of each other. Besides interdependence and differentiation, the concept requires closure, the system must have boundaries and this leads directly to the third concept, the region."

[47] There is a growing bibliography on these Castilian towns. For some of the key works on the subject see: for Valladolid, Bennassar (1967); for Segovia, García Sanz (1977), Bennassar (1968), Barrio Gozalo et al. (1987); for Toledo, Weisser (1973), Ringrose (1983: 253–280), Martz and Porres (1974); Montemayor (1987); for Salamanca, Fernández Alvarez (1975); for Medina del Campo, Marcos Martin (1978); for Ciudad Real, Philips (1979); for Talavera de la Reina, González Muñoz (1975).

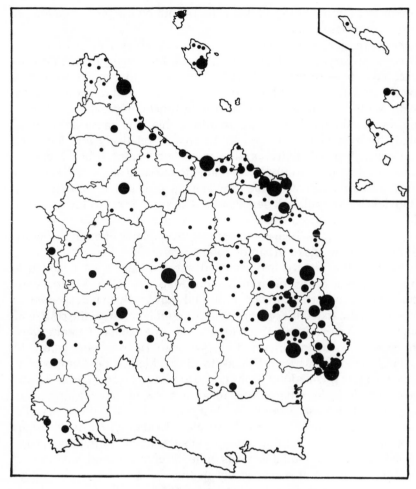

Map 2.3 Urban Spain, 1787

5,000–9,999
10,000–19,999
20,000–49,999
≥ 50,000

towns had special links to other centers both on the peninsula and in other countries of Europe.

However, it had important structural weaknesses which would only become apparent at a later date. Among these we can mention an excessive dependence on wool and textiles as the major source of wealth and an ill-defined distribution of political and religious power, with Madrid in the process of usurping functions previously carried out by Toledo and Valladolid. To add to this, it is important to note that this system was located in an area of relatively low levels of agricultural productivity, and was isolated from other areas of alternate agricultural supply.[48] Finally, in the rural areas of the central and northern parts of Castile, prevailing social structures, with fairly high levels of population density and widespread and secure access to land, did little to contribute to the creation of a flexible, market-oriented economy which could have been adaptable enough to readily support high levels of urban population.

By 1787 the picture had changed substantially. Castile had disappeared as a center of urbanization (Map 2.3). Only Madrid continued to be important. In fact, most of the areas which had seemed so vibrant in the sixteenth century had lost population over the course of almost 200 years. Some of the losses were spectacular: Cuenca went from near 14,000 inhabitants to 8,753; Segovia, from near 25,000 to 9,865; Toledo, from around 50,000 to 18,021; Medina del Campo from 12,000 to 3,454; Valladolid, from 37,000 to 21,099; Palencia, from 14,000 to 9,563; Alcalá de Henares from 10,500 to 5,688, etc. From Map 2.4 it is apparent that most of the towns lost population, and those that did not, showed almost no growth at all.[49] Evidently, Castile's urban system had ceased to exist, at least in its traditional form (Table 2.4).

The situation in Andalusia was quite different. It continued to be a highly urbanized area, especially in the Guadalquivir river valley. Important changes, however, had occurred. Overall levels of urbanization were down, though decline was spread unequally over the region. The provinces of Jaén, Córdoba and Seville had stagnated, many of their urban centers had lost population. This is most apparent with the city of Seville whose population, despite healthy growth

---

[48] Supplying towns with basic foodstuffs was always a major worry, whether the town was huge like Madrid or small like Cuenca. For works on the problems of transportation and the supply of urban centers, see Ringrose (1970; 1983: 143–163), and Castro (1987).

[49] It should be remembered that the second population estimate comes after an eighteenth century of population growth. In other words, had we been able to have reliable estimates of size towards the end of the seventeenth century, the decline would have been far greater.

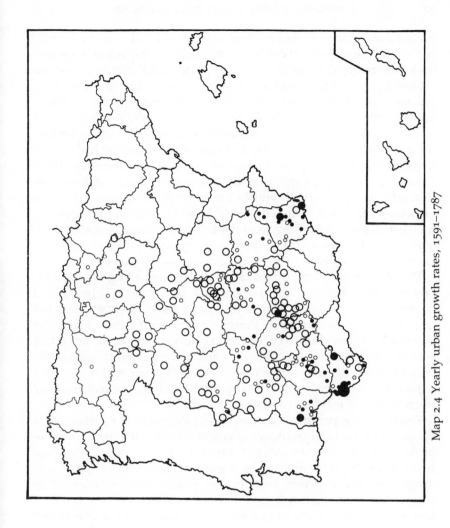

Map 2.4 Yearly urban growth rates, 1591–1787

during the eighteenth century, had not grown at all over the period. For Seville the stagnation can be attributed to the decline of American trade, the removal of the trade monopoly to Cádiz after 1650 and the disastrous epidemic of 1649 which killed off a good proportion of the town's population precisely at a time of economic hardship (Domínguez Ortiz and Aguilar Piñal, 1976: 21–25). In 1787 it still remained by far the most important city in Andalusia and the fourth largest on the peninsula, but demographic and economic dynamism had passed to the area of Cádiz. Spurred on by the monopoly of American trade granted in 1650, Cádiz and its surrounding towns made up what was clearly the most important conurbation in Spain at that time.[50] The rest of Andalusia, which included the old Moorish kingdom of Granada, was less densely urbanized than the low-lying valley of the Guadalquivir river, but contained a number of very important towns such as Granada (56,541), Málaga (51,098), and Antequera (20,266).

The other area of high urbanization was located along the Mediterranean coast, between the present-day provinces of Murcia and Barcelona. The Valencia–Murcia area (50.1 per cent urban) was the most highly urbanized, while Barcelona continued to be a major city that did not as yet seem to be the center of any sort of significant urban system. The immense agricultural wealth of the Levant facilitated this type of urban density, though it is unclear the extent to which this region was also highly urbanized at an earlier date. Indirect evidence suggests that it was less so than Andalusia.

The rest of the peninsula was practically devoid of any sort of urban system, and the rural landscape was only occasionally marked by the presence of an important town (Saragossa, Madrid, Valladolid, etc.). In other words, in these areas there seems to have been no significant urban structure in which large central places were surrounded by progressively smaller towns, each of which fulfilled certain specialized functions.[51] Large parts of the peninsula, mainly in the center and North, had no towns at all. The process whereby the periphery, from Cádiz to Barcelona, became the key demographic and economic area of growth in Spain was rapidly becoming a historical reality. It is unfortunate that we do not have reliable data regarding city size for much of the periphery of Spain before 1787. It is plausible, however,

---

[50] This conurbation, located around the shores of the bay of Cádiz included the following towns: Cádiz (71,080), San Fernando (28, 138), Puerto de Santa María (16, 429), Rota (6,789) and Puerto Real (8,438). Other major towns located within 25 km of Cádiz were Jerez de la Frontera (45,506), Sanlúcar de Barrameda (14,840) and Chiclana (7,450).

[51] The work of Christaller (1966, first published 1933) set the cornerstone for the central place theory of urban systems.

Table 2.5   *Yearly urban growth rates, by region*

Region	1591–1787			1787–1857			
	urban[a]	urban[b]	rural	urban[a]	urban[b]	rural	total
Andalusia	−0.09	0.28	0.25	0.49	0.67	0.91	0.71
New Castile	−0.13	0.04	0.07	0.23	0.44	0.39	0.44
Old Castile/ Leon	−0.23	−0.12	0.06	0.48	0.49	0.43	0.30
Estremadura	−0.17	−0.03	0.02	0.59	0.70	0.73	0.77
Valencia/ Murcia			0.46	0.49	0.83	0.94	0.71
Aragon			0.16	0.47	0.47	0.61	0.52
Basque Country/ northern coast			0.48	1.04	0.97	0.44	0.82
Catalonia			0.44	0.77	1.04	1.06	1.04
Balearic Islands				0.54	0.63	0.57	0.57
Canary Islands				0.10	0.42	0.49	0.48
Galicia			0.51	0.90	1.38	0.39	0.40
Total			0.23	0.48	0.70	0.59	0.57

Notes Urban growth rates are based on the unweighted averages of the towns in the region. Rates are calculated in two ways: (a) are based on towns with at least 5,000 inhabitants in the starting year (1591 or 1787, depending on the period), and (b) are based on towns with at least 5,000 in the finishing year (1787 or 1857). Rural data for 1591–1787 are based on series of baptisms (Nadal, 1988: 47–54). Total growth rates 1787–1857 include both rural and urban areas.

that starting levels of urban population were somewhat lower, perhaps even lower than in Castile, but that urban growth here was much stronger, especially after the middle of the seventeenth century.[52]

What is evident is that two and possibly three divergent dynamics of growth appeared on the peninsula (Table 2.5). In New Castile, Old Castile and Estremadura, there was a persistent situation of economic and demographic stagnation.[53] In all three regions weak rural growth rates exceeded still weaker urban ones, thus suggesting an on-going

[52] Indirect evidence supports the idea of important urban decline in Catalonia during the fifteenth century, and a certain stagnation during the sixteenth. It is well known that the early part of the seventeenth century was negative throughout, especially in Valencia, though recovery was much more rapid along the coast than in other areas of the peninsula. See Vilar (1962), Pérez García and Ardit Lucas (1988).

[53] If Madrid were eliminated from the New Castile sample, growth would be still lower.

process of de-urbanization in those areas.[54] In Andalusia, the situation is less clear. The towns of the sixteenth century also lost population, but less so than in Castile; and other centers of more or less vigorous growth appeared. The net result for the urban system was a major rearrangement of its principal centers, which mainly benefited the smaller towns. Finally, indirect evidence based on rural growth rates suggests that between 1591 and 1787 urban growth in the Valencia–Catalonia region must have been considerably higher than in other parts of the country.[55] The similarity in growth rates in both rural and urban areas between 1591 and 1787 for the regions for which we have data suggests that something similar might have been at work in other areas of the eastern portion of the peninsula.

Everywhere growth benefited the smaller towns more than it did the larger ones, though this trend was most pronounced in Andalusia and Estremadura.[56] Here Spain's experience was partially divergent from that of Europe where before 1750 most growth was concentrated in the larger towns (de Vries, 1984: 69–73). It was only after that period that small towns tended to grow faster than larger ones, precisely when in Spain there was no longer any indication of preferential growth in smaller towns.[57] Yet slow urban growth, especially during the seventeenth century, was not just typical of central and southern Spain. At a European level, de Vries (1984: 76) has estimated that in 1600 there were 586 towns with more than 5,000 inhabitants, in 1650

[54] Rural growth rates shown on the table have been calculated in two different ways. For the 1591–1787 period, series of baptisms based on large regional samples of rural parishes have been used. These were compiled by J. Nadal at the University of Barcelona. Summary results were published in Nadal (1984: 76–85, 1988: 47–54). Earlier in this chapter we have already discussed the use of births as a proxy variable for total population. Since these series only go up to 1822, another method has been used for the 1787–1857 period. Here total urban population has been subtracted from total population in each region for both dates. The growth rates have been recalculated for the "rural" population. Only towns with over 5,000 inhabitants in both censuses have been used, and thus rural rates will tend to be higher than they would be had I used, say, only those towns with 5,000 inhabitants in either end of the period. Changes in the territorial definition of the different regions lend uncertainty to the calculations, though they would not seem sufficient to change the rather robust results.

[55] Another source of data which gives slightly lower growth rates for Valencia during this period (0.39) can be found in Pérez García and Ardit Lucas (1988: 202).

[56] In all regions growth rates (1591–1787) were negatively correlated with city size in 1591, but only in Andalusia (−0.374) and Estremadura (−0.627) were these correlations highly significant (<0.001).

[57] If we correlate growth between 1787 and 1857, with city size in 1787, the bivariate correlation coefficient is an insignificant −0.063.

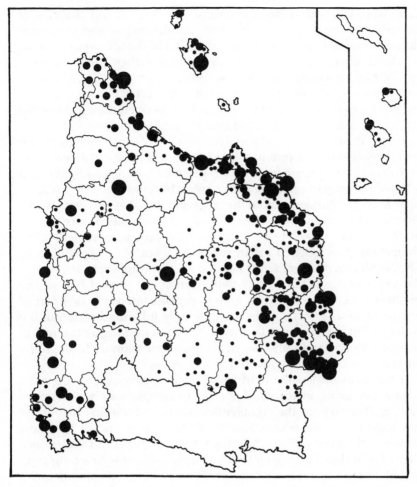

Map 2.5 Urban Spain, 1857

5,000–9,999
10,000–19,999
20,000–49,999
≥ 50,000

there were 538, and in 1700 there were only 557.[58] In this situation of diminishing urban population, the Mediterranean region mainly differed from northern Europe in that the decline of urban populations was far sharper between 1600 and 1650 than elsewhere (de Vries, 1984: 67). Notwithstanding the early seventeenth-century decline, what most clearly sets Spain apart from most of the rest of Europe is the fact that vast areas of the country really had not recovered until at least as late as the end of the eighteenth century, and some never did.

In 1787 the economic and social domination of the peninsula by the periphery had been a promise, by 1857 it was a reality. Between 1787 and 1857 consistent urban growth returned to all areas of Spain, and affected not only the existing urban areas, but stimulated the creation of new ones.[59] However, both the maps and the tables confirm that by 1857 the fastest growth and highest levels of urbanization were located in the coastal areas of the country. The center continued to be characterized by isolated urban centers in a sea of rural population. The North was predominantly rural, despite the appearance of urban density shown on Map 2.5.[60] Only during the second half of the nineteenth century did urban growth become intense in this part of Spain. Andalusia was still the most densely urbanized region of the country, but this was not to remain the case for long as the region between Murcia and Valencia, with a clear extension up through the coastal areas of Catalonia, would soon surpass it.

If we measure levels of urbanization by percentage of the total population living in towns, some ready comparisons with Europe emerge. Throughout the eighteenth century and the first half of the nineteenth, the arc from Cádiz to Valencia was one of the most densely urbanized regions in Europe. Only England and Wales, and then only in 1850, had higher levels of urbanization (de Vries, 1984: 39, 45–46). In 1787, Spain as a whole fitted somewhere in the middle, with levels below those of England and Wales, Scotland, the Netherlands, Belgium, but similar to those of Italy. By 1850, however, Spain's relative position had improved a bit, and it now surpassed both Italy

---

[58] De Vries emphasizes that the process of urbanization between 1500 and 1800 was generally a very slow one. In that period percentage urban only grew from 9.6 to 13.0 per cent (de Vries, 1984: 76).

[59] The example of Estremadura is eloquent on this point. In 1591 there were 14 towns in the region, in 1787 there were 8 and in 1857 there were 24.

[60] In 1857 in Galicia and Asturias, only Gijón, Oviedo, Lugo, La Coruña, Santiago de Compostela and Vigo can be considered true towns. Due to the specific nature of the administrative definition of "municipality" in that part of Spain, most "towns" were little more than the grouping of numerous smaller hamlets which had little in common save a municipal government. Thus the urban density for these two areas which appears on the map cannot be taken as such.

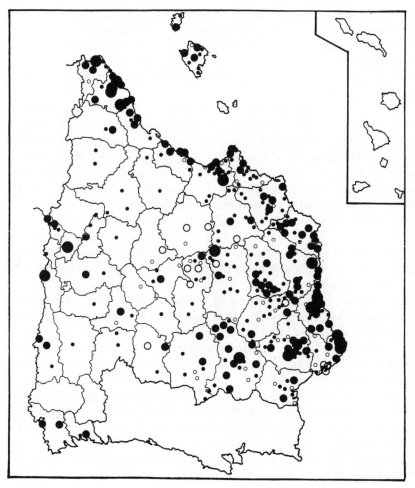

Map 2.6 Yearly urban growth rates, 1787–1857

O   <0.00

o   0.01–0.25

·   0.26–0.75

●   0.76–1.25

●   ≥1.26

and Belgium by a slight margin. The rate of increase, though, was lower than on the continent as a whole. The percentage of the total population living in towns of over 10,000 inhabitants increased in Spain between 1787 and 1857 by 47 per cent (from 14.7 to 21.6 per cent), as opposed to an increase in Europe of 67 per cent (from 10.0 to 16.7 per cent).

Barcelona was now the center of a major conurbation and included several medium-sized towns which had become focal points for considerable rural–urban migration thanks to the process of industrial expansion affecting the entire region.[61] This fueled extremely rapid population growth for most of the towns in the province, often in excess of 1.25 per cent per year.[62] However, the Barcelona area was still rivaled by Cádiz as the most important urban area on the peninsula. Cádiz, however, had fallen on difficult times since the early part of the century when Spain lost most of its American colonies. Eventually this led to its disappearance as a major urban center. Key growth areas of Andalusia had shifted to the district around Gibraltar, to Málaga and to Seville.

Growth rates in the central part of the peninsula lagged behind those along the periphery. The end result was that the differences in levels of urbanization between the two areas continued to increase.[63] What had happened to Cuenca was part of a much larger process which ended up changing the entire face of urban and rural Spain. The fact that population loss was far greater in Cuenca itself than in many other towns of the region merely emphasizes that having an economy which depended almost entirely on the wool industry, textile production and an ever-growing population to buy its products became a liability during the seventeenth century.

By all accounts, size should not be the only defining characteristic of urban areas. Towns also tended to have specialized functions and active populations which distinguished them from the surrounding rural areas. The debate between size and function arises whenever geographers discuss the definition of towns, and it is never easily solved.[64] Thus far I have used size as the sole defining characteristic of

---

61 For a recent study of this type of migration, see Camps Cura (1987).

62 Average population growth between 1787 and 1857 for towns in the province of Barcelona was 1.27 per cent per year, by far the highest in Spain.

63 Of the nearly 60 towns in both New and Old Castile, 9 of them (including Cuenca) continued to lose population between 1787 and 1857, and another 12 grew at a very slow pace. At a regional level it is apparent that all regions growing faster than the national average were located on the periphery.

64 De Vries (1984: 21–22) argues that "Cities...are places that have populations, population densities, percentages in the work force in non-agricultural occupations and a measure of diversity in occupationnal structure, all of which are sufficiently

towns because, despite its obvious shortcomings, it is the least ambiguous and most accessible data present in the historical documentation I have been using. Very little is known about the economic structures of the urban systems in Europe before the late nineteenth or even the early twentieth centuries. Spain, however, has an enviable source which enables us to circumvent at least partially this problem for the eighteenth century. Here I am referring, once again, to the Census of Floridablanca (1787) which contains a rudimentary division of the population by economic category. Apart from local studies, little systematic use has been made of this census for the study of the economic aspects of urban systems in Spain.[65]

In the Census of 1787 active population is divided up into a series of very rudimentary categories. These include different types of ecclesiastical occupations, nobles, lawyers, notaries and other legal authorities, students, farmers, day laborers, merchants, manufacturers, artisans, servants, military and other royal employees. Apart from servants, the military and some of the ecclesiastical categories, data refer mainly to household heads. Unfortunately, this is not always the case. A basic constraint arises when working with servants, nobles and, in a different sense, day laborers. The case of servants is especially problematic because in the census they do not seem to be classified in any consistent way. By and large, as one might suspect, servants in urban areas refer to domestic servants who were unmarried, lived in the households of their masters, and were more involved in the maintenance of the appearance of wealth than with production itself. However, there are enough towns in which the numbers of servants is so high that one is forced to suspect salaried urban workers were included as well. The problem is that these ambivalent categories make it impossible to establish the extent to which towns were, say, service towns. The solution I have adopted in this case has been to eliminate servants from all calculations and thus the active population of a town will normally refer only to household heads.

The nobility presents still other classification problems due to the basic social make-up of the northern part of the peninsula, especially the area extending from the Basque Country to Asturias. Here most or even all of the inhabitants were *hidalgos*, and this was often shown on

large." In practice, however, he settles on a size threshold (10,000 in practice, 5,000 in theory) for his definition of cities. This admittedly inadequate procedure is the one which most analysts of past urbanization have ended up adopting.

[65] One of the few studies to use this source, albeit superficially, to look at the economic nature of towns in Ancien Régime Spain can be found in Reher (1986: 44–46). Our knowledge of the economic structures of individual towns is, of course, much greater.

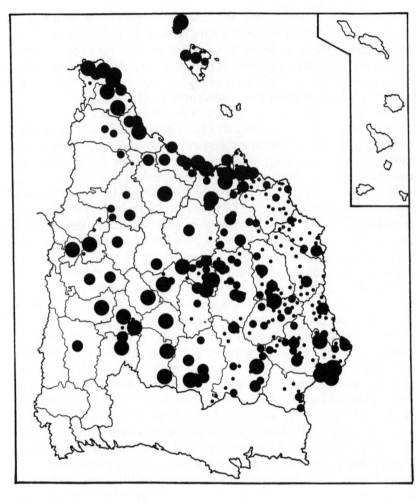

Map 2.7 Percentage of active urban population in industry and commerce, 1787

0–14
15–24
25–34
> 35

Table 2.6   *Active population in urban areas in 1787, by region*

Region	n	Eccle-siastical	Farmers	Day laborers	Total agricultural
Andalusia	72	3.23	10.57	58.99	69.56
New Castile	24	4.38	16.40	43.39	59.79
Old Castile/ Leon	12	9.05	13.98	27.81	41.79
Estremadura	24	5.80	14.91	39.62	54.53
Valencia/ Murcia	34	2.88	24.53	41.15	65.67
Aragon	6	5.24	18.41	33.34	51.75
Catalonia	12	4.62	9.66	34.03	43.70

Region	n	Industry	Commerce	Liberal professions
Andalusia	72	14.89	1.66	2.69
New Castile	24	18.40	3.90	4.79
Old Castile/ Leon	12	28.39	4.28	7.23
Estremadura	24	20.43	2.05	2.38
Valencia/ Murcia	34	16.04	1.09	2.53
Aragon	6	23.35	2.69	7.27
Catalonia	12	36.05	2.40	10.18

Note Expressed as percentage of total active population, excluding servants. Total ecclesiastical population does not include the population living in convents, which could at times be quite large. Total agricultural population is the sum of farmers and day laborers. Industrial population includes "artisans" and "manufacturers." Liberal population includes lawyers, notaries, and students. See text for further explanations.

the census itself. Active population data taken from the Census of 1787 for this part of Spain is useless and therefore these areas were eliminated from our calculations. Another difficult problem with no simple solution is the definition of day laborers as agricultural or industrial laborers. As I did earlier in this chapter, I have chosen to consider them as being occupied fundamentally in agricultural activities, though this is a forced interpretation of the data. For this reason, the magnitudes of different categories expressed in Map 2.7 and Table 2.6 should be considered as relative rather than absolute values.[66]

[66] Had I controlled for the relative weight of farmers and day laborers in regional populations, and ended up attributing "excess" day laborers to the industrial sector,

Doubts as to the precise interpretation of the data notwithstanding, the results give a clear-cut portrayal of the marked regional differences existing in Spain at the end of the Ancien Régime. Throughout the southern third of the country many, indeed most, of the towns were made up almost entirely of populations dedicated to agricultural activities. This was and is the legacy of the basic structure of land-holding in these areas where there was very restricted ownership of property, very large estates (*latifundios*), and large sections of the population with only their labor power to sell. Consequently it was an area of few but sizeable places where the day laborers lived.[67] The origins of this type of settlement are uncertain, but it could date from Muslim times and possible considerably earlier.

Agrotowns were most common in the highly urbanized regions of Andalusia, Murcia and the southern part of Valencia. In the southern half of the peninsula, apart from certain important exceptions, mainly in the Guadalquivir river valley, around Cádiz and in certain key cities, towns were large but otherwise had few of what one might consider the basic prerequisites for being urban. Patterns of urban settlement, however, were not uniform in this area. In most of Andalusia, the agricultural population lived within the limits of the town, as opposed to Murcia where it was often the consequence of farmers living outside the town walls themselves, but well within the municipal boundaries. From the perspective of a census, the result was basically the same: there were few distinctions between rural and urban social structures.

What then of urbanization in Andalusia and Murcia? Can one still speak of the existence of an urban system? By definition systems are based on the exchange of goods and services through a fairly well-defined urban hierarchy. Did these towns play a specific role in that hierarchy or not? A brief glance at Map 2.7 suggests that there was indeed a fairly well-defined hierarchy of functions, at least in the Guadalquivir river valley. Elsewhere, graduated differences in functional specialization are much more difficult to perceive. Based simply on the data at hand it is very difficult to advance more than tentative ideas, though it would certainly seem unwarranted to discard the existence of such a system just because of the presence of these agrotowns.[68]

industrial weight in Andalusia would have diminished, as opposed to everywhere else where it would have either increased or remained the same. Thus the fundamental differences already visible in Spain would not have changed at all.

[67] In 1787 in Andalusia, day laborers outnumbered farmers by a margin of 7.3 to 1. For one of the best studies on social structures in the south, see Malefakis (1970).

[68] The extent to which smaller towns performed specifically urban functions for other smaller settlements is unclear.

Rural–urban differences in demographic behavior seem to persist independent of the economic structure of the towns in question, thus suggesting that the density of settlement might also be a necessary part of any definition of a town, at least insofar as its behavioral implications are concerned.[69]

Industrial towns were the norm in the central and eastern parts of the peninsula, yet any similarity between Castile and the regions of the Levant is more apparent than real. The industrial towns in Castile had been the backbone of a viable urban network in the sixteenth century. If we could calculate active population data for 1591, the industrial weight of most of these towns would be far higher than it was in 1787.[70] Yet this was the part of urban Spain which had lost its vitality during the seventeenth century, and, by the time the Census of Floridablanca (1787) was carried out, it seemed to show little or no sign of recovery. On the other hand, towards the end of the eighteenth century, the industrial towns between Catalonia and Valencia clearly contained the seeds of Spain's economic transformation. Here, contrary to Castile, an important industrial sector was the hallmark of growth and transformation. This pattern was especially apparent in Catalonia where the percentage of people involved in industry was by far the highest in Spain. Both in terms of city size and active population, the eastern part of Spain, especially Catalonia, was destined to become the most dynamic part of the country.

Thus far I have placed considerable emphasis on the regional characteristics of city size, active population structures and growth patterns for Spanish towns. I have spoken a number of times of regional urban systems without offering any conclusive proof of their existence. Geographers have designed ingenious methods for modeling structures of entire urban systems and to test for the existence of integrated urban hierarchies. This method is based on the rank-size distribution of the towns in a given region.[71] If the urban system is well-integrated, then plotting the rank and size of all towns on a

[69] These differentials have appeared quite clearly in a number of recent studies about Spain. None of these, however, include smaller agrotowns, and so evidence is as yet tentative. See, for example, Reher (1986, 1989); Iriso Napal and Reher (1987).

[70] In 1561, 58 per cent of Cuenca's active population (including members of the clergy) was working in the industrial sector, as opposed to around one third in 1787. In 1561, the industrial sector in Segovia included 68 per cent of the active population (including clergy), as opposed to 56 per cent in 1787. For 1561 data on Segovia, see Bennassar (1968: 185–203); see also Barrio Gozalo et al. (1987: 173).

[71] The rank-size distribution can be expressed by the following equation:

$$P = K(R)^{-q}$$

Where R is city rank, q and K are constants, and P is city size.

logarithmic graph will yield an almost straight line, with a slope (−q) given as a simple linear regression by least squares. In this case, it can be called a lognormal distribution and suggests the existence of an effective urban integration. Some years ago, Zipf (1949) pointed out that city size distribution in the United States had a lognormal distribution with a slope of −1.[72] Since then, this specific type of lognormal distribution has been considered to be typical of economically mature and integrated urban systems.[73]

The use of these models for interpretation of historical data is not simple. Many of the predictive pretensions so often attached to them should be avoided because, in fact, there are many types of integrated urban systems, not just "mature" and "immature" systems. This is especially true when dealing with historical realities, where specifically economic factors are not the only forces determining the nature of these systems.[74] Here I will only use this method to give a systematic description of the different systems on the peninsula which, in fact, will complement much of what was already visible in the maps.

As de Vries (1984: 93) has aptly pointed out, one of the major problems with using rank-size models and interpreting their results, is the definition of the boundaries of different urban systems. Ultimately, there is no simple way to do this, nor can it be rigorously affirmed that a given set of towns belongs to only one system. De Vries in his pioneering study used national, regional and continental levels of analysis (de Vries, 1984: 95–120). In the case of Spain he has not, however, attempted any sub-national analysis.[75] And yet a brief look at any of the maps in this chapter suggests the existence of more than one system in Spain. Basically three seem to emerge from the data: a Castilian one (at least in the sixteenth century), an Andalusian one, and another which includes most of the historical Crown of Aragon (Aragon, Catalonia, Valencia and the Balearic Islands). There is, of course, no unassailable process by which the boundaries of urban systems can be arbitrarily established, and the present case is no exception. My basic criteria have been based on the empirical data emerging from the maps themselves, and these are certainly subject to criticism. Doubts may arise as to the specific boundaries of this or that

---

[72] In other words, each city in the system had a population which was the equivalent of that of the largest city system divided by its rank.

[73] Zipf's own work makes considerable use of the theoretical advances of Auerbach (1913) and Lotka (1941).

[74] For a critical review of these issues, see de Vries (1984: 85–95; 1989). Some of the most interesting work with rank-size models has been done by Carol Smith (1982, 1989).

[75] This was probably because he only had data on towns of more than 10,000 inhabitants, and therefore his samples were very small. For the present study, the sample includes all towns of more than 5,000 inhabitants.

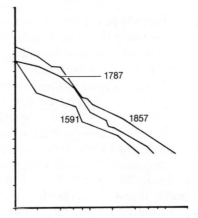

Figure 2.4 Rank-size distribution of towns in Andalusia

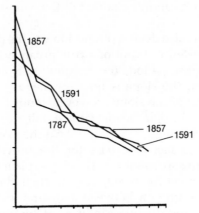

Figure 2.5 Rank-size distribution of towns in Castile

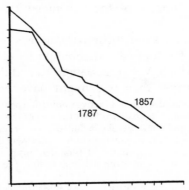

Figure 2.6 Rank-size distribution of towns in Aragon-Levant

system, but I feel that these three capture the essential networks of Spanish urban development over the period under study.[76] Finally, it should be remembered that use of rank-size models is a very elementary approach to the study of a far more complex subject. The basic task here is to show the essential traits of these systems.

The data shown in Figures 2.4. 2.5 and 2.6 suggest that all of the regions chosen had viable urban systems, though the degree of integration varied sharply among them and over time. Castile, much as I have already suggested, had a fairly well-developed system in the sixteenth century, when its rank-size distribution is nearly lognormal, though the slope is fairly shallow ($-.58$).[77] Thereafter, however, any suggestion of lognormality is lost.[78] It is clearly a case of a primate city (Madrid) dominating an entire system; or, rather, an entire urban system, as a system, apparently ceasing to exist. As already seen, the demise of Cuenca was an integral part of the demise of the Castilian urban system.

Rank-size analysis also deals a serious blow to the doubts expressed earlier as to the existence or not of a true urban system in southern Spain. Over the entire period, the distribution is almost lognormal though, once again, the slope is not very steep (-0.63, -0.66 and -0.59). The stability of the slope, however, tends to mask a definite evolution over time. In 1591, Seville fairly dominates the distribution, being higher than we might expect it to be if the slope is fitted to the smallest towns. The fact that data for the provinces of Málaga, Granada and Almería are missing, may help explain this distribution. In 1787 the situation was reversed, due mostly to the fact that Seville shared scarcely any growth between 1591 and 1787. The stronger growth of smaller towns doubtless influenced this distribution as well. In 1857 the distribution is much closer to lognormality and suggests that the disturbing effects of the seventeenth century had been overcome.

The Mediterranean system encompassing most of the eastern part of Spain shows a "flat-topped" distribution in 1787 when the four largest towns (Barcelona, Valencia, Saragossa and Palma de Mallorca) are clearly much larger than one might have predicted using an

---

[76] With respect to Murcia the disparities in active population of its towns as compared to the rest of the Levant and its distance from the center of the Andalusian system convinced us that it could not be readily included in either regional system.

[77] This evidence is in direct contradiction to Braudel's statement that the peninsula, and concretely Castile, were under-urbanized (Braudel, 1972: 2:726). In fact, as will become apparent later, at the end of the sixteenth century precisely the contrary was true.

[78] In 1787 the slope is -0.39 and in 1857 it is -0.33. If Madrid had been eliminated from the regression, the slope would have been still less.

equation based on the medium-sized and smaller towns. This could very well be due to the fact that talking of one system for the entire region at that time is stretching empirical reality. In 1857, however, the distribution comes much closer to lognormality, though the most important towns are still slightly larger than predicted. This progressive lognormality suggests that the economic and functional links underlying the system were much more operative than in the eighteenth century.

Surprisingly, the slope of the overall distribution in the Mediterranean region declines (from −0.56 to −0.49). This result is the same as the one seen in Andalusia, and in both cases is due to the fact that throughout the period small towns grew just as fast, or faster than larger ones. This could be considered a sign of immaturity within the system as a whole because it shows that much urban growth was a product of natural growth and non-selective migration. In a "mature" system, people should move about freely in search of the most advantageous jobs, normally in progressively larger towns. This automatically tends to make the slope of the distribution steepen, and had been considered a sign of a "mature" urban system.[79] During the period under study this sort of freedom of movement was not a possibility: large towns did not have enough economic "pull," living conditions in the countryside were not desperate enough to "push" the peasants off their land, and the institutional and cultural preconditions of high long-distance permanent migration had not yet been laid. Thus, while the existence of integrated urban systems in Spain as early as the sixteenth century is beyond question, their appearance was far from being modern.

Urban and rural patterns in New Castile

Let us return now to the more vexing question of the decline of urban Castile, a decline epitomized in the disaster which befell Cuenca. By now the general outline of that demise should be clear, both for the town of Cuenca and for the urban system of which it was an integral part. We also know that Cuenca suffered more or less the same fate as other Castilian towns; data on overall population totals are evidence enough of that. Yet many important questions still remain unanswered, or have only been touched on in a very general manner. To what extent was the rhythm of decline similar in different towns? Were there similarities in rural and urban population swings? What role did Madrid play in the demise of Castilian towns? Ultimately

[79] On the subject of the economic integration of urban systems, see C. Smith (1989).

these questions bring us up against other still more puzzling ones: why was the crisis so lasting; why was recovery so late in coming and so weak when it did?

The most cogent explanation for the downfall of the Castilian urban system has been given by David Ringrose in his brilliant but often speculative *Madrid and the Spanish Economy, 1560–1850* (1983).[80] Ringrose lays the blame for the decline of urban Castile squarely on the shoulders of Madrid, in his opinion a fundamentally parasitical imperial capital. Making use of the central place theory outlined by Christaller (1966), he sees the Castilian urban network during the middle part of the sixteenth century as a well-ordered urban hierarchy, with differing functional specializations. Toledo and Valladolid were the visible heads of this hierarchy. Below them there were a number of towns whose economic ties linked them both to the major urban centers of Castile, or to other areas on the peninsula and abroad (Ringrose, 1983: 253–258). Cuenca was one of those towns fulfilling specialized economic functions within the Castilian urban hierarchy.

The emergence of Madrid as the major city of Castile upset this balance. Being the center of a kingdom and of an empire, its functional relation with central Castile was one of providing governmental and ecclesiastical services, in return basically for food and rents. Since central Spain was not an agriculturally wealthy area and transportation was difficult and expensive, Madrid ended up becoming a parasite on the Castilian economy.[81] It purchased foodstuffs from its own hinterland and expensive products from abroad, encouraged subsistence economies in rural areas and ended up taking over many of the specific functions of the smaller central places in the Castilian urban system (Ringrose, 1983: 12–16). Toledo was the first to feel the negative effects of Madrid's influence, and its elites were emigrating *en masse* to Madrid by the early seventeenth century (Ringrose, 1983: 257). The other Castilian towns followed suit. Toward the latter part of the seventeenth century, there was a timid reaction on the part of the internal economy, but by that time the fundamental source of economic dynamism on the peninsula lay in the peripheral regions.

It would be historically inaccurate to blame Madrid exclusively for the downfall of an entire urban system.[82] This decline must be viewed

---

[80] For his basic argument see pp. 1–16 and 215–321.

[81] These factors were essential in preventing Madrid from being a stimulus for the Castilian economy, much as London had been for the English economy. See Wrigley (1967).

[82] Ringrose, in a personal communication, has insisted on the fact that there were multiple causes for the decline of Castile, and that Madrid became the "agency through which the negative pressures of taxation, inflation, imperial policy, and

within the general context of the seventeenth-century crisis in Castile whose most salient aspect was, perhaps, the practical disappearance of a once vibrant textile industry, victim of inflation, imperial policies, royal taxation and popular tastes. Without viable industries, or with little rural economic activity to coordinate, towns lost their ability to attract excess rural populations. This ability, of course, was the key to growth or stagnation of urban population. As is well known, natural growth rates tended to be negative in most towns, and Cuenca was no exception.[83] This being the case, a town's population growth was strictly dependent on its ability to attract rural migrants and, if this was undermined, as it was in Castile, its population could only stagnate or decline.[84]

A key element in this fundamentally straightforward process was the existence or not of "excess" rural population. As far as one can tell, people with land and jobs were seldom among the migrants to towns, at least not among those who stayed. Permanent migrants tended to be those who could better their lot in towns.[85] This could be the consequence of excessive population growth in rural areas, lack of jobs or land in the countryside, the absence of a place in the local marriage market, etc. However, this entire process was predicated on the fact that the rural sector of society could generate these potential migrants. It is from this perspective that I would like to examine the fate of urban Castile in greater detail. Just how closely were urban dynamics linked to rural population trends? If the ties were close, then the trends will probably reveal more similarities in short-and medium-run fluctuations in urban and rural areas of Castile than one might have suspected.

In essence Ringrose's interpretation of this aspect of Spanish history is based on an urban to urban, or urban to rural type causality. In the final part of this chapter I would like to make use of the results of some

growing lack of competitiveness were transmitted into the regional urban system and to the market-oriented sectors of the countryside." See also Ringrose (1988).

[83] This has often been called the "urban graveyard effect." On this subject, see Sharlin (1978: 127–138), van der Woude (1982) and, de Vries (1984: 277–297). Not all towns had negative natural growth rates. Berlin, for example, between 1711 and 1900 only showed negative rates before the middle part of the nineteenth century. Even here, though, the great bulk of urban growth came from migration. Both Amsterdam and Stockholm showed similar patterns (de Vries, 1984: 235–237). In urban Spain between 1887 and 1930, growth by natural causes was extremely weak, normally averaging less than 0.10 per cent per year (Reher, 1989).

[84] This is shown quite clearly by de Vries (1984: 221–231) by use of a three-sector pre-industrial migration simulation model.

[85] The process of migration was not a simple one; migrants had many reasons for doing what they did, and there were many types of migration. See Chapter 7 for further discussion.

more recent research to explore the possibility that some of the causality at work in seventeenth- and eighteenth-century Castile ran in the opposite direction, or at least was not unidirectional. The analysis will be based, once again, on long series of baptisms for a number of areas of New Castile. I will concentrate on data from New Castile because it is the most pertinent to the subject at hand. Vital statistics have recently been published from several towns of the region (Madrid, Toledo, Ciudad Real, Talavera de la Reina and Cuenca), as well as from a sizeable sample of rural villages in the area.[86] While these data do not provide any definitive answers as to the causes of urban decline in Castile, they open a perspective which heretofore had received little attention.

As seen earlier, the fundamental reversal of the fortunes of urban Castile took place during the first part of the seventeenth century. Figure 2.7 provides striking evidence of the fact that the evolution of our sample of towns in New Castile was practically identical. While there are slight differences in some areas, the basic patterns are common to all. Between approximately 1580 and 1590 there was a pronounced growth in population everywhere, with increases of up to 20 per cent in a period of around 10 years. The stagnation of the last third of the century noted by many authors quite simply did not exist, at least during this decade (Ringrose, 1983: 255). The period of euphoria was followed by a decline – greater in Cuenca, visible elsewhere – and then a leveling off of trends, with no growth at all between 1595 and the first years of the seventeenth century. The real crisis hit between 1603–1606. The use of five year moving averages makes it impossible to pinpoint an exact date, but the coincidence in the timing of the inflection point of the trends in all of the towns is striking. There was a pronounced and terrible population loss until at

---

[86] Data come from the following sources: Toledo (Martz, 1983: 79; see also Martz and Porres, 1974: Graph 1); Ciudad Real (Philips, 1979: 121–125); Madrid (Carbajo Isla, 1987: 257–287); Talavera de la Reina (González Muñoz, 1975: Appendix 1). The data from Toledo were taken directly from a graph, and some slight inaccuracies might be present. There are also data from part of the town of Ciudad Real for the eighteenth century, but their quality is subject to serious doubt. Rural data are taken from Nadal (1988: 40–45). The villages in the sample are: Barajas, Motilla, Tribaldos, Villarejo de Fuentes and Zafra de Záncara (the present-day province of Cuenca); Cereceda, Chiloeches, Hontanillas, Mantiel, Mochales (province of Guadalajara); Alcobendas, Anchuelo, Arganda del Rey, Colmenar Viejo, Griñon, Horcajo de la Sierra, Matalpino, Los Molinos, Soto del Real, Torrejón de Ardóz, Villaviciosa de Odón and Valdilecha (Madrid); Mascaraque, Orgaz, El Toboso, Villaseca de Sagra, Yepes and Yébenes (province of Toledo). This rural sample is heavily weighted toward the northern part of the region, especially the province of Madrid. On the whole, however, we have found little to suggest that it does not reflect the basic evolution of the non-urban population of the region.

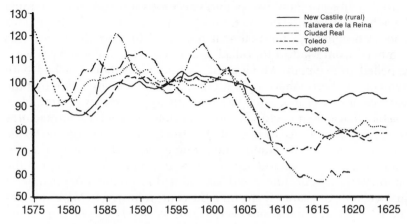

Figure 2.7 Baptisms in urban and rural New Castile, 1575–1625

least 1610, followed by a more gradual decline until 1615 or even later. Decline seemed to stop by the 1620s. By then, however, urban populations were somewhere between 15 and 25 per cent below levels holding at the beginning of the century.

The precise timing of this phase of the urban collapse does not have a ready explanation. It has often been said that the major mortality crisis of the end of the sixteenth century and beginning of the seventeenth century played a decisive role in the downfall of Castile. For urban New Castile, however, this timing is simply not correct. The bout with the plague, for all its gravity, was gravest in other parts of the peninsula and in New Castile outbreaks were almost entirely limited to the 1599–1601 period, considerably before the 1603–1605 crisis point (Pérez Moreda, 1980: 263–265, 278).[87] Other elements were at work undermining the structures of urban Castile. In general terms, the situation could not have been worse. Apart from the recent epidemic, the textile industry had been in crisis since the 1590s or earlier, rural population was declining and there was a generalized loss of confidence in Castile's ability to cope with adversity.[88] The future of Castilian towns was certainly not bright.

[87] In the towns of Old Castile, the effects of the plague were much more severe than in New Castile, and in places like Segovia it must have dealt a crippling blow to its textile industry.

[88] It is truly unfortunate that so little is known about actual fluctuations in textile production or even about the amounts of wool sold during this period. Due to this, ideas regarding the evolution of urban economies can only be approximations at best. For the period in question the demographic information we possess, despite its superficial nature, is far more complete than economic data.

In this dire situation, two political decisions were taken which must have had detrimental effects for the towns themselves, for their elites and, consequently, for potential migrants. In 1602 the Court was removed from Madrid to Valladolid, and in 1609 the Moriscos were expelled from Spain. Moving the Court to a distant city had both symbolic and economic implications. Apart from being a sign that the balance of power in Castile had definitively shifted away from New Castile, it also eliminated Madrid as a viable market for manufactures from New Castile. Apart from all the structural problems of the textile industry – inflation, taxation, investment, etc. – its basic markets in rural areas and in Madrid seemed to be drying up: population in the countryside was declining and Madrid had lost half its population in just a couple of years. By the time the court returned to Madrid it was too late; urban populations were down by nearly 15 per cent, there were no longer enough skilled artisans, and all investment capital had fled. The expulsion of the Moriscos was yet another blow in this string of crises and must have had similar, albeit less spectacular, effects.[89] It would be foolish to suggest that these two political decisions alone caused a downfall of Castilian towns which would have occurred in any case; they only hastened decline and made its timing more uniform.

At a more general level, parallel trends observed in all the towns suggest that there was a basic pattern holding in the entire region. Rural population development may be the reason for the overall uniformity observed earlier. It is extremely interesting to note that the growth period of the 1580s was also one of rural population growth. Subsequently rural areas showed a downward trend between 1595 and 1618; urban decline started a bit later, and lasted just about as long. Rural and urban trends are quite highly correlated (Table 2.7). Though we know distressingly little about the mechanisms under-lying these rural population trends, the correlation between the rural and the urban worlds is not difficult to explain within the context of rural to urban migration. As will become clear in chapter 7 of this book, in-migration to towns could be extremely intense, and was matched by similar rates of out-migration.[90] There is no reason to believe that these rates (based on nineteenth-century data) did not hold during the first part of the seventeenth century as well. Even a slight reduction in

---

[89] The Morisco population of the town of Cuenca was not very large. According to the Inquisition records, in 1594 only 53 Moriscos lived in Cuenca. In rural areas of the province of Cuenca their numbers were considerably higher. For more on this subject, see García Arenal (1978a: 15–18; 1978b: 191–199). The classic work on the expulsion of the Moriscos is Lapeyre's *Géographie de l'Espagne morisque* (1959).

[90] In a small town like Cuenca levels could exceed 10 per cent of the population per year.

Table 2.7   *Bivariate correlation coefficients of baptisms in several towns of New Castile*

Period: 1585–1623

	Cuenca	Talavera	Toledo	Ciudad Real	New Castile
Cuenca	1.00	0.92	0.69	0.71	0.66
Talavera		1.00	0.87	0.85	0.83
Toledo			1.00	0.92	0.79
Ciudad Real				1.00	0.79
New Castile					1.00

Period: 1595–1700

	Cuenca	Talavera	Madrid	New Castile
Cuenca	1.00	0.65	−0.55	0.79
Talavera		1.00	−0.63	0.35
Madrid			1.00	−0.48
New Castile				1.00

Period: 1701–1802

	Cuenca	Talavera	Madrid	New Castile
Cuenca	1.00	0.83	0.31	0.50
Talavera		1.00	0.61	0.68
Madrid			1.00	0.83
New Castile				1.00

Note   All data are five year moving averages.
Sources Talavera, González Muñoz (1975: Appendix 1); Madrid, Carbajo Isla (1987: 257–287), Ciudad Real, Philips (1979: 121–125). The sample for New Castile was compiled by Jordi Nadal. Summary results were published in Nadal (1984, 1988).

the in-migration rates could have tremendous effects on urban populations. Potential migrants from rural areas were basically made up of excess rural population, yet it turns out that from the mid-1590s, population was declining in rural Castile. There could not have been very much "excess" population in the countryside which would have made up the pool of potential migrants. In Castile, urban decline ceased only when the rural population started to grow once again.

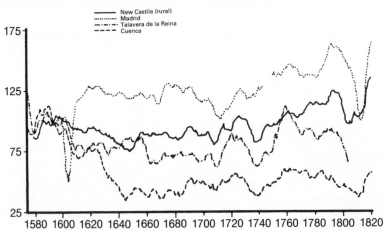

Figure 2.8 Urban and rural population development in New Castile, 1575–1820

The mechanisms of urban depopulation were probably the combination of a slow-down of in-migration coupled with the out-migration of the more productive social groups. As the Castilian towns lost their economic vitality, they lost their ability to attract or retain servants, artisans or unskilled labor. Only a marginal shift in the prevailing rates would, as seen earlier, have been enough to provoke the urban crisis.[91] Towns, however, did not develop independent of their surrounding rural areas. Towns and migrants were linked to their rural origins, and these links persisted whether a family lived in the town or not. In other words there was a continual flow of migrants from the countryside to the town, and back again. Within this context, the demise of Castilian towns probably mainly involved a return to the rural areas of New Castile.[92]

Once the period of crisis and readjustment had passed, rural and urban population trends continued to be linked, though perhaps less clearly than during the earlier period. Similarities also persist in the development of the Castilian towns of Cuenca and Talavera, though Talavera seems to have weathered the storm somewhat better than

[91] A population loss of 15 per cent in 10 years meant a decline of nearly 1.6 per cent per year. Given likely in- and out-migration rates of approximately 10 per cent per year, only an 8 per cent drop in in-migration rates (to 9.2 per cent per year), coupled with similar increase in out-migration rates (to 10.8 per cent) would have been sufficient to explain the entire loss.

[92] Except for the 1602–1607 period, a certain number of these urban out-migrants probably went to Madrid, and would probably have been members of the local bureaucracies, rather than of the productive groups in urban society.

Cuenca (Figure 2.8). While Cuenca continued its slide until mid-century, population losses were curtailed in Talavera and there was even some recovery. As opposed to Cuenca which was heavily dependent on the textile industry for its wealth (58 per cent of its active population), Talavera was a town in an agriculturally rich valley where textiles had less importance than in Cuenca.[93] Once the textile industry had been destroyed forever as a source of wealth, Cuenca, unlike Talavera, had little to fall back on.

After 1645, the similarity in urban and rural trends returns and persists until the 1760s (Table 2.7). At that point urban populations seem to stagnate while rural areas continue to show population increases, though this rate of growth is certainly slower. Castile was again reaching the limits of the carrying capacity of its agriculture. Once this had been surpassed, decline set in everywhere. These patterns of growth suggest the continued sensitivity of urban populations to rural trends. They also indicate a prolonged process of de-urbanization in New Castile, excluding Madrid. Holding relative populations of the 1590s equal, a century later Talavera was 17 per cent below rural levels, and Cuenca was 39 per cent below. By the 1790s this progressive de-urbanization had not shown any indication of stopping, as Talavera had fallen to 25 per cent below rural levels and Cuenca to 50 per cent below. Apart from Madrid, the ruralization of New Castile was complete.

The evolution of Madrid was, of course, different, though it too was generally subject to the existence or not of excess rural population. The exception to this was the period between 1600 and 1625, when fluctuations in Madrid were radically different from those of any of the other towns or rural areas of New Castile. After that point, Madrid's population remained faily constant throughout much of the century.[94] Once the new urban–rural equilibrium had been reached and the urban hierarchy readjusted by mid-century, Madrid also became subject to rural population trends, though in a more advantageous manner than other Castilian towns. Trends during the eighteenth century were largely similar everywhere. In the seventeenth century, fluctuations in Madrid's population were clearly different from those in both rural and urban areas; in the eighteenth century, this was no

93 In 1561 in Talavera, textiles occupied 15.5 per cent of the active population, and agriculture 38 per cent (18.1 per cent "farmers" and 20.4 per cent "day laborers"). This structure persists throughout the period under study. See González Muñoz (1974: 163, 254, 343–345).

94 This contradicts Ringrose's (1983: 25–33) "revised" population estimates for the town whereby Madrid lost nearly 40 per cent of its population between 1630 and 1700.

longer the case. This can be seen in the correlation coefficients on Table 2.7.

Underlying the mechanisms, causes and timing of the seventeenth-century change, there is also reason to believe that by the latter part of the sixteenth century urban Castile had outstripped the carrying capacity of rural Castile. Earlier it was shown that 22.7 per cent of the total population of New Castile (perhaps 18 per cent for both Castiles together), lived in urban areas. Agricultural productivity in much of Old and New Castile was not nearly high enough to support this density of urban population consistently. As towns grew, they put increasing pressure on rural areas to provide them with foodstuffs. Rural surplus could not always be guaranteed and subsistence crises probably became more frequent as rural population density grew and percentage urban increased even faster.[95] Moreover, the growth of populations in both towns and countryside fueled the inflationary processes already at work in Spain, with far-reaching economic consequences. In the long run all towns were tied to the productivity of their hinterlands, especially when long distances and deficient transportation systems made supply from other sources an unreasonable proposition. This was the case of urban Castile throughout the entire early modern period.[96]

The crisis in the seventeenth century produced a new equilibrium in Castile. The medium and large towns had lost much of their population, Madrid's had increased sharply. However, despite Madrid's growth, by the second half of the seventeenth century the percentage living in urban areas must have been well below the levels holding a century earlier. Even by the end of the eighteenth century, after a long period of urban and rural growth, the percentage urban in both Castiles combined was really no larger than it had been in 1591. Only in 1857 could some modest changes by perceived, though once again the lion's share of growth was concentrated in Madrid. It seems unlikely that at any time during the early modern period could Castilian agriculture have supported a greater proportion of urban population, and thus a type of ceiling to potential urbanization

---

[95] As far as we know, there is nothing published on the frequency and intensity of subsistence crises toward the end of the sixteenth century, but it is not unreasonal be to assume that these increased decisively. It should be remembered, however, that the rate of urban growth in Castile during the second half of the sixteenth century must have been extremely fast, especially if we take into account the likelihood that Madrid's population trebled between mid-century and the 1590s (from 30,000 to 90,000 inhabitants).

[96] This problem has become a central theme of analysis in the work of Ringrose (1970; 1983). The only town in central Spain to partially overcome this problem was Madrid, and then only much later. For more on this, see Castro (1987).

existed. The seventeenth century, then, was a period of adjustment with lasting consequences: the urban hierarchy had been rearranged and overall urban population declined, until such time as rural population growth and rural production could once again support urban growth. Once the ceiling had been reached, towards the end of the sixteenth century and then again at the end of the eighteenth, de-urbanization was the only solution.[97] Castile was prisoner of its own geographical reality, and technological change was unable to overcome this handicap until well into the nineteenth century.[98] By the same token, Cuenca's fate was only special to the people from Cuenca. Otherwise it was simply an integral part of the fate of an entire urban system, which could probably have been predicted as early as 1580 had anyone had a mind to do so.

[97] Increasing agricultural productivity, stimulated in turn by excellent transportation systems, enabled English urbanization patterns to break the stranglehold on urban (and rural) growth. England, however, was an exception in Europe where levels of productivity seemed to remain fairly stable throughout much of the early modern period. For the best overview of this subject, see Wrigley (1985; 1987: 167–193); see also Daunton (1978).

[98] On this subject, see the classic work by Boserup (1981).

3

Demographic dynamics in an urban context

Introduction

Somewhat hidden by the long-term oscillations in the town's fortunes, there was a demographic system whose development was often quite out of step with that of the town itself. A clear definition of the parameters and determinants of urban demographic behavior is certainly a major goal of this study, as it will shed light on the reproductive capacity of the population and help define many characteristics of urban life. However, any study of urban demography raises the question as to just how specifically urban it was. It is reasonable to suspect that demographic behavior was strongly influenced by a number of variables, some of which were typical of the central meseta of Spain, and others common to all urban areas independent of their cultural and economic context.

In other words, within an urban context we might expect to see a mixture of regional, mainly rural, and specifically urban factors or characteristics. If not, what explanation can be offered for the following apparent contradiction in urban demographic behavior? In most of Europe persistently lower levels of nuptiality and marital fertility, and higher levels of mortality characterized most towns of the pre- and early industrial era. Conversely though, if one were to juxtapose two maps of regional patterns of, say, fertility in urban and in rural areas, they would look remarkably similar. In other words, towns with relatively high fertility as compared to other towns tended to be located in provinces of relatively high fertility as well. In fact, we might well expect to see both regional and specifically urban forces at work in possibly contradictory ways. In this sense Cuenca ceases to be simply

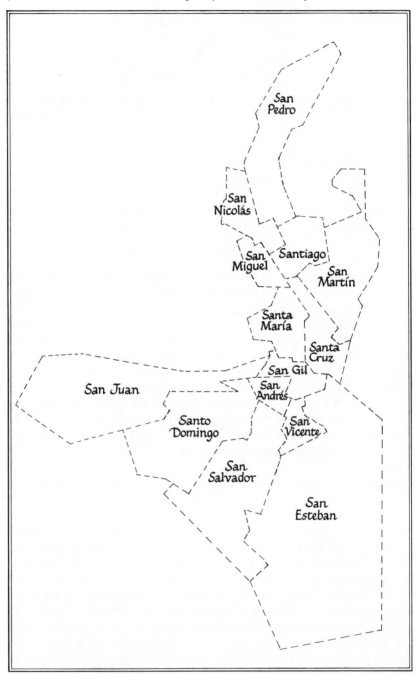

Map 3.1 Division of Cuenca by parishes

our protagonist and becomes a microcosm in which urban behavior patterns and their determinants can be studied.[1]

While a general discussion of both the regional and the urban context of demographic behavior in Cuenca will be a central part of this chapter, no less important is a precise definition of the basic parameters of the system itself.[2] Much of the present chapter is based on the results of a family reconstitution covering 7 of the 14 urban parishes which themselves represent approximately 30 per cent of the town's population.[3] These parishes are concentrated in the upper part of town and can be seen on Map 3.1.[4] Despite numerous problems stemming from the high mobility inherent in all urban populations, coupled with the fact that the data base only included a part of the population, I was able to make acceptable estimates of a number of basic demographic parameters.

The demographic indicators derived will be systematically compared to both regional and urban patterns, in order to ascertain the extent to which they were purely "urban" in nature. While distinctive urban behavior will certainly become apparent, it will also be clear that towns were always immersed in a rural world in which regional attitudes, structures and dynamics played an important role in urban life. In fact, given the importance of local migration for urban economy and life, it could be no other way.

---

[1] The pioneer work on urban demography was written many years ago by Roger Mols (1954–1956). More recently, the French school of historical demography has produced a number of monographs on the subject. In particular Jean Pierre Bardet (1983) and Alfred Perrenoud (1979) have published excellent studies of major cities. A useful review of the major issues of urban demography can be found in de Vries (1984: ch. 9) and Hohenberg and Lees (1985: 74–98). For examples of other studies of urban demography, see Lachiver (1969) and Garden (1970).

[2] This is especially important if we bear in mind that very little is known about urban demographic behavior in pre-industrial Spain. While a good number of urban monographs do exist, few deal directly with the basic nature of demographic behavior. Some examples of the monographs which give some importance to demographic aspects of towns are: Mauleón Isla (1961), Yun Casalilla (1980), Sanz Sampelayo (1980), Marcos Martín (1978), Philips (1979), Fortea Pérez (1981), Salas Auséns (1981), Alvarez Santaló (1974), Carmona García (1976), Chacón Jiménez (1979), Martz and Porres (1974), González Muñoz (1975), Ringrose (1983), Carbajo Isla (1987).

[3] Among the urban studies which make use to a greater or lesser extent of nominative record linkage techniques are Bennassar (1967), Ansón Calvo (1977), Rodríguez Sánchez (1977), Rodríguez Cancho (1981).

[4] They are San Pedro, San Nicolás, San Martín, Santa María, Santa Cruz, San Gil and Santiago. These registers are all housed in the Archivo Diocesano de Cuenca. A yearly index of vital statistics also exists for the parish of San Esteban and will be used in other parts of this study.

Nuptiality

The importance of nuptiality has long been a central theme in historical demography. While perhaps not the first, certainly the most eloquent statement of this was given by Malthus who showed that nuptiality was the only socially determined mechanism by which some sort of equilibrium between population and resources could be maintained. Though proponents of this view have never been lacking, in recent years the study of nuptiality has been considered a key area for an understanding of past population dynamics. John Hajnal was the first to attempt to look at the nature and geographical distribution of marriage patterns in Europe and, more recently, the work of Wrigley and Schofield and many others has gone a long way towards seconding Malthus' original formulation to the effect that marriage was indeed the chief determinant of fertility levels and of population growth in past societies.[5]

Recent research in the field of historical demography has contributed to our theoretical and empirical understanding of the relationship between nuptiality and fertility. Its role in society as a whole is both complex and multidirectional. It is closely tied to a veritable plethora of social, demographic, economic and cultural realities (the marriage market, economic structures, economic fluctuations, inheritance patterns, people's attitude towards marriage, mortality levels, etc.), though the specific weight of each factor has never been convincingly ferreted out. What is more, we are often far closer to understanding the determinants of nuptiality than many of its implications, especially those unrelated to the process of biological reproduction.

The study of nuptiality within a Spanish context has not kept pace with many of the theoretical and empirical advances made elsewhere in Europe. Recently, though, two thoughtful attempts have been made to reassess the existence or not of distinctive Spanish marriage patterns. Though the authors have based their analysis on somewhat differing time periods and data sets, they agree on the fact that marriage patterns in Spain (and in Portugal) differed quite markedly from those in most of the rest of Western Europe, revealed far greater regional variability than had been previously thought, and were marked by a generalized stability between the sixteenth and the

---

[5] See Hajnal (1965). Much of this interest stems directly or indirectly from the work of Wrigley and Schofield (1981). Two examples of this are Weir (1984a) and Goldstone (1986). For a succinct and eloquent statement of the importance of the role of nuptiality, see Wrigley (1981).

nineteenth centuries (Pérez Moreda, 1986; Rowland, 1988). Despite varying emphasis, both authors ultimately seek to explain both the stability and the variance of nuptiality within the context of socially determined institutions (inheritance patterns, agricultural labor, etc.) and demographic regimes.

Both articles should have a considerable influence on scholarship in Spain though, unfortunately, in both cases, their attempts at a global synthesis may as yet be somewhat premature. First of all, before the latter part of the eighteenth century we know only a little about age at marriage thanks to a few scattered local studies, and almost nothing about celibacy. Even after that period, information is restricted to census-based singulate mean age at marriage and permanent celibacy, and then only for widely separated intervals (1787, 1887, 1900, etc.) and for large aggregates of population (provinces and provincial capitals).[6] Hardly the stuff for a thoroughgoing understanding of nuptiality![7] One of the principal – and modest – purposes of this chapter is to bring to light new information regarding marriage patterns in Spain.

Yet in other areas of Europe where more abundant data are available, a sensible understanding of marriage patterns, their determinants and consequences, is still a sought-after goal. For example, the issue of nuptiality within an urban context, which has thus far received relatively little attention from historians, poses some ticklish issues for more general theories of marriage. It is commonly felt that inheritance patterns and the availability of land played an important role in the timing and incidence of marriage in northwestern Europe. People would not get married until such time as they could make a gainful living and, in a rural world, this could mean considerable delays in marriage (Smith, 1981a; 1984b). It is likely, then, that land and inheritance would play a sharply reduced role in an urban environment in which wage labor and job mobility were common. Yet most studies of urban nuptiality have shown that it was nearly always more restricted than in the surrounding rural areas.[8] The often skewed marriage market in towns has been used to explain this reality. Unfortunately, this explanation is only partially correct since an unbalanced marriage market should intensify nuptiality for one sex, just as it restricts it for the other. However, it is far from clear whether

---

[6] Age at marriage is calculated from census tabulations using the method pioneered by John Hajnal in 1953. More recently, Robert Rowland has proposed some adjustments to this method in order to compensate for male out-migration (Rowland, 1987b).

[7] Spanish material, however, is of far greater quality than in many other countries.

[8] For Spain, see Reher (1986: 46–55; 1989) and Iriso Napal and Reher (1987).

or not urban marriage was more restricted for only one, or for both sexes.

What cannot be disputed, though, is that in towns many of the basic mechanisms determining nuptiality worked differently than they did in rural areas. Marriage markets, job mobility, the availability of housing, the effects of migration and even the influence of the Church would not necessarily be the same. The extent to which the social context of nuptiality was specifically urban is a question of considerable interest since, apart from the obvious implications for an adequate understanding of urban society, it may help explain some of the reasons why towns played the role they did in the transition of nuptial patterns between the nineteenth and early twentieth centuries in Europe.[9] These and other similarly vexing questions will become recurrent issues throughout much of this section.

Our analysis will support the view that indeed there were specifically urban determinants of nuptiality, though these acted within a larger regional, or cultural, context in which the basic parameters of marriage were similar in both rural and urban areas. Urban migration, the marriage market, job availability and profession, all specific to pre-industrial towns, teamed with inheritance patterns, familial relations and even attitudes towards marriage which clearly transcended urban life. In this situation, prevailing levels of mortality would seem to have had little direct or short-run influence in nuptiality, though in the long run they too helped determine prevailing patterns. Finally, the importance of the basic social context of nuptiality will become clear as religious influences and geographical constraints on the choice of a mate end up playing a key role in characterizing nuptiality.

A map of eighteenth-century nuptiality patterns in Spain would show considerable regional contrasts.[10] Nuptiality was most restricted in the North and the Northwest, and most intense in the southern half of the country. Strong, albeit indirect evidence exists to the effect that this basic regional distribution had existed since at least the sixteenth century, and continued to exist at the end of the nineteenth. In other words, the Spanish marriage system (or systems) showed considerable stability over time and pronounced variability at any one

---

[9] For an overview of this change, see Coale and Treadway (1986: 52–76), Watkins (1981). For an earlier transition in nuptiality in France, see, Henry and Houdaille (1978 and 1979).

[10] A number of authors have made use of the Census of Floridablanca (1787) in order to establish a regional view of nuptiality in Spain. What I am saying here is merely a superficial summary of many of their viewpoints. See Rowland (1988), Livi Bacci (1986) and Pérez Moreda (1986). For a useful compilation of data, see Valero Lobo (1984).

Table 3.1   *Mean age at first marriage*

	Males			Females		
Period	mean	median	n	mean	median	n
1560–1600				21.6	21.0	32
1601–1650	23.6	23.4	44	20.7	20.3	65
1651–1700	25.2	25.3	36	21.8	22.8	64
1701–1750	25.6	24.5	68	22.4	21.9	75
1751–1800	25.5	24.2	88	22.6	21.9	100
1801–1852	25.6	24.2	97	24.3	23.6	81
1841–1852[a]	26.9	25.0	60	24.6	24.0	63

Sources Parish registers.
Note [a] Data for 1841–1852 are taken from the declared age at marriage.

moment.[11] The area of the southern half of the central meseta, where Cuenca is located, was one of moderately low age at marriage and even lower celibacy. Data from the town itself help confirm the validity of a regional approach to nuptiality in Spain. In Cuenca, age at marriage for men oscillated between 23.6 and 26.9 years between the sixteenth and the nineteenth centuries, while for women it went from 20.7 to 24.0 (Table 3.1). At the end of the eighteenth century, age at marriage in the town of Cuenca was 25.5 for men and 22.6 for women, while in the region of New Castile, it was 24.9 and 23.0.

A similar situation appears when we look at permanent celibacy, though here there is considerably greater variability. For men in the city it was 11.7 per cent in 1752, 15.9 per cent in 1800 and 6.6 per cent in 1844, while for women it was 13.3 per cent in 1752, 10.3 per cent in 1800 and 10.6 in 1844. For New Castile in 1787 the percentages were considerably lower (10.1 males and 7.5 females). The greater disparity here is not surprising and often characterizes urban nuptiality (Reher, 1986: 46–55). Yet the 10 per cent permanent celibacy in Cuenca is considerably lower than that of other regions. Both celibacy and age at marriage data confirm that nuptiality in Cuenca showed strikingly similar levels to those holding in the region of New Castile.

Central to the existence and stability of regional marriage patterns were the inheritance practices common to Cuenca as well as to much of the remainder of central Spain.[12] The basic system, which had been

---

[11] For example, female age at marriage in 1787 was as high as 25.2 in the Basque Country and as low as 22.2 in Andalusia. See Rowland (1987b: 58).

[12] Much of what is going to be said in the ensuing paragraphs is taken from the wills housed in the Notarial Archives section of the Archivo Histórico Provincial, as well as

largely unaltered since the Laws of Toro (1505), was based on the widespread existence of partible inheritance. Upon the death of either of the two parents, all of the goods which they had contributed to the marriage would be divided in equal shares among the surviving children, or, if there were no children, among the next of kin. By law, 80 per cent of the total property had to be bequeathed to the legitimate heirs.[13] This property division was always rigorously equal and no sex preference was ever shown. Only a small part of a person's property (20 per cent before 1889) could be disposed of freely.[14] This was normally given either to the spouse, some more distant relative, the Church or to increase the inheritance of one or more of the heirs.

When a family decided not to draw up a formal will (as few did), then all of the inheritance, once outstanding debts had been removed, would go to the legitimate heirs. Legally, each spouse bequeathed his own possessions upon death. Even though it is difficult to be completely sure on the matter, it seems that the dead spouse's part of all communal property was also willed at the time of death, thus considerably complicating property rights, at least before the death of the surviving parent. In fact, though, children did not necessarily have to wait for the death of one or more of their parents in order to get married, as there were multiple informal mechanisms of property transfer which could take place at time of marriage or when the parents felt they were too old to continue working.

These inheritance practices were typical of both rural and urban areas, though their importance was clearly reduced in towns where landed property was important to only a small part of the population. It is, however, interesting to note that rural property was often a central part of the wills of urban families, suggesting the existence of on-going economic ties between the urban and rural worlds. Perhaps the most noteworthy aspect of this system was a flexibility which tended to lessen the importance of inheritance in conditioning the timing and incidence of marriage. In this way, inheritance itself was really not an obstacle to relatively early marriage. Once early marriage had become the custom (thanks to inheritance, high mortality, land

---

from different legal texts. For a more in-depth discussion of Cuenca inheritance practices, see Reher (1988a: ch. 5).

[13] This 80 per cent stipulated by the Laws of Toro, was divided up in two unequal parts. One third of the total inheritance could be used to "benefit" one or more of the legitimate heirs. The rest of the inheritance (46.7 per cent) was to be divided equally among all of the heirs. The third set aside for "benefiting" one or more heirs to the exclusion of the others was, in fact, seldom used.

[14] After the establishment of the Civil Code in 1889, inheritances were divided into exact thirds: one third to the legitimate heirs, one third to those legitimate heirs chosen to be "benefited," and one third to be freely used by the person giving the will.

availability), it also became a central part of people's expectations in life. This last element certainly played a key role in the centuries-long stability of the system.

This is not to say that there is no indication of change in marriage levels in the town. Over the almost three centuries for which we have data, age at marriage was increasingly late, especially for women. The most pronounced increase took place during the seventeenth century and in the transition between the eighteenth and nineteenth centuries. This pattern has also been observed for a number of villages in the central meseta, and for much of the country between 1787 and 1887 (Pérez Moreda, 1986: 4–7). The rise in age at marriage in much of Spain during the nineteenth century was offset by a decrease in permanent celibacy, with a net effect of almost stationary general levels of nuptiality.[15]

The reasons for this progressive restriction of nuptiality are of considerable importance and can be found both at a larger regional and even national level, as well as in a more specifically local context. Before the eighteenth century, regional data are too sparse to offer much security as to the rate or timing of the trend, or the reasons behind it. After this period, though, consistent population growth, at least from the second half of the seventeenth century led, by mid-eighteenth century, to increased pressure on land availability and probably by the end of the eighteenth century, even lower living standards in much of the central part of the country.[16] Moreover, the plague had disappeared in the seventeenth century and by the eighteenth century, some areas of Spain had experienced a significant decline in crisis mortality . The effect of both of these interrelated processes was to force young couples to wait longer for their inheritance as they found it increasingly difficult to acquire the necessary land to support a family. thus marriage was delayed and, in all probability, celibacy increased.[17]

Between 1815 and 1877 Spanish population experienced its greatest rate of growth before the twentieth century (Reher, 1986; Pérez

---

[15] Overall celibacy went from 11.9 per cent in 1787 to 7.3 in 1887 (males) and from 11.4 per cent to 10.9 per cent (females). Age at marriage for men went from 25 to 27 years of age, and for women from 23.4 to 24.2. See Pérez Moreda (1985a: 64–71) and Cachinero Sánchez (1982). Further restriction of nuptiality gathered speed after 1887 and has continued throughout much of the twentieth century, quite contrary to the trends experienced in many other European countries.

[16] The major crisis of 1804 was due in part to an overall decrease in food surpluses in much of the center of the peninsula. The downturn in economic fortunes can be traced to the last two decades of the eighteenth century (Reher, 1980; Ringrose, 1970).

[17] Before the end of the eighteenth century I can unfortunately only speculate on this last point.

Moreda, 1985a; 1985b). This time, the continued increase in age at marriage was not paralleled by increased celibacy which was temporarily reduced due at least partially to the effects of legislative reform between 1833 and 1855 which dispossessed the Church of much of its property and forced a number of priests and nuns out of convents and into the marriage market.[18] This divergent pattern ended during the second half of the century as the process of restriction accelerated, aided now by an important increase in out-migration which further increased imbalances in local marriage markets. By the end of the century marriage was once again becoming both later and more restricted.[19]

Many of these general constraints affected Cuenca, though there were also factors specific to the town itself. It is difficult not to ascribe progressively restricted nuptiality during the first part of the seventeenth century to the decline in the economic fortunes of the town at that time. Economic decline itself, with its correlate of reduced job availability and lower incomes, tended to make marriage increasingly difficult for urban inhabitants. More important would seem to be the change in the social make-up of the town after that period. As was stated earlier, the decline in the textile industry in Cuenca led to a major upheaval in its social structure. The relative weight within the urban social fabric of weavers and other artisans, who had traditionally shown earlier marriage, diminished sharply and was replaced by that of local, royal and ecclesiastical bureaucracies. The data available regarding nuptial practices by social category, all from the nineteenth century, suggest that these groups had markedly higher age at marriage than the rest of society, a fact that might well have held during earlier centuries. Moreover, these groups brought with them an increase in the relative importance of domestic service as well, with imbalanced marriage markets and delayed marriage as a result. The basic change took place during the seventeenth century, which was precisely the period in which female age at marriage showed greatest increase.

The foregoing discussion raises the more general, and more interesting, question of the determinants of nuptiality in urban areas. The fact that in a given town, in this case Cuenca, marriage patterns strongly resembled regional ones, does not mean that urban nuptiality was the same or that it responded to the same set of determinants. It is

---

[18] On this point, see, for example, Artola (1973: 136–161).
[19] Throughout much of the twentieth century, celibacy and age at marriage have moved in consonance.

Table 3.2. *Urban and rural nuptiality in Spain*

| Spain | I_m | | Age at marriage | | | |
| | | | female | | male | |
Date	urban	rural	urban	rural	urban	rural
1787	0.464	0.561				
1887	0.487	0.617				
1900	0.457	0.599				
1920	0.432	0.541				
Cuenca						
1850–1875			24.6	23.2	26.9	25.8
1876–1900			25.0	23.3	27.1	26.0
Regions (1787)						
Andalusia (South)			22.2		24.3	
Estremadura (lower meseta)			22.0		23.6	
New Castile (lower meseta)			23.0		24.9	
Murcia (Southeast)			22.2		23.6	
Valencia (East)			22.7		24.9	
Catalonia (Northeast)			23.2		24.5	
Aragon (Northeast)			23.2		25.0	
Old Castile (upper meseta)			23.8		24.6	
Leon (upper meseta)			24.8		25.2	
Basque Country and Navarre (North)			25.2		26.3	
Asturias (North)			24.4		24.5	
Galicia (Northwest)			25.0		25.2	

Note The Spanish data for 1787, 1887, 1900 and 1920 are taken from Census material. Rural data have been derived by subtracting the general census totals for the provincial capital from those of the rest of the province. See Iriso Napal and Reher (1987: 50, 81). The data for mean age at marriage for rural and urban Cuenca are based on declared age at first marriage in both the Civil and the Parish Registers. Rural data are from a sample of 5 villages for 1850–1875 and 31 villages (1876–1900). Urban data for 1850–1875 are based on Table 1. The 1787 data are taken from Rowland (1988: Table 2).

not difficult to identify strong differences between rural and urban nuptiality. For example, if one uses urban and rural data aggregated at a national level for the period 1787–1930, it can be seen that a general indicator of female nuptiality (I_m) was between 18 and 23 per cent lower in towns than in rural areas (Table 3.2), while celibacy in towns was often twice that of rural levels.[20] A closer look at the data also reveals that, though age at marriage was generally higher in towns, the majority of the I_m differences were based on celibacy (Reher, 1986: 48–49; 1989). The comparative urban and rural data for different dates between the late eighteenth and early twentieth centuries clearly reveal that the urban/rural differences noted elsewhere held in Cuenca as well. Explaining both regional similarities and urban and rural differences is, then, a task of considerable importance.

Perhaps the single most important factor distinguishing urban from rural marriage patterns was the volatile and often unfavorable marriage market in urban areas. As is well known, and as will be shown later in this book, urban areas were subject to strong migrational flows. This was especially so in those towns where there was little industry to attract young men, and much of this migration was made up of female domestic servants. The nature of domestic service itself tended to delay marriage for servants, and make marriage impossible for some. Furthermore, the skewed urban marriage market, itself a partial by-product of female-dominated domestic service, is a reality which cannot be overlooked. In the town of Cuenca, for example, the sex ratio in marriageable ages ranged between 71 and 86 between 1752 and 1860.[21] Even though at a provincial level, mostly male-dominated emigration also tended to depress overall sex ratios, this was never so unbalanced in rural as it was in urban areas.[22] In a recent study, results from a multiple regression analysis showed the marriage market to be consistently the single most important determinant of female nuptiality in rural areas, and one of the most important in towns (Iriso Napal and Reher, 1987: 64–69, 83–87).

The marriage market also helps explain the fact that lower urban nuptiality was mainly the result of higher levels of celibacy. The "marriageable ages" were more than a semantic concept, since girls were constrained to get married within a fairly reduced age span, and this was hindered in towns by the relative lack of potential partners. At a later age, their possibilities of marrying diminished sharply

[20] In 1787 permanent female celibacy in urban areas was 17.1 per cent as opposed to 10.0 per cent in the countryside; in 1900 it was 12.9 per cent and 5.4 per cent; and in 1920 it was 14.3 and 9.2 per cent respectively.

[21] It was 71 in 1752 (ages 20–29), 86 in 1787 (ages 16–25), 75 in 1800 (20–29), 71 in 1844 (20–29) and 75 in 1860 (21–30). The source for these data comes from municipal listings of inhabitants (1800, 1844), the *Catastro del Marqués de la Ensenada* (1752), the *Census of Floridablanca* (1787) and the *Census of 1860*.

[22] In the Province of Cuenca, the sex ratio at marriageable age was 104 in 1787 (ages 16–25), 94 in 1860 (ages 21–30), 96 in 1887 and 95 in 1900.

Table 3.3. *Age at first marriage by sex and occupational status*

Category	Heute (1885–1909)		Cuenca (1890–1899)	
	M	F	M	F
Day labourers	25.5	23.6	26.3	24.9
Farmers	26.1	24.7	27.2	24.7
Artisan/industry	26.9	25.7	25.1	23.6
Services	27.3	25.6	27.8	25.6
Professional/privileged	29.5	25.9	29.3	26.0

Note Sample based on declared age.
Source Civil registers.

and the likelihood of being life-long celibates increased.[23] On the other hand, at least in theory, the marriage market was bound to act in two ways. The dearth of men would diminish women's possibilities for marriage but, *ceteris paribus*, it should have enhanced men's. This, however, does not seem to be the case. Once again, the data in Table 3.2 suggest that age at marriage for men was also higher in Cuenca than in the surrounding rural areas, though not to the extent that it was for women. Other reasons must have intervened in reducing nuptiality levels for both sexes.

Active population in towns was characterized by a heterogeneity not found in most rural areas. For Cuenca in the eighteenth and nineteenth centuries, for example, approximately 7 per cent of the active population in rural areas was occupied in industry and 7–9 per cent in the services sector, including the wealthy and the liberal professions (Reher, 1988a: 28–34). In town, these same groups represented between 55 and 70 per cent of the active population. Services and liberal professions, who comprised over one third of Cuenca's active population, were traditionally those which showed the most restricted nuptiality. Table 3.3, which contains data from two cities in the province of Cuenca during the later part of the nineteenth century, bears eloquent witness to this fact. The divergence is most keenly evident for professional men whose age at marriage was often more than two years higher than that of other social groups. The reasons for this differential behavior are relatively straightforward and concern both the length of time involved in training and educating members of this group, as well as the more clearly defined economic strategies both of the young couples and of their families. Both led to later age at

[23] Between 1751 and 1852 in Cuenca only 18.8 per cent of all female first marriages took place after 27 years of age.

Table 3.4. *Age at first marriage for migrant couples*

	1680–1750 (1701–1750)			1751–1815 (1751–1800)		
Category	mean	median	n	mean	median	n
Migrant males	25.0	25.0	48	24.3	25.1	59
Sedentary males	25.6	24.5	68	25.5	24.2	88
Migrant females	24.0	24.3	64	23.9	24.0	60
Sedentary females	22.4	21.9	75	22.6	21.9	100

Note Sample based on reconstituted families. Years in parenthesis refer to years of marriage of mobile persons linked to baptisms in their villages of origin; other periods refer to Cuenca-born persons.
Source Parish registers, Archivo Diocesano de Cuenca.

marriage. The presence of these groups in an urban setting contributes to explaining urban marriage patterns, especially higher urban celibacy.

One of the most visible aspects of urban society was the high degree of turnover of its population. I have already mentioned the fact that the presence of migrants tended to skew the marriage market in town. A certain number of these migrants were active in professions which imposed, almost by definition, a delay in nuptiality (servants). Here we would like to raise the possibility that mobile people, no matter what their profession, tended to marry later. The reason for this in some cases might be the uprootedness of all migrants, and in others the fact that high proportions of these migrants came from social groups where nuptiality tended to be more restricted. The net effect was similar. This idea receives at least partial confirmation from the data in Table 3.4.[24] While no clear pattern can be discerned for men, female age at marriage among migrants was nearly two years higher than it was for women born in Cuenca. This interesting result confirms our notion that, at least for women, migration tended to restrict nuptiality. It should be noted here that nearly 60 per cent of all marriage partners were migrants, and thus the marriage behavior of

[24] In this Table, mobile people are taken to be those people married in Cuenca but born in rural areas of the province. The data were compiled by searching out, one by one, the baptismal records in the registers of the village of origin, as declared on the marriage certificate in Cuenca. It should be noted that not all of these people were true migrants because, as will be seen shortly, some merely came to Cuenca to be married in the cathedral and returned subsequently to their village of residence. I am confident that the data at hand are reliable.

Table 3.5. *Prior marital status of Cuenca couples*

Period	n	celibate male/ celibate female	celibate male/ widow	widower/ celibate female	widower/ widow
< 1600	511	92.8	3.3	2.2	1.8
1601–1651	1,058	90.5	2.8	3.5	3.2
1651–1700	851	78.0	3.8	11.8	6.5
1701–1750	912	72.6	4.4	17.4	5.6
1751–1800	1,000	74.3	6.0	13.8	5.9
1801–1852	887	71.3	6.0	16.3	6.4
Total	5,219	79.2	4.5	11.3	5.1

Source Parish registers, Archivo Diocesano de Cuenca.

this sub-group could have a decisive influence on overall levels of nuptiality in town.

Other aspects of urban society also contributed powerfully to conditioning nuptiality, though not all of them tended to restrict it. Abundant rental housing, considerable job availability above the category of domestic servant, and the fact that inheritance could hardly act to delay marriage for most urban dwellers, all tended to facilitate nuptiality in town. These, however, were not sufficient to offset the delaying effects of the other factors we have just discussed, and thus nuptiality ended up being consistently more restricted in the towns than in the countryside.

The selection of a marriage partner and the seasonality of weddings were essential aspects of urban marriage patterns though they had little influence on the fundamental parameters of nuptiality. The basic biological purpose of marriage determined that most weddings would take place between celibate partners, and that remarriage had considerably less importance for widows than for widowers. What is noteworthy about the prior marital status of marriage partners is that the basic parameters changed decisively over time (Table 3.5). Before 1650, over 90 per cent of all weddings involved celibate persons, but by the nineteenth century this figure had descended to near 70 per cent.[25]

[25] It is interesting to note that after 1700 the proportion of marriages among celibate persons was not dissimilar to that of other rural areas of the central meseta (Pérez Moreda, 1986: 19). Due to insufficient data, it is unclear whether or not these areas underwent similar changes during the seventeenth century. In the town of Medina del Campo, located on the upper meseta, 68 per cent of all marriages were between celibates (Marcos Martín, 1978: Table 34).

In other words, before 1600 5.1 per cent of all weddings involved widowers and 4 per cent widows, whereas by the nineteenth century these figures had risen to 12.4 and 22.7 per cent respectively. Before 1650, evidence suggests that widow remarriage was at least as common as male, though this situation changed sharply after that period.

The increase in widow remarriage, which affected both sexes somewhat differently, is not easy to explain and apparently went against the advice of many of the Church fathers.[26] The difference for women, while evident, are too slight to be explained with any certainty. For men, however, they seem to respond, once again, to the changing social and economic structure of the town. Before 1650, when Cuenca was a dynamic textile town, the sex ratio of the population was probably far more balanced than at later dates when its artisan population had diminished drastically and services and Church-dependent sectors had become important components of its active population.[27] These new groups, as was mentioned earlier, probably changed the nature of migration to the town, thus skewing the sex ratio decisively in favor of men. In this new situation, the urban marriage market had plenty of single women available who would have made ready and willing mates for widowers.

Geographical constraints also had a considerable influence on the selection of a marriage partner. In Cuenca, as might well be expected, geographical exogamy at marriage was high. 60.9 per cent of all male spouses and 57.4 per cent of all females were not natives of the town, and only 22.3 per cent of all marriages were completelly endogamous.[28] Some, though by no means all, of the spouses from outside the town came from villages which were not too distant.[29] 14.6 per cent of all males and 10.3 per cent of all females came from outside the province. These levels of marriage-induced migration were typical of most urban areas.[30]

Selecting a mate was not only conditioned by family intervention,

26 The teaching of the Church counseled against second marriages. See, for example, Pineda (1589) and Arbiol (1791). Pérez Moreda (1986: 13–17) sums up many of these ideas.
27 The change in the structure of active population in Cuenca is unquestionable, though that of the nature of migration and the marriage market before 1650 is inferential.
28 The geographical endogamy of Cuenca marriages was slightly lower than that holding in the town of Segovia where 57.1 per cent of male spouses and 47.8 per cent of females were not natives of the town. See Pérez Moreda (1986: Table VI).
29 34.4 per cent of all males and 37.3 of all females came from villages lying within a radius of 50 kms of Cuenca.
30 This movement is not strictly speaking the equivalent of marriage-induced migration because, as will be seen shortly, a fair proportion of couples came to the city to be married in the cathedral, only subsequently to return to their villages of origin.

Table 3.6. *Urban residence of groom, by residence of spouse*

Residence of Bride	Residence of groom (%)		
	Same parish as bride	Same or adjoining parish	All seven parishes
Santa Cruz	64.8	88.7	92.6
San Gil	46.4	72.5	78.2
Santa María	53.9	67.8	79.7
San Nicolás	42.6	65.7	78.8
San Pedro	37.1	52.5	77.4
San Martín	42.6	60.6	79.2
Santiago	50.1	74.9	83.4
Total			81.6

Note This table only includes marriages in which both bride and groom are residents of the city of Cuenca. It is based on female residence.

The data show per cent of total Cuenca grooms from a given parish or group of parishes. The percentages have been weighted for the population of the groom's parish. The seven parishes for which we have data are all located in the upper part of town and represent approximately 30 per cent of the urban population. The total unweighted percentage of grooms from this group of parishes would be 65.7 per cent.

Sources Parish registers.

social group, and personal preference. Spatial considerations existed as well. As will be seen in a later chapter, considerable numbers of marital unions were established within the town among people of the same district or village, as migrants tended to recreate regional or local networks of social contact in the distant city. Similar spatial constraints continued to exist within the town. An attempt to estimate the urban residence of male spouses by current residential status of their brides brings this reality into clearer perspective (Table 3.6). This table estimates the relative importance of the urban residence of grooms in the weddings with brides who lived within the district for which parish registers exist.[31] The results suggest the undeniable importance of spatial proximity when seeking a mate. This spatial aspect of the marriage market probably reflects both the relative social homogeneity of the upper part of town, and a reality whereby young people tended to make social relationships with neighborhood youths before stray-

[31] As has been explained earlier, this district comprises seven parishes grouped together in the upper part of town and represents about one third of the urban population.

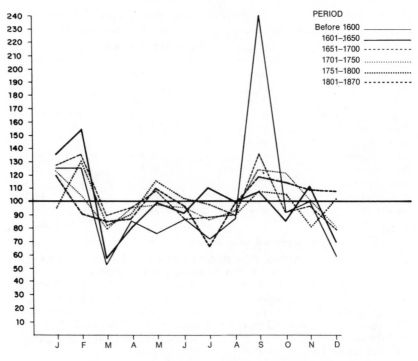

PERIOD
Before 1600 _____
1601–1650 _____
1651–1700 - - - - - - - - - -
1701–1750 ....
1751–1800 ....
1801–1870 - - - - - - - - - -

Figure 3.1 Seasonality of marriages, by period

ing further afield within the town itself. Naturally some partner choices not reflected in the Table involved people residing outside town. Both realities were certainly complementary and contribute to clarifying some of the spatial constraints influencing the functioning of the marriage market which was clearly more complex than a simple sex ratio would suggest.[32]

Religion also played an important part in people's decisions about when and whom to marry. There is little need to insist upon the fact that in Spain, and Cuenca, religious feeling had extremely deep roots in society. It has already been mentioned that the extent of remarriages seems to indicate that Church teachings were not altogether heeded. The picture is very different, though, if one looks at the seasonality of nuptiality where religion becomes the single most

---

[32] Unfortunately my data are not complete enough to enable me to estimate the relative importance of current residence (not origin) outside the town. Much still remains to be done in the study of marriage markets and their implications. Examples of attempts to define them methodologically can be seen in J. E. Smith (1981) and Henry (1981).

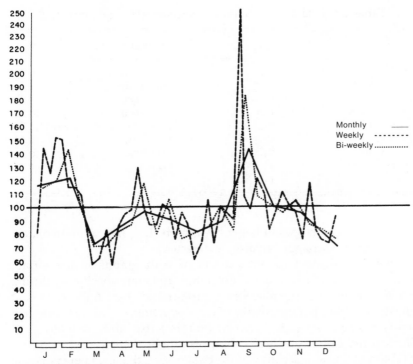

Figure 3.2 Monthly, weekly and bi-weekly seasonality of marriages

important determinant of behavior (Figure 3.1). Apart from a slight rise in early autumn marriages (not including 1601–1650) the most noteworthy aspect of the graph is the Lenten and Advent shortfall in marriages, along with a strong January and early February increase. Economic determinants seem to be singularly absent. This religious-inspired seasonality does seem to decrease over time and practically disappears by the nineteenth century, when it is replaced by a July shortfall and an autumn surplus. This is an indication that the religious influence on behavioral practices was diminishing.

If seasonality is viewed on a bi-weekly and a weekly level, certain nuances stand out quite clearly (Figure 3.2). Perhaps the most interesting is that the post-Advent increase in marriages does not occur until after the first week of January. Despite the fact that there was a slight upturn in marriages at Christmas, throughout the Christmas season (until Epiphany) marriages continued to be markedly below average. The rest of January and the first part of February had very high nuptiality, clearly the result of young couples hurrying to get married

Table 3.7. *Relative importance of September marriages, by period*

Period	%	Period	%
1561–1570	7.1	1651–1660	10.8
1571–1580	5.3	1661–1670	14.9
1581–1590	7.1	1671–1680	7.7
1591–1600	12.5	1681–1690	10.3
1601–1610	21.7	1691–1700	10.8
1611–1620	17.7	1701–1710	12.6
1621–1630	24.1	1711–1720	10.9
1631–1640	19.6	1721–1730	9.7
1641–1650	14.0		

before the Lenten season began. An interesting rise in immediately post-Lenten marriages can also be detected.

One of the most salient aspects of both graphs is the strong concentration of marriages in September, and more specifically during the first week of September between 1601 and 1650. A closer look at the data reveals that the custom of early September marriages began in 1591, reached its height between 1621 and 1640 and gradually diminished thereafter, practically disappearing by the end of the century (Table 3.7). Further scrutiny of the data reveals that 61.7 per cent of all September marriages during the first half of the seventeenth century were concentrated on 5 September. Once again, religious motives explain behavior patterns of the people of Cuenca. In 1595 the Pope gave San Julián, the patron saint and first bishop of Cuenca, his "own prayer" (*rezo propio*), which initiated a popular devotion to the saint whose feast day was celebrated on 5 September.[33] Many of these marriages affected the cathedral parish, Santiago, and involved couples who had come to Cuenca from the neighboring villages specifically for the purpose of getting married in the cathedral.

Before ending this section on the social context of nuptiality, I would like to look a bit more closely at the seasonality of marriage. It has already been affirmed that there was an evident shortfall of Lenten marriages, sandwiched between high points both before and after. Yet the variable date of Easter prevents any more precise estimation as to the extent of this shortfall. Moreover it suggests that both Lent and the subsequent Easter season should be taken as a whole, especially when

[33] Though San Julián continues to be venerated today, the special cult only lasted a few decades. See Mateo López (1787 [1949–1953]: 199–201) and Nalle (1981). He was also the patron of foundlings and often their namesake.

there is no theoretical or historical reason for not doing so. The Church discouraged marriages during Lent and especially during Holy Week, though it certainly did not prohibit them. To be more precise, marriages were composed of two parts: the marriage itself (*desposorio* in Spanish) and a Church blessing (*velación*). Normally both took place during the same ceremony, except during Lent when the Church refused to give the blessing. Thus any couple getting married during Lent was obliged to hold a second ceremony at a later date, possibly in the parish of the spouse not resident in the parish where the wedding took place. An attempt to avoid the double ceremony was probably a major reason for the Lenten shortfall of marriages. During Holy Week marriages were not generally celebrated. Beyond Lent itself, the Church calendar had a rhythm of its own in which both Lent and the entire Easter season, up until Pentecost, had a number of significant periods or days.[34]

In order to gain a clearer idea of its importance, I decided to control for the exact date of Easter after 1582, thus creating an exact Lenten and Easter season.[35] The results can be seen in Figure 3.3 and they underscore the enormous importance that religion had for the timing of marriage in Cuenca.[36] The dearth of Lenten marriages is confirmed, and the shortfall was approximately 28 per cent.[37] What is perhaps even more interesting is the fact there was little uniformity of behavior throughout the Lenten or the Easter season. There was a veritable burst of pre-Lenten activity, as couples scurried to beat the upcoming social pressures against marriage. Immediately thereafter marriages dipped to very low levels, which became still lower during Holy Week. In between, while there continued to be fewer marriages than normal, the effect of Lent was not nearly so noticeable.

Contrary to what might have been expected, the high points of the Easter season (Ascension and Easter) actually showed lower relative levels of marriages which reached their peak during the second week after Easter and then again in the week after Pentecost. Clearly moments of special religious importance both before and after Easter

---

[34] Lent had two key moments of sorrow and fasting, around Ash Wednesday and during Holy Week; the Easter season acquired special significance in the week immediately following Easter and the period between Ascension Thursday and Pentecost.

[35] The Gregorian calendar took effect in 1582. The Enciclopedia Espasa Calpe (vol. 10, pp. 724–725) has a table with the exact date of Easter between 1583 and the beginning of the twentieth century.

[36] The total number of marriages for each sub-period was divided by 7, except for Ash Wednesday–Saturday (by 4), and Easter Sunday (by 1).

[37] Measuring the shortfall in a different manner, there were 44 per cent fewer marriages in the seven weeks preceding Easter, than in the following ones.

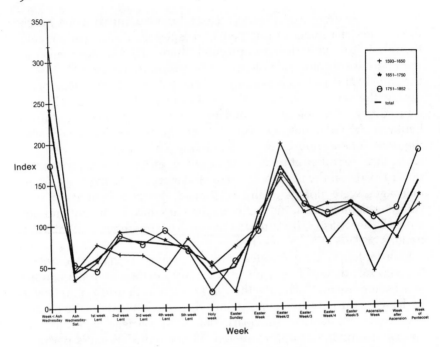

Figure 3.3 Seasonality of Lenten and post-Lenten marriages, 1583–1862

discouraged marriage among young couples, who preferred to delay their weddings until more socially and religiously acceptable moments. Over time it is difficult to discern clear patterns, except the greater irregularity of the curve for the late sixteenth and early seventeenth centuries, possibly indicating a more rigid socio-religious context of marriage. In sum, it would be difficult to evaluate properly the social context of marriage without taking into consideration the Church and the deep roots of popular religion in Cuencan society.

Marital fertility

Apart from a seminal article by Massimo Livi Bacci (1968) and a smattering of family reconstitution studies, very little is known about fertility patterns in Ancien Régime Spain. For the nineteenth century some aggregate studies do exist which enable us to identify basic regional fertility patterns and will be useful as benchmarks for comparison with the Cuenca data.[38] Once again a clear regionalization of

[38] See especially, Iriso Napal and Reher (1987). See also, Arango (1980); Pérez Moreda (1985a; 1985b).

fertility appears. Generally speaking, the areas of lowest marital fertility were located along the Mediterranean coast, in much of the South and in parts of the Northwest. Highest fertility was in the upper meseta (Old Castile) and along parts of the northern coast. Cuenca and much of New Castile were in an area of intermediate marital fertility. How the different regions reached those levels is a matter of speculation. There is some indication of a marginal decrease in fertility between the latter part of the eighteenth and the middle of the nineteenth centuries, but the evidence on the matter is far from clear.[39] Generally, though, there is little sign of decisive fertility decline anywhere in Spain before 1900, except in Catalonia, and even there pre-1860 decline is still a matter of debate.

It is well known that marital fertility in towns tended to be considerably below levels holding in rural areas.[40] In the countryside in Spain fertility was consistently 7–10 per cent above urban levels (Reher, 1986; 1989). At the end of the nineteenth century, lower levels of urban fertility seemed to be, in part, the result of the make-up of active population in towns, with considerable numbers of socially displaced individuals (migrants) as well as the presence of groups which traditionally had lower fertility levels (wage laborers). A recent attempt to identify systematically determinants of marital fertility in urban areas at an aggregate level has also suggested that in towns traditional demographic factors influencing marital fertility (nuptiality and infant mortality), which were so vital in rural areas, had little or no importance. Thus high infant mortality and relatively low nuptiality did not have the fertility-boosting effects they would have had in rural areas (Iriso Napal and Reher, 1987: 96–97). This general explanation probably identifies some of the societal constraints which were evident in the behavior of specific groups in society. The end result was consistently lower marital fertility in towns.

In this section, I will attempt to situate levels and evolution of marital fertility within their proper regional and social context. Due to the veritable dearth of fertility studies in pre-industrial Spain, one of my main tasks will be to present fertility data for the town. Much of these data are the product of a family reconstitution study which, despite evident problems, gives a fairly reliable picture of women's reproduction behavior over time.[41] Attempts will be made to define

---

[39] Livi Bacci (1968; 1988) was the first to suggest the existence of this gradual decline.

[40] See, for example, Livi Bacci (1977: 121), (Knodel, 1974: 89–101) and Sharlin (1986).

[41] The success of the project was hindered by high urban mobility and the fact that we were only able to use parish registers for slightly less than one third of the total population (7 of the 14 parishes). The reduced size of the population at risk, perennial nemesis of all reconstitutions, was the result and advises great caution in the

Table 3.8   *Age-specific marital fertility rates*

Age at marriage	1600–1750					
	15–19	20–24	25–29	30–34	35–39	40–44
15–19	349	447	343	283	181	58
20–24		432	418	365	276	119
25–29			441	494	375	103
30–34				412	371	161
Total	349	442	388	358	240	100

Age at marriage	1751–1850					
	15–19	20–24	25–29	30–34	35–39	40–44
15–19	427	483	424	397	277	147
20–24		543	422	400	262	147
25–29			546	459	242	77
30–34				457	406	181
Total	427	513	445	418	276	133

Note Rates adjusted in order to compensate for birth–baptism interval.

Table 3.9   *General marital fertility rate by period*

Period	Age of mother						
	15–19	20–24	25–29	30–34	35–39	40–44	45–49
< 1650	515	455	400	325	243	74	11
1651–1700	203	440	424	411	248	93	10
1701–1750	355	436	363	348	234	121	18
1751–1800	420	523	463	438	285	126	0
1801–1850	431	497	417	390	262	140	12

Note Adjusted for birth–baptism interval.

interpretation of results. An unwanted and possibly unavoidable by-product of the high mortality levels which existed in Cuenca is the tendency to overestimate women's fertility.

specifically urban aspects of women's reproductive behavior and the existence of any evidence of fertility control. The picture which will emerge suggests that fertility did indeed seem to undergo a long-term evolution, though no indication of parity-dependent control will ever be present. In fact, nineteenth-century women still had marital fertility levels as high as at any time before. A more thorough look at fertility will also show the influence of age at marriage on many aspects of reproductive intensity, the existence of low levels of illegitimacy, and the importance of migrational status, social group and religion for fertility.

This study of fertility will concentrate on marital fertility because extramarital fertility never seemed to have been very important in Cuenca. It is extremely difficult to generate illegitimacy data for the pre-industrial period due mainly to the creation of Foundling Homes (Casas de Niños Expósitos) as early as the sixteenth century.[42] These institutions took in abandoned children, cared for them for a short time, attempted to find them wet nurses and even foster homes. Often the abandoned children were illegitimate, though evidently this was not the case with all foundlings.[43] Nineteenth-century census and Civil Registration data, though, confirm that, while extra-marital fertility was appreciably higher in the town than in the rural areas, in neither place could it be considered significant for overall reproduction.[44]

One of my principal tasks, then, is to identify prevailing levels and trends of marital fertility. Tables 3.8, 3.9, 3.10 and 3.11 convey these data for Cuenca between the sixteenth and the mid-nineteenth centuries. All data have been adjusted for under-registration.[45] Sample

[42] There is a growing body of literature on the subject of *niños expósitos* in Spain. See, for example, Fernández Ugarte (1988); Egido (1973), Alvarez Santaló (1977, 1980). Within a more general context of aid to the poor see also Marcos Martín (1985); Martz (1983); Callahan (1980: ch. 1); Soubeyroux (1978).

[43] Even if all of these children had been illegitimate, their baptisms or the registration of their arrival at the home could not be an indicator of the extent of illegitimacy because they did not come only from the town itself, but were brought to Cuenca from all over the province.

[44] When it is possible to estimate illegitimacy at a local level, it is so low that it is hardly worth mentioning. In the town of Talavera de la Reina, also located on the lower meseta, where it is somewhat easier to follow the incidence of illegitimacy, it seldom surpasses 10 per cent of the total number of births and is frequently a good deal lower. It is highest, though, at the end of the sixteenth and the beginning of the seventeenth century. See González Muñoz (1975: 423–432).

[45] This adjustment has been based primarily on the length of the birth-baptism interval. Date of birth only begins to appear at the beginning of the seventeenth century. Between that moment and approximately 1740, the average and median intervals oscillate between 10 and 11 days. From 1740 on there is a decade by decade reduction of the interval. By 1820–1830, it is only two days and birth registration can be

Table 3.10. *Marital fertility, women married 20–24, by period*

Period	Age of mother				
	20–24	25–29	30–34	35–39	40–44
< 1650	336	435	288	206	82
1651–1700	491	505	447	300	112
1701–1750	452	361	351	307	145
1751–1800	546	447	395	260	127
1801–1850	535	391	402	263	170

Table 3.11. *Total marital fertility ratio, by age at marriage and period*

Age at marriage	1600–1750	1751–1850
15–19	7.34	9.21
20–24	6.77	7.51
25–29	5.79	5.26
30–34	3.60	4.08

Period	Married 20–24
< 1650	5.90
1651–1700	8.05
1701–1750	6.95
1751–1800	7.51
1801–1850	7.47

Note The totals are the result of multiplying the cumulative marital fertility rate by 5, except for the first age group (× 2.5). Thus it represents the completed fertility of a woman married at the outset in the absence of mortality. For the 15–19 year age group, we have used the actual average number of children per woman in the sample.

size has counseled the grouping of data into rather long periods, though general levels and overall trends should be clear.[46] One of the most noteworthy results is that fertility did not show any sign of decreasing over time, though it would not be appropriate to consider it

considered almost complete because all children considered to be in danger of death, tended to be baptized almost immediately.

[46] The periods used refer to the date of marriage.

invariable.[47] There is rather clear evidence of an appreciable increase in fertility between the first and second half of the seventeenth century, followed by a slight decrease during the first half of the following century. Another rather noticeable increase takes place during the second half of the eighteenth century, subsequently leveling off or turning slightly downward during the first part of the nineteenth century. Possibly part, though not all, of this evolution may have been due to improving registration of births. It is quite clear, however, that fertility levels after 1750 were at least 10–15 per cent higher than those holding at the beginning of the seventeenth century.

Since our knowledge of fertility determinants in pre-industrial societies is still somewhat sketchy, speculations as to the reasons for the observed trends would be gratuitous. Showing the changes, however, is certainly not. It is interesting to note the similarity in the evolution of the female age at marriage and marital fertility after 1750. Declining nuptiality offsets rises in marital fertility with the end result of lower completed family size (see Table 3.13).[48]

If one compares marital fertility levels in Cuenca to those holding in the few other areas of Spain where data are available, it becomes clear that they were only moderately high by pre-industrial standards. A total marital fertility ratio (TMFR) in Cuenca of around 6.1 after 1750, was exactly the same as that of the only other urban area on the meseta for which I have data (see Table 3.12). These levels are somewhat higher than those in Catalonia or Galicia, and similar to those from other rural areas of the meseta.[49] They were lower than those holding in the eastern part of France, though considerably higher than in England. Circumstantial evidence suggests the possibility that by at

47 Evidence of declining fertility, especially after the latter part of the eighteenth century, has been abundant for both rural and urban France. Certain groups in Geneva participated in fertility reduction as well. The literature on the subject is extensive. See, for example, Henry (1972, 1978); Henry and Houdaille (1973); Houdaille (1976); Wrigley (1985); van de Walle (1978); Bardet (1983); Perrenoud (1979).
      Other countries, among them England, show little or no indication of significant changes in marital fertility levels. See, for example, Wrigley and Schofield (1983), Wilson (1984).

48 This supposes unchanging adult mortality levels. Once again, something similar seems to have occurred in wide areas of France prior to the major declines in marital fertility. See, Henry and Houdaille (1978, 1979). See also, Pérez Moreda and Reher (1985).

49 The information from Galicia is suspiciously low and suggests the possible existence in eighteenth-century Galicia of a sharply different demographic regime from any other on the peninsula. Problems with data cannot be discarded either. On this subject see, for example, Eiras Roel (1984), Barreiro Mallón (1973), Pérez García (1979).

Table 3.12. *Total marital fertility ratio for women married between 20 and 24 years of age*

Period	TMFR
Cuenca (1600–1650)	5.06
Cuenca (1651–1700)	6.92
Cuenca (1700–1751)	5.82
Cuenca (1751–1800)	6.15
Cuenca (1800–1850)	6.21
Cáceres (eighteenth century, Estremadura)	6.13
Palomós (1740–1779, Catalonia)	6.21
Palomós (1780–1819, Catalonia)	5.44
El Grove (1695–1727, Galicia)	4.99
El Grove (1760–1793, Galicia)	4.67
Xallas (eighteenth century, Galicia)	5.12
Northwest France	6.03
Northeast France	6.90
Southeast France	6.33
Southwest France	5.75
England (1600–1799)	5.02

Note Completed family size is cumulative fertility × 5, except first age group which is not counted. This has been done to facilitate comparison.
Sources All ratios were calculated from original data from the following sources: for Cáceres, Rodríguez Cancho (1981: 216); for Palomós, Nadal and Sáez (1972: 109); for El Grove, Pérez García (1979: Table 4.19); for Xallas, Barreiro Mallón (1973: 196); for France, Henry (1978: 886), Houdaille (1976: 353), Henry and Houdaille (1973: 889), Henry (1972: 979); and for England, Wrigley and Schofield (1983: 179).

least the eighteenth century, the basic regional fertility patterns were already in existence.[50] Moderate fertility levels characterized both urban and rural Cuenca data, as well as those of all of New Castile until well into the twentieth century.

Reproduction was, of course, subject to the constraints of nuptiality and adult mortality. In Cuenca the effects of both of these factors tended to reduce actual completed reproduction sharply (Table 3.13). Despite the increase in fertility in the latter part of the eighteenth and the beginning of the nineteenth centuries, actual reproduction hardly varied or even diminished slightly. The progressive reduction of the intensity of marriage offset any implications that higher marital fertility might have had.

[50] Lack of adequate studies makes any sort of convincing verification of this postulate impossible at the present time.

Table 3.13. *Children per marriage*

Period	Family size
1680–1729	6.2
1730–1774	5.7
1775–1815	5.6

Note Actual number of children born to families married in Cuenca. All ages at marriage.

Table 3.14 *Age specific marital fertility*

	Age group	
Age at marriage	30–34	35–39
15–19	340	229
20–24	383	269
25–29	477	314
30–34		389

Age at marriage had considerable influence on the intensity of fertility. Here I am not speaking merely of completed fertility where the timing of marriage was, beyond any question, the most important factor in determining final family size (Table 3.11). Rather, the timing and duration of marriage seemed to have had other, perhaps more pervasive effects on women's reproductive behavior. More precisely, evidence suggests that the duration of marriage was inversely correlated with the intensity of marital fertility. This pattern can be seen in many studies of contemporary and historical fertility patterns, and seems to be related to a series of factors which range from biological fatigue to coital frequency. In Cuenca, despite certain misgivings due to sample size, this same basic relation emerges from the data. In other words, women married in higher age groups generally tended to show higher age specific marital fertility rates. If we consider marital fertility at different ages by age at marriage for the entire period under study the differentials shown in Table 3.14 emerge.

The end of the reproductive period of women was also dependent on the duration of marriage; the longer the duration, the earlier reproduction stopped (Table 3.15). The increase in age at last birth

Table 3.15. *Age at last birth*

Age at marriage	Age at last birth
15–19	36.3
20–24	38.2
25–29	39.7
< 30	41.0
Period	
< 1750	37.7
1750–1850	38.4

Table 3.16. *Birth intervals in large families, by age at marriage*

Age at marriage	Mean birth interval						
	0–1	1–2	2–3	3–4	4–5	second to last	last
15–19	19.8	25.4	25.3	28.2	26.9	30.5	31.0
20–24	16.5	23.7	29.9	27.2	30.0	30.7	37.7
< 25	15.5	25.7	21.8	24.4	20.7	25.7	24.3
Total	17.4	24.8	26.4	26.9	26.6	29.5	32.2

Note Married women with five or more live births.

before and after 1750 would plausibly then seem to be the result of the increasing age at marriage, which we have already mentioned earlier. Much the same can be said of the increase in fertility after 1750, especially in higher age groups (35–44) shown in Table 3.9 which was quite possibly the indirect product of ever-later female age at marriage. This negative correlation between nuptiality and the intensity of marital fertility has emerged in other Spanish studies based on nineteenth- and twentieth-century data as one of the most noteworthy aspects of Spanish demographic patterns (Reher, 1989; Iriso Napal and Reher, 1987: 60–62, 64–69).

Age at marriage also affected other aspects of women's fertility, this time related to birth intervals. First intervals were always longer for women who married young than it was for those marrying at later ages (Table 3.16). Temporary teenage sterility was most certainly the cause for the longer first intervals among teenage brides. Yet it is also

Table 3.17. *Premarital conceptions and first birth intervals*

Period	Premarital conceptions		First birth interval
	A	B	
< 1650	8.2	10.2	16.8
1650–1700	5.9	5.9	15.0
1701–1750	6.1	8.2	15.5
1751–1800	20.0	22.9	15.9
1801–1850	13.6	22.7	12.7
Age at marriage			
15–19	9.0	11.7	19.8
20–24	7.6	11.0	16.5
25–29	15.2	19.6	15.2
30–34	19.0	23.8	15.8

Note All data expressed as mean duration in months of each type of interval. A = births taking place within seven months of marriage. B = births taking place within eight months of marriage. All first birth interval calculations exclude all births taking place within seven months of marriage.

noteworthy to see that intervals for brides between 20 and 24 years of age were also longer than for those in higher age groups.[51] This same pattern also emerges for many of the other birth intervals, reiterating once again the positive relation which exists between the age at marriage and the intensity of marital fertility.

The importance of marriage, however, went considerably beyond age specific fertility rates and birth intervals. The likelihood that a woman would already be pregnant when she was wed also increased sharply with age. The proportion of pre-nuptial conceptions, for example, was nearly twice as high for women married over 25 years of age, as it was for younger brides (Table 3.17). Whereas the earlier results can plausibly be explained by the existence of factors related to the biological capacity of women, these data are entirely unrelated to biological constraints, and only refer to behavioral patterns. The older a woman was, the more likely she was to conceive a child out of wedlock. We do not have further information on the matter, but quite possibly the rate of illegitimacy was also higher among older women. The lack of sexual contact in a sexually repressive environment, as well as the fear of permanent spinsterhood in a society which frowned upon spinsters, led many women to regard traditional sexual mores

[51] In this last case, though, the differences are not great enough to be considered truly robust and thus are subject to some doubt.

with increasing liberality as they grew older. Once married, the need and desire of the couple to have a sizeable family, together with other possible physiological factors, tended to make fertility intensity far higher among those women marrying at an older age.

Another important result which can be derived from the data in Table 3.17, is that a considerable amount of the increase in age specific fertility levels after 1750 mentioned earlier is directly attributable to the rise in pre-marital conceptions after that date, and to a complementary, albeit marginal, decrease in the duration of the first birth interval. Even though the evidence on this last point is not altogether conclusive, the growing incidence of pre-marital conceptions points to changes in behavior. Was it a response to changing moral attitudes, or the effect of an ever-increasing age at marriage? It was probably both, though here our analysis must remain somewhat speculative.[52]

One of the salient aspects of the Cuenca fertility data has been the decisive role played by nuptiality. Not only was the timing and extent of female marriage the foremost determinant of the final reproductive capability of society, it also influenced more basic behavioral patterns. It must be emphasized that its effects on fertility were, at least apparently, contradictory. Even though the age at which women married was a key factor for the number of children they would bear, from a sociological perspective of human behavior, early marriage led to numerous fertility inhibiting mechanisms. In other words, even though younger brides normally had more children, the intensity of fertility at higher age groups tended to be inversely correlated with years of exposure to pregnancy risk. Even though the net effect of these mechanisms was of subsidiary importance for overall fertility, they formed a part of the social context of reproduction and it would be unwise to underestimate their significance for society and for women.

The understanding of rates, levels and trends is a necessary part of understanding reproduction, though not a sufficient one. While systematically probing the complex web of fertility determinants in urban areas is a well-nigh impossible task with the data at hand, certain aspects of fertility are certainly subject to further scrutiny. If a thorough understanding of reproduction is to be achieved, fertility

---

[52] There is conflicting evidence for this period of Spanish history. Whereas Church institutions were strongly, though often indirectly, attacked both by enlightened thinkers and by the State, there is also evidence of the fact that much of the population continued to be strictly orthodox in their religious attitudes. On this subject, see Herr (1958) and Sarrailh (1954).

   It is also most interesting to note how the rate of premarital conceptions decreased appreciably in the transition between the sixteenth and the seventeenth centuries, precisely the time of the height of the Counter-Reformation in Spain.

must be approached within a wider social context. Identifying some of
the specifically cultural, urban and economic aspects of fertility is the
major goal in this section.

It is normally felt that natural fertility patterns prevailed in most
pre-industrial societies and the data from Cuenca certainly suggest
that there was little evidence of conscious control.[53] This should
mitigate, but certainly not eliminate, the effects on fertility of such
social and economic factors as profession, religion, income, etc.[54] A
study of the seasonality of conceptions will enable us to see the extent
to which social and cultural constraints are discernible for fertility
patterns.[55] These were evident in people's marriage practices, though
one should not therefore necessarily expect a similar reality for
reproductive behavior.

A perusal of the basic seasonality of conceptions for Cuenca reveals
that there were pronounced oscillations over the calendar year (Figure
3.4). Throughout the period under study, the months of April to July
showed higher than average intensity of conceptions, as opposed to
the rest of the year in which the relative importance of conceptions
was generally below average.[56] During this latter part of the year
conceptions were lowest between August and October, and again
during the months corresponding to Lent.

Factors related to mortality, nuptiality and religious sentiment seem
to underlie this pattern of seasonality. Economic constraints, mainly in
the form of seasonal migration, probably played a role in lowering

[53] There is an abundant literature on the subject of "natural fertility" and its existence or
not in pre-transitional societies. See Henry (1961), Coale (1971, 1986: 8–17), Coale and
Trussell (1974).
[54] On this subject, see Lesthaeghe (1980).
[55] Our study of seasonality is based on the seasonality of baptisms rather than of births
because this enabled us to use sixteenth-century documentation and it does little to
change the basic seasonal distribution of conceptions. In this case, our sample size is
fairly large and the results offer a high degree of accuracy.

Period	Sample size
1560–1600	2,790
1601–1650	3,163
1651–1700	2,280
1701–1750	2,472
1751–1800	2,853
1801–1870	3,415
Total	16,973

[56] Our general discussion would not be helped here by a detailed commentary of
several aspects of seasonality mostly related to trends over time. Nonetheless, these
are visible in the data.

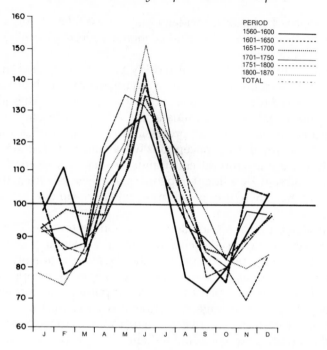

Figure 3.4 Seasonality of conceptions, by period

September and October conceptions.[57] The incidence of mortality was probably even more important. As will become apparent later, mortality was highest between August and October. This was not only the case for infant and child mortality, but for other age groups as well. The great majority of epidemic-related deaths (plague, malaria, cholera, typhus, etc.) occurred during the late summer and early autumn. It is well known that conceptions tended to be inversely correlated to mortality during periods of crisis and perhaps during other periods as well, though the reasons for this are not totally clear. We can postulate that high mortality with the frequent presence of epidemics during these months tended to depress coital frequency and was the principal factor behind the decrease in conceptions.[58] The

---

[57] Seasonal migration was probably most intense during these months as day laborers participated in the grape harvest carried out in areas to the south and west of town.

[58] A strikingly similar dynamic of summer and fall conceptions appears in studies of other urban areas in Spain, as well as in several rural parishes. All of these parishes are located in areas of high summertime temperatures and mortality. See, for example, Rodríguez Sánchez (1977: 96–102); Ansón Calvo (1977: 77); Pérez Moreda (1980: 212–214). Recent analyses of short-term fluctuations have shown a clear negative

slight upturn of conceptions in November seems to be the partial result of the wave of marriages taking place during the months of September and October (see Figure 3.1). The seasonal variations throughout the rest of the year seem mainly to coincide with the religious calendar: Advent and Lent are periods of few conceptions, and the post-Lenten season is precisely that of greatest number of conceptions. For this last period however, the more general effects of spring cannot be totally discarded either.

Refining this analysis further will bring the behavior patterns of the *conquenses* into far better focus. As with nuptiality, I have once again endeavored to pinpoint the exact dates of the Lenten and Easter seasons so as to see more clearly the possible influence of cultural and religious constraints on behavior. We should emphasize that, in the absence of evidence of widespread fertility control, the effects of Lent should only be moderate and should reflect the downturn in marriages during the same season as well as the probable, though unproven, effects of decreased nutrition, itself the result of Lenten fasting. There is a greater degree of uncertainty attached to the analysis since conceptions can only be approximately measured in time.[59]

Notwithstanding the precautions taken, these results are eloquent and reflect significantly wide-ranging behavioral differences in the weeks preceding and following Easter (Figure 3.5, Table 3.18). The shortfall of Lenten conceptions is noteworthy. There are almost 27 per cent fewer conceptions in the weeks preceding Easter than in the weeks of the Easter season. It might be argued that a good part of this shortfall is due to first births which followed the seasonality of nuptiality more closely. Even if one controls by these first births, however, the shortfall continues to be appreciably higher than 20 per cent.[60] The shortfall of Lent and the surplus thereafter are not by any means uniform.

The expected spurt of conceptions just prior to Ash Wednesday fails to materialize. After the beginning of Lent the number of conceptions diminishes until it reaches its nadir during the second week. From that

correlation between mortality and fertility at a 0 lag (Galloway, 1986a, 1988). The analysis carried out in the next chapter will confirm this same reality for Spain.

[59] For this part of the study, conceptions have been taken to have occurred exactly 38 weeks prior to birth and therefore the data will only give an approximate idea of the importance of Lent itself.

[60] If one compares it to the seasonal average for the entire year, the shortfall is 13 per cent. The method for neutralizing the effects of nuptiality is as follows: 20 per cent of the conceptions were considered first conceptions and were arbitrarily given no seasonality at all. In other words, their index was made equal to 100. The adjusted index includes these de-seasonalized first births.

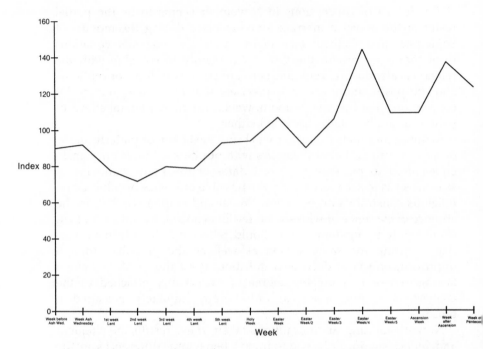

Figure 3.5 Seasonality of Lenten and post-Lenten conceptions, 1583–1862

point onwards there are increasing numbers of conceptions though not until after Easter do they turn into "surplus" conceptions. Even during the Easter season, the second week after Easter and the period just prior to Ascension Thursday are characterized by relatively fewer conceptions. The reasons for these last fluctuations are not at all clear. What is clear, beyond any reasonable doubt, is the existence of a marked seasonality of fluctuations just around Easter, only explicable by the religious nature of the season.

The observed decrease in conceptions during Lent cannot evidently be explained by economic realities. While factors such as nutritional levels (possible amenorrhea), couples at risk (nuptiality, adult mortality, etc.), spousal separation and biological fecundity may have affected conceptions, they could not possibly explain such a consistent pattern of Lenten decline and post-Easter recovery.[61] Coital frequency clearly decreased during Lent due to either physiological or psycho-

[61] For amenorrhea, see Le Roy Ladurie, 1969. To my knowledge the subject of variations in biological fecundity during Lent has never been the subject of systematic analysis within a historical context.

Table 3.18. *Lenten and post-Lenten conceptions*

Week	Conceptions	Index	Adjusted index
Week before Ash Wednesday	155	90	92
Week of Ash Wednesday	159	92	94
1st week of Lent	134	78	82
2nd week of Lent	123	72	77
3rd week of Lent	137	80	84
4th week of Lent	136	79	83
5th week of Lent	160	93	94
Holy Week	161	94	95
Easter week	184	107	106
2nd Easter week	155	90	92
3rd Easter week	182	106	105
4th Easter week	247	144	135
5th Easter week	187	109	107
Week of Ascension Thursday	187	109	107
Following week	235	137	129
Week of Pentecost	211	123	118
Total	2,753		
Shortfall of Lenten conceptions:	A	26.7%	22.0%
Shortfall of Lenten conceptions:	B	16.0%	13.0%

Note Conceptions take place 38 weeks prior to birth. In the adjusted index, 20 per cent of all conceptions (theoretically, first conceptions after marriage) are considered to have no seasonality at all (= 100). A = conceptions. B = percentage shortfall of pre-Easter conceptions as compared to entire average (100). See text for further details.

logical factors, or to rational choice. We are inclined to believe that some couples voluntarily refrained from normal sexual activity (either totally or partially), and did so for religious reasons. The Church itself counseled sexual abstinence during Lent out of a sense of Christian asceticism, and the behavior of the people in Cuenca reflects the importance of popular faith in their lives.

Indirectly, the issue at hand is whether or not people were able to turn their reproductive capacities on or off at will. Cuenca evidence certainly suggests the distinct possibility that this was, indeed, the case. This issue is not a simple academic diversion because it brings up a whole series of other questions. Even though we might accept the hypothetical absence of any sort of systematic fertility control, does this mean that the ability to control reproduction did not exist and was not used when deemed necessary? Clearly the primary means of control would be abstinence, and was probably only used occasionally. Yet in times of crisis, as well as in those of religious penitence, this rudimentary method was probably used as a common and socially acceptable (or even socially mandated) form of limiting reproduction.[62]

Other elements related to urban society also played an important role in shaping fertility patterns in Cuenca, and possibly in all cities. Towns differed from rural areas primarily because of their economic make-up and the intensity of migratory movement which characterized them. The extent to which these factors influenced fertility continues to be a matter of speculation, expecially within a Spanish context.[63] Unfortunately, the parish registers are not adequate for this type of analysis since social class rarely if ever appears, even during the nineteenth century. Also, the sample of mobile families whose age at marriage we were able to obtain in their parishes of origin was too small to be used for a study of fertility.

Yet the subject seems too important not to be addressed at all and so an alternate approach to the fertility of migrants and of different social groups has been devised. It is based on the numbers of children aged 0 to 4 and present in households headed by married couples on the municipal *padrones* of 1800 and 1844, which also contain data on migratory status and profession. The lack of differential mortality and nuptiality estimates made it impossible to carry out a full-fledged "own-children" analysis.[64] It can be assumed that migration of children in this age group was very low, and so, with certain reservations, my estimates of the child/mother ratio can be considered as proxies for marital fertility. It must be remembered that these estimates are subject to variations of nuptiality and, especially, of mortality whose effects we have been unable to compensate for. In this way, differences observed are subject to serious reservations.

These methodological points notwithstanding, the results of my analysis offer strong evidence of the existence of differential fertility

---

62 Massimo Livi Bacci (1978) already argued some years ago that during times of crisis there were clear indications of conscious fertility control.

63 This is not the case for the towns of Rouen in France and Geneva in Switzerland, where the pioneering studies of Bardet and Perrenoud have done a great deal for our understanding of differential fertility. See Bardet (1983), Perrenoud (1979).

64 For a basic statement of the own-children method of analysis, see, Cho (1973), Grabill and Cho (1965), United Nations (1983). For use of this method with historical data, see Harevan and Vinovskis (1978), Reher (1988a: 114–136).

Table 3.19. *Child–mother ratios, profession and migration*

Professional category	1800	1844
Day labourers	79	80
	(82)	(204)
Farmers	125	113
	(167)	(103)
Artisan/industry	105	105
	(330)	(156)
Services	101	99
	(88)	(119)
Public administration/nobility/	82	115
liberal professions	(198)	(151)
Total	100	100
	(865)	(733)

Migrational status	1844
Both natives of Cuenca	96
	(309)
Male native/female migrant	109
	(122)
Male migrant/female native	108
	(113)
Both migrants	96
	(203)
Total	100
	(733)

Note 100 = index corresponding to the average number of children aged 0–4 present in households headed by married couples in the sample. The numbers in parenthesis indicate the number of households in the sample for each category. All child–mother ratios have been standardized for the general age distribution of each sample.

patterns in Cuenca (Table 3.19).[65] The lowest marital fertility belongs to the day laborers, and the highest is shown by farmers and, at one date, by the privileged sector. These results are not at all surprising since other studies have confirmed that in nineteenth- and early twentieth-century Spain marital fertility levels were generally highest in those provinces where there was a widespread access to land ownership, and lowest in regions where day laborers predominated.[66]

[65] Similar patterns appeared in Rouen and in Geneva. See, Bardet (1983: 276–288) and Perrenoud (1979).
[66] See, Iriso Napal and Reher (1987: 52); and Livi Bacci (1968). Within an urban context, day laborers were occupied in both the agricultural and the industrial sector.

The fact that day laborer families probably experienced higher levels of infant and child mortality would hardly offset the fertility differences with farmers (more than 32 per cent lower). The high percentages of day laborers in most towns help explain the lower levels of fertility which have been observed there.

The high fertility among farmers and the urban privileged and educated is not surprising either and has been observed elsewhere (Reher, 1988a: 132–135). More surprising, though, is the evolution shown by the privileged who in 1800 had one of the lowest levels of marital fertility, and in 1844 one of the highest. Data problems notwithstanding, this could indicate some sort of incipient control in 1800 which was halted thereafter.[67] While it is difficult to doubt the pioneering role played by these groups during the onset of the demographic transition, in a pre-transitional setting lower fertility need not necessarily have characterized their behavior.[68]

Migratory status substantially influenced women's fertility as well. Here, however, a precise interpretation of the data is quite difficult. Theoretically we would expect urban natives to have lower fertility than migrants, who would be bringing rural patterns of higher fertility with them when arriving in town. This would probably have offset any potentially fertility-diminishing effects which the unsettled nature of migrants' lives might bring (Zarate and Unger de Zarate, 1975). Once in town, however, their fertility would rapidly diminish until more typically "urban" levels had been reached. The Cuenca data seem to confirm this hypothesis at least partially. Fertility among couples born in the town was generally lower than among couples where one of the two was not a native of the town. Surprisingly, fertility among couples where both spouses were migrants was markedly lower than for mixed couples. This result is contrary to expectations and suggests that fertility behavior among migrant popu-

---

[67] All of the other groups show similarities between one listing and the other.

[68] In Rouen this was also the case until it became immersed in its own peculiar demographic transition during the eighteenth century, when the role of the privileged was quite different (Bardet, 1983: 279–283). See also Livi Bacci (1986). In Cuenca, it must be remembered that the urban elite was a heterogeneous group which included both the nobility and low-level civil servants, whose one common denominator is that they had probably all received some formal schooling. It is interesting to note that a strong positive correlation between literacy and fertility has been seen in Spanish provincial level data for the latter part of the nineteenth and the beginning of the twentieth century, though the extent to which aggregate results can be directly applied to different social groups is not clear. On this see Iriso Napal and Reher (1987).

lations was not uniform over time and does not conform well to simple models of migration.[69]

At a more general level, the reality of differential fertility in towns is beyond question. It is unclear whether the spread between high and low fertility groups was greater in towns than in rural areas, though the more complex economic and social make-up of towns gave behavior patterns a far greater diversity. Urban fertility levels were, of course, subject to strong rural influences. This is shown by the regional similarity of both urban and rural fertility which has appeared in other studies of urban and rural Spain. Yet urban fertility was indeed lower, and this must have been the consequence of specifically urban factors involving high population densities, wage labor and highly mobile populations.

Before concluding, the issue of conscious fertility control should, once again, be raised. I have stated before that there is little or no evidence that any sort of systematic fertility control was being practiced in Cuenca during the period under study. Yet a close look at the seasonality of conceptions has suggested that people were aware of how to control fertility (abstinence in this case) and were willing to use this ability at special moments (Lent, times of crisis, etc.). The extent to which this form of primitive control was also practiced during other periods of people's reproductive lives is not at all clear. Yet there is nothing at all to suggest that this was not the case. In this way, the differing levels of fertility observed among different social groups can be seen in a new perspective. Even though my data do not afford a clear answer to this question, there is a distinct possibility that the fertility differences among economic or migratory groups was also the product, to a certain extent, of the more or less widespread use of abstinence as a conscious form of family limitation.

Mortality

The study of mortality is a perpetual source of frustration for historical demographers in Spain. The quality of parish death registers is significantly lower than that of baptism or marriage registers. Before the middle part of the seventeenth century, they are actually registers of wills rather than of deaths. Thereafter, until the eighteenth century when deaths of *párvulos* or children under 7 years of age begin to

---

[69] Probably higher mortality among new migrants would tend to diminish the child–women ratios, and thus their fertility would be underestimated. It is impossible to calculate this differential mortality and as a consequence I am unable to adjust the ratios in the table.

appear, by and large, only adult deaths are included. In most parishes registration of infant mortality does not begin to approach acceptable completeness until some time between the end of the eighteenth and the middle of the nineteenth centuries. While the condition of the burial registers may vary from parish to parish and from region to region, it is safe to say that their overall quality is substandard. A consequence of this has been the almost complete lack of serious studies of mortality in Spain before the nineteenth century.[70]

The Cuenca registers are no exception. Before the nineteenth century, it is practically impossible to establish a global vision of mortality patterns and even then this must be done with great care. Even so, a number of important issues can be tackled for the nineteenth century, not the least of which is the identification of the general levels of non-crisis mortality. In this section, the experience of Cuenca will again be placed within a larger Spanish context in which regional and urban determinants of mortality will become clear. In addition, an analysis of cause of death by seasonality, sex and age structures will enhance our understanding of the nature of urban mortality patterns.

The town of Cuenca, like most of the central and southern parts of Spain, was characterized by high levels of non-crisis mortality. Infant and child mortality were high, and life expectancy relatively low, though there are some indications that the severity of this regime was lessening during the first half of the nineteenth century. The structure of this mortality, though, can be clearly differentiated from that of other areas of high mortality elsewhere in Europe.

Infant mortality was high, but not surprisingly so. In Cuenca itself, and allowing for some under-registration, it was 228 per thousand around the central part of the nineteenth century. If one compares these figures with those elsewhere in the country during the eighteenth and the beginning of the nineteenth centuries, it is clear that the Cuenca levels are similar to those in other parts of the central meseta and points further south, but somewhat higher than those in the northern part of the country (Table 3.20). Once again we are confronted by the reality of a well-defined regional distribution, this time of mortality, which persists until well into the twentieth century. Areas on the northern coast and parts of the eastern seaboard show relatively low infant mortality, as opposed to those located on the central meseta and in the South where mortality is high and shows little inclination to decline before around 1900.

---

[70] The study of crisis mortality has fared somewhat better. This will become evident in the next chapter of this book. See, for example, Pérez Moreda (1980).

Table 3.20   *Infant mortality in Spain*

Place	Region/province	Date	$_1q_0$
Village data for the eighteenth and nineteenth century			
Los Molinos	Madrid	1710–1739	277
Plencia	Basque Country	1740–1799	308
Plencia	Basque Country	1790–1799	152
Palomós	Catalonia	1790–1818	192
Otero de Herreros	Segovia	1780–1816	317
Villacastín	Segovia	1820–1850	274
Hervás	Cáceres	1801–1810	282
Longares	Zaragoza	1804–1813	240
Mantiel	Guadalajara	1819–1837	264
Cuenca and its province (village, district, etc.)			
Valdeolivas	Cuenca	1818–1837	305
Cuenca	Cuenca	1842–1862	228
Alcarria (district)	Cuenca	1860–1869	266
Sierra (district)	Cuenca	1860–1869	192
Mancha (district)	Cuenca	1860–1869	226
Province	Cuenca	1859–1861	217

Sources For Los Molinos, Soler Serratosa (1985: 186); for Plencia, Fernández de Pinedo (1974: 116); for Palomós, Vilar (1965); for Otero de Herreros, Villacastín, Hervás, Longares and Mantiel, Pérez Moreda (1980: 148); for Valdeolivas, Reher (1980: 69); for Alcarria, Sierra, Mancha, Reher (1988a: 98) The provincial data for Cuenca are taken from published census material.

Table 3.21   *Patterns of infant and child mortality*

Region	$_1q_0$	$_4q_1$
North	148	137
Upper Meseta	203	214
Lower Meseta	208	212
South	207	229
East/Northeast	161	187

Table 3.22. *Survivors at different ages*[a]

			Age			
Place	Province	Period	1	5	10	15
Otero de Herreros	Segovia	1820–1829	839	639	610	590
Otero de Herreros	Segovia	1840–1849	838	691	646	631
Villacastín	Segovia	1820–1829	731	471	425	401
Valdeolivas	Cuenca	1818–1827	695	465	446	437
Cuenca	Cuenca	1842–1848	772	587	560	545
Alcarria (district)	Cuenca	1860–1869	753	541	524	510
Sierra (district)	Cuenca	1860–1869	814	610	557	542
Mancha (district)	Cuenca	1860–1869	766	532	506	492
Province	Cuenca	1859–1861	786	579	550	535

Notes [a] Per thousand born.
   Provincial totals based on official statistics. If based on a sample of local level
data, the survival rates would be: 778, 561, 526 and 512.
Sources See Table 3.20.

In much of Spain child mortality ($_4q_1$) was as high or even higher
than q_0. This fact has been noted elsewhere, is amply corroborated by
both rural and urban data for Cuenca, and differs substantially from
mortality structures in much of the rest of Europe.[71] In the city itself $_4q_1$
was 240 per thousand, 5 per cent higher than q_0. Similar results appear
in most of the other examples we have used. Official estimates (*c.* 1900)
for provinces (Table 3.21) show the following patterns of infant and
child mortality.

The consequence of this is that the probabilities of survival beyond
childhood were far lower than we might have imagined had we used
only $_1q_0$ as a guideline (Table 3.22). Only slightly more than half of
children born were going to reach the age of puberty, thereby relying
heavily on fertility to ensure acceptable growth rates. If one uses
aggregate data from a later date, it appears that only in the northern
part of the country were survival probabilities much higher. While it is
impossible to pinpoint the exact levels of mortality at earlier dates, the
sparse information suggests that its basic structures were in place by
the eighteenth century and possibly earlier.

Explaining this reality is an important task and involves a close
examination of mortality in the first year after birth as well as an

[71] See, for example, Reher (1988a: 96–101). The mortality schedules underlying Coale
   and Demeny's South model life tables, based on Mediterranean mortality structures,
   reflected the same pattern. See Coale and Demeny (1983).

understanding of the infant feeding practices. In the province of Cuenca, as well as in much of the rest of the central part of Spain, children were breastfed for a relatively long period of time. If no health problems arose, the duration of breast-feeding was considerably more than a year. The period of breast-feeding was not uniform, and supplemental feeding was utilized during the first year of life, normally some time after the fourth or fifth month.[72] Supplementary food, mostly paps made up of wheat or rye, water, and honey or sugar, was not generally prepared with any great care and the water used was not boiled. The result was a sharp upturn in infant deaths after six or seven months of life. The protection afforded by the mother's milk had been neutralized, at least in part. If mortality by month during the first year of life is graphed in order to estimate levels of endogenous and exogenous causes (by Bourgeois Pichat's biometric method), there is a perceptible upturn after six months.[73]

High child mortality, which mainly affected one-year-old children, was also related to breast-feeding and subsequent weaning practices. Weaning could take place after a child's second birthday, though some time between 12 and 20 months was more likely. This was precisely the time when the child was in the process of teething. Since infant and child hygiene was not a relevant issue in the popular culture of the period, it is not difficult to see why so many children died of intestinal infections during the late summer months. Clearly, the availability of pure water and the rigor of the climate, especially the summer heat, played a role in a child's chances of surviving, though ultimately the persistence of high infant and child mortality must be viewed in the light of cultural constraints.[74] Until hygiene assumed a more important role in people's awareness, it was impossible to reduce rates of infant or child mortality. In the province of Cuenca, this does not occur until after the beginning of the twentieth century.

As suggested by the relatively low probabilities of survival of

[72] This information has come to light in in-depth interviews with elderly peasants from the province of Cuenca (Reher, 1988a: 105–109). For an interesting study of infant feeding practices in much of Europe and especially in England, see Fildes (1987).

[73] For the period 1842–1847, 21.3 per cent of all infant deaths (48.6 per thousand births) were due to endogenous causes. The distribution of deaths over the first year of life is similar in rural areas of the province during the second half of the nineteenth century. See Reher (1988a: 104–107).

[74] Season of birth, and thus the age at which children went through their first and second summers, could influence probabilities of surviving the first two years of life by as much as 26 per cent (Reher, 1988a: 107–111). For the influence of climate on mortality at young ages, see also Breschi and Livi Bacci (1986a, 1986b). Several authors have found a significant relation between climate and overall levels of mortality as well (Lee, 1981; Galloway, 1985). For a general discussion of the relationship between climate and population growth, see Galloway (1986b).

Table 3.23. *Life expectancy at different ages; Cuenca,*
1842–1848

Age	e_x
0	29.1
1	36.6
5	43.5
10	40.5
20	33.5
40	22.2
60	10.4

Sources Municipal listings of inhabitants, 1843–1847; Municipal registration of vital events, 1842–1862 (children), 1842–
1847 (adults).

children, the overall mortality regime of Cuenca was quite severe. Life
expectancy at birth was a low 29.1 years around the mid-nineteenth
century (Table 3.23).[75] Once childhood had passed, chances of survival increased appreciably, but mortality was always severe. Cuenca
belonged to what could be termed a "high pressure" demographic
regime in which mortality levels were perhaps the key determining
element.[76]

The seasonal distribution of mortality showed considerable stability
over time. As one might expect from a Mediterranean population, the
concentration of mortality during the months of August and September throughout the period studied is clearly its most noteworthy
aspect and can be attributed to two factors (Figure 3.6).[77] Most infant
and child mortality was concentrated in those months, and the
seasonality of the majority of the major epidemics during the period
under study was concentrated during the late summer and early
autumn.[78]

[75] This is, however, somewhat higher than estimated levels for Spain as a whole in the
eighteenth century or for the village of Valdeolivas, located in the province of
Cuenca, where e_0 was 25.8 years. See Livi Bacci (1968), Reher (1980: 69).

[76] For a discussion of some of the implications of high and low pressure demographic
regimes, see, for example, Wrigley and Schofield (1981: 457–466), Pérez Moreda and
Reher (1985: 318–324).

[77] It is not difficult to find numerous examples of similar seasonal patterns of mortality
in central and southern areas of Spain. For Murcia, see Pérez Picazo (1981: 572); for
the central meseta, Pérez Moreda (1980: 206–211); for Aragón, Ansón Calvo (1977: 99)
and Salas Auséns (1981: 203).

[78] The apparent increase in late summer mortality during the second half of the
eighteenth and the first half of the nineteenth centuries is, in reality, a product of the
beginning of systematic registration of infant and child deaths. On the other hand,

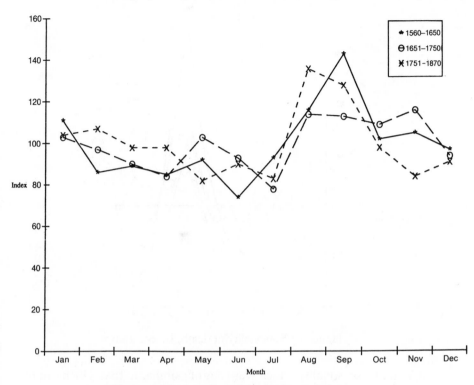

Figure 3.6 Seasonality of death, by period

Further disaggregation reveals a distribution of mortality subject to considerable heterogeneity. Only the mortality peak of August and September affects all age groups, but even then its intensity is strikingly different (Figure 3.7). For infants and especially for young children, it was a period of extremely intense mortality, whereas for other groups this was not the case.[79] Infant mortality itself was subject not only to the effects of late summer, but also mirrored the seasonality of births quite closely. This can be seen more clearly in the April peak which coincides with the period in which most children were born. Other age groups show less seasonal variability. Of these only those over 50 and to a lesser extent those between 15 and 49 years of

the sixteenth and early seventeenth centuries peak during the autumn, partially due to the presence of the plague in town which tended to be most intense during these months.

[79] While the seasonal pattern of infant deaths is quite similar to that holding in nineteenth-century London, that of young children is radically different (Buchan and Mitchell, 1875: 228–230).

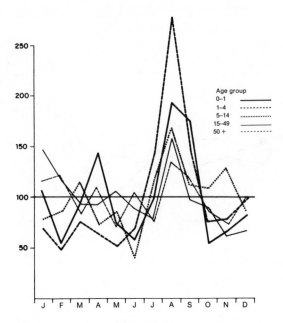

Figure 3.7 Seasonality of death, by age group

age, had a seasonality which was roughly similar to that which can be observed in other parts of Europe during the nineteenth century, and in Spain after the middle part of the twentieth century.[80] Clearly the seasonality and intensity of mortality at younger ages were the key distinguishing marks of mortality patterns in central Spain during this period.

The prevailing causes of death along with their characteristic seasonal and age distributions underlie the patterns we have just seen. In

[80] The seasonal distribution of mortality in the northern regions of Spain during this period differed sharply from that in central and southern parts of the country. The areas of greatest concentration of summer deaths were also those of most intense infant and child mortality. In 1900, when seasonal variation was presumably considerably lower, this same pattern emerges, as can be seen in the following table based on provincial civil registration data:

Percentage of infant and child deaths (0–4) taking place between July and September (based on unweighted averages of provinces)

North	24.9
Upper Meseta	30.6
Lower Meseta	34.1
South	33.5
East–Northeast	30.0

Table 3.24. *Cause of death by general groups and sex in two Spanish towns*

Cause of death (general typology)	Cuenca			Segovia
	Males	Females	Total	
General pathology	35.7	43.9	39.6	30.3
Infectious disease	28.7	26.4	27.6	41.9
Disorders				
Digestive	11.8	11.0	11.4	7.4
Respiratory	17.9	13.2	15.6	27.1
Cardiovascular	1.1	0.3	0.7	1.1
Nervous	17.9	18.6	18.2	7.1
Psychiatric	1.8	1.8	1.8	1.5
Gynecological	0.0	3.2	1.6	0.7
Rheumatic	0.4	2.3	1.4	0.7
Urinary	1.0	0.4	0.7	0.0
Otolaryngological	2.1	1.8	2.0	0.4
Pediatric	0.4	1.2	0.7	0.0
Non-medical causes	14.8	8.3	11.7	5.1
No classification/ others				6.1
Total deaths (number)	840	770	1,610	816

Note Totals are expressed as the percentage of all deaths which correspond to a given category. Double classification of certain disorders (281 male deaths, 250 female) means that the sum of all groups does not equal 100. See text for further explanations.
Sources Cuenca, parish death registers between 1830 and 1870; Segovia, 1807–1856, a personal communication from Vicente Pérez Moreda, reworked by author.

Spain, a systematic evaluation of the incidence of different diseases has been hindered by inadequate death registers. Fortunately, beginning in the 1830s the Cuenca registers begin to list cause of death consistently. It should be remembered that during this period the popular understanding of causes of death was at best approximate, and this can be seen in the nature of the data. A precise classification of certain causes of death has been unavoidable.[81] Finally, cross-

[81] The categories used are very general and are based on standard medical classifications. An example of double classification would be, say, cholera which is both an intestinal disorder and an infectious disease. Since this classification problem has been unavoidable, all tables have been designed so as to reflect only the exact weight of each category. In other words, double classifications are not counted twice, and the columns of the table do not add up to 100. A total of 1,610 causes has been classified,

classification of cause of death by category, sex, age and seasonality has sharply reduced our sample sizes. All of these aspects counsel a cautious and limited analysis dealing only with the most noteworthy aspects of the data. The results, though, are quite interesting.[82]

Infectious disease has traditionally been considered to be the prime cause of death in pre-twentieth-century societies, and our data amply confirm this notion (Table 3.24).[83] Apart for those causes classified as General Pathology, in both Cuenca and Segovia, infectious diseases accounted for the greatest proportion of deaths.[84] These were followed in importance by nervous, respiratory and digestive disorders.[85] No category is entirely sex-specific, except of course gynecological disorders, though respiratory problems seemed to affect men considerably more than women. It is not clear whether differences observed between the Cuenca and the Segovia data reflect a different disease structure (affecting infectious diseases, digestive and especially respiratory disorders) or are the result of small sample size.

The basic seasonality we have seen is also largely the result of the importance of infectious and digestive disorders within the prevailing mortality structures. Only these disorders showed pronounced late summer peaks (Figure 3.8). The rest showed little or no seasonality at all, except for disorders of the respiratory system which were concentrated during the winter months. A closer examination of certain of the most common causes helps bring this picture into sharper focus. As can be seen in Table 3.25, some causes of death were sex-specific, all showed a marked preference for certain age groups, and most had a more or less well-defined seasonality. The precise etiology of many of

531 of which were classified in more than one category. My thanks to Dr. Javier Gavilán for his assistance in this classification. See World Health Organization (1948). The best Spanish account of causes of death in a historical context can be found in Hauser (1902). Medical historians in Spain have recently carried out considerable research on the historical classifications of cause of death. See, for example, Bernabeu Mestre and López Piñero (1987).

[82] There is a singular lack of many of the most traditional causes of epidemic death, such as plague or typhus, which had all but disappeared by this period. For an overall look at epidemic disease and its evolution over time, see McNeill (1976).

[83] The importance of infectious diseases and their decline are central to much of the history of nineteenth-century mortality in Europe (McKeown, 1976: ch. 3).

[84] General pathology includes disorders such as "fevers," "teething," "pain," "dropsy," etc. While in some cases this category includes disorders which affect the general system, in other cases it reflects imprecise definitions. The principle components of the infectious disease category are cholera, typhoid fever, "lung," consumption, pneumonia, measles, typhus, and smallpox.

[85] The chief nervous disorders are apoplexy, "cerebral attack," epilepsy and palsy. Respiratory disorders include many different types of lung ailments, most important of which is pneumonia. The range of digestive diseases goes from summer diarrheas to cholera.

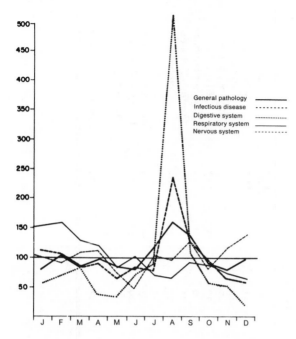

Figure 3.8 Seasonality of death, by cause

the prevalent diseases was, in fact, the underlying factor for the age structure and seasonality of mortality which was so characteristic of much of central Spain.[86]

Most of the causes of death showing special prevalence among the young were almost invariably strongest during the summer months. Epilepsy was typical only in the very young and was slightly more important among boys, much as occurs nowadays. Measles was most intense among young children during the summer months. Naturally, "teething" was important only for the young children. In fact, the term "teething" probably referred to the combined effects of teething and weaning, and to the frequent diarrheas which often followed the confluence of both events. The generic concept of "fevers" was the most common cause of death and included what were known as "gastric fevers," which were probably associated, once again, with the

---

[86] It is unfortunate that diseases such as malaria, plague and typhus which had earlier been so important in this part of Spain, are not present in our sample. For malaria, see Pérez Moreda (1980: 74–76; 1982).

Table 3.25 Age, sex and seasonal structures of principal causes of death; Cuenca, 1830–1868

Cause of death	% male	Age (%)					n	Seasonality
		0	1–4	5–14	15–49	>50		
Epilepsy	51	66	26	8	0	0	63	July
Apoplexy	48	5	2	2	21	70	64	unclear
"Cerebral attack"	60	4	11	17	19	50	55	October
"Fevers"	48	13	42	9	16	20	120	July–September
Cholera	42	2	17	7	37	37	43	August
Teething	44	14	86	0	0	0	48	July–September
Typhoid fever	47	0	11	16	51	22	38	August–October
Dropsy (Ascites)	35	0	6	5	27	62	83	October
"Chest"	63	4	4	4	27	62	62	January
Palsy/Paralysis	45	0	0	0	7	93	56	November–December
Pneumonia	57	14	9	1	29	47	86	January–February
Measles	46	23	77	0	0	0	24	August–October
Tuberculosis	52	0	0	10	75	15	25	unclear
Smallpox	73	13	39	35	13	0	33	December–January

Note See text for further explanation.

entire process of teething and weaning.[87] Since all of these were most intense during the summer, the timing both of births and of the termination of breast-feeding ended up having important implications for a child's probabilities of surviving beyond the age of 1 or 2 years.

Other disorders were frequent among other age groups and evidenced a considerably different seasonal pattern. Apoplexy or stroke syndrome, which is also a nervous disorder, affected older people almost exclusively and showed no seasonality at all. "Cerebral attack," which in popular parlance probably referred to something akin to apoplexy, was also concentrated in older age groups. Cholera epidemics, strongest among adults, were, of course, typical of the summer months.[88] Typhoid fever, like many of the other diseases related to contaminated food and water, was most intense among adults during the summer months. Dropsy or ascites, a liver disease related to cirrhosis of the liver, was especially prevalent among adults and older people. It was prevalent in October, though the reasons for this are unclear. Lung disorders, including pneumonia, "chest" disorders, and the first appearances of tuberculosis were especially frequent among adults and older people and were typical of the winter months.

On the whole adult-specific diseases showed a very mixed seasonality and, with the evident exception of typhoid fever and cholera, were mostly unrelated to hygienic conditions. Quite the contrary was true for those disorders typical of younger ages. In fact, of all childhood diseases, only smallpox was common outside of the late summer months, and it was on the wane as a major cause of death during this period. Another common characteristic of most childhood disorders was their relation to prevailing hygienic conditions, summer heat, feeding and weaning practices and, ultimately, diarrhea.

The first inroads into the prevailing mortality structures came with the gradual elimination of most great epidemics, and this process was quite advanced by the second third of the nineteenth century. It is interesting to note, however, that once this had been done, the next major reduction in mortality in Spain took place much later, affected younger age groups, was basically concentrated on exogenous

---

[87] If all types of fever are lumped together ("bilious," "gastric," "nervous," "verminous," "rotten," "slow," etc.), nearly 13 per cent of all deaths in my sample were caused by fevers. This count does not include typhoid fever or typhus.

[88] Since registration of cause of death only begins after the middle 1830s, our data only include one relatively mild cholera epidemic in 1855. For more on cholera in Cuenca, and especially on the epidemic of 1885, see Troitiño Vinuesa (1982, 1984: 267).

mortality, and seemed unrelated to prevailing nutritional levels.[89] The decline, rather, began in large towns and was paralleled by increased awareness on the part of mothers of the importance of hygiene, itself motivated in part by government efforts to educate and give assistance to mothers with young children.[90]

At a more general level, it is clear that as the importance of infectious and digestive disorders decreased during the twentieth century, the characteristic seasonality pattern of mortality also changed. The basic differences in seasonality which can be observed between areas of northern and southern Europe, or even between the northern coast and the central and southern parts of Spain, are attributable to the prevalence of digestive and/or respiratory ailments in each area. This, in turn, seemed to be linked to the relative importance and structure of mortality in the 1–4 year age group. While infant death was also important, it was perhaps less specifically distinctive of Spanish mortality patterns than was child mortality. In the light of this, it is particularly distressing to see that child mortality has been practically ignored by population historians and demographers of Spain.

[89] For a detailed account of this stage of the mortality transition in Spain, which occurred in the first decades of the present century, and especially for its effects on infant mortality, see Gómez Redondo (1987). The prime exponent of the hypothesis relating nutritional levels to mortality decline is, of course, McKeown, (1976: 128–142). For an iconoclastic view of this same issue, see, for example, Livi Bacci (1983, 1987) or Pérez Moreda (1988b).

[90] A good example of this were the *gotas de leche*, where mothers could find quality milk and other foods to supplement their children's diets. See Gómez Redondo (1985, 1987). These ideas are very close to those of McKeown (1976: 110–127) with respect to the period after 1850 in Europe.

4

Economic fluctuations and demographic behavior in urban Spain

Introduction

The relationship between economic realities and demographic behavior has occupied center stage in most demographic research since Malthus, with enlightened clarity, pointed to its importance nearly two centuries ago. For Malthus, the "invisible hand" whereby population growth was kept in line with economic realities was materialized through the relation between economic well-being and fertility and mortality. While the basic postulates of Malthus' model are difficult to deny, operationalizing it is not an easy task for population historians because of the inherent difficulties in defining and empirically showing the relations implicit in his theory. Malthus set his model in the medium and long term, but, if his postulates are correct, it is likely that they would be visible in the short term as well. Short-term analysis of fluctuations has certain advantages over other types of analysis because adequate indicators are more readily accessible, have a more straightforward interpretation and can enable one to verify statistically the relationship between economic and demographic fluctuations.[1]

In pre-industrial societies people's immediate economic situation was determined mainly by the available food supply and the proportion of family income dedicated to food-related expenditures. In turn, the available food supply was fundamentally influenced by fluctuating and insecure harvests whose effects might be mitigated by the

---

[1] One of the principal advantages of short-term analysis is that it tends to minimize the importance of migration. In other words, from one year to the next variations in births, deaths and marriages are a fairly good proxy of fertility, mortality and nuptiality of the resident population. Naturally the effects of migration cannot ever be completely eliminated, especially when looking at mortality. See Galloway (1988a: 275–276).

existence or not of inter-regional grain markets and the ability of municipal and national institutions to curb periods of shortage by importing grain effectively. Among the possible indicators of available food supply, and therefore of short-term economic well-being, the price of wheat seems to reflect economic conditions with perhaps less ambiguity than other indicators such as the tithe (Le Roy Ladurie and Goy, 1982). The interpretation of this indicator is not always simple because, for example, those farmers who had wheat and therefore could either sell it at a profit or did not need to buy it on the market, would be comparatively unaffected by price increases, or would perhaps even have benefited by them. Nevertheless, for the great majority of people, and especially those living in urban areas, the market price of grain was a powerful indicator of their short-term economic well-being and an indirect proxy for the relative bounty of the harvest.

The relationship between harvest fluctuations (prices) and vital events has been the object of abundant historical speculation.[2] This has been especially the case with mortality where many historians have pointed to the often simultaneous rise in both prices and mortality, suggesting that there was a causal link between the two (Goubert, 1960; 1968: 68–82). At another level, authors such as Thomas McKeown (1976) have suggested that nutritional levels and mortality were closely correlated. Despite the fact that a good deal of current scholarship tends to minimize the direct importance of nutrition (prices) for mortality, the link between prices and vital events remains a traditional though often ambiguous theme in the field of historical demography.[3] Even though fertility has not received nearly so much attention in this context as has mortality, its links with prevailing economic conditions are equally as important if we are to understand the true meaning of the type of homeostasis originally postulated by Malthus (Lee, 1987).

The present chapter will attempt to analyze the basic structure of the links between grain prices and vital events in a number of Spanish towns during the pre-industrial era. The results will enable us to evaluate the direction, magnitude and temporal structure of the responses of vital behavior to grain prices. My analysis will also include a long rural series corresponding to New Castile which will contribute to defining the specificity or not of urban responses which,

[2] See, for example, Schofield (1985); Meuvret (1946); Lebrun (1980); Bruneel (1977); Del Panta and Livi Bacci (1977); Pérez Moreda (1980; 1985c); Post (1985); Livi Bacci (1978).

[3] McKeown's theories have come under criticism by scholars who point out that the relation between nutrition and mortality is neither simple nor evident. See, for example, Livi Bacci (1983; 1987); Pérez Moreda (1985c; 1988b).

at least in theory, should be different in intensity, if not in direction, from those of more isolated rural areas.

Methodology and data

Some years ago Ronald Lee (1981: 356–401) attempted to estimate systematically the relationship between prices and vital events by means of a distributed lag regression model. His work showed that discernible links between the two did exist, though the overall importance of prices in determining fluctuations was often not great. Lee's pioneering work has been followed by a whole host of scholars who have gone a long way towards consolidating and deepening Lee's original understanding of the problem.[4] All of these authors have used similar distributed lag models, though not all have used the same number of lags, so as to best reflect the structure of the effect of prices over a period of time.

This analysis follows Lee's method closely, using, in particular, many of the improvements shown in the recent work of Patrick Galloway (1987). All series used have been detrended by dividing each point in the series, x, by an eleven-year average of points centered around x. The mean of the resulting series will be nearly 1.0 and thus the coefficient of variation of each series is practically the same as the standard deviation. The present study uses a five-year distributed lag model. In other words births (or marriages or deaths) of year 0 are made a function of prices (and other variables) in that and in the four previous years. The use of a distributed lag model is designed to show delayed effects of the explanatory variable or variables, which might well be very important as will be indicated later. The method also corrects for second-order autoregressive disturbances by using Cochrane and Orcutt's iterative procedure (Pindyck and Rubinfeld, 1981: 152–157).[5] R^2 and corrected R^2 are calculated for untransformed variables. The significance of the sums of the regression coefficients are also estimated. The regression results are shown in Tables 4.2, 4.3 and 4.5 and in Figures 4.1–4.5, and will be discussed in the following sections.

The data used for this study are based on the vital statistics of four urban centers, of varying size and importance, and one rural region.

---

[4] See, for example, Galloway (1985; 1986a; 1988; 1989), Bengtsson (1984; 1986), Weir (1984b), Richards (1983), Hammel (1985), Bengtsson and Ohlsson (1985), Pérez Moreda (1988c), and Reher (1989b).

[5] If the series is sufficiently long, this procedure should have little effect on the value of the regression coefficients, but will provide a better estimate of their significance. (Galloway, 1988; Harvey, 1981: 189–199)

During the period under study, Madrid was a major city, and Granada a relatively large one (52,375 inhabitants in 1787). On the other hand both Cuenca and Talavera were small towns with fewer than 10,000 inhabitants. The vital statistics for New Castile are taken from a differing number of parishes from the entire region. For Granada, the price series used corresponds to wheat in Granada itself. All other areas utilize prices from Toledo and Alcalá de Henares, complemented, where necessary, by wheat prices from Villacastín.[6] While it is unfortunate that I did not have price series available for each town, it should be noted that the series I have from New Castile are fairly highly correlated. Wherever data availability requires the use of more than one period to make up an entire series, the detrended sub-series were spliced together.[7] In order to get a better idea of the differential

[6] The basic price series is taken from Hamilton (1934; 1947). Since the detrended Toledo prices end in 1795, for some of the areas analyzed it was necessary to use prices for the first part of the nineteenth century. I was able to choose from two series, one from Villacastín and another from Almadén. The series from Villacastín was preferred because only two years had to be estimated between 1790 and 1835, as opposed to 10 estimations with the Almadén data. See Doblado González, 1982: 372 and Llopis Angelán, 1982: 90. It should be noted that wheat from Villacastín, located in Old Castile, was normally sold on the market in Madrid. Both of these series are significantly correlated (0.689).

[7] All births are, in fact, baptisms. In the parish registers I have personally worked with, before approximately 1730 the mean interval between birth and baptism is approximately 10 days. Subsequently, this interval diminishes to between two and four days at the end of the century. By and large deaths are non-infant deaths, though in some towns this is because of under-registration of deaths of children under seven years of age (*párvulos*) rather than a specific recording of non-infant deaths.

Vital records from Granada are taken from Sanz Sampelayo (1980: 546–608) and refer to 16 of the 23 parishes. Deaths in Granada are fundamentally adult deaths, though the registration does not specify this. Granada prices come from Sanz Sampelayo (1982).

For Madrid all vital data come from Carbajo Isla (1987: 256–324). The author of this book estimates the values for some parishes for certain periods based on the general totals. We have not utilized any parish whose values have been estimated. There is a distressing gap in the Madrid data for 1746 and 1747. This is why my analysis is divided into two different sub-periods. The first period, 1650–1745 for the raw data, includes 8 parishes. For the second period, 1748–1812, the data correspond to 15 parishes. The second period was ended at this date (the detrended series goes to 1807) so as to avoid the perturbing effects of the War of Independence (1808–1812) which were most serious in Madrid. All deaths are specifically non-infant deaths.

Talavera de la Reina data come from González Muñoz (1975: 420–453). They refer to seven of the town's parishes. Adult deaths are specified. Cuenca data refer to vital events in 8 of the towns 14 parishes. Deaths are not specifically non-infant deaths.

A number of different parishes are included in the New Castile series. The origin of these data is the following. Professor Jordi Nadal provided me with the data for Móstoles, Griñon, Torrejón de Ardoz, Yepes, El Toboso, Orgaz and Colmenar Viejo. Vicente Pérez Moreda provided the series for Chiloeches, Mantiel, Cereceda, Motilla del Palancar and Barajas. All data for the following villages was taken from the Archivo Diocesano de Cuenca: Arcas, Albaladejo del Cuende, Atalaya del Cañavate, Buenache de Alarcón, Castejón, Cervera del Llano, La Peraleja, La Ventosa, Leganiel,

Table 4.1. *Means of raw series and coefficients of variation of the detrended series*

| Place | Period | Mean of raw series | | |
		Births	Marriages	Non-infant deaths
Madrid				
Rich	1661–1740	1,425.4	564.3	890.1
Poor	1661–1740	1,206.3	449.0	674.1
Total	1661–1740	2,631.7	1,013.3	1,564.2
Madrid				
Rich	1759–1807	2,083.8	715.2	924.3
Poor	1759–1807	2,223.4	806.0	927.9
Total	1759–1807	4,307.2	1,521.2	1,852.2
Granada				
Rich	1712–1795	1,345.3	341.3	615.1
Poor	1712–1795	327.5	73.3	93.8
Total	1712–1795	1,672.8	414.6	708.9
Talavera				
Rich	1711–1785	96.7	39.9	60.1
Poor	1711–1785	109.3	37.7	75.3
Total	1711–1785	206.0	77.6	135.4
Cuenca				
Rich	1673–1777	51.2	19.0	41.2
Poor	1673–1777	46.1	15.7	29.2
Total	1673–1777	97.3	34.7	70.4
New Castile				
1	1583–1682	770.0	178.8	288.0
2	1650–1750	517.5	144.2	278.0
3	1730–1830	1,265.1	273.8	812.3
Total	1583–1830	850.9	198.9	459.4

Mohorte, Olmeda del Rey, Priego, Puebla de Almenara, Valdecabras, Valdemeca, Valdeolivas, Villalba de la Sierra, Villanueva de Guademejud. For this last group of villages we only have series for the period 1775–1825, whereas all of the rest date back to the sixteenth century. All deaths are total deaths, and reflect the aforementioned under-registration of infant and child mortality. There are approximately 12 villages included in the first period (1583–1683), 10 in the second (1650–1750) and 28 in the third (1730–1830).

Prices for New Castile are based on the work of E. J. Hamilton (1947) and complemented by those compiled by Llopis Angelán (1982). The year missing in Llopis' series (1812) was based on the data from Almadén (Dobado González, 1982: 372).

Table 4.1. (*cont.*)

Place	Period	Coefficient of variation of detrended series			
		Births	Marriages	Non-infant deaths	Wheat prices
Madrid					
Rich	1661–1740	0.046	0.076	0.122	
Poor	1661–1740	0.052	0.084	0.137	
Total	1661–1740	0.044	0.073	0.125	0.320
Madrid					
Rich	1759–1807	0.036	0.070	0.119	
Poor	1759–1807	0.047	0.067	0.150	
Total	1759–1807	0.035	0.060	0.132	0.325
Granada					
Rich	1712–1795	0.056	0.115	0.205	
Poor	1712–1795	0.072	0.192	0.254	
Total	1712–1790	0.056	0.117	0.206	0.259
Talavera					
Rich	1711–1785	0.110	0.250	0.280	
Poor	1711–1785	0.114	0.204	0.272	
Total	1711–1785	0.089	0.184	0.271	0.269
Cuenca					
Rich	1673–1777	0.132	0.262	0.391	
Poor	1673–1777	0.169	0.328	0.495	
Total	1673–1777	0.114	0.221	0.401	0.300
Castilla la Nueva					
1	1583–1682	0.069	0.116	0.262	0.292
2	1650–1750	0.077	0.109	0.250	0.299
3	1730–1830	0.073	0.169	0.212	0.342
Total	1583–1830	0.074	0.139	0.247	0.317

Notes In the cases of Madrid and Talavera all deaths are specifically non-infant deaths. In all other cases, the deaths correspond to total registered deaths during periods when, by and large, the death of children under 7 years of age was not recorded. The disparities in the raw series for New Castile are due to the fact that each subperiod is integrated by a different number of parishes. For the total detrended series this is not a problem because the partial series have been spliced together. See text for further details.

effects of prices by social group, all urban areas have been divided into rich and poor districts. Given the lack of data on wealth or income in most pre-industrial Spanish towns, the divisions by district have invariably been based on the active population data.[8] While less perfect than other types of wealth measure, these divisions reflect substantially different levels of wealth.

The means of the raw series and the coefficients of variation of the detrended series can be seen in Table 4.1. The variation in deaths and prices is always the greatest and that of births the least; variation among the poor sectors of the urban population is considerably greater than for the rich. Finally, the variation in the price series corresponding to Toledo-Villacastín clearly increases during the eighteenth and nineteenth centuries.

Prices, mortality and fertility

Since high prices were often accompanied by periods of high mortality, their effects on fertility could well be confounded. In order to sift out the relative weights of both, the present study has made fertility dependent both on prices and on mortality. The regression equation used is as follows:

$$B_t = a + \sum_{k=0}^{4} b_k P_{t-k} + \sum_{k=0}^{4} c_k D_{t-k} + e_t$$

Where B = births, P = prices, D = non-infant deaths, a is a constant, b and c are coefficients, e is an error term and t is time. Remember that all series have been detrended. The coefficients estimated are, in fact, elasticities and reflect the percentage increase or decrease of the

---

[8] For Granada, this division is based on the Census of 1787 and effectively isolates the behavior of the most rural and poor of all Granada parishes, San Ildefonso. In 1787, 87.7 per cent of the active population of San Ildefonso was either a tenant farmer or a day laborer (normally occupied in urban activities). This distribution was provided by Juan Sanz Sampelayo.

The division in Talavera, based on sixteenth- to seventeenth-century data, isolates the parishes filled with farmers and day laborers (Santa Leocadia, El Salvador, San Clemente and San Andrés) from the more well-to-do parishes (San Pedro, San Miguel, Santa María) (González Muñoz, 1975: 162–163, 254–255, 394–397).

In the case of Madrid, the administrative and noble districts of town in 1787 (Barrio del Palacio, de San Francisco, de la Plaza and de Maravillas) are distinguished from those of San Gerónimo, Barquillo and Lavapiés (Ringrose, 1983: 37–40; Larquié, 1974; 1978; Jiménez de Gregorio, 1980: 182–220).

The available data for Cuenca have enabled us to divide the town into two districts. One of them corresponds to the upper part of town and includes the seven parishes for which I have parish registers. I have also used the index of vital events for the parish of San Esteban which was located in the lower part of town.

Table 4.2 Regressions of fertility on grain prices and non-infant mortality

Place	Dependent variable	Period	n	Constant	Grain prices				
					Lag 0	Lag 1	Lag 2	Lag 3	Lag 4
Madrid									
Rich	Births	1661–1740	80	1.265 a	.028 d	−.020	−.007	−.001	.025 d
Poor	Births	1661–1740	80	1.238 a	.003	−.054 b	.008	−.018	.026
Total	Births	1661–1740	80	1.250 a	.017	−.036 c	.001	−.010	.027 d
Madrid									
Rich	Births	1759–1807	49	.799 a	.014	−.047 b	−.020	.007	.040 c
Poor	Births	1759–1807	49	1.197 a	.025	.039	.016	−.010	.053 c
Total	Births	1759–1807	49	1.030 a	.012	.005	−.010	−.012	.049 b
Granada									
Rich	Births	1712–1795	84	1.199 a	−.126 a	−.052 b	−.061 b	−.020	−.008
Poor	Births	1712–1795	84	1.184 a	−.113 a	−.024	.021	−.075 b	−.005
Total	Births	1712–1795	84	1.202 a	−.123 a	−.043 c	−.050 c	−.024	−.014
Talavera									
Rich	Births	1711–1785	75	1.229 a	−.079 d	−.027	−.022	−.019	−.012
Poor	Births	1711–1785	75	1.380 a	.011	.009	−.122 b	.049	.032
Total	Births	1711–1785	75	1.270 a	−.040	−.001	−.092 b	.000	.005
Cuenca									
Rich	Births	1673–1777	105	1.198 a	.041	.164 a	.084 d	.005	−.054
Poor	Births	1673–1777	105	1.033 a	.026	.013	−.021	.029	.061
Total	Births	1673–1777	105	1.126 a	.014	−.057	.027	.007	−.002
New Castile									
1	Births	1583–1683	101	1.291 a	−.049 c	−.063 b	.000	−.001	−.006
2	Births	1650–1750	101	1.365 a	.010	−.097 a	−.015	.015	−.017
3	Births	1730–1830	101	1.330 a	.008	−.074 a	−.049 b	−.010	−.017
Total	Births	1583–1830	248	1.317 a	−.004	−.084 a	−.026 d	−.000	−.003

| Place | Non-infant mortality | | | | | R^2 | Corrected R^2 | Grain prices lag sum | Non-infant mortality lag sum |
	Lag 0	Lag 1	Lag 2	Lag 3	Lag 4				
Madrid									
Rich	-.109 b	-.080 d	.002	-.032	-.071	.67	.62	.024	-.291 a
Poor	-.087 c	-.043	-.005	-.016	-.053	.60	.53	-.035	-.204 b
Total	-.100 b	-.063 d	-.002	-.021	-.064 d	.68	.62	-.001	-.249 a
Madrid									
Rich	.066	.054	.038	.024	.029	.73	.64	-.006	.211 d
Poor	-.134 b	-.090 b	-.068	.097 c	-.118 c	.74	.66	.123 b	-.313 b
Total	-.051	-.031	-.011	.080 c	-.057	.77	.70	.044	-.070
Granada									
Rich	-.043 d	-.022	.088 a	.010	.034	.82	.79	-.267 a	.067
Poor	-.093 a	.050 c	-.008	.017	.045 d	.49	.41	-.196 a	.011
Total	-.053 c	-.017	.078 b	-.001	.043 d	.80	.76	-.254 a	.050
Talavera									
Rich	-.087 c	-.054	.026	-.019	.059	.55	.46	-.158 c	-.075
Poor	-.152 a	-.112 b	-.041	-.065	.007	.58	.50	-.021	-.363 b
Total	-.110 a	-.065 c	-.005	-.033	.067 c	.70	.64	-.127 c	-.146 d
Cuenca									
Rich	-.059 c	-.051 d	-.012	-.037	.048 d	.40	.31	-.088	-.111 d
Poor	-.054 d	-.060 d	.053 d	-.075 c	-.009	.54	.48	.107	-.145 d
Total	-.060 b	-.073 b	.045 d	-.045 d	.016	.64	.59	-.011	-.117 d
New Castile									
1	-.051 d	-.042 d	-.001	-.034	-.039 d	.75	.71	-.119 b	-.167 b
2	-.094 a	-.062 b	.002	-.061 b	-.045 d	.56	.50	-.104 c	-.260 a
3	-.077 b	-.103 a	.013	-.002	-.020	.81	.79	-.142 a	-.189 b
Total	-.063 a	-.066 a	.009	-.038	-.040	.78	.77	-.117 a	-.198 a

Notes The trend has been removed from each series by dividing each data point, call it x, in a series of an eleven year average of data points centered around x. The regressions are corrected for second order autoregressive disturbances using the iterative Cochrane–Orcutt procedure. R^2 and corrected R^2 are calculated for the untransformed variables. The significance level of the test statistics is: a 1%, b 5%, c 10%, d 20%.

dependent variable in reaction to a 1 per cent increase in the independent variable. The empirical results can be found in Table 4.2 and Figures 4.1 and 4.2.

High prices would tend to depress fertility levels in a number of different manners. They could often lead to acute food shortage and undernourishment, as well as to times of stress and "calamity" as many contemporaries termed them. In such a situation fertility would suffer for several physiological, psychological and behavioral reasons, which would affect women's reproductive behavior both immediately and during the ensuing years. Spontaneous abortions, amenorrhea, decreases in coital frequency due to spousal separation or decreased libido, or even voluntary restriction of coitus as an immediate response to the situation, could probably all play an important role (Le Roy Ladurie, 1969). While it is very risky to attempt to isolate the effects of any one of those factors, it is clear that the timing with which they affected fertility would differ. During the first moments of the crisis, only spontaneous abortions would directly affect the number of births. The consequences of other factors would become visible only later in the first year or in successive years. For this reason, the postulated downturn in fertility should last at least two years, and should then be followed by a more or less significant rebound in births.[9] This time, however, the recovery would probably only be partially due to improved nourishment and increased coital frequency, and would also be the result of the rapid recovery of marriages which typically followed most subsistence crises.

If the data are ordered by social group, the reaction of fertility to price increases is not easily predicted. The poorer sectors of society would probably suffer the effects of undernourishment far more directly than the rich. Thus spontaneous abortions, amenorrhea and other physiological and psychological factors might well be greater among these groups and fertility lower. On the other hand, however, the sectors in pre-modern societies traditionally most willing to restrict their nuptiality and the pioneers of fertility control were the well-to-do. If conscious choice entered into fertility behavior, the more wealthy sectors of society might well react more negatively to changes in prices than the poorer, even though they suffered rela-

---

[9] It is important to bear in mind that the method used here only gives an approximate estimate of the timing of fertility swings. Yearly data of vital events and price series in which only one price estimate is used for the entire year do not allow for more precise analysis.

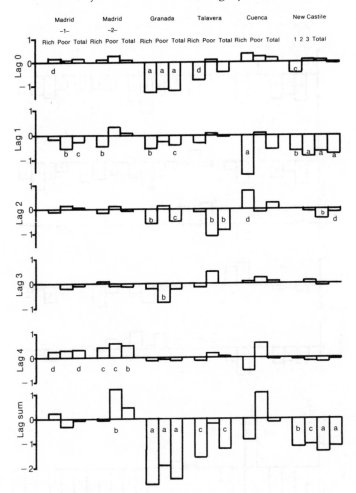

Figure 4.1 Response of births to fluctuations in grain prices, controlling non-infant deaths

tively less at times of high prices. Thus far results from other studies on short-run fluctuations have been contradictory.[10]

Periods of high mortality, which often accompanied increases in prices, could also have a decidedly negative effect on fertility. The

[10] Galloway (1986a: 287) found that the urban poor reacted more to prices than the rich. The same author (1988: Figures 3–5) suggests that wealth had nothing to do with fertility response in a number of European countries. It should be mentioned that in each article, Galloway is dealing with different units of analysis, with different population densities and different socio-economic characteristics. His results, therefore, may only be apparently contradictory.

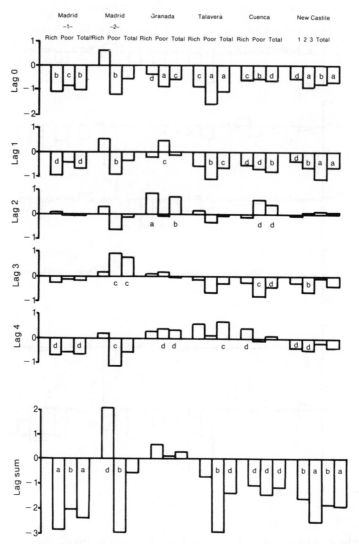

Figure 4.2 Response of births to fluctuations in non-infant deaths, controlling grain prices

impact on fertility of the death of pregnant women would be immediate, whereas that of adult women (and men), leading to broken marriages and a depletion in the stock of available women, would only show up at lag 1 and would be more lasting and pervasive. When mortality levels were sufficiently high so as to significantly depress the supply of adults in the population, its negative effects could well be prolonged far beyond the first two years (Livi Bacci, 1978: 78–86). Insofar as the area studied was characterized by generally high levels of adult mortality and epidemics were recurrent, this effect would have been far greater than in those areas of relatively lower and more stable levels of mortality. Consequent to this, we can also hypothesize that among the poor the fluctuations in mortality would have a greater effect on fertility than among the rich. Finally, the influence of mortality on fertility would end up being partially neutralized via increases in marriages subsequent to periods of high mortality.[11] This effect would become visible only at higher lags in our model.

The empirical results of this study have given support to some of these theoretical postulates, and have contradicted others.[12] In the first place, prices unquestionably tended to depress fertility levels. Taking overall urban totals as a basis, it is clear that generally prices are negatively correlated with births at lags 0 and 1, as well as for the overall lag sum. While this confirms my basic postulate, it should be noted that at lag 1 the negative relationship is weaker than expected and overall it is slightly lower than in a number of other European areas (Galloway, 1988: Appendix, Table 1). In rural areas, in New Castile and in other regions of Spain, on the other hand, the results are identical to those postulated: an initially negative correlation, increasing at lag 1 and significant overall (Pérez Moreda, 1988c: 94–96).

There is also a significant negative relation between deaths and births at lag 0 in every case; at lag 1 it is somewhat weaker, though still often significant. The rebound effect that I had postulated hardly materializes in urban areas, and does not exist at all in rural New Castile. An important characteristic of most of the Spanish data is that, by and large, mortality plays a greater role in influencing fertility than do prices.[13]

Certain clear differences emerge if the population is divided by social category. Response to prices among the rich sectors is consistently more negative than among the poor, especially at lag 1. If the sum

11 This last point is touched upon only tangentially in our analysis. It would be unwise to attribute too much importance to the potential reaction of nuptiality. For more on this, see Lee (1981: 369).

12 The results of these regressions are not always uniform and so I will only comment on their most salient aspects. The numerous disparities observed caution extreme care in the interpretation of the Madrid data.

13 This is especially true if one takes both lags 0 and 1 together. On average, the negative effect of mortality is more than three times greater than that of prices. On the other hand, over lags 2–4 there is a certain rebound in births with respect to deaths, as opposed to prices where there is none. The greater significance of mortality was also found in Rouen (Galloway, 1986a: 287–288).

of lags 0 and 1 is taken, this response is 2.1 times more negative among the rich. These differences contradict the findings in Rouen and seem to indicate that the wealthy sectors of society were more inclined than the poor to restrict their fertility, either directly or through nuptiality (Galloway, 1986a: 287).

This should not be construed to mean that the rich suffered more from moments of dearth than the poor, as was evidently not the case, but that they seemed more willing and able to adjust personal behavior in such situations. It should be remembered that times of dearth (often accompanied by the presence of epidemics) were times of generalized woe for the entire urban community, and this general atmosphere affected all social groups.[14] In these situations, even though the effect of direct physiological factors would probably be far greater among the poor, the behavioral response to dearth could certainly be utilized more amongst those groups most likely to regulate their behavior in the light of rational economic criteria.[15] Finally, temporary migration to towns, so important in times of dearth, was probably concentrated in the poorer areas of town and was yet another factor which would tend to stimulate births in poorer neighborhoods, thus mitigating some of the direct effects of the price increase on the native population.

The response of births to deaths was as expected. The rich were always less negatively affected by mortality than were the poor, and the rebound in births among them was clearly stronger. This is particularly evident if one takes the sum of lags 0+1 which was twice as negative among the poor; or that of lags 2–4 which among the rich showed a 4.1 per cent rebound, as opposed to the poor where births continued to be negatively related to deaths (−2.7 per cent). Clearly, the rich and the poor areas of town were caught in differing demographic realities. While mortality played a predominant role in fertility among the poor, economic realities held sway among the more well-to-do.

Finally it should be mentioned that R^2 and corrected R^2 suggest that a good part of the variance of the dependent variables is not explained either by prices or by mortality. This is not surprising and shows that

---

[14] While it is true that certain numerically insignificant segments of urban society controlled wheat stores and might therefore benefit from times of dearth, the specificity of their behavior would hardly be reflected in my data sets in which towns are divided into two large sectors by levels of wealth.

[15] In the previous chapter I found no real evidence of any fertility control among these groups, though in specific periods it could well have existed. In Rouen itself those were the first groups to use fertility control within marriage (Bardet, 1983: 276–286).

the universe of fertility determinants is more complex than allowed by the model.[16] It does not, however, invalidate my method, which does not pretend to delve into the vast structure of causality, but rather looks for systematic variations among indicators.

Nuptiality, prices and mortality

Much like the fertility model, the model for nuptiality attempts to show the systematic relation holding between nuptiality and prices and mortality. The equation used is as follows:

$$M_t = a + \sum_{k=0}^{4} b_k P_{t-k} + \sum_{k=0}^{4} c_k D_{t-k} + e_t$$

Where M = marriages, P = prices, D = non-infant deaths, a is a constant, b and c are coefficients, e is an error term and t is time. The empirical results can be found in Table 4.3 and Figures 4.3 and 4.4.

Prices should tend to depress marriages, at least at lag 0, because the timing of marriage was in part subject to certain economic constraints (Smith, 1981a; 1983). After lag 1 there should be a discernible rebound due to the celebration of marriages which had been put off for economic reasons. Mortality, on the other hand, should tend to depress marriages at lag 0 because of the death of potential spouses and, perhaps more important, to the traditional putting off of marriage in times of crisis. After the first lag, mortality should have a clear and significantly stimulating effect on marriages due not only to those marriages which had been postponed earlier, but to abundant remarriages. On the whole I postulate that mortality will prove to be an important stimulus for marriage.

In accord with my original postulates, in towns prices are generally negatively related to nuptiality at lag 0 and, to a lesser extent, at lag 1. Subsequent lags are characterized by a rebound in nuptiality and the result is that the lag sum is only modestly negative in most towns.[17] Deaths also confirm expectations: lag 0 is negative, and all subsequent lags are clearly positive, especially lag 1 which is strongest of all. On the whole, as occurred with fertility, mortality plays a greater role in

---

[16] The R^2 values compare favorably to those appearing in other studies using a similar methodology. See Galloway (1986a: 300–301; 1988: Appendix, Table 1), Lee (1981: 375).

[17] The results here are similar to those found for the town of Rouen by Galloway (1986a: 290–291) save that the influence of prices is far clearer in the Spanish data.

Table 4.3 *Regressions of nuptiality on grain prices and non-infant mortality*

Place	Dependent variable	Period	n	Constant	Grain prices				
					Lag 0	Lag 1	Lag 2	Lag 3	Lag 4
Madrid									
Rich	Marriages	1671–1740	80	.854 a	-.041 d	-.042	.029	-.019	.045 d
Poor	Marriages	1671–1740	80	.875 a	-.044 d	-.072 b	.109 a	-.033	.038
Total	Marriages	1671–1740	80	.868 a	-.043 d	-.054 c	.062 b	-.020	.043 d
Madrid									
Rich	Marriages	1759–1807	49	.890 a	.110 a	-.031	.077 c	.028	.000
Poor	Marriages	1759–1807	49	.907 a	.139 a	-.018	.091 b	.067 c	.078 b
Total	Marriages	1759–1807	49	.955 a	.129 a	-.033	.085 a	.051 d	.039
Granada									
Rich	Marriages	1712–1785	84	.746 a	-.292 a	.040	-.027	.030	.049
Poor	Marriages	1712–1785	84	.785 a	-.240 b	.094	.068	.011	.027
Total	Marriages	1712–1785	84	.747 a	-.291 a	.049	-.028	.021	.037
Talavera									
Rich	Marriages	1711–1785	75	1.023 a	-.040	-.217 c	.115	.124	-.042
Poor	Marriages	1711–1785	75	.621 b	-.021	-.077	.009	.305 a	-.074
Total	Marriages	1711–1785	75	.845 a	-.058	-.143 c	.057	.198 b	-.045
Cuenca									
Rich	Marriages	1673–1777	105	.640 a	-.182 c	.003	.113	-.004	-.072
Poor	Marriages	1673–1777	105	.863 a	.042	-.146	.041	.053	.083
Total	Marriages	1673–1777	105	.733 a	-.073	-.084	.059	.022	-.011
New Castile									
1	Marriages	1583–1683	101	.988 a	.020	-.091 c	.061	-.009	.064
2	Marriages	1650–1750	101	.969 a	-.024	-.169 a	.027	-.030	.028
3	Marriages	1730–1830	101	.917 a	-.125 b	-.158 a	-.029	.041	.059
Total	Marriages	1583–1830	248	.969 a	-.056 c	-.138 a	.031	.025	.053 c
Granada									
Remarriages (total)		1712–1795	84	·334 b	-.336 a	-.024	.028	.077	.046
Talavera									
Remarriages (m)		1711–1785	75	.032	-.004	.021	.108	.346 a	-.020
Remarriages (f)		1711–1785	75	.407	-.117	-.169 d	.077	.333 b	.058

Place	Non-infant mortality					R²	Corrected R²	Grain prices lag sum	Non-infant mortality lag sum
	Lag 0	Lag 1	Lag 2	Lag 3	Lag 4				
Madrid									
Rich	−.097	.159 b	.143 c	−.020	−.011	.49	.40	−.027	.174
Poor	−.037	.053	.139 b	−.086	.057	.42	.32	−.001	.126
Total	−.060	.115 d	.136 b	−.057	.010	.49	.40	−.012	.144
Madrid									
Rich	−.031	−.076	.029	.069	−.056	.35	.14	.183 c	−.065
Poor	−.127 c	−.039	−.105 d	.023	−.013	.56	.41	.357 a	−.261 d
Total	−.093	−.050	−.054	.028	−.051	.46	.29	.271 a	−.220
Granada									
Rich	.034	.282 a	.099 d	.041	−.003	.68	.63	−.200 d	.453 a
Poor	.068	.094	.039	−.037	.096	.27	.15	−.040	.260
Total	.035	.259 a	.092 d	.040	.039	.65	.59	−.212 d	.465 a
Talavera									
Rich	−.133	.041	.028	.218 c	−.113	.22	.07	−.060	.042
Poor	−.028	.116	.057	.040	.057	.35	.22	.142	.242
Total	−.091	.088	.070	.103	−.020	.36	.24	.009	.150
Cuenca									
Rich	−.044	.250 a	.043	.216 a	.039	.22	.11	−.141	.504 a
Poor	.004	.181 b	−.006	−.058	−.061	.15	.03	.073	.060
Total	−.031	.239 a	.049	.108 c	−.011	.24	.14	−.087	.354 b
New Castile									
1	.038	−.099 c	.015	.101 c	−.088 c	.48	.41	.045	−.033
2	−.071 d	.071 d	.080 c	.105 b	.013	.35	.27	−.168 c	.198 d
3	−.022	.187 b	.231 a	.011	−.115 d	.53	.47	−.212 d	.292
Total	−.021	.054 d	.077 b	.053 d	−.048 d	.53	.50	−.085	.115
Granada Remarriages (Total)	.162 b	.550 a	.168 c	.058	−.039	.79	.76	−.236 d	.899 a
Talavera									
Remarriages (m)	.091	.157 d	.224 c	.145	−.084	.43	.32	.451 c	.533 c
Remarriages (f)	−.019	.331 a	.084	.198 d	−.168 d	.37	.25	.182	.426 d

Notes See Table 4.2.

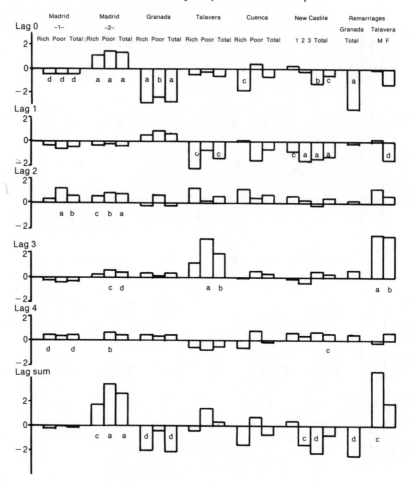

Figure 4.3 Response of marriages to fluctuations in grain prices, controlling non-infant mortality

nuptiality than prices. These results are very closely replicated by those based on rural data from New Castile and in other regions of Spain (Pérez Moreda, 1988c: 98).

If the data are organized according to social groups, the results are quite interesting and confirm some of my hypotheses. Whereas the effect of prices on marriages at lags 0 and 1 shows little difference between the rich and the poor neighborhoods, the lag sum generally shows that prices had a far less negative effect on the marriage patterns of the poor than on those of the rich. Though the overall relation between prices and nuptiality might vary by town, it is clear

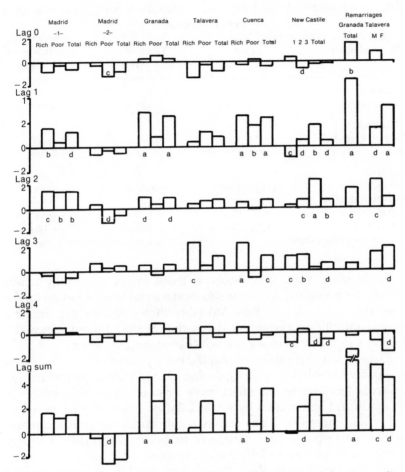

Figure 4.4 Response of marriages to fluctuations in non-infant mortality, controlling grain prices

that nuptiality was far less hurt (or more stimulated) by high prices among the poor. If one divides the lag structure into two parts (0–1, 2–4), on average the negative reaction among the rich is over double that of the poor during the first part, and the positive rebound over lags 2–4 is 2.2 times greater among the poor than among the rich. In other words, the rich felt the negative effect of the first years more, and the positive rebound of subsequent lags less than the poor. These results suggest that nuptiality among the rich was more sensitive to short-run economic stress and less flexible thereafter than among the

Table 4.4   *Means of raw series and coefficients of variation of additional detrended series*

Place/category	Period	Mean of raw series	Coefficient of variation
Granada			
Remarriages	1712–1795	125.8	0.165
Talavera			
Remarriages (m)	1711–1795	13.9	0.296
Remarriages (f)	1711–1785	14.0	0.205
Madrid			
Hospitalized	1757–1802	20,982.4	0.134
Hospital deaths	1757–1802	2,427.3	0.143
Total deaths	1757–1802	4,238.4	0.116
Foundlings	1757–1802	448.2	0.081

poor. In many ways they duplicate those found for fertility where clearly the prevailing economic situation was far less important for the poor than it was for the rich. Mortality shows no clear lag structure when controlling for economic status, though the rebound (lags 2–4) is far more significant among the rich than among the poor.

Earlier it was hypothesized that the basic pattern of the response of nuptiality to mortality was largely due to the incidence of remarriage. In order to estimate this effect more precisely, total remarriages in Granada and remarriages by sex in Talavera have been regressed on prices and mortality.[18] The results amply confirm our expectations. While the response of remarriages to prices is difficult to assess, deaths have proven to be a major stimulus for remarriage. Understandably, lags 1 and 2 show the greatest reaction, as couples whose households had been severed by periods of high mortality, hurried to remarry. The reaction of remarriages to fluctuations in deaths is evidently far stronger and more immediate than that of first marriages. It is also much more apparent in Granada, and this might well reflect a greater flexibility in remarriage in a part of Spain already characterized by more intense nuptiality. By sex, the data suggest that both prices and deaths were more inclined to stimulate and accelerate remarriage

---

[18] The Granada data refer to the total number of widows or widowers remarried and are taken from Sanz Sampelayo (1980: 626–631). For Talavera de la Reina they are distinguished by sex and, once again, refer to the total number of widowed persons remarrying (González Muñoz, 1975: Data appendix). For means of raw series and coefficients of variation of detrended ones, see Table 4.4.

among men than among women.[19] These results confirm many of the conclusions derived from historical studies in other areas of Europe which emphasize a greater flexibility of male remarriage, due to biological, economic and social reasons.[20] More generally they underscore, once again, the key role played by nuptiality in the mitigation of the effects of periods of high mortality in pre-industrial Europe (Dupâquier, 1979a; Livi Bacci, 1978: 76–77; R. Smith, 1981b: 109–110).[21]

Mortality and prices

Mortality has been made dependent on price levels. The following equation has been used:

$$D_t = a + \sum_{k=0}^{4} b_k P_{t-k} + e_t$$

Where D = non-infant deaths, a is a constant, b is a coefficient, e is an error term and t is time. The results can be found in Table 4.5 and Figure 4.5.

Mortality fluctuations can be hypothesized to be positively and significantly related to prices. This is not to say, however, that people died of outright starvation. While this might occasionally happen, as we shall see in the next chapter, it was clearly an exception.[22] Prices increased mortality for other reasons. Firstly, moments of dearth also tended to be moments of epidemic disease. The causality here is not clear or unilateral because epidemics themselves often seemed to stimulate dearth. The fact that both phenomena often coincided accounts for a good deal of the positive postulated relation between

---

[19] Male remarriages receive no negative impact whatsoever from high prices as opposed to females who certainly do at lags 0 and 1. After this, there is hardly any difference by sex. Economic fluctuations played no role in men's decision to remarry, whereas for women it could be a powerful initial impediment (−.286 for females as opposed to +.017 for males).

[20] Greater incidence of male remarriage and a shorter duration of widowhood among males has been emphasized by several authors. A number of case studies are included in Dupâquier et al. (1981). See, for example, Livi Bacci (1981: 351); Marcílio (1981: 369); Corsini (1981); Cabourdin (1981: 280–282).

[21] Both the intensity and pattern of these responses are quite similar to those found by Galloway for Sweden (1987: Figure 4.2). The only difference is that in Sweden the overall response of nuptiality to mortality is greater among females, whereas the opposite is true for Talavera.

[22] Peter Laslett (1983: 122–152) posed the question: "Did the peasants really starve?" and reached a similar conclusion to ours.

Table 4.5   Regressions of non-infant mortality and other related variables on grain prices

Place	Dependent variable	Period	n	Constant	Grain prices					R²	Corrected R²	Grain prices lag sum
					Lag 0	Lag 1	Lag 2	Lag 3	Lag 4			
Madrid												
Rich	Non-infant deaths	1661–1740	80	.850 a	.112 a	.100 b	.006	−.081 c	.011	.55	.51	.148 d
Poor	Non-infant deaths	1661–1740	80	.892 a	.058	.149 a	−.028	−.050	−.024	.45	.39	.106
Total	Non-infant deaths	1661–1740	80	.867 a	.089 b	.122 a	−.008	−.068 d	−.004	.52	.47	.131 d
Madrid												
Rich	Non-infant deaths	1759–1807	49	.869 a	.153 a	.043	.026	−.035	−.064	.53	.45	.131
Poor	Non-infant deaths	1759–1807	49	.809 a	.208 a	.073	.034	−.004	−.127 d	.66	.60	.191 c
Total	Non-infant deaths	1759–1807	49	.839 a	.181 a	.058	.029	−.022	−.094 d	.60	.53	.161 d
Granada												
Rich	Non-infant deaths	1712–1795	84	.915 a	.443 a	−.056	−.118 d	−.116 d	−.076	.43	.38	.085
Poor	Non-infant deaths	1712–1795	84	.880 a	.424 a	.035	−.165 d	−.165 d	−.020	.30	.24	.120
Total	Non-infant deaths	1712–1795	84	.905 a	.446 a	−.046	−.124 d	−.120 d	−.067	.42	.37	.095
Talavera												
Rich	Non-infant deaths	1711–1785	75	1.040 a	.080	.132	.037	−.177 d	−.110	.12	.03	−.038
Poor	Non-infant deaths	1711–1785	75	.681 a	.195 d	.140	.123	−.105	−.034	.10	.01	.319 d
Total	Non-infant deaths	1711–1785	75	.906 a	.138	.117	.063	−.154	−.074	.20	.11	.088
Cuenca												
Rich	Non-infant deaths	1673–1777	105	.848 a	.197	.053	−.071	.073	−.106	.14	.07	.152
Poor	Non-infant deaths	1673–1777	105	.650 b	.406 b	.112	−.371 b	.313 d	−.116	.13	.06	.350
Total	Non-infant deaths	1673–1777	105	.787 a	.279 c	.078	−.190	.162	−.120	.14	.08	.213
New Castile												
1	Non-infant deaths	1585–1683	101	.976 a	.194 c	.130	.047	−.162 d	−.184 c	.46	.42	.025
2	Non-infant deaths	1650–1750	101	1.148 a	.127	−.052	−.033	−.113	−.082	.13	.07	−.148
3	Non-infant deaths	1730–1830	101	.750	.159 b	.188 b	.013	−.042	−.071	.49	.45	.250 b
Total	Non-infant deaths	1585–1830	248	.947 a	.162 a	.121 b	−.020	−.093 c	−.117 b	.45	.44	.053
Madrid												
Admitted to hospitals		1759–1802	44	.610 b	.109	.151 d	.172 c	−.036	−.007	.62	.55	.390 c
Hospital deaths		1759–1802	44	.568 b	.153 c	.164 c	.201 b	−.002	−.084	.57	.49	.432 c
Total deaths (including hospital deaths)		1759–1802	44	.679 a	.154 b	.113 d	.148 b	−.003	−.089 d	.83	.79	.321 c
Foundlings		1759–1802	44	.795 a	.056	.045	−.009	.072	.038	.58	.50	.205 c

Notes: See Table 4.3

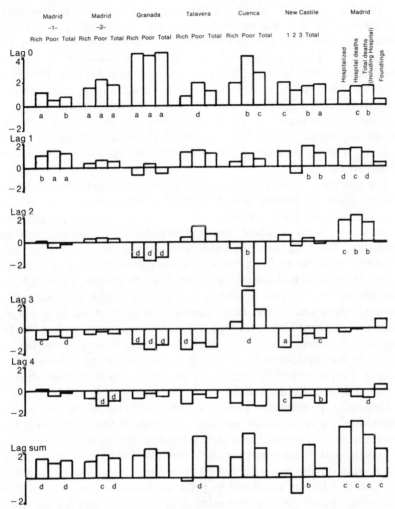

Figure 4.5 Response of non-infant deaths and other variables to fluctuations in grain prices

the two. Nutritional status also worked at another level because undernourishment tended to decrease the ability of people's immune system to resist disease, though this was only the case in periods of extreme dearth.

Due to the nature of both epidemics and price levels, the positive relation between prices and mortality should be strongest at lag o and, to a lesser extent, at lag 1. Thereafter, some sort of rebound should be evident because many of the weaker or more infirm people in society would have died in the original onslaught. The predicted result by economic standing leaves little doubt. Insofar as there was a general coincidence of high prices and mortality, the relationship should be positive everywhere. Since, however, the nutritional status of the rich districts would not have suffered nearly so much as that of the poorer neighborhoods, high positive correlations should certainly be class-specific. Finally higher levels of population density in towns, themselves a powerful factor for the spread of disease, should make a positive relation between prices and mortality generally stronger in urban areas.

The empirical results confirm most of these theoretical postulates, though there are certain aspects of the lag structure in Spain which warrant consideration. At lag 0 the response is strongly positive everywhere, lag 1 is mixed and lags 2–4 show a strong decrease in mortality. The end result in most areas is a lag sum which is only modestly positive and is generally weaker than that found in other European regions (Galloway, 1985: 293; 1988: Appendix, Table 1).[23] As postulated, the response among the poor is always considerably stronger than among the rich. Among the poor, it is, on average, nearly 50 per cent higher for lags 0–1 and it is 2.4 times higher for the lag sum. This clear difference, which has appeared in other studies, is not only the product of lower living standards among the poor, but also of the presence of migrants in the poorer areas of town during times of dearth (Reher, 1989).

Generally, patterns are similar in both rural and urban areas, with prices tending to stimulate mortality, though in the countryside the overall effect of prices on mortality is weaker than in urban areas, due at least in part to lower population densities.[24] In fact, in New Castile the results for the period between 1650 and 1750 are surprising and suggest that factors unrelated to price fluctuations played an important role in determining mortality levels.[25] Only during the final

---

[23] Though the empirical results are evident, their explanation is a matter of speculation. Part of this pattern of response of mortality to prices could be attributed to varying quality in the registration of deaths, which might diminish in times of crisis. Should this be the case, it would tend to minimize the positive fluctuations during the first lags. However, at least in Cuenca, I have not found any indication of selective under-registration of deaths in times of crisis.

[24] Results from other regions of Spain suggest that this pattern does not always hold (Pérez Moreda, 1988c: 102).

[25] An examination of the residuals has shown 1684 to be the principal outlier for the period and probably responsible for a good part of the low levels of variance explained in the model. It is important to note that in 1684 there was a major epidemic in most of New Castile which was much more severe than price trends would have predicted. More generally, the possible effects of a colder climate cannot be ruled out

period, when the major diseases show far clearer links to nutritional status (typhus, malaria, etc.) and when the variation in price fluctuations increases sharply (Table 4.1), does the lag sum become clearly positive.

The presence of hospitals was an important characteristic of most pre-industrial towns. Generally, urban hospitals were filled with the poor and, more specifically, the migrant poor who often filled towns in times of crisis (Martz, 1983: 159–200). Hospital deaths, therefore, are a good proxy indicator for deaths among the poorest sectors of society, including in-migrants, and thus are probably far more closely linked to price fluctuations than deaths as a whole. In order to estimate the effect of prices among these sectors of society, we have utilized data corresponding to the hospitals of Madrid which is the only urban center included in this study to list hospital deaths. In addition to this the annual fluctuations of the numbers of people admitted to Madrid hospitals are also included and should help us estimate the effect of prices on prevailing levels of poverty and, to a lesser degree, on morbidity. Finally, the yearly fluctuations of those foundlings baptized in Madrid's Inclusa (foundling home) will be another proxy indicator for the relation between prices and poverty.[26]

The results confirm my expectations and reaffirm many of those postulated earlier. The effect of prices on deaths is sharply higher in hospitals than in any other urban group. While lower overall health levels and greater population density in hospitals contribute to the observed effect, the role of living standards should not be forgotten either. The same pattern holds true when regressing fluctuations in those hospitalized on prices. At lags 0, 1 and 2, the increases are normally significant, and these are followed by a very modest negative correlation at lags 3 and 4. In addition, the number of abandoned children from specifically urban households shows a significant overall positive relation to prices. This, in turn, tended to increase levels of child mortality in urban areas. Quite clearly, mortality among the poor was far more sensitive to price fluctuations than it was among other urban groups. If hospital deaths in Madrid are added to all other deaths, the lag sum for the entire town nearly doubles. This suggests

either (Galloway, 1985: 496–500; 1986b). Similar patterns emerge from English data for the same period (Lee, 1981: 376; Galloway, 1988; Appendix, Table 1).

[26] All data are taken from Carbajo Isla (1987: 273–279, 327–329). The data on foundlings generally refer to those born in Madrid who were baptized in the *Inclusa*, rather than to those babies who were known to come from outside town (Carbajo Isla, 1987: 52–58, 370).

The first of the indicators chosen (hospital deaths) is certainly subject to problems of heterogeneity, the other two, much less so.

that part of the weaker relation between mortality and prices that had been observed earlier was due to the absence of hospital deaths from the available totals.

Conclusions

Certain insights into the mechanisms linking demographic behavior and economic realities in pre-industrial society have become clear in the course of this analysis. Prices have proven to have a net depressing effect on fertility and on nuptiality, at least in the very short run. In both cases, vital rates have tended to rebound toward the end of the five year model and thus the net effect of prices has been somewhat weakened. Mortality has also played a key role in depressing fertility, especially at lag 0 and, to a lesser extent, lag 1, and has been an important stimulant of nuptiality, especially after its initial negative impact at lag 0. On average, mortality fluctuations have seemed to exert a greater influence of fertility and nuptiality, than have prices.

Clear differences have also appeared when controlling the data for neighborhood wealth. By and large, in the poorer districts of the towns we have studied, fertility and nuptiality have proven to be less sensitive to price fluctuations than the richer ones. It has been argued that this reaction should not be interpreted to mean that the rich suffered the effects of economic fluctuations more than the poor, which they clearly did not, but rather that more well-to-do social groups were more willing and able than the poor to adjust their vital behavior in response to economic fluctuations. In the case of fertility, this reaction would seem to take place, at least partially, through more or less flexible marriage and remarriage behavior. Mortality has had a far greater effect on fertility among the poor, and has been a greater stimulant to marriage among the rich. Both of these results conform to expectations.

The consequences of high prices have been most clearly visible when analyzing mortality fluctuations. Periods of high prices tended to provoke strong increases in mortality at lags 0 and 1, which were partially neutralized by below average mortality after lag 2. All of these patterns confirm my theoretical postulates, though the lag sums were lower than those holding in some other areas of Europe. By social group, mortality among the poor was far more dependent on prices than it was among the rich. Periods of high prices were also related to a growth in the general levels of poverty and the numbers of abandoned children in society which, in turn, contributed to increases in morbidity and mortality.

Ultimately my data have shown the existence of an equilibrium-based demographic system in which price fluctuations have ended up having a net overall effect close to 0. As we have seen, prices have tended to depress fertility either directly, or through the intervening variables of nuptiality and mortality.[27] Conversely, high prices have also tended to stimulate fertility by means of the strong net effect which mortality has on nuptiality. Indeed, on average the strongest links in the entire model have been between prices and mortality (+), mortality and nuptiality (+) and, probably, nuptiality and fertility (+). In a very real sense, economic factors were at the very foundation of the short-run fluctuations of the pre-industrial demographic system in Spain. The variance not explained by prices either directly or indirectly within the model suggests that other exogenous factors (cultural, epidemiological, structural, etc.) also played an important role in determining reproduction.

[27] High prices lead to higher mortality and thus to lower fertility; and they lead to lower nuptiality and thus lower fertility. The effect of nuptiality on fertility has not been specified in my models, but it certainly exists.

5

Dearth, death and epidemics: towns in times of crisis

Introduction

Great crises periodically devastated the towns of early modern Spain. In relatively short periods of time, large proportions of a town's population might go hungry, or even die. The specter of dearth or epidemic mobilized urban populations and put institutions to their most serious test. A typical scenario involved a period of scarcity and rocketing grain prices, followed or accompanied by the appearance of epidemic disease with its corollary of rising death rates and declining fertility. Frantic efforts by municipal officials to ensure the supply of grain, to stave off epidemic disease and to curtail a spreading feeling of panic and isolation felt by the entire populace were, in many ways, the most characteristic hallmarks of these times. For a period of time the town was forced to combat the crisis more or less on its own. During times of subsistence crises, towns received little help from the outside; during times of epidemics they received none. Not all food shortage was followed by disease; nor did fevers always attack an ill-nourished populace. Yet the pattern of subsistence crisis/epidemic is recurrent, and certainly warrants further examination.[1]

The subject is complex and requires analysis at a number of levels. In the first part of the present chapter I will analyze the frequency, intensity, and consequences of crisis mortality with specific reference to the town of Cuenca. This will be followed by a more general non-quantitative discussion of the human and institutional behavior patterns which arise in moments such as this. Since these patterns

[1] Despite the theoretical possibility of epidemics without any sort of dearth, in fact instances of this pattern are rare in Spain during this period. A useful discussion of this issue can be found in Post (1976), Appleby (1977; 1978), and Walter and Schofield (1989).

were common to all pre-industrial towns in Spain, my analysis will cover all of urban Spain rather than a single town. In the final section of the chapter I will attempt to combine both types of analysis in our discussion of the crisis of 1804, clearly the single most important demographic crisis in the history of Cuenca. The chapter concludes by underscoring the stability over time of certain patterns which only during the nineteenth century were beginning to break down.

Cuenca was no exception to the rest of urban Spain and suffered from periodic bouts of crisis mortality. Before continuing our discussion it would be useful first to acquire a clear and precise idea of the frequency and importance of these periods of crisis. The measurement of crisis mortality has been attempted by numerous authors with only relative success. The basic problem has always proven to be the definition of exactly what intensity of mortality constitutes a crisis.[2] For the present study, my definition based on an average of 25 years around the crisis year will be used. Only years in which mortality at least doubled the average will be considered as years of true crisis. This will eliminate the random variations so characteristic of small populations like Cuenca's.

From this perspective, the quantitative aspects of crisis mortality are quite clear. During the 280 years over which I have been able to observe the fluctuations of mortality in Cuenca, there were 12 years of major mortality crises. In eight of them, mortality levels doubled, and in the other four, they more than trebled (Table 5.1). The incidence of crisis was greatest during the seventeenth century, and diminished sharply after 1735. While this tendency seems to parallel that observed in many parts of Europe, the gravity of the crisis of 1804 and the incidence of years in which mortality increased by more than 50 per cent (six between 1749 and 1809) suggest that Cuenca (and Spain) participated only incompletely in the more general European trends (Pérez Moreda, 1980: 370–374).

Most of these crisis years were marked by the classical rise in mortality accompanied by an almost simultaneous decline in conceptions and marriages.[3] The period of most intense mortality was often quite short (sometimes lasting only for a period of weeks) and, once passed, conceptions and marriages tended to rebound, thereby initiating a period of excess births and demographic recovery. These built-in

---

[2] There is never complete agreement on this subject. For different approaches, see, for example, Hollingsworth (1979: 21–28); Pérez Moreda (1980: 102–103); Dupâquier (1979b: 81–112); Del Panta and Livi Bacci (1977: 401–446); Wrigley and Schofield (1981: 331–342); Moll Blanes *et al.* (1983).

[3] Goubert termed these the "crises démographiques de type ancien" (1968: 68–82).

Table 5.1   *Years of crisis mortality in Cuenca*

Year	% of excess morality
1606	372.7
1804	351.6
1684	332.6
1647	307.9
1585	255.4
1710	250.7
1631	218.9
1706	218.4
1781	218.0
1735	205.1
1695	202.1
1599	201.3

Note Based on percentage of mortality above a 25 year average around the date of the crisis.

recovery mechanisms tended to mitigate the long-run demographic impact of most crises.[4]

Crises tended to be accompanied and often preceded by sharp increases in the price of foodstuffs. As we saw in the previous chapter, much of the behavior of both mortality and fertility so typical during times of crisis can be attributed to price fluctuations.[5] Yet it would be rash to extrapolate from this in order to suggest that price fluctuations (and dearth) were the single most important cause of crisis mortality. Price fluctuations only explain a small part of the variance observed over long periods of time.[6] There is also evidence to suggest that often in times of crisis, the crisis itself and the measures taken to mitigate its effects, were more the cause than the consequence of radical increases in the price of food.[7]

Whatever the originating cause, epidemic disease was the direct executor of mortality crisis.[8] Some of the diseases were more sensitive

[4] See, for example, Livi Bacci (1978: 66–69); Dupâquier (1979a: 381–391).
[5] Both the positive relation between prices and mortality, as well as the negative ones linking prices and mortality to births and marriages, especially at a o lag, have already been shown for many urban centers of Spain (chapter 4) as well as for many other areas of Europe.
[6] Walter and Schofield (1979) have summarized much of the current research on this matter.
[7] On this subject, see Dupâquier (1979a: 377–378); Wrigley and Schofield (1981: 313–332); Pérez Moreda (1980: 77–82, 373–374).
[8] Here I do not include temperature variation as an important factor since, apart from the impossibility of measuring it for the period under study, it probably played a far

to economic conditions than others.[9] Typhus, which was more closely linked to prices than others, proved to be the most important cause of crisis mortality in the town of Cuenca.[10] The crises of 1606, 1631, 1710, 1735 and 1804 can be safely attributed either exclusively or primarily to typhus.[11] Plague was the principal cause of crisis mortality in 1599, 1647, and possibly in 1684.[12] The bad years of 1775 and 1781 can be attributed to the presence of malaria, while that of 1855 was due to cholera.[13]

The social response to crisis in urban Spain

Most losses in population could be replenished within a relatively short period, either by the mechanisms of demographic recovery, which I have already mentioned or, perhaps more likely, by rapid in-migration from rural areas. In the short run, however, these crises probably constituted the single most trying moments for urban populations. When a crisis struck, or while it approached, all efforts were concentrated on avoiding it, neutralizing its impact or mitigating its consequences.

My discussion of these moments will center on the two principal distinguishing characteristics of all crises: the problem of the price and supply of food during times of shortage, and the reaction of all sectors of urban society to epidemics. A careful examination of both these situations will enable us to see the responses of the different groups

more important role for normal mortality levels than in moments of crisis. On this see, Galloway (1985), Lee (1981).

[9] Cholera, for example, was closely tied to nutrition. For typhus, the relation is somewhat more vague and for plague, typhoid, smallpox and malaria there does not appear to be any at all (Livi Bacci, 1987: 55).

[10] On this, see Galloway (1985: 498); Appleby (1973: 413); Post (1976: 36).

[11] We know this thanks to contemporary accounts from Cuenca and other areas of central Spain (Villalba, 1802: II, 17, 97; Muñoz y Soliva, 1860: 289; Pérez Moreda, 1980: 295–296, 298–300, 364–365). It can also be corroborated by the basic seasonal pattern of death during those years where peak mortality generally occurred between May and September, coinciding in part with the moments of highest grain prices. We have abundant information about prior harvest failures in every one of these years.

[12] See Bennassar (1969); Pérez Moreda (1980: 245–293, 301–303); Fortea Pérez (1980: 182); Nadal (1984: 35–43); Kamen (1964: 72–73). There is some doubt as to whether the mortality crisis of 1684 in central Castile was due to plague or to typhus (Pérez Moreda, 1980: 303–306). In Cuenca seasonality of death, which for all plague epidemics was concentrated during the second half of the year, suggests that plague was the cause.

[13] For Malaria in Castile, see Pérez Moreda (1980: 336–360; 1982). For Cuenca, see Muñoz y Soliva, 1860: 485. Cuenca's brisk climate and relative lack of swampy land (except for the area on the other side of the Huecar River) contributed to a relatively lower incidence of malaria than in other districts located in New Castile. For cholera in Cuenca, see Troitiño Vinuesa (1984: 247–249).

and institutions which made up the fabric of the pre-industrial urban community. It will become apparent that during periods of crisis, though frequently and momentarily overwhelmed, towns were not completely defenseless. In such situations a series of mechanisms for meeting the situation was activated. Some were effective, others were not. My analysis will stretch from the series of crises beginning the sixteenth century, to the other even more deadly one beginning the nineteenth century. The basic responses of towns to crisis during these three centuries will prove to be much the same. While some changes will take place, the old evils will be found to be just as evident in 1800 as they were in 1500.

Subsistence crises
In Spain, as in the rest of early modern Europe, bread, and more generally, cereals, constituted the staple of people's diets. Despite their importance, other food products were never the cause of the same sort of consistent worry as was the supply of wheat. In times of shortage, this supply had to be guaranteed at all costs. It is safe to say that this was one of the chief concerns of all local governments. Unfortunately for these governments, wheat was a product whose supply was subject to periodic and abrupt fluctuations. Harvests were irregular at the best of times, and often almost total failures. A year of sub-normal rainfall could create a shortage, and if this situation was repeated a second or a third year, the shortage turned into famine.

Scarcity was also exacerbated, or even created, by two other related factors, one of them specifically human, and the other structural. Producers were accused of hoarding their products so as to take advantage of the highest possible prices, or to boost already high ones. Furthermore, the lack of national or regional grain markets until well into the nineteenth century prevented areas not suffering from bad harvests, or those with ready access to imported cereals, from mitigating price and supply irregularities, so typical of the central part of the peninsula.[14] During times of scarcity, the central government would intervene to ensure grain supplies, though often legislation never got beyond the drawing board. Invariably it was left to local authorities to implement the central government's programs. Thus the heavy responsibility for providing the populace with food supplies lay principally with the municipalities.

In times of scarcity rural areas tended to fare slightly better than

[14] Disparities in price fluctuations are especially noticeable when comparing the interior and coastal towns (Anes Alvarez, 1969: 59–60; Domínguez Ortiz, 1976: 504; Palop Ramos, 1977: 29–30).

urban centers because they were producers of wheat. But in times of famine towns had an edge because those who controlled the greatest amount of wheat in society, such as the bishop or certain nobles, lived in towns and were the first to be called upon to help in times of crisis. The town also commanded much larger sums of money and could exercise power over neighboring villages, thus enabling it to survive truly severe crises more easily. This is why recurring features of early modern Spain are that towns tended to fill up with the hungry in times of dearth and there were invariably attempts to expel the non-resident poor during these times.[15]

The prevailing system of grain supply in Spain before the nineteenth century was cumbersome and by and large inefficient.[16] Normally small and medium-sized towns received their wheat from the surrounding municipalities. Local producers would bring grain to the town's market and in a normal year this would be sufficient to keep the town supplied. Wheat from more distant sources was avoided, except when absolutely necessary, because its transport increased the price considerably. In 1627 a ship-load of wheat in Alicante from Naples, doubled in price before it reached Madrid. Overland transportation costs could easily more than double the price of wheat over a distance of less than 300 kilometers (70 leagues) (Domínguez Ortiz, 1973b: 32–35). Another important obstacle to the immediate supply of wheat from distant sources was the time it took to get it there. In the sixteenth century it took wheat purchased in Estremadura seven months to reach Córdoba (Fortea Pérez, 1981: 209–210).

The location of the town conditioned the nature of its wheat supply. If it was located in a particularly productive region, such as Valladolid or Medina del Campo, or along the coast, wheat prices tended to be lower and more stable (Marcos Martín, 1978: 213–216). Towns in other regions, such as Guadalajara or Soria, had much greater difficulty in ensuring supplies. Furthermore, if a town's natural zone of wheat supply fell within the area of influence of a larger city, it normally had to look for its wheat elsewhere. This was the case of Cuenca and Toledo, for instance, with respect to Madrid. Finally, the social characteristics of the system of supply also depended on where a town was located. In the South the nobility controlled the supply of wheat, as opposed to parts of Castile and the North, where wheat was mainly supplied by local peasant farmers. Only Madrid had a full-blown

[15] Córdoba in 1506, Cuenca in 1766 and Santiago de Compostela in 1852 are but three examples of this. See Yun Casalilla (1980: 72); Jiménez Monteserín (1977); Rodríguez Galdo (1977: 333).
[16] The best work on this subject is by Concepción de Castro (1987). See also Ringrose (1983: 144–153).

system of long-distance supply (Castro, 1987: 267–278). In all cases, however, certain nobles, the local bishop and other ecclesiastical authorities who resided in the towns controlled large, albeit dispersed supplies of grain.

Most towns had a number of mechanisms designed to ensure the supply of wheat at reasonable prices. The market price was regulated, at least in theory, by a price ceiling called the *tasa* (Castro, 1987: 69–86). Introduced in 1502 as an exceptional measure, the *tasa* became common practice during the reign of Philip II. Even though the *tasa* was periodically altered, its purpose was to limit market fluctuations (Domínguez Ortiz, 1973b: 27). Municipal *pósitos* or storage granaries were also key elements in a system designed to control prices and guarantee supplies. Most of them were founded during the reign of Philip II, but their greatest importance was reached during the eighteenth century. At that time there were two principal types of *pósito*.[17] The rural ones, a kind of grain bank which would loan seed to farmers for the autumn planting in years of shortage, were normally controlled by ecclesiastical institutions. Urban *pósitos* were supposed to guarantee the supply of wheat in times of shortage, and were designed to influence market prices as well.

In moments of severe scarcity, the urban *pósito* was unable to fulfill this function satisfactorily due mainly to two structural aspects of the supply of wheat. Firstly, hoarding of grain was a common occurrence. Those who either produced or possessed it tended to keep it off the market until the *meses mayores* (March to June) when the prices were highest, demand least elastic, and families most willing to pay whatever necessary in order to ensure their personal supply of wheat. In contemporary documents, these hoarders were blamed over and over again as the instigators of dearth. Who were they? Here, once again, the location of the town was important. In Castile the hoarders were local farmers, while in Andalusia they were invariably nobles. In all areas, suspicion often fell on local authorities (*regidores*) or even on the Church. In other words, locally it was both those in power and the rather more modest local producers who were involved in hoarding.

A further structural constraint was the lack of any sort of fluid regional or inter-regional grain market. If this had not been the case, hoarding would have been prevented because poor harvests were normally local and rarely affected large geographical areas. A primitive transportation system hindered the establishment of great distri-

---

[17] For studies of *pósitos* see, for example, Anes Alvarez (1968), López Yepes (1971: 75–77), Ruiz Martín (1970: 169–173), Guillamón (1980: 5–7), Castro (1987: 95–108, 237–267).

bution networks for agricultural products. An immediate result of this was that, despite the Declaration of Free Trade for Cereals in 1765, there were few important grain merchants in central Spain before the end of the eighteenth century, and even then they were almost exclusively involved with the supply of grain to major cities like Madrid (Ringrose, 1970: 42, 135, 187–192; 1983: 151–152). Vested interests and lack of information at a local level often led, in times of shortage, to the uneconomic purchase of wheat from unnecessarily distant sources. An example of this could be 1766 when the Council of Castile accused the town of Cuenca of having purchased grain in Aragon when Aragon had purchased grain in Castile.[18]

The immediate consequence of these structural and human constraints was that the *tasa* was a dead letter whenever there was the slightest problem with supply. In moments of crisis only the clergy paid it any heed and even they did not always do so (Anes Alvarez, 1976: 26; Castro, 1987: 86–95). A generalized and persistent lack of confidence seems to exist with respect to any government effort to control prices. During the sixteenth and seventeenth centuries, there was a feeling that the *tasa* in reality provoked more hoarding and less supply, and its derogation was repeatedly requested. Ironically, during the eighteenth century after the Decree of Free Trade for Cereals (1766), moments of shortage (especially 1803–1804), brought with them requests for a return to the *tasa*.[19] Contradictory requests were the reaction to a problem as simple to explain as it was difficult to solve for towns in pre-industrial Spain. The nature of the product itself was fluctuating and those who speculated with it, the hoarders, were frequently tied to municipal government. The situation was complicated by the fact that the demand for bread was not at all flexible. It always had to be purchased, and in times of shortage the psychological need to have bread at home, even in excess of the most basic physical needs, placed the consumers completely in the hands of those in possession of wheat (Domínguez Ortiz, 1973b: 30–31). Unfortunately we are not in a position to estimate the extent to which the hoarders themselves, as their contemporaries believed, actually instigated crises, or merely took advantage of a situation caused by climatic variability and deficient transportation systems.

The period between 1765 and 1810 is an excellent example of the permanence of centuries-old problems and the unsuccessful attempts of enlightened reformers to solve them. For the ministers of Charles III

---

[18] Archivo Histórico Nacional, Consejos, legajo 17801, *Asonadas*.
[19] On this subject, see, for example, Yun Casalilla (1980: 72); Fortea Pérez (1981: 213–214); Anes Alvarez (1970: 405); Guillamón (1980: 7).

(1759–1788), the problem of radically fluctuating prices, hoarding and their corollary, subsistence crises, could be solved or at least mitigated in two ways. Firstly, the reformers felt that the storage of sufficient wheat in municipal *pósitos* would help offset speculation. Secondly, they believed that if all hindrances to the commercialization of cereals were removed, the effects of the market place would take over and shortages would be virtually eliminated (Guillamón, 1980: 139–145; Castro, 1987: 216–236). Unfortunately, neither of these two policies were to prove effective. In 1766 and then again in 1802–1804 the same problem reappeared, except that this time the hoarders were not acting illegally. Why did this happen? While free trade and storage of wheat were clearly forward-looking measures, there was no economic infrastructure to support them. Towns continued to be supplied essentially from local sources and, at a local level, fluctuating harvests and hoarding were a way of life. With no commercial network for agricultural products, it was impossible for grain from other regions to offset local speculation effectively. The proof of this is that, with the exception of Madrid, until well into the nineteenth century imported grain rarely if ever effectively mitigated periods of dearth in the interior.

Coming on the heels of the Declaration of Free Trade for Cereals, the dearth of 1766 and the events accompanying it proved the optimistic predictions of the reformers to be erroneous. This time, however, scarcity helped spark widespread unrest in several places and, though their cause was certainly more complex, the famous Esquilache riots in Madrid (Anes Alvarez, 1974: 219–224).[20] In the aftermath of the protests, the government, to its credit, never revoked the decree of free trade for cereals completely, though attempts were made to mollify its effects. *Pósitos* and the requisitioning of grain, which had existed since the sixteenth century, were utilized to help curb further hoarding. Neither of these had proven effective in the past, though prolonged years of good harvests after 1766 gave the impression that things had changed. They had not; the period of inflation and great crises marking the final decade of the eighteenth and the first few years of the nineteenth century confirm this beyond a doubt. Let us briefly examine these mechanisms.

The maintenance of free trade for cereals obliged a rather subtle change in the role ascribed to the *pósito* in the regulation of municipal

---

20 The standard interpretation of the riots of Esquilache is that they were essentially bread riots (Vilar, 1972: 199–249; Rodríguez, 1973a and b). This exclusively economic interpretation has been strongly questioned, at least with respect to Madrid by Teófanes Egido (1979: 125–154).

grain distribution.[21] Now that the price of wheat could no longer be directly controlled, at least in theory, by the municipal authorities, the *pósito* added a new function to its previous one of storing wheat, that of subtle price fixing. It sold grain to a series of contracted bakers who, in turn, were obliged to sell bread to the public in certain locations at a price stipulated by the town council. The free trade of grain continued, though there were semi-official bakeries which helped to maintain prices.[22] At least in principle, the *pósito* could exercise a slight though not unimportant influence on the price of grain in the town.

The *pósitos* were never able to fulfill this role adequately, primarily because of lack of adequate funding, along with the physical impossibility of storing enough grain for sufficiently long periods of time to offset local speculation. As grain began to disappear from town, the town council began to worry about keeping the *pósito* stocked. Spurred on by fears of a possible repetition of the riots of 1766, the *pósito* purchased wheat wherever it could, often from distant sources. Municipal records are filled with these efforts which became increasingly frantic as the local price of wheat rose. Ultimately the towns were obliged to purchase grain at high prices because they literally could not afford not to do so. Petitions would also be sent to nobles, certain city councilmen, and to the Church requesting, or rather imploring, them to sell wheat to the *pósito* at fair prices. The funds of the *pósito* would soon be exhausted and repeated authorizations to dip into other sources of municipal income in order to purchase grain would ensue. There was always resistance to this sort of measure because invariably the money was not returned, with ruinous results for municipal finances. If, however, dearth was sufficiently serious, all obstacles to the purchase of wheat were rapidly overcome.

The grain bought by the town at high prices to meet short–term needs invariably ended up being sold at equally high prices (Guillamón, 1980: 169–172). Whenever the price of municipal grain reached a certain level, or when the up-coming harvest seemed promising, grain reappeared on the market. This immediately caused a decline in the prices and the *pósito* would be abandoned by its own bakers who could find less expensive grain elsewhere. Generally there was considerable resistance in the town council to lowering prices. Eventually, however, complaints that the grain was rotting in the *pósito* could force

21 Much of what follows is taken basically from the municipal deliberations of the town council of Cuenca. There is, however, little to suggest that behavior in Cuenca did not reflect more general patterns throughout most of the central part of Spain.

22 There was no obligation on these bakers to buy the *pósito*'s grain if its prices were not competitive. This system is not dissimilar to that existing in major cities like Madrid (Castro 1987: 185–216).

the town to lower the price of its own grain. The result was normally serious damage to municipal finances.

Thus the *pósito* did not adequately fulfill either of its roles. It was unable to store enough wheat to supply the town for more than a very short period of time and it had little if any effect on the price of bread. When there was abundant and cheap grain, there was no need for it, and when dearth set in, there was a run on its supply. The *pósitos* always seemed about to run out of grain. Since the need to keep the town supplied was perceived to be crucial, wheat was ultimately purchased regardless of source or price. This, in turn, forced the *pósito* to raise the price of bread. When the price had risen sufficiently, additional wheat appeared on the market, prices dropped and the town ended up attempting to maintain the price of bread artificially high. Eventually it gave in, sold grain at a loss and seriously compromised its own budget. What was happening was that the *pósito* had far less flexibility than the market itself to adapt to new situations of price and supply. Though pretending to do the contrary, it was really controlled by the market and was constantly at a disadvantage.

In times of acute crisis, towns made use of other exceptional measures which often entailed an increase in the coercive powers of local governments. Making the sale of grain to non-residents illegal or even expelling them were frequent though not normally very effective measures. Imploring local notables and Church authorities to sell grain to the town at reasonable prices was a recurring phenomenon in periods of dearth. Other more drastic measures were also possible. For example, in 1766 the authorities of a town in La Mancha illegally detained two wagon-loads of wheat destined for Madrid. In Bilbao and other towns, no pack teams were allowed to enter town if they did not bear foodstuffs for the populace.[23] The strongest internal measure that municipal authorities could take in times of dearth was the requisitioning of grain. As early as the sixteenth century, royal *cédulas* exist which oblige individuals and even the Church to sell "excess" grain at reasonable prices to the town.[24] This measure was put into effect in Cuenca in 1803–1804. A house to house search under the direction of the corregidor and other local authorities was initiated, but to no avail. People only admitted to having just enough grain for their personal consumption and, since ultimately the inspectors and the

---

[23] Archivo Histórico Nacional, legajo 6774, expediente no. 7. See also Anes Alvarez (1974: 223); Domínguez Ortiz (1973b: 26).
[24] An example of this is the Royal Decree of 1790 which obliged people possessing grain exceeding the amount absolutely necessary for the maintenance of their homes and families and for the autumn planting, to sell it at a "reasonable" price (Anes Alvarez, 1970: 402–407).

inspected belonged to the same social groups, the search rendered no positive results.

The Crown also intervened in order to guarantee the supply of grain to towns. The most frequent measure used was authorizing the import of foreign grain. Once again, though, these initiatives were fraught with obstacles and were seldom if ever effective for smaller urban centers far removed from the coast. The grain tended to arrive in very poor condition, several months after it had been ordered. The ports of distribution often hindered its distribution.[25] In addition to the political and administrative impediments to the effective distribution of grain, authorization of imports was normally given so late that by the time the grain arrived it was often no longer needed.[26] With the exception of Madrid, throughout our period grain imports never seemed to reach the interior in any effective manner, and when prices did go down, it was normally because of good harvests.

In conclusion, these periods of scarcity in urban areas do seem to share certain common characteristics. A latent fear seemed to underlie all governmental action: a fear of running out of wheat and a fear of possible political and social tensions. This turned the question of the supply of bread into the most important municipal issue and often led to ill-timed measures with extremely negative consequences for municipal finances. Moments of scarcity were also accompanied by a generalized increase in social tensions. These not only affected the relations between the hungry populace and the municipal officials, a tension which rarely overflowed into violent action, but also those within the local elites of the town, between the town and its surrounding countryside, between the town and the larger cities, between the town and central government. The concrete measures taken tended to be few and ineffective. This was partly due to poor public administration and partly to lack of preventive action. Despite its shortcomings, the reform of 1765 was a step forward. Unfortunately, simple remedies were impossible since immediate problems were the product of a key structural weakness: as long as the agricultural economy was essen-

---

[25] This was the case of Seville in 1507 which impeded further circulation of the imported grain to the rest of Andalusia because, if not, prices would plummet and certain wealthy citizens and the town itself would lose money. A rather absurd situation existed in which there was abundant grain in the port of Seville, but there were people in Seville and especially upriver in Córdoba dying of starvation (Yun Casalilla, 1980: 140–144).

[26] This happened during the crisis of 1803–1804. The import of grain was authorized in September of 1803 but by the time the grain arrived to port towns in late spring and early summer of 1804, the Council of Castile discovered that most villages no longer needed it (AHN, Consejos, legajos 49,195, 11,506 and 11,500). See Anes Alvarez (1970: 413–423); Peset and Carvalho (1972: 245).

tially one of subsistence farming and the transportation networks were deficient, recurring harvest failures and market manipulation were inevitable facts of life.

Epidemics

Subsistence crises, terrible as they might be, were often accompanied by the much more frightening threat of epidemic disease. It is important to insist on the tandem dearth–disease because, while there were moments of shortage not accompanied by epidemics, one seldom finds instances of epidemics not escorted by periods of inflation and dearth (Post, 1976; 1977; 1985). Throughout the period we are studying, the diseases changed. Whereas plague was the chief killer during much of the sixteenth and seventeenth centuries, malaria, smallpox, typhus, yellow fever, and finally cholera replaced it during later centuries.[27] Though these diseases may have been epidemic or endemic in origin and could provoke quite divergent die-offs in the populations affected, the dynamic they followed was largely the same. The arrival of the disease in town was normally sudden, terrible and total; at times the great mortality took place in a question of a few days or weeks. During this more or less brief period, the town was totally isolated and frequently administrative chaos ensued. In this section we will examine the manner in which urban institutions attempted to confront epidemics.

While the disease was far away, there was considerable interest on the part of the Crown and the local authorities to keep well-informed.[28] Once closer to the town, however, there was widespread resistance to recognizing the existence of the epidemic. There was a fear of calling the plague by its name, and the word was reserved for times past or for other towns. At home it tended to be called the "illness" or some other similar euphemism (Bennassar, 1969: 23). While most prevalent during the sixteenth and seventeenth centuries, it is not unusual to find examples of this type of reaction in the nineteenth century.[29] Vacillation born of fear hindered but did not necessarily prevent the adoption of effective measures. Indecision and

---

[27] For more on the evolution of epidemic disease in Spain, see Pérez Moreda (1980: 69–85); Peset and Peset (1972). For a broader perspective, see McNeill (1976: chs. 4–6); Walter and Schofield (1989); Flinn (1974).

[28] There are abundant examples of this for different towns or regions between the sixteenth and eighteenth centuries. See, for example, Riera and Jiménez Muñoz (1977: 283–295); Peset, Mancebo and Peset (1971); Vincent, (1976: 23; 1969: 1511).

[29] In order to "avoid alarm," news of the first yellow fever deaths were hushed up in Barcelona (Danón, 1977: 120). As late as 1865 during the cholera epidemic in Madrid, we find similar tactics being utilized by local officials (Fernández García, 1979: 156, 176, 184).

dispute often marked the medical diagnosis of the disease, its causes and any preventive, medical and sanitary measures to be taken. These disputes tended to affect the relations among doctors, between doctors and the authorities, between doctors and the townspeople or between the authorities and the populace, and proved to be further obstacles to decisive action (Peset *et al.*, 1977a: 218–221).[30]

The struggle against the epidemic tended to be concentrated in certain general areas. Effective isolation of the town from the outside world was one of the chief concerns of the authorities. Towns were closed, especially to travelers coming from areas known or suspected to be infected by the disease. In order to ensure the effectiveness of this isolation, the gates of the town were guarded by officials and citizens whose help was often forcibly demanded.[31] Those coming from infected areas were quarantined outside the city limits and all travelers were obliged to prove that they had not been exposed to infection. This was normally done by means of a type of passport or certificate of health which was signed by each town a traveler passed through.[32] Non-resident poor and vagabonds were always expelled if they were believed to be a source of pestilence or of its spread. Efforts were also made to place all possible foci of disease such as hospitals or jails outside the walls of town. Well-organized and harsh as some of these measures might have been, they were seldom successful because keeping a town completely isolated from the outside world was a practical impossibility. Such measures severely handicapped economic activity, spelled immediate dearth and met with subtle resistance on the part of the citizenry, no matter how many lashes the violators might be given or how "reasonable" isolation might have seemed.

From the very beginning diverse commissions were established both at a local and a national level. The local ones were composed of representatives of different sectors of municipal life and were nor-

[30] Among the multiple examples of these sorts of disputes we can cite the resistance of the authorities in eighteenth-century Valencia to its implementation of measures limiting the cultivation of rice, which was known to be important for the spread of malaria (Peset and Peset, 1972: 47–49); the disturbances in 1676 in Cartagena protesting about the declaration of the state of plague (Casal Martínez, 1951: 77); or, finally, the controversy between the corregidor and the doctors of the town of Cuenca in 1804 as to whether the fevers in town were or were not infectious.

[31] Burgos in 1493, Córdoba in 1507, Cáceres at the beginning of the seventeenth century, Talavera in 1597, Valencia in 1647 and Cuenca in 1804 are all examples of this. See Jiménez Muñoz (1974: document 5); Fortea Pérez (1981); Rodríguez Sánchez (1977: 74); González Muñoz (1974: 155); Peset *et al.* (1977b: 244); and Archivo Municipal de Cuenca, Municipal deliberations for 1804.

[32] In Córdoba in 1600, all poor were required to wear slates around their necks where the names of all places they had visited were to be written (Fortea Pérez, 1981: 202).

mally headed by the royal corregidor and coordinated by doctors.[33] Acting as more than simple consultants, they normally had the authority to coordinate the battle against the illness. This included financing the defense, a major headache for early modern urban societies, and organizing the municipal food supply which was directly affected by the epidemic. To help centralize the battle against epidemic disease, Bourbon reformism created the Junta Suprema de Sanidad which was to be the major coordinator of national public health, with authority over local juntas. Apart from its capacity to isolate entire regions, as occurred in the Levant in 1720 and in Andalusia at the beginning of the nineteenth century, it was normally plagued by an excess of bureaucracy and a shortage of doctors (Peset and Peset, 1972: 44–45). As late as the early nineteenth century, the battle against epidemic disease continued to be mostly a local one.

The concrete measures taken were similar to those utilized elsewhere in Europe at the time and can be classified into two general categories: social-hygienic and therapeutic measures. Apart from the expulsion of indigent non-citizens and the restriction of entry for all those coming from infected areas, social measures covered several fronts. There were significant attempts to ensure the food supply of the poor, since malnutrition was always considered to be a principal cause of disease. Severe restrictions were also placed on public gatherings: fairs, bull fights and fiestas were normally cancelled as, at times, were certain manifestations of religious fervor. In 1803 and 1804, the churches of Málaga were closed on the advice of Dr. Arejula and with the approval of the head of the Junta de Sanidad and the bishop.[34] In 1649 in Córdoba, good sleeping habits and moderation in sexual activity were even advised.

Early modern towns were not noted for their cleanliness, and in times of epidemic disease concerted efforts were made to improve public hygiene. From the end of the fifteenth to the middle of the nineteenth centuries certain measures were consistently employed. Citizens were made responsible for the cleaning and washing down of

---

[33] The Junta del Morbo, established in Castellón in 1647, was composed of two nobles, two citizens, two artisans and two farmers (Granjel, 1977: 21). The same year in Valencia, the Junta de Sanidad was composed of the viceroy, the archbishop, two judges, the archdeacon, a Dominican, a knight and a canon (Peset *et al.*, 1977b: 246). In Osuna in 1600, doctors, pharmacists, priests and sacristans were on the local junta (Vincent, 1976: 22). These local juntas continued to organize the battle against disease in the nineteenth century where, in the case of Cuenca, all effective actions by the national Junta de Sanidad or the Junta de Socorro were taken at a local level.

[34] Carrillo and García Ballester (1977: 80–95). Many centuries earlier, similar measures were taken in Orvieto during the Black Death (Carpentier, 1962: 131–133).

the streets in front of their houses; the clothes and belongings of the dead were burned and their houses re-plastered; dumps were removed from the town, and the quality of food sold in the market was controlled and certain types might be prohibited, though little consistency can be found in the foods chosen. In 1599, under the threat of fines and jail, Málaga prohibited the sale of cod, lima beans, cottage cheese, snails and milk. The sale of vegetables was forbidden in Valencia in 1647–1648. Medina del Campo took hens and fresh fish off the market in 1599. Jails were traditionally considered to be agents in the spread of disease and were cleaned or even moved outside the city limits. The purification of the air by means of bonfires of aromatic wood was also a recurring phenomenon throughout early modern Spain.[35]

The burial of the dead was a cause of worry for the municipal authorities. Multiple edicts exist which regulate the hiring of pall-bearers, the depth of graves, the time elapsed between death and burial, and the separation of the diseased dead from the other deceased. When the situation was particularly serious, burials in churches were prohibited and all graves had to be covered with quicklime. Sometimes cemeteries would be walled in and slaves and prisoners called on to act as grave diggers. There were also attempts to bury the dead outside the limits of the towns. This, however, did not become a widespread practice until the 1830s (Goldman, 1979). All of these measures had one aspect in common: they were applied during epidemics, but never before or after. The inability of the authorities to take truly preventive action is a testimony to the fact that public health was perceived as important by municipal officials only when faced with the immediate presence of epidemic disease. It is also a major reason why defense against disease was never truly effective until comparatively recently.

If social and hygienic measures met with limited success in the battle against epidemic disease, medical ones met with almost none. Throughout the period under study, the only qualitative improvement in the treatment of the ill came from an increase in the use of quinine during the eighteenth century. From the very beginning, hospitals were set up, normally outside the city limits. They were financed and staffed by local Church and civil institutions and, even though their effectiveness has been called into question, they were

---

[35] Still stranger measures could be taken to purify the air. In January of 1597 in Santander, 15 cows, 10 lambs and 20 goats were walked about the town "to consume and spend the poor quality and corruption of the air" (Bennassar, 1969: 25).

considered a major bulwark against disease.[36] On the whole, however, it can be said that before well into the nineteenth century medicine won few if any battles against major diseases (McKeown, 1976: ch. 5).

All efforts against disease carried out at a local level were subject to certain constraints which conditioned any possible effectiveness. While some were specifically human and others were related to the structures of pre-industrial society, all persisted throughout the period we are dealing with. It is to these more general and perhaps more pervasive aspects of epidemic disease that we will now turn our attention.

Fear was understandably an ever-present factor in moments of epidemics.[37] The town was alone, besieged by an unseen enemy; it had become a hostage to fate or the whims of an enemy who could not be effectively combated. In such a situation, the only reasonable reaction, according to a famous proverb, was to flee as quickly, as far and for as long a time as possible.[38] And flee they did! Our epoch is filled with cases of overt flight by municipal, royal and ecclesiastical authorities, along with other local elites.[39] Despite the fact that those who stayed and organized the struggle were esteemed in the eyes of their fellow citizens, no special stigma seemed to be attached to flight (Jiménez Muñoz, 1974: 351; Vincent, 1977: 356). Once the epidemic had run its course, most of those who had fled seemed to fit back into local life without provoking any noticeable tensions. In fact, the only restriction on flight seemed to be one's physical and economic ability to leave. In 1647 we find that citizens of Cartagena had fled to the hills

[36] Though financing could be either civil or ecclesiastical, or a combination of both, hospitals were normally under the control of the town, staffed by the regular clergy and under the supervision of doctors (Peset *et al.*, 1977b: 245; Marcos Martín, 1978; García Guerra, 1977: 162–164).

[37] In 1599, Juan de Arroyo, parish priest of Talavera de la Reina, described the fear provoked by the epidemic in these terms: "El miedo era tal que ni padre a hijo, ni hijo a padre no abía quien diere una jarra de agua a los enfermos ... Los curas ... sacramentando, huyesen no se pegase tan mala enfermedad" (González Muñoz, 1974: 160) ("The fear was such that nobody, neither sons for their fathers nor fathers for their sons, were willing to give so much as a pitcher of water to the ill ... Instead of administering the sacraments, priests fled lest they catch such a terrible disease.") In 1506, in Córdoba, Bernáldez described much the same terror: "non podian valer los padres a los hijos, ni los hijos a los padres é los vivos huian de los muertos" (Yun Casalilla, 1980: 111) ("Parents could not help their children nor children their parents, and the living fled from the dead.")

[38] "Huir luego, lejos y por largo tiempo" (the spelling here is modern).

[39] A good example of flight is given by the corregidor of Murcia who was not only willing to abandon his plague-stricken city, but also insisted on breaking the isolation imposed by Cartagena which also came under his jurisdiction. In order to gain entry into Cartagena he lied about the state of health in Murcia. Needless to say, he was refused entry (Casal Martínez, 1951: 47–49).

and were squabbling over who should have which cave in a desperate effort to get out of the path of the epidemic (Casal Martínez, 1951: 50–54).[40] Municipal government and the organization of the defense suffered from this tendency of people to flee. Government could be crippled or even disappear for weeks during the peak of the disease (Yun Casalilla, 1980: 110–111). This was a serious handicap because, apart from structurally limiting the capacity for reaction, all those who fled became potential agents of the spread of the disease. The presence of the epidemic also produced the contrary human reaction of solidarity. During these times certain dedicated individuals shouldered the major part of the struggle. Many examples of efficient organization of local solidarity during moments of crisis mortality can be found. While fear conditioned all forms of reaction to epidemic disease, solidarity also existed and became the basis for the struggle against the disease.

Another important factor present in most epidemics was the fact that the appearance or the mere rumor of disease had disastrous effects on the local economy. Efforts to isolate the town brought commercial activities to a halt, created a shortage of labor, stimulated inflation and otherwise tended to undermine most economic activity (Granjel, 1977: 19–20; González Muñoz, 1974: 155). This situation might be prolonged beyond the period of the epidemic itself and compromise the future of the town's economy. Doubtless the incidence of the plague of 1596–1602 played an important role in the decline of urban populations and economies during a large part of the seventeenth century.[41] Economic paralysis, however, had more immediate effects and was present during all epidemics. Those affected by economic hardship (a great proportion of the town's population) initiated subtle, albeit steadfast, resistance to most sanitary measures, especially those concerning the isolation of the town. Smuggling was but the most visible form of resistance; other more subtle forms also existed. The frequent delay in declaring the state of plague and the haste in declaring a bill of good health were efforts by the authorities to protect the economic interests of the town.[42] While

---

[40] Both in terms of morbidity and especially the ability to escape, it is hard to dispute the "class-specific" nature of epidemic disease. If we are to explain the relatively scant incidence of social and political upheaval in the wake of crisis mortality it will be necessary to rethink the meaning of flight from epidemics.

[41] In 1600 Martín González de Cellorigo, a lawyer at the *Audiencia* of Valladolid, wrote to Philip III relating the plague of 1598–1600 to the "decline of Spain," and proposed both medical and economic solutions to remedy the situation (Carreras Panchón, 1973).

[42] This practice was not uncommon in the rest of Europe as late as the latter part of the nineteenth century. The famous case of Hamburg and the cholera epidemic of 1892 is

this concern and resistance is understandable, it undermined most local defense efforts. Early modern towns were never able to achieve total isolation because not even their own populations desired it.

A corollary of this was the town's general inability to finance its own defense efforts. Enforced loans, special taxes on the rich and the Church, and other extraordinary measures were adopted with only limited success, and often produced very adverse reactions among the people. The ruinous state of municipal finances would be at least partially alleviated in the wake of the crisis by royal intervention. This help might take the form of loans, freedom from payment of the *alcabala* for short periods of time or temporary suspension of debt payments.

A frequent explanation of the causes of epidemic diseases and, more generally, of periods of hardship was that they were a type of divine punishment for the sins of society. This type of explanation was invariably present in times of crisis and did not seem to preclude more secular forms of analysis. Times of crisis mortality almost always seemed to be accompanied by an increase in popular religious senti-ment. Processions to saints such as San Roque and San Sebastián during times of disease as well as *Te Deums* to celebrate their end were undeniable elements of popular culture in moments of distress.[43] At times, as in Valencia in 1647, in Málaga in 1803, or in Cuenca in 1804, the bishop was obliged to curtail such activities lest they contribute to the spread of the disease. Measures of this nature were normally extremely unpopular. These aspects of religious fervor fulfilled a very important psychological need for populations besieged by an unseen enemy. An explanation, albeit spurious and ineffective, offered con-solation to an otherwise terrorized populace. The fact that no attempt was ever made to discredit this manner of combating epidemics leads one to believe that even the most enlightened authorities felt that the spiritual consolation offered by popular religion was as or even more important in the battle against the epidemic than isolation and other hygienic and medical measures.

Apart from this role, the Church fulfilled many other functions in times of crisis. Some priests were the first to flee or take economic advantage of the distress, while others cared for the ill or helped organize the defense until they too fell victims.[44] The Church also

an excellent example of official vacillation in the face of the economically negative consequences of epidemics. On this case, see, for example, Evans (1987).

[43] For more on this subject, see Bennassar (1969: 26); Vincent (1977: 356–357); Maza Zorilla (1978: 380–381).

[44] See, for example, Vincent (1977: 351–352); Bennassar (1969: 76–77); Castellanos and Reguero (1977: 112).

fulfilled certain structural roles in the fight against death. Care for the ill fell to the clergy (especially the regular clergy) and the bishop and other ecclesiastical officials played key roles in the coordination of defense efforts. All local juntas were staffed in part by clergy and often founded by them, and it is not unusual to find the bishop collaborating with the civil authorities in the publication of certain edicts.[45] Finally, there were times in which the Church was also called upon to bolster weak municipal finances. This dual material and spiritual role made the Church a vital part of all municipal efforts to stem the tide of crisis mortality.

Doctors were the key figures in the battle against epidemics. While their medical contributions to the elimination of disease were severely limited, they were the chief organizers of defense efforts. Few if any measures were taken either by the Juntas de Sanidad or the municipal government without their advice.[46] This does not, of course, mean that doctors were either universally respected or well-paid; widespread mistrust made them the butts of many jokes (Domínguez Ortiz, 1973d: 320–321). Doctors were in constant demand despite deplorably low salaries, which improved somewhat only in the nineteenth century. Here towns were better placed than rural areas because they were able to pay more and consequently had a greater concentration of doctors.[47] Whereas from a strictly medical standpoint there was little doctors could do, their contribution to the organization of municipal defense efforts made them essential elements in the battle against epidemic disease.

Before 1700 the role of the Crown during times of epidemics was actually quite limited, though afterwards it adopted increasingly effective interventionist policies. The often inefficient Junta Nacional de Sanidad represented for the first time the possibility of standardizing policy and amplifying isolation techniques. While there was plague in Marseilles in 1720, it directed the defense of the entire Levant coastline; during the yellow fever epidemic in Andalusia at the beginning of the nineteenth century, efforts were made to establish a cordon sanitaire in order to isolate the entire region.[48] Had that progressive rationalization of the central administration in the face of

---

[45] See Castellanos and Reguero (1977: 111–113); Riera (1977: 310–315); Zubiri and Zubiri (1981: 72–75); Carrillo and García Ballester (1977: 85–90).

[46] See Bennassar (1969: 77–80); Peset *et al.* (1977a: 232–235).

[47] For information on the wages of doctors, see Domínguez Ortiz (1973d: 317–319); Peset and Peset (1968: 235–239).

[48] Reference to this attempt to isolate all of Andalusia can be found in Cuenca sources (Archivo Municipal de Cuenca, legajo 1,354: Documentos sueltos de 1800). For a thorough study of this epidemic, see Arejula (1806).

epidemics, that "critical variable" in the words of John Post, been reached?[49] Probably not. Towns were still essentially on their own in the struggle against disease. Even so, Bourbon reformism stimulated the beginning of a slow change which was to gather increasing intensity during the nineteenth century.

Some additional considerations
Up to this point the effects of subsistence crises and epidemics on urban societies in pre-industrial Spain have been considered separately. These were the moments in which urban institutions were put to their greatest test. The social and economic ties which held Ancien Régime society together suffered severely during these periodic onslaughts. Towns were composed of a number of groups and institutions, and each had its own particular and often divergent interests.

Municipal government was itself a manifestation of the vested interests of the wealthiest sector of the town, and this tended to inhibit its effectiveness in both types of crisis. The connection between *regidores* (town councilmen) and those hoarding grain in times of dearth was often suspected; the first ones able to flee from an approaching epidemic came precisely from members of that elite. Yet it would be very risky to affirm that government did not have the interests of its citizens at heart during these times. Indeed action was probably less hindered by the social origin of the *regidores* than it was by lack of money, scant scientific knowledge and a mentality which seemed often to exclude any preventive action against what was surely conceived of as an unavoidable fact of life. A careful examination of the evidence suggests that the commonweal was the foremost concern of early modern municipal governments in times of crisis.

It was in times of crisis that urban government came closest to wielding truly dictatorial powers. Whatever measures might be enacted, it was done under the threat of severe punishment for offenders. Normally fines, lashes and the galleys were threatened, but capital punishment was not uncommon. This, however, was not the only manifestation of the coercive powers of local government. Arbitrarily interfering with trade, appropriating grain shipments, requisitioning grain from its own citizens, forceful entry into people's residences and breach of contract were all examples of this. While the extent to which these practices were carried out to their fullest consequences is not entirely clear, they were bound to produce social tension. Direct evidence of strained relations among the town's elite or

[49] See Post (1976: 26–37; 1977: 159–175).

between the municipal government and different groups within the urban context is most difficult to come by, yet they must have been typical of moments of crisis.

Relations between a town and the villages lying within its radius of influence suffered considerably as well. Each was constrained to defend potentially conflicting interests. A relationship existed in which the villages had the grain, and the towns had the money, force and legal means to get it. Villages did their best to defend what little wheat they had. It is not uncommon to see rural officials embargoing grain destined for the city, local *justicias* refusing to turn over previously purchased grain, mayors impeding the transport of wheat, and even the illegal requisition of wheat in transit.[50] The towns, in turn, could retaliate by prohibiting the taking of food out of town, by sending their police to embargo grain in the surrounding areas, by cutting transport with other areas unless food was bought in return and, much as the villages, by requisitioning wheat bound for other cities. It would be difficult to imagine a time where urban–rural relations were more strained than in times of crisis.

A substratum of tension permeated social and economic relations during periods of crisis. Many historians have felt that this situation could lead to a more or less direct breakdown in the social and political order. Despite some spectacular exceptions, this situation seldom if ever arose. We have even seen cases in which the town could be without any sort of government for a prolonged period of time and no disintegration of the social and political order occurred. Why? There appear to be two reasons for this; one inherent in the dynamic of group behavior and the other related to the nature of crisis itself. Disturbances take place when individuals or groups successfully make use of latent tensions for very specific ends. Though this did occur (1506– 1507 in Córdoba, 1647–1652 in Andalusia, 1765–1766 in Madrid and elsewhere), it happened so seldom that it would seem safe to say that social institutions normally emerged unscathed from periods of crisis. Those moments of intense suffering for the great majority of the populace tended to provoke a passive attitude of prostration rather

---

[50] The judge of the village of Vera embargoed pre-purchased grain destined for Cartagena in 1647 (Casal, 1951: 40). In 1802 the town of Cuenca complained that the local *justicias* were preventing the shipment of grain which had already been paid for (AHN, Consejos, leg. 4,021, no. 60). In 1581 the town of Córdoba complained to the Cortes that the mayors of local villages were preventing the transport of previously paid wheat to the city (Fortea Pérez, 1981: 212). Wheat bound for Madrid was appropriated by authorities in several villages of La Mancha in 1765. In this last case there is clear reference to a factor which must have existed every time: the local authorities acted under pressure from the people (AHN, Consejos, leg. 6,744, exp. no. 17 in Anes Alvarez, 1974: 223).

than any sort of anger or rebelliousness. This was certainly more so in the case of epidemics where the enemy was unseen and it was not possible to place the blame on any individual or group. Protest was more frequent in the case of subsistence crises where hoarders were held responsible; though they too tended to blend into society and could not be readily singled out. Seldom, however, did it overflow into active disturbances. The fear of political unrest, however, did play an important and ever-present role in the minds of municipal officials and tended to underlie most of their decisions. In the final analysis, normally crises were more an onerous fact of life and a major test of government than a serious challenge to the stability of Ancien Régime society.

The crisis of 1804 in Cuenca and its province

Up until this point, our analysis has focused on both the demographic and the socio-economic implications of periods of crisis within the general context of urban Spain. Many of the aforementioned structural and behavioral patterns characteristic of these moments will be brought into sharp focus in a detailed analysis of the crisis of 1804 in Cuenca. The experience of the town and its surrounding rural areas will be discussed together so as to compare the effects of the same crisis in both the urban and the rural worlds.[51]

The crisis years of 1803–1805 followed the familiar pattern of so many demographic crises. A prolonged period of sharp inflation in the prices of foodstuffs culminated in 1803 in a major subsistence crisis whose effects were amplified and worsened by the appearance of epidemic fevers. The crisis affected most of the province of Cuenca and widespread areas of Spain; there was even news of its presence in Andalusia (where urban areas seemed to be spared), the Levant, and much of the central meseta (New and Old Castile). I have not found any indication of crisis in the northwestern or the northeastern parts of

---

[51] The data for this study come from the parish registers of the town of Cuenca, complemented by material from the Archivo Municipal de Cuenca (AMC) and the Archivo Histórico Nacional (AHN). Rural data come from a sample of 18 villages widely distributed throughout the province of Cuenca. This sample includes the following villages: Arcas, Albaladejo del Cuende, Atalaya del Cañavate, Buenache de Alarcón, Castejón, Cervera del Llano, La Peraleja, La Ventosa, Leganiel, Mohorte, Olmeda del Rey, Priego, Puebla de Almenara, Valdecabras, Valdemeca, Valdeolivas, Villalba de la Sierra and Villanueva de Guadamejud. I am confident that this sample is fairly representative of the experience of the province as a whole. Annual growth rates for the 1787–1857 period were 0.14 per cent for the entire province, and 0.134 per cent for our sample of villages.

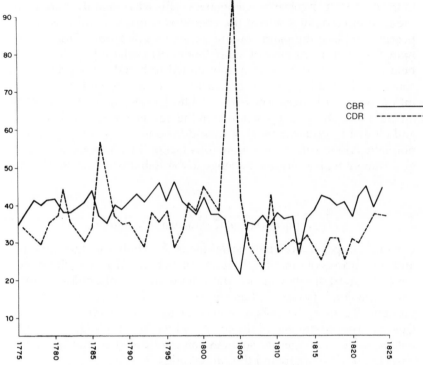

Figure 5.1 Crude death rates in eighteen Cuenca villages

the peninsula.[52] In the province itself, 1803–1805 were years of crisis in 14 of the 18 villages in the sample, and the period 1799–1805 showed negative natural growth rates in all of them (Figure 5.1).

The typical demographic structure of mortality crises in Ancien Régime Europe can be seen in 1803–1805 in Cuenca (Walter and Schofield, 1989). Conceptions, which had been gradually declining for some years, decreased sharply in the third quarter of 1803, reached their lowest level during the winter of 1804 and did not begin to recover until the second quarter of 1805 (Figure 5.2). During the same period, mortality increased drastically and reached two moments of

[52] Arejula (1806) gives testimony of its presence in Andalusia and the Levant. It badly affected Segovia but was much less intense in Salamanca (García Sanz, 1977: 89; Peset and Carvalho, 1972). Bilbao had excess mortality during the decade 1801–1810 (Mauleón Isla, 1961: 130), but Galicia (Pérez García, 1979: graphs 3–7) and Catalonia (Nadal, 1963) seemed to escape it. It was quite severe in other parts of La Mancha, Madrid, Talavera de la Reina and vast areas of Old Castile (López-Salazar Pérez, 1976: 280–281; González Muñoz, 1975; Pérez Moreda, 1980: 375–389; Carbajo Isla, 1987: 321).

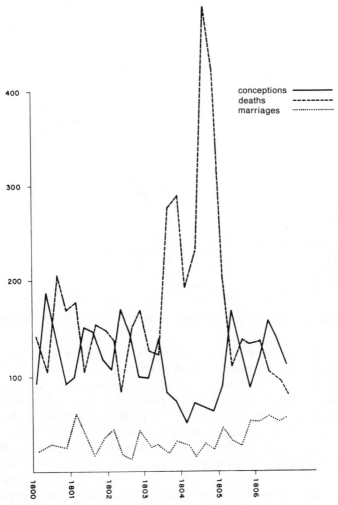

Figure 5.2 Quarterly vital events in eighteen Cuenca villages

great intensity: the second half of 1803 and, even more so, the second half of 1804. Peak mortality occurred during the summer of 1804 and did not decline to "normal" levels until the second quarter of 1805. Marriages were also below normal from the beginning of 1803 until the first months of 1805.

In the town of Cuenca the crisis lasted for a shorter time, but mortality peaks were more intense than in rural areas. The first appearance of mortality in 1803 was hardly visible and the real blow

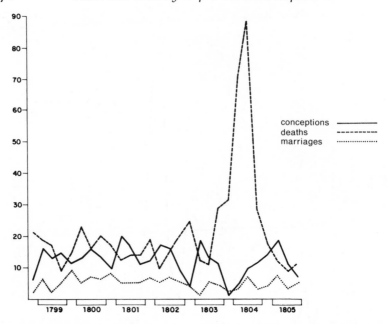

Figure 5.3 Quarterly vital events in the town of Cuenca, 1799–1805

came during the spring and summer of 1804. It was significantly more intense than in the province and practically disappeared during the autumn of that year (Figures 5.3 and 5.4). During a period of less than two years both the town and the rural areas of the province lost about 11 per cent of their population and during the second half of 1804 there was a net loss of population of 6.4 per cent. Most of the victims of the fevers were adults. During the worst moment of the epidemic, only 34 per cent of all deaths during that period were of infants and children (*párvulos*), as opposed to the 50 to 60 per cent which was normal.[53] Of the 227 persons for whom we know the exact age at death, 40 per cent were between the ages of 16 and 50, as opposed to the 13 per cent in normal times. This last aspect acquired considerable importance in prolonging the effects of the mortality because it slowed the recovery of subsequent births after the crisis (Livi Bacci, 1978).

In 1804 we see a combination of a severe subsistence crisis and epidemic disease. By 1803 prices of basic foodstuffs had been on the

[53] This preference for adults generally coincides with that shown by the yellow fever epidemic in the South at the beginning of the century, though it is not nearly so intense. In Málaga in 1803 and 1804, or Cádiz in 1804, 90 per cent of all those dying were adults, as opposed to the slightly less than 70 per cent in the province of Cuenca (Arejula, 1806: Estados 1, 3 and 4).

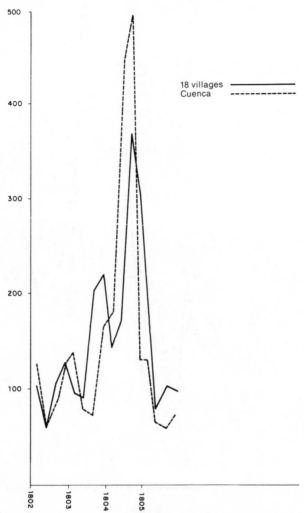

Figure 5.4 Mortality in rural and urban Cuenca by quarter, 1802–1805

rise for more than 15 years (Figure 5.5).[54] Wheat, the most essential of all products, showed the sharpest increase. In 1804 it nearly trebled levels reached between 1780–1790. The first years of the nineteenth century were inflationary in most of Europe, though the levels reached

[54] The price series underlying Figure 5.5 is based on urban data and shows a striking similarity to those used by Anes Alvarez (1970: 489, 495). The price of wheat is based on the average price regulated by the town council for the sale of wheat by the *pósito* to the official bakers. The rest of the prices are based on the official bids given by suppliers to the town. When these bids were altered during the year at the request of

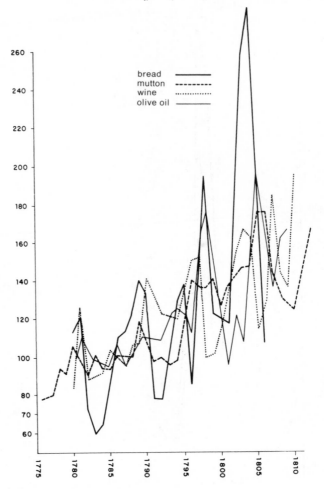

Figure 5.5 Prices of certain foodstuffs in the town of Cuenca

in Cuenca and elsewhere in central Spain were truly extraordinary
(Fontana, 1979: 59–60). Years of substandard harvests, combined with
the lack of a national market, created a situation of hardship possibly
never before reached in Castile, at least since the early seventeenth
century.

The gravity of the situation becomes clear if we look at the municipal
deliberations of the town council of Cuenca. Dearth or at least
problems of wheat supply were mentioned in 1791, 1793, 1797, 1798,

the suppliers, the changes were reflected in the overall prices. In all cases the prices
are the average for 12 months.

1800, 1801 and in 1802, a year of great hardship. The situation worsened noticeably because the harvest of the summer of 1803 was a complete failure. On 28 May of that year there was a petition for *Rogativas de Aqua* (prayers for rain) by local farmers who also complained of the continuing frosts between 16 and 25 May. What had promised to be a good year after the horrible crop of 1802, now "in the opinion of the experts will be sterile and fruitless," especially if "mild and gentle" rains did not arrive soon.[55] By mid-June the rains had still not arrived, then, later, floods washed away almost the entire crop of summer wheat.[56]

News of extreme dearth came from every corner of the province. The situation was extremely serious and many documents affirm that there was no grain, not even for bread. The situation in the jail of the town of Cuenca says it all. On 25 January, the parish priest of the parish of Santa Cruz and the chief doctor in town visited the jail where 20 gravely ill prisoners were kept. In their report, they cited the cost of food among the causes and aggravating aspects of the prisoners' situation. They stated that each prisoner received 11 *cuartos* per day which before had been enough for 1.5 or 2 pounds of bread.[57] With this allowance, there were normally 3 or 4 *cuartos* per day left over that the prisoners used to buy vegetables and other foodstuffs. Now, since a pound of bread cost 11 *cuartos*, many prisoners ate their pound of bread as soon as they received the money, and had nothing left over for more food. At the end of their report and after requesting an increase in the allowance given to each prisoner, they say: "These poor devils, on top of being deprived of their freedom, may also die of starvation."[58]

At least in the eyes of their contemporaries, people were dying of starvation, especially during the *meses mayores* (March to June) of 1804. "She died of poverty"; "an unknown woman who had come begging with her two children died of starvation"; "after having fainted in the fields, he was brought in dead."[59] It is not difficult to find references like these to the cause of death in the burial registers. In fact, of all the known causes of death during 1804, 14 per cent were directly attributed to starvation.

Further aggravating an already dramatic situation, dearth was accompanied, or rather followed by the appearance of endemic fevers

55 Archivo Municipal de Cuenca, Actas for 1803, f. 39v. and 40.
56 Archivo Histórico Nacional, Consejos, legajo 4025, no. 94.
57 The value of a *cuarto* was 4 *maravedís*; one *real* was worth 8.5 *cuartos*.
58 AMC, Municipal deliberations of 1804, f. 21v, 22 and 23. According to Muñoz y Soliva (1860: 485), that year in Cuenca bread reached the price of 15 *cuartos* per pound.
59 For more on this subject, see Laslett (1983: 128–136).

whose nature was the subject of some controversy. Some called it
tabardillo (typhus), others *tercianas* (malaria), and the parish priest of
Osa de la Vega even called it *cuartanas* (fevers); all called it the
"epidemic" and never referred to any diseases not already known in
the province.[60] Its origin and nature might not have been clear to the
people of Cuenca, but its effects certainly were. In 68 per cent of the
121 deaths whose causes were listed, the parish priest noted either
typhus (45 per cent) or malaria (23 per cent) as the principal cause of
death.[61]

This was not the first attack of fevers in the nineteenth century. The
doctor and physician of the village of Palomares del Campo, at the
behest of the president of the provincial Junta de Sanidad, stated in
1801 that there had been "continuous fevers from the last part of 1798
until the end of 1800, and intermittent fevers from the spring of 1800,"
and that some 60 or 70 people had been brought to him. At present the
fevers seemed to be receding. Some 230 people had been ill and about
10 per cent of them had died.[62] Evidently, epidemic proportions had
not yet been reached. The village of El Provencio wrote to the Council
of Castile requesting a greater supply of quinine in 1802 due to the
presence of malaria.[63] Indeed, the death statistics for 3 of the 18
villages reflect a situation of excess mortality during 1801 and 1802,
though crisis levels were not reached.[64] These localized outbreaks
seemed to decline and be forgotten; the Junta de Sanidad, which had
been formed to monitor the progress of the epidemic in Andalusia,
was even disbanded.

This respite did not last long, and fevers returned during autumn
1803, only to reach their peak between June and October of 1804. In
Cuenca, infectious fevers had been in the town since September of
1803, but people paid little heed to them. After all, they were part of
the typical late summer surge in mortality. During the second week of
December, the military prisoners in the Casa Cuartel were stricken.[65]
At this point disagreement arose between the local authorities and
some doctors, as to whether or not they were epidemic fevers. In
January some affirmed that they were due to deficient sanitary

[60] AHN, Consejos, legajo 4025, no. 94.
[61] The same epidemic, though in a more benign form, reached Salamanca (Peset and
   Carvalho 1972: 250). Pérez Moreda (1980: 374–384) considers the crisis mortality to be
   primarily caused by malaria, though in the concrete case of Cuenca the numerous
   cases of typhus suggest a more mixed epidemic, with malaria in rural areas and
   typhus in the town itself.
[62] AMC, legajo 1355, *documentos sueltos*, 1801.
[63] AHN, Consejos, legajo 2022, no. 29.
[64] These villages are La Peraleja, Villanueva de Guadamejud, and Puebla de Almenara.
[65] AMC, legajo 1359, *documentos sueltos*, 1803.

conditions and not to the feared epidemic.[66] Yet one month earlier, 11 recruits had already received the Last Sacraments.

All doubts soon disappeared because the fevers spread to the municipal jail. On 21 January the head doctor of Cuenca affirmed that 17 prisoners had fevers which seemed to be typhus. He proposed a number of remedies, which I will mention shortly, and ended by affirming that "the town is exposed to a great contagion. . .and it would be terrible if the fevers spread even more." According to this doctor, they were caused by the conditions of the jail with the "poverty, filth, uncleanliness and ill-treatment of all who inhabit it"; and this situation was worsened by the custom of not separating the healthy prisoners from the diseased ones.[67] In the Casa Cuartel at the beginning of January, the authorities felt that the worst had passed, when in reality it had only just begun.

Within a few months, the disease had spread to the entire town. The town council called 5 doctors and 2 surgeons to an urgent meeting on 11 April, "in order to curb the progress of the epidemic which has just broken out."[68] The number of deaths did not abate, especially between the months of July and September, both in the town and in the rest of the province. During the autumn the epidemic finally left the town, though it continued in the rest of the province until the end of 1804 or even the beginning of 1805.

As we have seen in the case of Cuenca, death caught everyone by surprise. The fears of an epidemic back in 1800 and 1801 seemed far away. This was (and is) possibly the most important point of people's conceptualization of epidemics: once the problem had disappeared, it was forgotten. In that way, it could only take them by surprise. An example will help illustrate this point. The jail in Cuenca, which was one of the original foci of infection within the town, had been the object of a report to the Council of Castile in 1790 in which its unsanitary state counseled either a total remodelling of the building or its removal from the center of town. The same complaints were voiced again in 1803 and 1804 by the municipal architect Mateo López.[69] It was only then that the authorities became truly concerned. In other words, reform was seriously contemplated only when the jail *already was* a focal point of infection, but not when it was a possible point of infection. Otherwise, conventional wisdom related the causes of disease to poor living standards and unhygienic conditions. In the

[66] "This typhus cannot come from the Casa Cuartel because those who enter there do not come down with the illness." AMC, legajo 1360, no. 1; 10 January 1804.
[67] AMC, Municipal deliberations of 1804; 21 January, f. 18, 19.
[68] AMC, of 1804; f. 51, 52.
[69] AHN, Consejos, legajo 2155, no. 2.

light of this, the Junta de Socorro distributed bread to the poor and to the prisoners, enacted measures to assure a general clean-up of the town's streets, had bonfires lit to purify the atmosphere, and attempted to expel from town the many paupers who came every winter in search of alms.[70] Other than this, there was little else pre-industrial Spanish towns could do to fight epidemics.

The following text underscores the gravity of the situation in Cuenca and its province. In September of 1803 a group of farmers from the village of Villar de Cañas, when writing to the Council of Castile asking for seeds for the autumn planting, managed to give a terse and eloquent description of their plight.

Some have not been able to sow what they planned to, and others after having sown, have ended up without any wheat or any of the other grains which are totally necessary for them, their families and their work; and in this way they are in the direst of straits and misery without any way out and not knowing where to turn from now on. In order to survive this year it is not enough to have land if there are no seeds, or even money, because even if they should want to sell their property, there is normally nobody to buy it, and if there is, they must get rid of farms of great value at the most infamous prices. The recourse to loans, even those with usurious interest rates, high financing or mortgages, is also shut off because no one has any money, or because he who has it is jealously guarding it. In this way the farmer has no choice but to die if he is not helped in this moment of need. In order partly to alleviate this misery, and so that the charitable intentions of His Majesty be fulfilled, we request the fair distribution of grain among the farmers in proportion to their property . . .[71]

These farmers pointed to the essential ingredients of their situation: the impossibility of seeking help from those who had more grain, because it was precisely these people who were most interested in aggravating the crisis; the absolute need to acquire seeds for the autumn planting; the on-going lack of savings which might help meet situations such as these; and, finally, the fact that the only possible help would have to come from the government.

Let us turn to the town of Cuenca where the entire problem of governmental intervention in the supply of wheat will become clear. It must be remembered that the province of Cuenca, and especially its southern part, falls within the area of influence of Madrid and therefore wheat bound for the capital tended to receive priority treatment from the Council of Castile. For example, in February of 1804 when the suppliers of wine to the town of Cuenca were loading wine in the village of Sisante, their wagons and their services were

[70] It is interesting to note that none of these measures were ever enforced when there was no epidemic present.
[71] AHN, Consejos, legajo 2155, no. 2.

requisitioned to go to San Clemente and participate "in the transport of wheat to the Court."[72] The mayor of Belmonte complained that the *justicias* "with the greatest amount of liberality, allowed the export to the very needy Court of Madrid of grain which might be completely necessary for the people here."[73] In fact, the person who controlled most wheat in the province, who was suspected of hoarding, and whom the town of Cuenca asked for help, was Don Santiago González y Noriega, the agent of the Court of Madrid for the purchase of wheat in the province. Being a breadbasket for Madrid put considerable pressure on local wheat production, especially when harvests were not abundant.

The supply of wheat was considered a political issue of the highest importance by the authorities who feared a repetition of the popular unrest which had taken place in 1766.[74] Even though the Decree of Free Trade of Cereals (1765) was never overturned, the authorities did whatever was in their power, both by ordinary and extraordinary measures, to ensure the supply of wheat at the most equitable prices possible. In their own opinion, the great enemies were the powerful who hoarded wheat. On 2 February 1804, the authorities of the town of Belmonte complained:

Even though some of the rich have behaved with the greatest generosity when faced with this situation of dire need, others have taken advantage of the situation to push the price of wheat even higher. These people are not content with the price of 100 *reales* per *fanega* and have no compassion for the poor victims of starvation . . .[75]

With this in mind, he ordered wealthy farmers to sell all available grain to the municipal bakery at the price of 100 *reales*.[76]

There were more or less veiled accusations that other groups also participated in the hoarding of wheat. In 1802 the municipal government of Cuenca indirectly suggested that even the Church was not selling all the wheat it could to the town. The deacon of the cathedral responded immediately and alleged that the accusations were not fair and that the Church had always sold wheat to the town at fair prices.[77] In the final analysis, the incident seems to suggest that all social

[72] AMC, Municipal deliberations of 1804, f. 36, 29 February.
[73] AHN, Consejos, legajo 2343, no. 11.
[74] AMC, Municipal deliberations for 1797, f. 60, 24 June.
[75] A *fanega* was a measurement of volume in Castile which varied by region but which contained about 55.5 liters or 1.56 bushels.
[76] AHN, Consejos, legajo 2343, no. 11; see also, AMC, Municipal deliberations for 1804, f. 69; 9 June.
[77] The dispute lasted for some months during the summer and fall of 1802 (AMC, Municipal deliberations for 1802, several pages). See also Peset and Carvalho (1972: 237).

groups might have been participating in this practice, or at least were perceived to be doing so by those attempting to manage the crisis. Perhaps still more revealing is the fact that local officials from nearby villages were also actively encouraging their own citizens to keep what little wheat they had from leaving their villages, even if it had already been purchased. A testimony of the extent of dearth between 1802 and 1804 is that as the crisis worsened the entire structure of the wheat trade began to crumble.

In many ways the municipal authorities had their hands tied and there was not much they could do. In order to curb hoarding, the Royal *Cédula* of 16 July 1790 was repeatedly reactivated. In it local officials were authorized to force all citizens with stored grain exceeding what was necessary "to support the household and family, and for the autumn planting," to sell it at fair prices.[78] In Cuenca, representatives of the town council accompanied the corregidor and the head constable in a house by house search for stored grain. Yet, as might be expected, these inspections, which were carried out in April of 1803 and repeated in June of 1804, were never successful. Everybody alleged that he had just enough for his own household.[79] About all the central government could do was to threaten fines of up to 30,000 *maravedís*.[80]

Another institution which might have helped to alleviate shortage and control prices was the *pósito*. Originally they had been created to act as grain reserves in rural areas, and as a means of ensuring supply and influencing prices in towns. By the beginning of the nineteenth century they were unable to fulfill either purpose. Royal intervention during the latter part of the eighteenth century forcing rural *pósitos* to help finance the war effort had depleted their grain reserves to such an extent that they proved to be practically useless during these years of scarcity.[81] Unfortunately, the *pósito* was unable to store enough grain, or to influence prices effectively.[82] Ultimately, relief came from the following year's harvest. This was what happened in 1804.

Two extraordinary measures were also taken by the Council of Castile during the 1802–1804 crisis. Faced with the horrendous harvest of the summer of 1803, on 2 September of that year the Crown renounced its share of the tithe and a number of other taxes on grain

[78] See, for example, the Royal Order of 11 November of 1802 cited in Anes Alvarez (1970: 401–2).
[79] AMC, Municipal deliberations for 1802, f. 55–7; Deliberations for 1803, f. 43–4.
[80] AHN, Consejos, legajo 4021, no. 60.
[81] This aspect of the rural *pósitos* is best studied in Anes Alvarez (1968; 1970).
[82] This mechanism was analyzed in considerable detail in the preceding section of this chapter.

and ordered that "it be distributed to needy farmers for the autumn planting."[83] Contrary to other measures, this one seemed to be effective and the harvest of 1804 was adequate. The most important government efforts, however, were concentrated on importing grain (Anes Alvarez, 1970: 413–423). In September of 1803 the government had ordered the importation of wheat which arrived at the coast during the first part of 1804. In July of 1804 when the Council of Castile requested information from villages as to whether or not they wanted wheat.[84] At least in the case of the province of Cuenca, the problem was that the measure came about one year too late. By the time the July request had arrived, there were indications that the crop of 1804 would not be bad and the price of bread in Cuenca had already begun to decline, and continued to do so throughout the autumn.[85] While it is possible that the prospect of the distribution of imported grain might have provoked a reappearance of hoarded wheat in the market, it was more probably due to the sure prospects of a good up-coming harvest.[86] Several villages in the province refused to receive the imported grain because the recent harvest had at least been sufficient.[87]

In times of crisis government action, be it local or national, was insufficient, ineffective and normally late. Perhaps the fate of Las Majadas, a mountain village not far from the town of Cuenca is a fitting example of this process. On 3 April 1804 its town council wrote to the Council of Castile, requesting the creation of supplementary jobs:

to come to the aid of sick and needy farmers with the most efficient means at their disposal to keep them from dying of starvation and poverty. In order to achieve these holy ends and to help relieve in any way possible the terrible problems of this village which had one of the worst wheat harvests in living memory. It is the only crop which can be farmed here and yet last year nothing was harvested, and so people are at this moment dying of starvation; this situation will only worsen if something is not done . . .

They asked the crisis management commission of the town of Cuenca (Junta de Socorro) for permission to cut down some 10,000 pine trees on municipal land. With this, "they could help out the needy day

---

[83] AHN, Consejos, legajo, 4024, no. 102.
[84] In the summer of 1803 there had been numerous affirmative replies to a similar inquiry.
[85] AMC, Municipal deliberations, f. 83v, 84 and 86; 11 and 14 July.
[86] The town council stated: "The harvest promises to be good and sufficient, and recovery will be fine if the grains are not used for anything else because of the scarcity." See, AMC, Municipal deliberations for 1804, f. 104v–106.
[87] AHN, Consejos, legajos 11500 and 11506. I have counted 16 of these villages and towns (including Cuenca).

laborers by starting the most necessary public works projects such as fixing the roads and streets in and around the village ..." The Junta had offered some money but it had said nothing about the trees. The Council of Castile was not able to decide either, and sent them to the corregidor who, in turn, said they had to go through the Navy Commission, who would decide the matter. In June this commission stated that it would have to find out if the cutting of the trees would hurt livestock farmers or not. The dossier ends on 12 June with no final decision having been taken, over two months after the village had affirmed that people were literally starving to death.[88] It is a good example of the gravity of the crisis and the inefficiency of government efforts to curb its effects.

From the standpoint of public health, the actions of the authorities were hardly more effective. In the first place, there was considerable hesitation on the part of the municipal authorities to admit that the disease was present in town. As early as December of 1803 some doctors stated that a clear danger of contagion existed and the town council asked the intendant to move the prisoners outside of town. He replied with a certain irony: "I was very moved to see the haste you showed in submitting your report, which I received yesterday afternoon, your willingness to declare the state of contagious epidemic based on the experience of the illness of some men in the Casa Cuartel of this town." He continued by saying that "the illness is clearly not contagious, poses no problem whatsoever to the rest of the town and can be cleared up by cleaning and feeding the prisoners ..." Then he suggests that the council should help him find some food and clothing for the prisoners. Despite the fact that 9 of the 50 sick prisoners had already died, he considered the actions of the town council to be "hasty and not well thought out." Despite this optimistic scolding, he must have had certain misgivings for he refused to move the prisoners because this might "extend the illness to the entire peninsula."[89]

The unwillingness shown by the intendant to cause alarm among the populace and his evident stubbornness provoked a dispute involving the municipal government, the intendant and the city doctors which ended up preventing any action, apart from finding clothes and food, until the month of January. By then, the disease had spread from the Casa Cuartel to the city prison, and from there to the rest of the population.[90] It is difficult to say whether or not decisive action on the

---

88 AHN, Consejos, legajo 2377, no. 14.
89 AMC, Municipal deliberations for 1803, f. 94v–99.
90 AMC, Municipal deliberations for 1803, f. 99–105; Legajo 1359, *documentos sueltos*, 1803.

part of the authorities might have been able to control the spread of the fevers, though clearly official vacillation did little to help matters.

Once the contagion had been declared, one of the first things done was to reactivate the Junta de Sanidad which had originally been formed to coordinate locally the battle against the spread of the epidemic in Andalusia. In Cuenca, it promoted a series of measures which tended to isolate the town, purify the air, and clean up its streets and buildings. The use of quicklime in burial sites was recommended and two chapels were closed because of "the number of bodies and repugnant smell which turns them into foci of pestilence."[91] The first serious attempt was made to establish a cemetery outside of town, and a place near the Cerro del Socorro was surveyed.[92] Yet many of the structural changes proposed, such as building a new jail beyond the city limits, were forgotten once the epidemic had passed. The epidemic only concerned the authorities when it was present in town. Once passed, most of the good intentions were forgotten until the next one came along.

Some conclusions

By 1804 there were few indications of any fundamental change in the management of crisis. Despite an increase in the role played by central government, the fight was still organized essentially from a local level. In many ways, in 1804 society seemed as vulnerable as it had been in 1506. The consequences, though, were certainly not the same. In 1804, the crisis had once again shown how inoperative Ancien Régime administration could be. What differed, though, was the fact that this took place against the backdrop of the French Revolution. In many ways, the crisis of 1804 must be seen within the context of the dismantling of Ancien Régime society in Spain.

Yet an administrative interpretation of crisis only covers part of the reality at hand. Subsistence crises were produced by radically fluctuating harvests in a society where few inter-regional grain markets existed, and the control of epidemics was clearly beyond the capabilities of early nineteenth-century technology. Profound changes would soon take place. 1804 marked the last catastrophic subsistence crisis on the peninsula, and, with the exception of the cholera epidemics of the nineteenth century, and the war-related deaths of

---

[91] AMC, Municipal for 1804, f. 46v–48, 11 April. Many of these measures have already been analyzed in the preceding section and therefore only brief mention will be made of them here.

[92] AMC, Municipal deliberations for 1804, f. 57, 58; 2 May.

1809–1812, it was also the last major general mortality crisis. The nineteenth century with its myriad administrative reforms was going to have an important impact on the traditional dynamics of crisis. Gradually a national grain market was created, thanks largely to the elimination of government controls on the wheat trade, to an overall increase in the production of cereals stimulated by the great Disentailment Laws, and, somewhat later, to the quantitative and qualitative improvement of land transportation. Subsistence crises gradually became a thing of the past. Similarly, the improvement in the effectiveness of public administration finally made defense against epidemics a feasible proposition. This, together with the sharp decrease in the incidence of typhus, itself dependent to a certain extent on price fluctuations, reduced the intensity and frequency of mortality crises. Only the massive cholera outbreaks remained, but here Spain was no longer at odds with most of the rest of Europe as it seemed to have been in 1804.

6

Household and family in Cuenca: a question of perspective

The study of the family and the "co-resident domestic group" is both one of the most attractive new fields of social history and one of the most frustrating ones. Interest in the family comes from the role it plays in conditioning such important factors for pre-industrial society as fertility, socialization of children, transmission of property and organization of the peasant domestic economy; all of which are parts of the prevailing system of economic production and social reproduction. Yet the study of the family has been an unending source of frustration, owing primarily to the practical impossibility of approaching it from all of the desirable and pertinent angles. Historians have been generally restricted to the examination of partial aspects of this elusive reality. The case in point here is the analysis of the "co-resident domestic group," whose relationship to the more ample and complex concept of the family is not always clear, but whose accessibility in historical documents has made it the object of a veritable torrent of historical literature (Wall, 1983a: 6–13).

Yet even here the breakthrough is comparatively recent and can be traced directly or indirectly to the work of Peter Laslett and other scholars who, in the late 1960s and early 1970s, developed a classification system which, for the first time, provided researchers with the tools to undertake a systematic approach to household structure.[1] Whereas in its origin the method gave overwhelming emphasis to the study of household structures, it has also stimulated more sophisticated forms of analysis where household and family are related to nuptiality or to the overall modes of social reproduction. From the beginning this approach to family and household became the focal point of numerous criticisms related not only to its underlying theo-

[1] The starting point for this approach really dates from the appearance of Laslett and Wall (1972). See also Hammel and Laslett (1974).

retical framework and to the somewhat imprecise relation between the family and the "co-resident domestic group," but also the the method itself and its avowed goals.[2] Regarding this last point, the most significant line of criticism has been primarily directed at the inadequacies of single cross-sectional types of analysis inherent in it. It has been suggested that such an undynamic approach to the household places key questions, such as the transformation of one type of household into another, beyond the methodological scope of any study. Clearly, more dynamic approaches to household and family are necessary and some more recent scholarship has attempted different modes of life-cycle studies which have brought an all too obscure reality into sharper, more dynamic focus by addressing such questions as the distinct forms of household transition, formation and dissolution.[3]

Strict period analysis is a valuable key to understanding the prevailing patterns of structure and other aspects of the pre-industrial household, and it provides data which can be readily interpreted in terms of prevailing inheritance patterns and socio-economic structures. It is a necessary starting point for any serious attempt to analyze the historical family. However, if a more finely tuned analysis of the nuances of different family "systems" is our goal, then single cross-sectional analysis leaves much to be desired. It may well become clear that some of the apparently less important nuances of people's life experience might just be essential for the understanding, not only of social and economic patterns, but also of socialization processes and reproductive behavior. The role of marriage in the formation of new households and in the parental home itself, residential patterns of newlyweds and of kin groups, kin circulation and the nature of structural transformations are all questions central to people's life experience and to the developmental cycle of the household itself. If these realities are to become clear, other complementary analytical tools must be used. In this chapter a systematic attempt will be made to utilize both types of analysis in order to obtain a more rounded view of the family in Cuenca.

In Spain the study of the family has been slow to take root and only recently have any worthwhile studies begun to appear.[4] Yet one of the

2 For a recent article on the possibilites and limitations of the field of family history, see Laslett (1987).
3 For examples of this type of innovative work see van de Walle (1976), Segalen (1977), Sieder and Mitterauer (1983), Danhieux (1983), Fauve-Chamoux (1984), Kertzer (1984), Lévy-Voelant (1988). For the demographic and economic implications of family structures within the context of England, see Schofield (1989).
4 For a good general overview of the field in Spain, Portugal and Italy, see, Kertzer and Brettell (1987). For some of the new work beginning to appear on the family in Spain, see Casey *et al.* (1987), Chacón Jiménez (1983; 1987a; 1987b), Rowland (1987a; 1987b,

first achievements of this admittedly young field has been the identification of a significant diversity of family forms on the peninsula. The existence of what amount to regional patterns of household structure, formation and dissolution is closely related to the relative homogeneity of inheritance practices and socio-economic structures within the different regions (Rowland, 1988). Furthermore, the heterogeneous regional patterns which characterize the Spanish family and household structures seem to be remarkably consistent within any given region. In most of central and southern Spain, household structures were always fundamentally simple, and where complexity existed, it was normally for reasons unrelated to inheritance. The only areas of Spain where some evidence of household complexity could be found lay above a line stretching from Northern Portugal in the West, along the Cantabrian coast, into the Basque Country, along the Pyrenees and swinging down into Catalonia.[5] Once again, as so often happens in studying Spanish population and economic history, regional patterns loom large, and it would be unwise to try to understand family and household in Cuenca without situating them within a regional context or taking into account the regional factors influencing their development.

Once within this general context, though, there are numerous specifically urban elements affecting families and households and these should lead to discernible differences between behavior and structures in the urban and the rural worlds. Understanding the pre-industrial family is largely a question of selecting the most appropriate perspective or perspectives, and the present inquiry into the nature of the family in Cuenca will make use of a number of different ones. My analysis is based on the systematic use of a series of municipal listings of inhabitants (*padrones*) dating from the eighteenth and nineteenth centuries. Data from the surrounding province are marshaled in order to determine the extent to which the observed patterns were specific to the town or were also rooted in the cultural and economic context of this region of Spain (Reher, 1988a: 5–14). More traditional cross-sectional analysis, controlling for profession, age or place of residence, is complemented by a life-cycle perspective of the development of the household based on nominative record linkage techniques and applied to population listings of the nineteenth century. The importance of economic, social and demographic

1988), Douglass (1988a; 1988b), Reher (1987; 1988a; 1988b), Martínez Carrión (1988), Perez García (1988), Lanza García (1988), Dubert García (1987), Moll Blanes (1987), Casey and Vincent (1987), and Pla Alberola (1987).

[5] In these areas inheritance practices and social and demographic structures differed markedly from the rest of the country (Douglass, 1988a; Kertzer and Brettell, 1987).

factors for household structures and development; the permanence of family forms over time; the existence of a lagged neo-local household formation system; the complexity and fluidity of household and family dynamics; the similarity of cultural norms in both urban and rural areas; and, finally, the impossibility of viewing the urban family solely through the household or as something physically, economically or even emotionally separate from its rural context, are among the most salient conclusions reached.

Regional and local contexts for the family in Cuenca

Certain regional and local realities provided what might be thought of as the background for the family in Cuenca, conditioned its existence, development and the structural forms it might take. In Cuenca, as well as in much of the remainder of central Spain, partible inheritance practices prevailed. Upon the death of either of the two parents, all of the goods which they had contributed to the marriage were divided in equal shares among the surviving children, or, if there were no children, among the next of kin (Reher, 1988a: 202–213; 1988b: 68–69).[6] This property division was always rigorously equal and no sex preference was ever shown. Only a small part of a person's property (normally 20 per cent) could be disposed of freely. This was normally given either to the spouse, some more distant relative, or the Church, or it was used to increase the inheritance of one or more of the direct heirs. Each spouse retained his or her own patrimony throughout their married lives, even though the husband normally administered the property as a whole, and willed it separately upon death. It seems that in the case of the dead spouse, all property acquired during marriage was also bequeathed upon death, thus considerably complicating property rights. It is interesting to note that rural property was often a central part of the wills of urban families, suggesting the existence of on-going economic ties between the urban and the rural worlds. The importance of these ties will loom large as this study of Cuenca society progresses.

The prevailing system of inheritance did little to inhibit marriage and household formation. It was flexible and provided relatively early access to at least the usufruct of property. Furthermore, there were numerous other ways, often by means of seasonal labor and temporary migration, in which young people could find the necessary income to establish new families. A key difference between the rural world and urban society was that property transfers were far less

6 For more on this subject, see chapter 3.

important in an urban context in which wage labor was common. Only within certain urban groups, such as artisans or the very wealthy, might the inheritance of a home or a trade prove to be an effective impediment to household formation.[7] Within an urban context we can expect to find nuptiality, household formation and family relations far less subject to the prevailing system of inheritance and property transfers than in rural areas. This situation was facilitated by the abundance of available housing, so prevalent in urban society.

In Cuenca, then, predominantly simple household structures and neo-local household formation rules should prevail. In a world of flexible job and housing markets, these households should be characterized by considerable movement of kin, in search of work and making use of family networks, based largely, though not exclusively, on the spatial proximity of other kin households. In fact, urban society might well facilitate the existence of higher proportions of both solitary and complex households than in rural areas, and yet there should be little or no incidence of more complex family forms in towns. Domestic service should be predominantly feminine and should involve young girls from both Cuenca and from the surrounding rural areas. Cuenca families as a whole can also be expected to show stable ties with the rural world. Verifying many of these postulates will occupy much of the rest of this chapter.

A matter of structure and content

In a town where a partible system of inheritance prevailed amid a geographically mobile population, household structure in Cuenca offers few mysteries: the preeminence of the nuclear family household is unquestionable. As can be seen in Table 6.1, between 72 and 75 per cent of all households were made up of nuclear families. This predominance not only persisted over the century-and-a-quarter for which I have been able to study household structure, but was also found among the different social groups in the town and in the rural areas of the province as well. This prevalence raises numerous questions concerning the relation between those nuclear households and economic and demographic variables, the reasons for complexity when it did arise, the underlying causes of the apparent stability over time, or, finally, the nature of the ties between these nuclear families and other kin households.

Within this general context, social, economic and demographic

---

[7] The wealthy showed far more restrictive marriage patterns than any other urban group.

Table 6.1. *Household structure by occupational category and date*

Household type	Cuenca[a] 1724	Cuenca[a] 1800	Cuenca[a] 1844	Rural[b] XVIIIth	Rural[b] 1800–1850
Solitaries	14.1	13.5	9.2	11.9	9.8
No-family	4.8	5.4	6.4	2.8	2.4
Simple	74.5	72.8	72.3	80.8	82.1
Extended	5.0	6.6	10.4	4.1	4.9
Multiple	1.1	1.7	1.6	0.4	0.8
Undetermined	0.6				
Total	100.1	100.0	99.9	100.0	100.0
Number	1,046	815	1,412	778	2,762

Household type	Agricultural/ day laborers	Industry/ artisans	1800 Services	Professionals/ administration/ privileged	Widows, others
Solitaries	5	5	8	4	43
No-family	2	1	1	2	8
Simple	85	85	82	80	46
Extended	5	8	5	11	2
Multiple	4	1	4	2	0
Total	101	100	100	99	99
Number	165	240	79	153	122

Household type	Agricultural/ day laborers	Industry/ artisans	1844 Services	Professionals/ administration/ privileged	Widows, others
Solitaries	3	4	5	4	22
No-family	2	5	5	7	12
Simple	84	81	71	73	56
Extended	9	10	14	16	8
Multiple	1	1	4	1	2
Total	99	101	99	101	100
Number	453	211	208	234	263

Notes [a] In the totals for the town of Cuenca, households headed by the clergy have been included. Most of these are types 1 and 2 and in 1800 were composed of 56 households and in 1844 of 43.
[b] The data here refer to rural households from the province of Cuenca. See Reher (1988a: 6).

variables tended to create discernible nuances in household structure. Household complexity was more common among the privileged; and it showed signs of increasing over time in all urban groups. However, multiple family households had little if any importance and the complexity which did exist was mostly made up of extended family households. These could be quite plentiful, especially among the higher income groups in 1844. There was an overall increase in complexity between 1724 and 1844 which affected all social groups without exception. This increase came at the expense of solitary households.[8] In Cuenca complexity was caused by kin who might have lived in solitary households but who decided in increasing numbers to live as a part of otherwise simple family households. The multiple households which did exist were probably related to marriage, but more on this later.

In rural areas of the province, the importance of nuclear households was far greater than in the towns. Here the differences are most noteworthy with no-family and extended households. No-family households were groups of often unrelated people sharing accommodation for the sake of convenience and closely dependent on the abundance of available housing and the importance of temporary residence. Not surprisingly these households were far more common in towns than in the villages. We can postulate that in rural areas lower levels of familial mobility and circulation of kin among kin households were the reasons for smaller proportions of extended families. This was related to the fact that in a town the availability of other kin groups beyond the immediate co-resident domestic group was greater than in the countryside. This tended to facilitate the existence of both solitary and complex family households as the extended family played an important role in meeting the potential needs of family members. Thus in town it was more feasible to live alone because there were other kin households close by, and that very proximity also made it easier to send a son or daughter to live in another kin household. In rural areas the kinship pool was not nearly so large or flexible as in town.[9]

The prevalence of simple household structures, within a demographic regime of relatively high fertility compensated for by high infant and child mortality, invariably led to reduced household size. Throughout the period under study, mean household size (MHS) hovered around 3.9 and only changed noticeably in 1800 owing to a temporary decline in the numbers of children per household, itself apparently the product of the economic difficulties which characterized the turn of the century in much of central Spain (Table 6.2)

[8] It should be remembered that most households headed by females do not receive a professional classification, but rather are listed as "widow" households. Therefore, the category, "widows/other," which has very high degrees of solitary and no-family households, includes families from all professional categories.

[9] For a discussion of the use of kin relationships for the welfare of individuals see Laslett (1988: 158–161).

Table 6.2. *Kin composition of households by date and occupational category*

Category	Agricultural/ day laborers			Industry/ artisans			Services		
	1724	1800	1844	1724	1800	1844	1724	1800	1844
Average no. as head or spouse	1.9	1.9	1.9	1.9	1.9	1.8	1.7	1.8	1.7
Average no. of children	2.1	1.8	1.7	1.8	1.5	1.6	1.8	1.6	1.9
Average no. of resident kin	0.0	0.2	0.2	0.1	0.1	0.3	0.3	0.1	0.3
Average no. of servants	0.2	0.1	0.1	0.2	0.2	0.2	0.3	0.4	0.6
Average no. of inmates	0.0	0.1	0.1	0.0	0.1	0.2	0.1	0.1	0.1
Mean household size	4.2	4.1	4.0	4.0	3.8	4.1	4.2	4.1	4.6

Category	Professionals/administration/privileged			Cuenca[a]			Rural[b]	
	1724	1800	1844	1724	1800	1844	Eighteenth century	1800–1850
Average no. as head or spouse	1.8	1.9	1.7	1.67	1.69	1.69	1.71	1.77
Average no. of children	1.8	1.7	1.9	1.59	1.40	1.61	1.57	1.59
Average no. of resident kin	0.4	0.2	0.4	0.20	0.19	0.26	0.09	0.09
Average no. of servants	1.2	0.8	0.7	0.45	0.42	0.35	0.18	0.12
Average no. of inmates	0.1	0.1	0.1	0.03	0.10	0.11	0.00	0.00
Unidentified				0.01				
Mean household size	5.3	4.6	4.8	3.95	3.80	4.02	3.57	3.58

Notes [a] Households of the clergy, widows and heads with no profession are included in the totals for Cuenca.
[b] The data here refer to rural households from the province of Cuenca. See Reher (1988a: 154).

(Reher, 1980). These households were mostly made up of children and their parents (82 per cent); other groups played a negligible role in determining household size. Co-resident kin represented between 5 and 6 per cent of total size, though their numbers did increase markedly in 1844; servants with between 8 and 11 per cent of the MHS declined in importance in 1844, and inmates had an entirely negligible effect on Cuenca households.[10]

Mean household size varied appreciably among different social groups, mainly owing to the importance of domestic service and, to a lesser extent, to the presence of kin in households. This was most evident in the well-to-do households where the presence of resident kin was numerically more important than in any other group, as was that of servants.[11] In all groups the nuclear family was the principal component of the MHS, an importance which was still greater in rural areas where it could be considerably more than 90 per cent of the total household. Despite some changes by social group or in the components of the household, stability was the keynote; overall household size hardly changed and was similar to levels found in other western European towns.[12]

Households were most frequently headed by married couples (69 per cent throughout the period), and, if not, they were normally headed by widows. This can be seen in the data shown in Table 6.3, in which I have estimated the marital status of household heads at three different dates.

This, of course, was a function of marriage and remarriage patterns in an urban population in which remarriage was typically easier for men than for women. Marital patterns can also be seen in the age difference between spouses which was never large (3 years), though it varied substantially by social group (Table 6.4). Since age at first marriage was approximately 1.5 years higher for men than it was for women, it can safely be concluded that in remarriage the age spreads or potential marriage partners were not normally very large.

Interesting differences emerge when we examine the data by social group since it is evident that the well-to-do sectors of urban society showed considerably greater age differences and, perhaps more important, a considerably higher variance than did other groups. In certain groups in society the age range of eligible partners was

---

10 Institutional populations are not included in this analysis of household size.
11 In the case of the professionals/privileged the presence of domestic servants represented 23 per cent of household size in 1724, but was reduced to 15 per cent by 1844.
12 For example, in the city of Rheims mean household size in 1802 was 3.88 (Fauve–Chamoux, 1983: 479–480).

Table 6.3. *Marital status of household heads at three different dates*

Marital status of head	1724	1800	1844
Married	70%	69%	69%
Widower	5	4	7
Widow	18	15	15
Never married male	2	9	6
Never married female	3	3	3
Unknown male	2	1	0
Total	100%	101%	100%

Table 6.4. *Age difference between spouses*

	1800		1844	
Category	Mean	Standard deviation	Mean	Standard deviation
Agricultural/ day laborers	3.2	6.1	2.1	6.6
Industry/ artisans	2.1	6.3	1.6	6.3
Services	3.7	8.3	4.3	6.6
Professional administration/ privileged	4.2	8.8	2.9	7.2
Total	3.1	7.3	3.0	6.9
Rural[a]	2.7	6.5		

Note [a] Rural figures are based on eighteenth and early nineteenth century data. See Reher (1988a: 159).

considerably less restricted than in others, and suggests that the marriage market worked differently by social category. An indication of this is the fact that not only was the age difference greatest among the professionals and privileged, but also that the percentage of men at least 10 years older than their wives or that of those at least 10 years younger was also highest in this group. This is brought out in the data in Table 6.5.

Clearly wealth helped lessen many of the typical life cycle restrictions on nuptiality. Much the same can be said for the rural areas of the province even though throughout the nineteenth century age differences at marriage were considerably smaller than in the town.

Table 6.5. *Percentage of men at least 10 years older or younger than spouse*

	1800		1844	
Category	Professionals/ administration/ privileged	Cuenca	Professionals/ administration/ privileged	Cuenca
% men at least 10 years older than spouse	19.6	12.1	19.4	16.8
% men at least 10 years younger than spouse	3.8	2.4	5.0	3.4

From a numerical standpoint, children were the single most important component of the household. With certain variations by social
status, residence or date, they generally represented around 40 per
cent of the total MHS during the period under study.[13] If we include
only those homes with children present as our denominator, then the
average number of children per household with children is 2.5 in 1724,
2.3 in 1800 and 2.6 in 1844. Even allowing for the distortion caused by
using women of all ages in our sample, this relatively small number is
the consequence of the demographic constraints on reproduction in
Cuenca, together with the patterns of mobility and nuptiality holding
in the town. Demographically, high infant and child mortality, with
only 52 per cent of children born surviving until five years of age,
meant that there were seldom more than three or four children at
home, even when a mother was 40 years old.[14]

As important as these basic demographic constraints were for the
number of children present in the household, they only tell part of the
story. The mobility of children could and did play an important role in
determining their numerical importance at home. This was especially
true in an urban population which, as we shall see, was characterized
by extremely high general levels of population mobility. The risk of a
child's leaving the parental home could occur at any time, though it
became especially high in towns after 10 years of age. Due to the

[13] In 1800, 36 per cent of household size was composed of offspring, and in rural areas in
both the eighteenth and the nineteenth centuries it was 44 per cent (Reher, 1988a:
154).

[14] In rural areas of the province, the peak period of offspring presence in the household
came when the head (male) was between 40 and 49 years of age and hovered around
an average of 2.7 children per household. The overall average in rural areas was 1.8 as
opposed to the 1.6 in town (Reher, 1988a: 185).

Table 6.6. *Percentage of children residing in parental household, by age*

| | Cuenca | | | | Rural | |
| | 1800 | | 1844 | | Both sexes | |
Age group	male	female	male	female	Eighteenth century	1800–1850
0–4	92.1	96.7	91.6	98.4	95.8	93.2
5–9	96.1	93.8	90.8	91.7	94.7	94.3
10–14	81.1	79.7	88.0	88.1	84.7	92.1
15–19	65.8	50.9	76.3	51.7	72.3	84.0
20–24	43.8	25.1	50.2	30.9		

Sources: Cuenca, Municipal listings; rural data, Reher (1988a: 167).

impossibility of controlling for people entering or leaving town, it is very difficult to measure this sort of mobility, but the data in Table 6.6 are sufficiently robust to confirm the significant existence of this type of movement of children.[15]

The mobility of the very young arose mostly from their presence as nephews or nieces in other kin households. In town, this might well involve living with members of the clergy. At these ages, there was little difference between urban and rural behavior. After 10 years of age, however, the situation changed substantially and mobility in towns became much more intense and took place at younger ages than in rural areas.[16] It can safely be said that in town there was a distinct probability that young people, especially young girls, would spend one or more years of their adolescence in other, often non-kin households.[17] This sort of mobility was stimulated by a lively job

---

[15] At least in the case of the women, the data in the Table overestimate the true level of mobility since they do not allow for the influx of female domestic servants into town, especially after 15 years of age. Conversely, I have been unable to estimate the numbers of urban-born who left town for one reason or the other. This tends to minimize my figures, though not enough, I feel, especially with women, to offset the first effect completely. The data in Table 6.4 represent the percentage of children of a given age group who are living with their parents. For similar and earlier work, see Wall (1978).

[16] As was suggested earlier, our cross-sectional examination tends implicitly to increase proportions of children not living at home unless, of course, out-migration of children equalled or surpassed in-migration of the children of other families as well as the number of children "left behind" by emigrant families. This same problem also makes direct comparison with rural results very difficult. Richard Wall (1978: 196) found higher levels of adolescent mobility in Colyton which was related to the importance of servants as a life-cycle activity in England.

[17] Since there is a built-in bias in our sample, it is impossible to estimate the exact probability of this occurring.

market, especially for domestic servants, and the often imperious need to supplement family incomes or to save for a projected wedding. The levels of local mobility were probably considerably lower among the well-to-do sectors in town where income supplementing was not a life-long necessity, though the nature of my data does not allow me to measure this.[18] Whatever the reason, the net effect was to reduce sharply the numbers of children residing in family households.

The life cycle nature of this mobility was, with certain noteworthy exceptions, similar for both urban and rural families. In both areas numerous families used the potential labor power of their children as supplementary sources of income either for the parental households themselves or as a means of saving for impending marriages. In town, however, there were far fewer opportunities for gainful employment within the household and thus children often resided elsewhere, working most often in domestic service, a job which was far more important in urban society than it was in the countryside where there were very few servants (Reher, 1988a: 172–175). Even though servants in Cuenca came primarily from rural areas, a propensity to enter into this sort of activity was certainly higher among urban youths, especially at younger ages. Ultimately adolescents from both worlds participated in the same sort of economically motivated mobility. Marriage put an end to this sort of itinerant life, and this occurred only after 20 years of age when the youths had spent a good number of years in the local job market.

As already seen, the presence of co-resident kin was at times appreciable Cuenca households, and was certainly greater than in rural areas. The presence of kin in Cuenca households was apparently unrelated to inheritance or any other sort of property devolution. At least in part, their presence was a type of hidden labor which was used by urban households instead of other sources of non-family manpower (servants). Mostly though, the data from Cuenca suggest that, more than anything else, the presence of co-resident kin in households proved the existence of family ties which transcended households.

Lateral and descendant extension was the typical form of complexity in Cuenca households. Siblings formed the most numerous groups of co-resident kin, followed by nieces and nephews and parents (Table 6.7). Sons- and daughters-in-law were only present in small numbers

---

[18] This is because a considerable proportion of the migrants from the lower classes would be living in the homes of the wealthy and thus the data for both groups would not be comparable.

Table 6.7. *Co-resident kin (%)*

Kin category[a]	1724	1800	1844
Parents	11.9	14.2	19.2
Siblings	37.4	25.8	35.9
Nieces/nephews	30.8	32.9	24.4
Sons-/daughters-in-law	2.6	7.1	7.9
Grandchildren	8.4	16.8	7.4
Other/unknown	8.9	3.2	5.2
Total	100.0	100.0	100.0
Number	228	155	365

Notes [a] Kin category refers to the familial relationship either to the household head or to his spouse.
Sources Cuenca, Municipal listings.

and, as we will see shortly, were mostly there as temporary co-residents immediately subsequent to their marriages. Grandchildren played a small but consistent role in kin households. Most kin were females as sex ratios of 53 in 1800 and 52 in 1844 indicate. Sex ratios in rural areas of the province during the nineteenth century were similar (Reher, 1988a: 171).

The circumstances under which kin were present in the household are not difficult to imagine. Co-resident parents were normally widows (rather than widowers), though some evidence does exist that they also circulated among kin households (Reher, 1988a: 227–230). Co-resident siblings were generally spinsters, though occasions do exist in which an adolescent brother or sister remained at home temporarily after the death of both parents and before they were able to get married and set up their own households. Nieces and nephews, whose presence could be quite significant, normally came from kin groups in rural areas and took up temporary residence in town. Classic host households here would be those of the clergy. Very few cousins, uncles or aunts were present in Cuenca households.

Rural and urban data present some interesting contrasts. Whereas in both areas co-resident siblings were the most important group, widowed parents play a far more important role in the countryside. Co-residence was far less important in rural areas, as is suggested by the fact that during the nineteenth century only 4 per cent of all households had co-resident kin in the rural areas as opposed to over 12 per cent in town (Reher, 1988a: 169). The practice of sending young

Table 6.8. *Co-resident kin: a numerical evaluation*

Category	% of total population			% households with co-resident kin		
	1724	1800	1844	1724	1800	1844
Agricultural/ day laborer		3.6	4.3		9.1	12.6
Industry/ artisans		3.7	6.6		10.4	16.6
Services		2.8	5.6		10.1	16.5
Professionals/ administration/ privileged		4.6	7.9		14.4	23.9
Clergy		18.7	16.4		37.5	26.7
Others[a]		4.5	8.1		9.8	17.9
Total	5.5	5.0	6.5	12.2	12.6	17.1

Notes [a] Includes households headed by widows and persons whose professions are not listed.
Sources Cuenca, Municipal listings.

children to town into kin households seems to underline the observed differences.

Social groups showed markedly different patterns of kin co-residence. Co-residence was strongly and positively related to social status both in 1800 and in 1844 (Table 6.8). This presence could become quite significant, especially for the clergy and, to a lesser extent, in households of other privileged groups in society. These patterns of co-residence were the proof of the existence of enlarged family ties and seem to have little specific economic significance. While co-resident siblings or nieces and nephews might well have been veiled domestic service, especially in the houses of the wealthy, the same cannot be said for other kin components of Cuenca households (parents, grand-children etc.). In fact I am inclined to believe that the greater proportions of co-residents in homes of the wealthy were related more to the spatial and economic capability of those households to receive other kin, albeit in a temporary fashion, rather than to any economic usefulness of those kin.

Domestic servants were the other important group in Cuenca households. Throughout the period under study, they were present in approximately 25 per cent of all households and represented around 10 per cent of the entire population (Table 6.9). Between 1800 and 1844 the numbers of servants diminished considerably in all social groups,

Table 6.9. *Sex ratios and numerical importance of domestic servants*

Profession of household head	sex ratio			% of total population			% households with co-resident kin		
	1724	1800	1844	1724	1800	1844	1724	1800	1844
Agricultural/day laborer		300	103		1.8	3.6		7.3	11.3
Industry/artisans		36	29		4.2	3.6		13.3	11.9
Services		84	30		11.0	12.5		31.6	36.5
Professionals/administration/privileged		21	13		16.3	13.9		44.4	49.2
Clergy		34	6		52.3	40.6		92.9	80.0
Total[a]	62	35	24	11.2	11.0	8.9	25.9	25.4	25.6

Note [a] Includes households headed by widows and males whose profession is unknown.

Table 6.10. *Age distribution of domestic servants*

Date and category			males	females
Cuenca				
1800	% <	20	43.0	34.0
	% <	30	75.0	73.5
1844	% <	20	40.8	39.2
	% <	30	84.5	83.6
Rural				
1800–1910	% <	20	27.3	33.9
	% <	30	59.1	71.9

	Both sexes			
	% < 20		% < 30	
	1800	1844	1800	1844
Agricultural/day laborer	50.0	43.8	75.0	86.1
Industry/artisans	42.1	40.6	73.7	84.4
Services	42.9	34.8	88.6	85.2
Professionals/ administration/ privileged	36.8	47.4	83.3	89.8
Clergy	28.7	16.9	59.8	56.3
Total	36.4	39.4	73.9	83.8

Sources Cuenca, municipal listings; rural data, Reher (1988a: 174–175).

though the same pattern was not paralleled by the proportions of households with servants. The result was a 17 per cent decrease in the mean number of servants per household (0.42 to 0.35), and was probably the consequence in part of the increase in offspring and co-resident kin during the same period. Servants were most likely to be present in the households of the privileged, especially the clergy, where they represented a large percentage of the total household size. Domestic service began some time in late adolescence and lasted intermittently until people were of marriageable age. Nearly 40 per cent of all servants were under 20 years of age and only between 15 and 25 per cent were above 30 (Table 6.10).[19] Clearly the "life-long

---

[19] This is a considerably younger age distribution than that found in Austrian towns for approximately the same period (Schmidtbauer, 1983).

servant" was an exception. In fact, only in households of the clergy could appreciable proportions of servants not involved in life cycle activity be found.

By and large servants were female, except among farmers where male servants were clearly used as additional farm labor. In all the other groups, however, they were involved primarily in household labor activities. There is indirect evidence that to a certain extent children and servants were considered as mutual substitutes. Table 6.11 shows percentages of different types of household structure for households with and without servants throughout the period under study. It shows that there was a far greater likelihood that a household without children would have servants. Even though small sample size keeps us from being able to see the extent to which these decisions were based on the age of the head or that of his children, the existence of a substitution effect between children and servants is quite evident.

It would seem that families with the economic means showed a greater tendency to have servants to perform household chores in the absence of their own offspring. This sort of effect was stronger among households headed by the elderly and among families with no adolescent daughters (servants were mostly female) than for, say, young couples. Co-resident kin seemed to play little or no role in these economic decisions; the presence of both kin and servants is positively correlated. Kin, then, must have circulated among Cuenca households for reasons other than economic utility and, much as I suggested before, should be interpreted as indicators of the existence of larger kin units which transcended individual households. Many of these points are vital to an understanding of the Cuenca family and will crop up repeatedly in the rest of this chapter.

A different perspective on household and family

As long as one maintains a rather rigid synchronic approach, the family and household in Cuenca reveal certain clear patterns which persist with little change for well over one hundred years. Household structure was overwhelmingly simple, though showing a slight tendency towards greater complexity with the passing of time. It was composed of a stable nucleus, the head and his wife, surrounded by three considerably more mobile groups: children who tended to leave home early, co-resident kin and finally a domestic service which was young and tended to stay in the household only for short periods of time. While its structure was apparently unaltered, a closer look at

Table 6.11. *Household structure by presence or absence of domestic servants*

Structural category	1724		1800		1844	
	with servants	without servants	with servants	without servants	with servants	without servants
Solitaries/no family/simple, no children	44.0	29.8	46.9	29.8	37.0	28.8
Simple households, with children	46.9	65.1	43.0	62.5	47.8	60.3
Complex households, with or without children	9.1	5.1	10.2	7.8	15.1	10.9
Total	100.0	100.0	100.1	100.1	99.9	100.0

Source: Cuenca, municipal listings, 1724, 1800, 1844.

the Cuenca households would seem to indicate that at least some of the elements contained therein might have been anything but stable.[20]

Yet this is about as close to the immensely complex reality of the family as a cross-sectional synchronic analysis can take us. Does it reveal all, or even most, of the reality of the family or the co-resident domestic group? A number of studies have already pointed to the fact that the household was in a continual state of development. The basis of the system was the household itself and its perpetuation, rather than merely the personal life cycle of its head, especially in the case of societies where more complex household structures predominated (Czap, 1983; Sieder and Mitterauer, 1983; Fauve-Chamoux, 1984). Evidently this would not be the case in an urban environment where the absence of the stem family is unquestionable. Nevertheless, here too it would seem reasonable to assume that, even though it is unlikely that long-term traceable evolution occurred in more than a limited number of cases, Cuenca households also underwent changes and these had a decisive influence on people's perception of what family and household were, as well as on the domestic economy itself within an urban context. If this is so, the role played by marriage, birth or death, or kin circulation in this family cycle becomes a matter of considerable importance. Moreover, if spatial aspects are also introduced into this discussion, we may be able to get closer to a more adequate understanding of the larger and more complex reality of the family. Is there any evidence in historical documentation to show the existence of a pool of kin relationships which transcends or, rather, underlies those of individual household boundaries and which, under certain circumstances, could give the larger kin group a discernible economic and social dimension (Anderson, 1971: 141; Laslett, 1988)? While for anthropologists this aspect of kin relationships is fundamental to their understanding of society, to what extent can it be shown to exist within a historical context?[21]

While definitive answers will evidently not be forthcoming, dynamic household analysis will confirm some of the more accepted ideas about the nature of the household, while discrediting others. This analysis is based on the nominiative record linkage of individuals, complemented by the construction of some genealogies. The data are taken from parish registers and from the annual series of listings of inhabitants (*padrones*) which exist for the town of Cuenca

[20] Parts of the following section were originally published in Reher (1987).
[21] See Pitt Rivers (1961: ch. 7), Kertzer (1984), and Lisón-Tolosana (1966: 151–157) (1983 paperback edition).

between 1843 and 1847.[22] Even though the time-span in which it is possible to trace individual families closely is short, it enables one to observe life cycles in great detail over that period. Individual genealogies have been illustrated by ideographs in which each household can be visually followed from one year to the next.[23]

Marriage and household formation
Marriage not only led to procreation, it set in motion a series of events which were essential to the survival of society. For example, marriage-related mobility was a source of the redistribution of active population and, as long as it was accompanied by some sort of devolution of property, heralded the foundation of separate family economies and perhaps even the diversification of previously existing ones. This indeed seems to be the case in much of western Europe where marriage implied certain property transfers in dowries or other types of marriage portions, and led to neo-local household formation. In so doing, marriage became an important catalyst for individual and household development, stimulating change not only for the newly-weds, but for their households of origin as well. Careful examination of the marriage and household formation patterns in Cuenca will illustrate a number of these points.

Marriage was closely related to household formation. The similarity of proportions married and proportions of household heads in each age group (Table 6.12) indicated that a marriage invariably led to the

[22] For a more detailed description of this data base, see the Appendix.
[23] Key to ideographs:
    –Triangles represent males; circles, females.
    –Bonds of direct kinship are shown by unbroken lines; between husband and wife the line is underneath the figures, and among siblings it is above the figures.
    –Indirect as well as suspected bonds of kinship are shown by broken lines. Indirect lines are also used to denote bonds of kinship which will eventually exist within a household, but which do not at a given moment.
    –Members of the household who are not members of the family are shown in the upper right hand corner of the rectangle.
    –A rectangle is used to indicate a household.
    –The head of the household is indicated by the presence of a darkened triangle or circle.
    –When there is movement of individuals between two households of the same figure, this movement is indicated by a directional line. The same holds true when the household changed physical location.
    –Household development is pictured yearly and thus one can normally visualize the same household in, say, five successive years. In order to convey more clearly the great mobility of kin, at any given moment all the potential members of a household are portrayed. Those actually present are represented by unbroken lines, and the ones who will be present or have been present before are shown by broken lines.
    –Every individual in an ideograph receives a number. In the corresponding note to the figure, personal data on the indicated individual are supplied.

Table 6.12. *Marriage and household formation in Cuenca*

Age group of household head	Proportion of males in age groups who are:		
	Ever-married[a]	Household heads	Ever-married household heads
		1800	
15–19	2	2	1
20–24	30	27	27
25–29	55	53	48
30–34	72	75	70
35–39	75	85	75
40–44	82	89	82
45–49	83	89	83
50–59	89	97	88
>60	78	93	77
		1844	
15–19	0	1	0
20–24	22	20	19
25–29	56	53	51
30–34	77	82	83
35–39	80	84	78
40–44	87	93	87
45–49	91	88	88
50–59	93	95	93
>60	79	86	73

Note [a] Includes the currently married and the widowed.

formation of an autonomous household.[24] Just what factors might condition this undeniably close relationship which is the principle reason for the predominance of simple family households in Cuenca? Firstly it is quite clear that household formation in Cuenca depended on two factors: the necessary economic independence and a prior marriage (single individuals rarely formed households, especially in younger age groups). Richard Smith (1981a: 618) has spoken of a "basic minimum living standard" as an essential element for marriage in a country like England. In the case of Cuenca, there is no reason to doubt that this "basic minimum living standard" was also a *sine qua non* for marriage. However, attaining this standard was not exceed-

---

[24] Here I am following the ideas of John Hajnal (1982).

ingly difficult where income did not necessarily have anything to do with property transmission.

In the year 1821/2, 83 per cent of Cuenca's families lived in rental housing, and this fact can be corroborated from wills where urban property was seldom transferred.[25] The average rent charged in this housing was 319 *reales* per year, though the median was considerably lower (172 *reales*). Even though rents could vary a good deal from year to year and people tended to change their living quarters frequently in search of optimum prices, these levels probably held true for the middle of the century. Urban income is more difficult to estimate, owing mainly to the fact that data available do not generally distinguish between net and gross income, or between wages and other sources of income. A small sample for 1837 shows agricultural earnings at an average of 788 *reales* per year; day labourers, 237 *reales* per year; artisans 810; services, 898; and professionals and public administrators, 1,833 *reales* per year. This gives an average wage per family head of between 800 and 900 *reales* per year. Unfortunately, this estimate is contradicted by 1841 data, which suggest that average income (*utilidades*) for resident households heads, excluding clergy and non-residents, was just under 650 *reales* per year.[26] Despite the uncertain nature of these data, and accepting a liberal margin of error, it is reasonable to conclude that the normal Cuenca family lived in rented living quarters which cost between one-fifth and one-third of the income of the household head. In this situation, it is conceivable that a young married couple would be able to have more or less ready access to cramped though adequate housing subsequent to marriage, even if one concedes that either or both of the parental families were likely to contribute some sort of monetary or other material support to the newlyweds as was the case in rural areas (Reher, 1988a: 215–227).

The custom of neo-local household formation subsequent to marriage, which by the beginning of the eighteenth century was typical of central and southern Spain, was common enough to be considered a normative cultural behavior pattern, and can be summed up in the aphorism *casada casa quiere* (a married woman wants a house) (Pitt Rivers, 1961: ch. 1). Originally the result of inheritance practices, economic needs and opportunities, housing and land availability, and other cultural attitudes, it had probably been in existence for centuries. Even though these economic and social factors might still influence the

[25] Some years earlier, during the middle part of the eighteenth century, 93.2 per cent of all families lived in rented housing (Troitiño Vinuesa, 1984: 69–70).

[26] Archivo Municipal de Cuenca, Relaciones de Utilidades, legajos 1199, 1200 (for 1820) and 1193, 1197 (for 1841). See also Troitiño Vinuesa (1984: 170–171, 207–221).

timing of marriage and were the basis of the system, to a large extent cultural behavior patterns seemed to transcend individual decisions. Moreover, these patterns could only be facilitated in an urban setting characterized by a lively rental housing market, relative job mobility and greater opportunities for income diversification than in rural areas. A noteworthy aspect of the situation in Cuenca is that, even though both marriage and household formation took place at a moderately young age, simple family structures predominated, as they had seemingly done so since at least the early eighteenth century, when age at marriage was younger (22.3 as opposed to 24.5 for women). This seems to be as least partially out of step with the early-marriage/complex household patterns recently pointed out by Hajnal (1982) and Wall (1983b: 16), and certainly has no place in Laslett's geographical distribution of household forms in Europe (Laslett, 1983: 525–531).

A closer look at the Cuenca data, however, reveals that the link between marriage and household formation was not necessarily an immediate one. This can be seen in the example of the family of Galo Peñalver, a 45-year-old merchant, and his wife Escolástica Pérez (Figure 6.1).[27] During the five years in which the development of the family can be followed, one of the children gets married, resides temporarily with her spouse within the household and subsequently leaves in order to establish residence in the immediately adjacent parish. This example suggests that perhaps our original impression of a strict relation between marriage and household formation should be revised in favor of a situation in which, indeed, marriage did lead to household formation, but frequently did so after a period of time in which the couple lived in the home of one of the parents. This dynamic is not contrary to what might have been suspected, and has been noticed by other researchers (Laslett, 1983: 532).

Just how frequent was this type of temporary co-residence and how long did it normally last? A systematic check of the data reveals that this form of sharing was not at all uncommon among the newlyweds. Between 1843 and 1847, 49.9 per cent of a small random sample of first marriages (72 in total) indicate co-residence of some kind in the household of one of the two parental families. In fact, this proportion should probably be substantially raised, since any form of co-residence ending before the next annual listing of inhabitants would go unnoticed. This practice might have affected well over half of all

---

[27] The ideographs used in this and other examples portray a good number of behavior patterns. In the interests of clarity, however, my comments will be limited to those aspects strictly pertinent to my discussion.

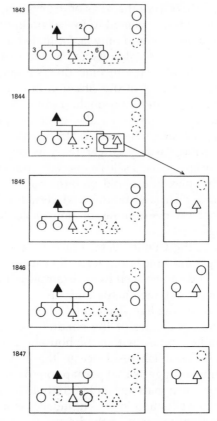

Figure 6.1 The family of Galo Peñalver

1. Galo Peñalver, merchant, married, 45 years old 2. Escolástica Pérez, his wife, 42 years old 3. Terese Peñalver, daughter of Galo Peñalver, single, 25 years old 4. Juana Peñalver, daughter of Galo Peñalver, single, 23 years old 5. Juan Peñalver, son of Galo Peñalver, single, 21 years old 6. Isabel Peñalver, daughter of Galo Peñalver, single, 16 years old 7. Antonio Dominguez, husband of Isabel Peñalver, 26 years old 8. Doretea García, wife of Juan Peñalver, 21 years old

first marriages and thus should be considered a common behavior pattern.

It is not easy to estimate the duration of these stays, since material on the very short stays is unavailable and we cannot usually follow couples for more than a couple of years. Nevertheless, during the period under study, we were able to locate 22 couples who could have had a maximum three year stay in a parental household. Of these, 41 per cent stayed one year, 23 per cent, two, and slightly more than one-third stayed all three years.[28] Once again one must emphasize two aspects of these data: the samples are too small to be more than mere indications of the temporary nature of co-residence, and the yearly intervals of listings tend to minimize the importance of shorter stays. It is interesting to note that momentary co-residence in the parental household of newly weds accounts for 43 per cent of all multiple family households in the town. Helping young couples just after their wedding, either with gifts, sharing table with them or by letting them stay in one of the parental households was a common practice in rural areas of the province and in many other areas of Europe (Reher, 1988a: 216–222). Evidence from Cuenca itself suggests that these same traditions existed there as well.

These data raise further questions regarding our understanding of the concept of neo-local household formation. Where it predominates, as is certainly the case in Cuenca, it suggests that the separate household is a fundamental organizing characteristic of society. Yet the fact that this physical separateness is not immediately established upon marriage, whether for economic or for personal reasons, or for a combination of both, is noteworthy because it could suggest that while neo-localism is a physical reality, in social and economic terms it may mean only a relative separation of households and kin groups. Just when are ties with the parental household completely severed, and to what extent do neo-local formation patterns contribute to the weakening of kinship ties and the diversification of economic activity? The matter is not simple and unfortunately the Cuenca data do little to clarify more than the risks inherent in an overly simplistic conceptualization of the household and the family. Yet one might speculate that a dual situation ensues upon marriage, in which household and kin group economies, kinship and support systems, authority structures, etc., coexist in a rather ambivalent fashion until the parental generation disappears entirely, or becomes too old or too distant to effectively exert any influence on the behavior patterns in separate households. Even then close relatives would continue to make the family web a permanent conditioning factor in society.

Marriage could also influence the household in other ways, as will become apparent in the following example (see Figure 6.2) which represents several branches of the same Fuero family. In 1843 this family was made up of four siblings living in two households: Manuela, 30 years old and single; Baltasar, 26 and single; Jacinto, 21 and single; and Matilde, 26 and married to Norberto Toledo who was the same age. In 1843 the first three lived together in the parish of El

[28] Laslett (1988: 155) suggests that this practice was probably quite common in Europe.

Salvador, on the Calle del Pósito, located in the lower part of town. Matilde lived with her husband and their two children in the same parish on the Calle del Corralejo, less than 75 meters from the other branch of the family. In 1844, Manuela Fuero married Nemesio Foreada and this marriage initiated the breaking up of the household on the Calle del Pósito. In the year of the marriage, Baltasar Fuero left what was probably his parent's home and took up residence with his married sister on the Calle del Corralejo. In this same household, the eldest daughter had died, but the loss was compensated the following year by the birth of another daughter. In 1846 both of the unmarried brothers of the Fuero family, Baltasar and Jacinto took up residence in the same household on the same street as their sister Manuela and her husband who, meanwhile, had a new addition to the family. Finally in 1847 Manuela had another child and moved to the adjacent parish on the Calle del Retiro, which was really only about two blocks away from the Calle del Pósito. Jacinto meanwhile had married Ramona Templado, who had been a maid in a different household in 1845 and 1846. At this juncture, at least in the opinion of the list compilers, Jacinto became household head instead of his older brother.

This is indeed a fruitful example, for, apart from illuminating many aspects of family mobility, it enables us to see other consequences of marriage which often appear in the Cuenca documents. In 1844 the marriage of the Fueros' elder sister initiated the breakup of the original family nucleus which had survived what we can only assume was the death of the parents just before 1843. At this point the siblings who still remained unmarried stayed on in the family home and this is how we find them in 1843. However, the marriage of one of them, in 1844, initiated the departure from the home of both siblings, one immediately and the other shortly thereafter. In this manner, the household became simple in structure. Similar behavior might also be expected in the third household, since in 1847 one of its members married, though unfortunately the chronological limitations of the documentation make it impossible to follow this development. The tendency for the marriage of one of the members of a family to begin the disintegration of the household was not uncommon and suggests that marriage initiated a period of transformation within a household, both for the married couple and for the remaining members of the family. The dynamic, whereby autonomous households of simple structure were created, was initiated at the moment of marriage, though it normally took some time before it became a reality. I can only lament the fact that the documentation sheds little light on the most crucial question as to the causes behind the exit from the household either of the rest of

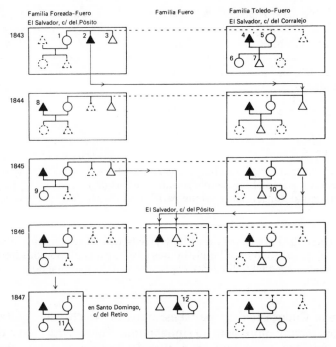

Figure 6.2 The Fuero family

1. Manuela Fuero, elder sister of the Fueros, single, 30 years old 2. Baltasar Fuero, brother of Manuela Fuero, shoemaker, single, 23 years old 3. Jacinto Fuero, brother of Manuela Fuero, single, 20 years old 4. Norverto Toledo, shoemaker, married, 25 years old 5. Matilde Fuero, wife of Norverto Toledo, 26 years old 6. Felipa Toledo, daughter of Norverto Toledo and Matilde Fuero, 2 years old 7. Agustin Toledo, son of Norverto Toledo and Matilde Fuero, 1 year old 8. Nemesio Foreada, day labourer, husband of Manuela Fuero, 29 years old 9. Eugenia Foreada, daughter of Nemesio Foreada and Manuela Fuero, 1 year old 10. María Toledo, daughter of Norverto Toledo and Matilde Fuero, 1 year old 11. Juan Foreada, son of Nemesio Foreada and Manuela Fuero, 1 year old 12. Ramona Templado, wife of Jacinto Fuero, 20 years old

the family or the newlywed couple, though evidently the cultural constraints underlying neo-local household formation patterns and ultimately tending to make structures simple were at work. What is certainly clear is that the role of marriage as catalyst of change looms once again as a key variable for the adequate understanding of Cuenca households.

Kin-related residential patterns and support systems
When establishing autonomous households, young couples showed a marked tendency to do so in the immediate vicinity of at least one of the parental households. It should be remembered that at this time the

Table 6.13. *Residence patterns of newlyweds, Cuenca 1843–1847*

Parental household	Men (%)	Women (%)
Same parish	35	33
Same district	11	13
Other district	32	32
Outside Cuenca	22	22
Total	100	100
Number	93	
At least one parental household in same parish (%)		57.0
At least one parental household in same district (%)		74.0
Both parental households in same parish (%)		11.8

Note These data are based on 93 newlyweds who at some point subsequent to marriage abandon their family homes to set up an autonomous household. The calculations refer to the relative proximity of the parental home to the new household.

town of Cuenca had 12 parishes, most of which were quite small, seldom having more than 400 inhabitants. This is why I have decided to divide the town into four districts of approximately the same population size.[29] In this way residential proximity can be measured in two complementary manners. The sample used is based on young couples, where at least one of the partners can be followed from his or her parental home to a separate residence within the city (Table 6.13). The results suggest that both men and women normally preferred proximity to the parental household to any other place of residence. What is more, numerous examples, some of which are given in this chapter, indicate that this pattern seemed to persist, albeit with diminishing intensity, throughout the life course of many families.

The ultimate significance of this behavior is, or course, a matter of speculation, though it speaks for the continued existence of family ties which spanned the separate nuclear households. The availability of family property or family-related job opportunities, and the desire or need to establish a network of family residences which might facilitate a mutual support system, or a combination of both, tended to reinforce the larger kin group. These factors are a token of the continued, though possibly weakened, existence of wealth flows,

[29] Two of the districts have but one parish, another has four and the final one has six. The maximum distance between any two households within the same district is approximately 150–200 meters.

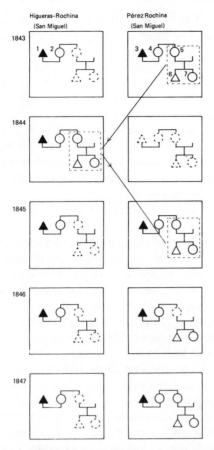

Figure 6.3 The Rochina family

1. Juan María Higueras, painter, married, 35 years old 2. Ursola Rochina, his wife, 40 years old 3. Pablo Pérez, notary, married, 34 years old 4. Ceferina Rochina, his wife, 42 years old 5. Joaquina Rochina, Ceferina's sister, married, 34 years old 6. Justo Pérez, son of Joaquina, 7 years old 7. Lucia Pérez, daughter of Joaquina, 7 years old

even after the apparent breaking up of the original household (Caldwell, 1981; 1982). Examples of this type of support system in Cuenca are not difficult to find.

The importance of spatial transfers and residential proximity which characterized a great number of urban households can be seen in Figure 6.3. Here we can see three sisters occupying two households. One of the sisters, Ursula Rochina, is married to Juan Higueras; another, Ceferina Rochina, is married to Pablo Pérez, and the last, Joaquina Rochina, has two children in her charge, but her husband does not appear. The two households are located in the same parish, separated by only one street. In 1843 Joaquina and her children live with Pablo Pérez, her brother-in-law, and Ceferina, her sister. In 1844, however, Pablo and Ceferina have left the town for unknown reasons and Joaquina and her children have moved in with the other sister. In 1845 once again all have returned to the household of 1843. In 1846 Joaquina has also left the town, leaving her children under the protection of her sister, only to return in 1847. Here the support offered by the family for the sister, whose husband is absent for unknown reasons, is evident, as is the fact that the family members live within close proximity, a reality which indubitably facilitates the sort of support seen in this example.

Familial relations within an urban context can, however, affect more than two households. Figure 6.4 gives a clear idea of this considerably more complex system of circulation of kin among different households. In the example one can observe three branches of the Martinez family. The first one, which lives in the parish of El Salvador, is the family of María Garcia, widow of a Martínez brother. In 1843 she is living with her three children, one boy and two girls. The second branch is the family of Domingo Martínez who, in 1843, lives with his wife and a nephew and niece at the other end of town, in the parish of Santiago. The third branch is the family of María Millán who is also a widow of one of Domingo's brothers and who lives in the parish of El Salvador, quite near her sister-in-law, María Garcia. We are able to follow the development of what is left of the families of three brothers whose households are distributed throughout the entire town. In 1844 the eldest nephew abandons the house of Domingo Martínez for a destination outside town, and he is replaced by a younger nephew. It is impossible to know whether these nephews were siblings or not. In 1845 the remaining nephew and niece leave the home of Domingo Martínez, who remains alone with his wife. The niece moves into the house of her aunt, María Garcia, in the parish of El Salvador, thereby indirectly suggesting the possible existence of a fourth branch of the Martínez family. The nephew moves into the home of his mother, María Millán, who in 1845 had moved into the parish of San Gil which is located in the middle part of the town. In 1846 the two persons who had abandoned the household of Domingo Martínez return to their uncle's home. Moreover, a daughter of María Garcia abandons home, while María Millán is once again living with her daughter but has moved to the immediately adjacent parish of San Andrés. Finally, in 1847, a niece leaves the home of Domingo Martínez for an unknown destination outside town, and another one enters.

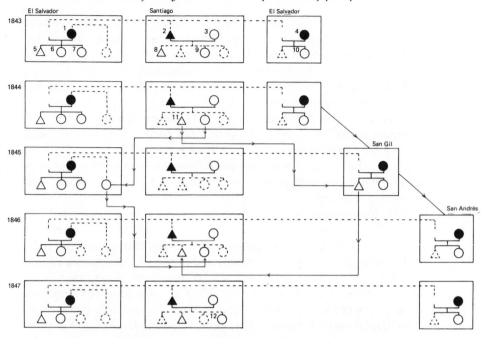

Figure 6.4 The Martínez family

1. María García, widow of a Martínez brother, 44 years old 2. Domingo Martínez, brother-in-law of María García, surgeon, married, 44 years old 3. María López, wife of Domingo Martínez, 26 years old 4. María Millán, seamstress, sister-in-law of Domingo Martínez, widow, 45 years old 5. José Martínez, sheep-shearer, son of María García, single, 16 years old 6. Ventura Martínez, daughter of María García, single, 15 years old 7. Irene Martínez, daughter of María García, single, 10 years old 8. Nicanor Martínez, nephew of Domingo Martínez, single 19 years old 9. Francisca Martínez, niece of Domingo Martínez, single, 11 years old 10. Gavina Martínez, daughter of María Millán, single, 11 years old 11. Santos Martínez, nephew of Domingo Martínez, single, 18 years old 12. Isabel Martínez, niece of Domingo Martínez, single, 26 years old

In this example the circulation of children and kin among the different households of the same extended family is more than evident and attests to the fact that, at least in this case, it would be wholly misleading to consider these are three separate families when, at least insofar as familial aid and mutual dependence are concerned, it is one family living in three distinct households. Furthermore, this mobility of household members takes place within the framework of a more general spatial mobility which was quite intense in Cuenca. It is unfortunately impossible to follow the histories of those individuals who left the town, though we feel that they may well have continued those same sorts of familial exchanges with relatives living in other villages.

In an attempt to summarize many of the aspects which have been pointed out regarding family behavior patterns in Cuenca, a considerably more elaborate genealogy taken from reconstituted families has been constructed. In it a family, the Recuencos, is followed over a period of five generations from the latter part of the eighteenth century until approximately 1860. This example eloquently illustrates the tendency of different kin households or family branches to maintain close spatial relations within the town, thereby suggesting once again that, despite the fact that households themselves are separate, the family ties among the different households of the same family were an ever-present conditioning factor of human and economic relations.

The protagonists of Figure 6.5 are several branches of what was surely the same Recuenco family. There is José Recuenco who is from the nearby village of La Melgosa, another José, though he could also be the same person who remarried, and finally, Antonio, who is most likely José's nephew and who also comes from the same village. Though these links cannot be established with total certainty, the coincidence of the surname and the minute village of origin (about 300 inhabitants) would indicate that they were relatives. On the other hand we have the family of Manuel Recuenco, which probably stems from the same Recuenco family since his father Gregorio was also from La Melgosa. During a short period at the end of the eighteenth century, all of these members of a single kin group are in Cuenca and take up residence in the upper part of town, in the parish of San Pedro. How might these branches of the same family have reached Cuenca? Unfortunately it is impossible to know with any certainty, though the marriage patterns of the distinct members of the family are revealing. In all cases the Recuencos married women from neighboring villages, all of which bordered on the municipal limits of the town of Cuenca, and all moved to the city, forming a large familial nucleus in one neighborhood of town. It is as though movement to town depended on kin links which, once established, conditioned residential patterns. Of course a good deal of what has just been affirmed is speculative, though my experience with highly permeable and fluid relations between the town and its own hinterland, as well as the continual movement in and out of town of different household members, leads me to believe that these conjectures are not at all unreasonable.

Once inside the town, the genealogy reveals that the families, or rather the different branches of the same family, tended to develop within a very restricted zone of the upper part of town. It could be alleged that the use of the parish registers of only seven of the 12 urban parishes (the only ones in existence) introduces a bias in the sample in favor of a greater spatial concentration. However, since not a single member of the family could be located outside the upper part of town in any one of the yearly listings of inhabitants between 1843 and 1847, the observed concentration seems to have sound evidence. Aside from the children who either died or left town, geography exerted a great influence on the patterns of residence of the extended Recuenco family. In the genealogy, the parish of birth of each child is noted in the upper portion. A brief glance shows that the vast majority were born in the parish of San Pedro and those who were not, came from the immediately adjacent parishes. It is useful to note that in Cuenca the distance between the parish church of San Pedro and that of Santa Cruz, the most distant point of residence of this family, is less than 200 meters.

While the fact that the family tended to reproduce itself within a limited compass is most noteworthy, so also is the slow but progressive extension of the original limits. All first generation descendants, without exception, were born in the parish of San Pedro. In the second, however, of the 30 children we can follow, three were born in neighboring parishes and another two outside town. In the third generation, of the 36 children who appear in the genealogy, a little over half (19) were born in the parish of San Pedro. This continued dispersion of the family is, in fact, a logical variant of a system in which the family tended to reproduce itself within the same district. A good number of the children of these families sought their respective spouses among residents of the same district in such a manner that distinct family networks became intertwined, thus creating a situation which itself stimulated this type of local marriage and residence pattern. Naturally the system was not perfect since a number of the children did leave town, as indeed might have been expected. Yet the fact that family members seldom took up residence in other districts confirms the specific nature of this behavior.

To sum up, in the example, several branches of the same family, originally from a nearby village and after a generation or more of marital relations with persons from villages equally close to the capital, came to Cuenca for unknown reasons at more or less the same moment. All took up residence in the upper end of the town and entered either into agriculturally related activities (tenant farmers) or became day laborers, occupations that they had probably held in their villages of origin. Once in the town, this kin group ended up reproducing itself within a well-defined zone. Property transmission and jobs, as well as the marriage patterns of the children who wed

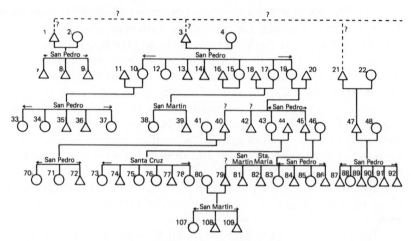

Figure 6.5 The Recuenco family

1. José Recuenco, from La Melgosa 2. María Fiel, his wife, from Palomera 3. José Recuenco, from La Melgosa, nephew of (1) (or possibly the same person as 1) 4. Teresa Pintor, his wife from Palomera 5. Manuel Recuenco, from Villardolalla, kin of (1), father from La Melgosa (same as 1 and 3) 6. María Dolores Herraiz, his wife, from Cuenca.

Family of José Recuenco (1) and María Fiel (2) 7. Francisco Santiago, born in parish of San Pedro, 1767 8. Pablo Miguel, born in San Pedro, 1770 9. Marcela María Josefa, born in San Pedro, 1772

Family of José Recuenco (3) and Teresa Pastor (4) 10. María Quintina, born in San Pedro, 1775; married in 1797 11. Bartolomé Titos, husband of María Quintina Recuenco 12. Perona, born in San Pedro, 1777 13. Fulgencio José, born in San Pedro, 1779, 14. Juan, born in San Pedro, 1780 15. Fausta, born in San Pedro, 1782, married in 1805 16. Aniceto Peñalver, husband of Fausta Recuenco 17. María Petra, born in San Pedro, 1784, married in 1807 18. Apolonio Liborio Calvo, husband of María Petra Recuenco 19. Simeón Ramón, born in San Pedro, 1786 20. Blasa Mayordomo, wife of Simeón Ramón Recuenco 21. Antonio Recuenco, from La Melgosa, nephew (?) of José Recuenco. 22. Julia Checa, his wife

Family of Manuel Recuenco (5) and María Dolores Herraiz (6) 23. Leandro José Manuel, born in San Pedro, 1806 24. Hilaria Juárez, wife of Leandro Recuenco 25. José Pelegrín Santiago, born in San Pedro, 1808 26. Antonia Olivares, wife of José Pelegrín Recuenco 27. Francisca Saturia, born in San Pedro, 1811, married in 1838 28. Victorino Cañas, husband of Francisca Saturia Recuenco 29. Ignacia Senena, born in San Pedro, 1813 30. Teresa, born in San Pedro, 1817, married in 1843 31. Clemente Gimeno, husband of Teresa Recuenco 32. Jacinta Josefa, born in San Pedro, 1819

Family of Bartolomé Titos (11) and María Quintina Recuenco (10) 33. Victoriana Tomasa, born in San Pedro, 1798 34. Francisca Basilisa, born in San Pedro, 1803 35. Atanasio Benito, born in San Pedro, 1805 36. Julián Felipe, born in San Pedro, 1811 37. María Isidora, born in San Pedro, 1811

Family of Apolonio Liborio Calvo (18) and María Petra Recuenco (19) 38. Aquilina Juana Teresa, born in San Martín, 1819 39. Ezequiel Anselmo, born in San Martín, 1811

Family of Simeón Ramón Recuenco (19) and Blasa Mayordomo (20) 40. Ignacio, born outside Cuenca, married 41. Francisca Barreña, wife of Ignacio Recuenco 42. Matías, born outside Cuenca 43. Sebastiana Petra Regia, born in San Pedro, 1820, remarried in 1848 44. Juan Torrecilla, husband of Sebastiana Recuenco 45. Joaquín, born in San Pedro, 1822 46. Nemesia Recuenco, his wife, from Villardolalla, possibly related to husband

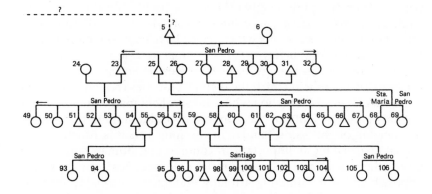

Family of Antonio Recuenco (21) and Julia Checa (22) 47. Faustino, born outside of Cuenca 48. Juana Saiz, wife of Faustino Recuenco.
Family of Leandro José Recuenco (23) and Hilaria Juarez (24) 49. María Ruvigis, born in San Pedro, 1825 50. Lorenza Justa, born in San Pedro, 1827 51. Esteban, born in San Pedro, 1829 52. Pablo Ignacio, born in San Pedro, 1832 53. Anastasia Teresa, born in San Pedro, 1835 54. Nicolás, born in San Pedro, 1838 55. Paula Pérez, wife of Nicholás Recuenco 56. Victoriana Benita, born in San Pedro, 1843 57. Pedro, born in San Pedro, 1846
Family of José Pelegrin Recuenco (25) and Antonia Olivares (26) 58. Rafael, born in San Pedro, 1827 59. Plácida Moya, wife of Rafael Recuenco 60. Isabel, born in San Pedro, 1830 61. Manuel Ignacio, born in San Pedro, 1833, 62. Marta Luis, wife of Manuel Ignacio Recuenco 63. Clemente Ignacio, born in San Pedro, 1837 64. Patricio Eugenio, born in San Pedro, 1840 65. Petra, born in San Pedro, 1842 66. José María, born in San Pedro, 1850 67. Marcelino, born in San Pedro, 1852
Family of Victoriano Cañas (28) and Francisca Recuenco (27) 68. Plácida María Josefa, born in Santa María, 1839 69. Estanisla Ascensión, born in San Pedro, 1842
Family of Ignacio Recuenco (40) and Francisca Barreña (41) 70. Eusebia Isabel, born in San Pedro, 1851 71. María Rosa Natalia, born in San Pedro, 1852 72. Nicolás Gregorio, born in San Pedro, 1855
Family of Juan Torrecilla (44) and Sebastiana Recuenco (43) 73. María Catalina Valentina, born in Santa Cruz, 1848 74. Francisco Santiago, born in Santa Cruz, 1850 75. Petra Dámasa Asunción, born in Santa Cruz, 1853 76. Francisca María Rosario, born in Santa Cruz, 1856 77. Pedro Antonio, born in Santa Cruz, 1858 78. Amalia Rufina, born in Santa Cruz, 1859
Family of Joaquín Recuenco (45) and Nemesia Recuenco (46) 79. Ramón, born outside Cuenca 80. María González, wife of Ramón Recuenco 81. Ruperto José, born in San Martín, 1843 82. Domingo José, born in Santa María, 1846 83. Liboria Filomena Josefa, born in San Pedro, 1850 84. Angel Benito, born in San Pedro, 1852, 85. Silveria Josefa, born in San Pedro, 1854, 86. Joaquín, born in San Pedro, 1856
Family of Faustino Recuenco (47) and Juana Saiz (48) 87. Alejandro Hipólito, born in San Pedro, 1847 88. Victoriana Florentina, born in San Pedro, 1849 89. Raimundo Luis, born in San Pedro, 1851 90. María Magdalena, born in San Pedro, 1852 91. Praxedes, born in San Pedro, 1855 92. Lucas, born in San Pedro, 1857
Family of Nicolás Recuenco (54) and Paula Pérez (55) 93. Eusebia Camila, born in San Pedro, 1868 94. Alejandra Ascensión, born in San Pedro, 1869

persons from the same neighborhood, contributed to this situation. Underlying these social and economic considerations, there existed other family-related reasons which might have been still more important in influencing behavior. The spatial development one can observe from the genealogy probably owes its specific form to the existence of a family in which the distinct branches created systems of mutual assistance: a situation whose most salient manifestation might be that spatial mobility of children and other kin among the distinct households of the same family. In the long run this function was probably every bit as important in conditioning human behavior as were other social and economic factors. Nonetheless, owing to the impossibility of maintaining a totally endogamic nuptiality (that is, within the same district), and owing to the existence of abundant rental housing in town which encouraged frequent changes in residence, the restriction of the family to one neighborhood slowly began to break down. Even so, it is instructive to observe how the family members still showed a marked tendency to take up residence in the adjoining parishes rather than on the other side of town.

The aforementioned examples of spatial proximity all point to the existence of a geographically separated kin group in nineteenth-century Cuenca. Could family economies also have existed beyond individual households? While there is no ready answer, it is quite likely that both individual household and kin group economies were present.[30] The extremely complex property arrangements implied by local inheritance practices (with both urban and rural possessions and mutual ownership of considerable property), the temporary absences of family members probably moving out of town to tend rural holdings and the circulation of kin among different households of the same family are all indirect indicators of a situation which most likely complemented, rather than negated, the reality of individual household economies. The existence of the support system is unquestionable and has its most visible manifestations in the circulation of kin (widowed parents, unmarried brothers and sisters, etc.) which itself, along with the temporary residence of newlyweds, was the principal source of household complexity. Could such a wider form of family also have influenced personal behavior patterns such as nuptiality or fertility, as Caldwell might suggest (1981: 177–179)? Evidently my data do not provide an answer, though they do help pose the question.

[30] This was certainly the case in the rural areas of the province (Reher, 1988a; 1988b: 68–71).

Household permeability

Circulation among related households was, in fact, an example of more general economically motivated movement. The imperious need to diversify family economies led to surprisingly high levels of movement of household members, and this had important effects on individual co-residential units. In order to gauge its intensity, an attempt has been made to measure familial movement in a systematic manner. An Index of Familial Change (I_{fc}) has been devised, which measures the propensity to change of different household components in any given person-year. In order to minimize what, for my purposes, are the potentially distorting effects of migration of entire families, which may or may not have affected their size and structure, only those which were present at the same address for the entire 1843–1847 period were included in the sample.[31] The results can be found in Table 6.14 and are divided by general kin category within the household, as well as by the occupation of the head. They bear eloquent witness to the fact that, despite the somewhat special nature of the families used as examples, change in structure and size was a common experience for Cuenca homes. Out of every hundred person-years, almost 15 family members were likely to enter or leave these homes in a given year and only 17.9 per cent of all households were able to survive the four years of possible movement (1844–1847) with no change at all. Forty per cent of those changes were due to births or deaths and 60 per cent represented actual movement of children and other kin.

Household members were affected unequally by this propensity to change. The core of the home, the head and his wife, was in fact quite stable and most changes detected were caused by the death of one of them. Offspring showed considerably higher levels of movement, as nearly one in five entered or left the home in any given year, and, even if one excludes births and deaths, levels of movement continue to be close to 12 moves per 100 children-years in the household.[32] Finally it

---

[31] The data I have register those present, those leaving and those entering the household in any given year between 1843 and 1847. The following procedure was used to derive the total person-years at risk (the denominator of the I_{fc} equation). Since movement was only possible in four years (1844–1847) (in 1843 everyone was present by definition), all those person-years present from 1843 to 1847 were reduced by 20 per cent. Furthermore I have supposed that all entries or exits from the household between 1844 and 1847 were, in fact, six month stays in that household (on the average). Thus the total person-years at risk were represented by the sum of entries and exits divided by 2 plus the total years present multiplied by 0.8. See the Appendix for further explanation.

[32] The concept of children-years measures the time during which a particular population of children was at risk of experiencing a particular event.

Table 6.14. *Index of familial change (I_{fc}): Cuenca 1843–1847*

Occupational category	Head, wife	Sons	Daughters	Resident kin (lateral + upwards)	Resident kin (downwards)	Total household	Total person-years at risk
Agricultural/day laborers	0.014	0.200	0.213	0.580	0.550	0.152	2,251
Industry/artisans	0.027	0.149	0.194	0.513	0.612	0.140	1,211
Services	0.035	0.155	0.162	0.634	0.792	0.140	850
Professionals/administration/privileged	0.020	0.150	0.096	0.329	0.504	0.121	846
Others						0.248	121
Total	0.021	0.176	0.186	0.517	0.560	0.144	5,279

$$I_{fc} = a + b/(c + \left(\frac{a+b}{2}\right))$$

where: a = number of entries into household, 1844–1847, b = number of exits from the household, 1844–1847, c = total number of years present in household, 1843–1847 (five years) × 0.8.

Note If births and deaths were not included in the I_{fc} for sons and daughters, the new I_{fc} would be 0.117 for sons and 0.123 for daughters.
Percentage of households which undergo no change between 1843 and 1847: 17.9.

was the other resident kin who showed the most intense patterns of circulation. Thus, we are presented with a household which, as had been suspected, was composed of a relatively stable nucleus, surrounded by ever more unstable elements. These include children who entered or left home either for strictly demographic events, marriage or, more likely, for work-related reasons. It is through these mobile children that, at least in part, households were able to diversify family economies, as for the most part they entered the labor force. Circulation of other kin is also susceptible to an economic interpretation and would affect both the sending and the receiving households: it is not uncommon to find young girls, for example, listed as "servant" one year and as "niece" the next. However, it would seem unwise here to belittle the role of the kin group as a network of mutual aid. I_{fc} levels of older kin not only reflect higher mortality among that group, but also the probable movement of widowed mothers and fathers among the households of their own children, and between the urban household and the family roots and possessions both in the town and in the surrounding villages. At least in rural areas of the province, the custom of widow and widower circulation among the homes of their children was widespread (Reher, 1988a: 227–230). It should also be pointed out that prevailing in- and out-migrational levels in the town affected over 10 per cent of the population per year of every age-group and sex, independent of occupational status. Such intense migration must have been, at least partially, an expression of urban–rural familial and economic links.

Finally it is revealing to see how occupational status could at times sharply affect propensity to movement. The clearest example can be seen in the daughters of the more well-to-do groups in town who were much less likely to move into and out of their households than were the daughters of day laborers or artisans. Once again the requirements of family economies proved to be a major conditioning factor in urban households, as the daughters of the lower classes often had little choice but to enter domestic service for a period of time.[33] In this manner, circulating kin become the agents of both the kin group and the diversification of family economies. On the one hand, when these kin moved among different familial households they became the physical manifestation of the existence of a larger family group. On the other, general movement of kin, either to another kin household, or perhaps more likely as servants or employed laborers in non-related urban and rural households, helped to supplement family incomes

---

[33] Unfortunately the reduced size of the sample advises against deriving important conclusions from the data on other co-resident kin.

either by bringing wages directly home, accumulating savings for marriage, or simply by ceasing to be consumers of family income. Prevailing I_{fc} levels for children attest to the fact that very few, if any, spent their entire adolescence at home, and this reality had definite implications not only for family economies but for the general process of socialization as well, where many of the formative years of life were likely to have been spent outside the parental home.

Household structures: a life course analysis

By now the enormous complexity of these "simple" Cuenca households should be evident. In this section still further implications of family realities will be explored. The nature of household structures will be analyzed in terms of the life-cycle experience of the household itself. In order to give this discussion a point of departure, a final genealogy is presented which also summarizes a number of points which have already been addressed. This genealogy is really not a genealogy in the strict sense of the word, since only one or two generations of the same family enter into our field of observation. In it the movements of all the children of Juan José Cantero and of María Santos García have been monitored between 1843 and 1847. All of these children were born in the parish of San Pedro between 1799 and 1820, and all of those surviving to 1843 resided in the parish at least temporarily between 1843 and 1847. Of course it is evident that this example is quite exceptional, since it enables us to follow the development of a family practically in the absence of any migratory movement either within the city or outside it. Yet it is hoped that the special nature of the family will illuminate many of the characteristics which have been mentioned throughout this study.

A brief description of its contents will be given, though a complete understanding requires a close perusal of Figure 6.6 Of the 13 children born to Juan José and María Santos, four died at a young age and the rest ended up marrying in the parish of San Pedro. Between 1843 and 1847 Matías, the eldest, lived with his wife and three children in the parish. María Margarita, the second child, also lived in San Pedro with her husband and five children. The parental home was occupied in 1843 and 1844 by Juan José Cantero, whose wife had already died, together with his third child, Florentino José, his wife and daughter, and with Dionisio, his youngest son. In 1845, Feliciano, the second youngest son, entered the household from outside town. In 1846 Feliciano married and moved in with the family of his wife, Basilisa Vindel, in the parish of San Pedro, remaining there until at least 1847. In 1847 Dionisio married María Soria and took up residence in the same district of town, while his father, Juan José Cantero, moved into the household of his now-deceased brother, Gil Cantero, who had been living with Juan José's daughter Remigia, her husband Tiburcio Nielfa, and their seven children. Blas Andrés, the fourth child, who had married María Peñalver in 1825, in 1844 lived with his second wife, Cipriana Martínez, and their three children who were joined by a fourth in 1847. The second daughter, Remigia, married Tiburcio Nielfa in 1837 and in 1843 lived, together with her husband and seven children, in the home of her uncle Gil Cantero and her 68-year-old aunt Antonina. In 1844 Gil died and Tiburcio became head of the household. Finally in 1847 Remigia's father, Juan José Cantero, entered the household of his daughter while, incidentally, Tiburcio's brother lived with his mother and three brothers in the same parish just one block away. This home was most probably the original Cantero residence some three generations earlier and, during the period under observation, was occupied by distinct elements of the families of three of the original Canteros: Juan José, Gil and their younger sister Antonina. Headship belonged to the eldest brother and, upon death, descended to the son-in-law of the second brother, rather than to Juan José's sister Antonina. When Juan José entered the household, his son-in-law continued to retain headship, probably owing to his age and to the fact that he was the prime economic producer of the household. Continuing my description of Figure 6.6, we find the third daughter of Juan José Cantero and María Santos Garcia, Tiburcia, who in 1838 had married Domingo Herraiz and during the period under examination lived on the outskirts of San Pedro in the household of Domingo's parents and brother. Finally, Baldomera, the youngest daughter, married Domingo Martínez in 1840 and lived with her husband and daughter in the same parish in 1843, leaving the town thereafter.

Despite the exceptional nature of this example, it obliges us to reassess the importance of nuclear family households in pre-industrial Cuenca. Here, owing both to the fluidity of interchange of members of the same kin group among the different households and to the concentration of all familial branches within a single district of the city, the family in Cuenca seems more like a vast and complex network of interdependent households. It might be pointed out that this example could have been considerably more complex if the genealogies of the families which eventually became related to the Cantero-Garcías through marriage had been included. And yet, if household structure is calculated for all the years within our field of vision, 62 per cent of the households are simple. Naturally, proportions of complex households do not make up 38 per cent of the total in the town, yet it is

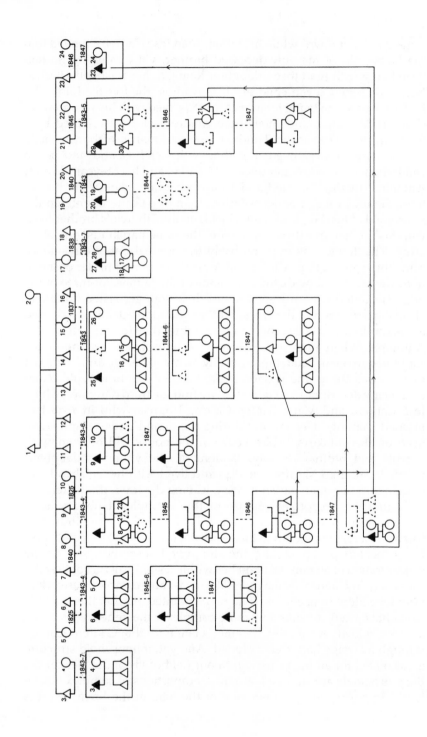

Figure 6.6 The family of Juan José Cantero and María Santos García

1. Juan José Cantero, horticulturist, widower, 78 years old in 1843 2. María Santos García, his wife 3. Matías Cantero, day laborer, born 1799 4. Josefa Casas, his wife, 44 years old in 1843 5. María Margarita Cantero, born in 1801 6. Pablo González, her husband, day laborer, 48 years old in 1843 7. Florentino José Cantero, horticulturist, born in 1803 8. María Viejobueno, his wife, 30 years old in 1843 9. Blas Andrés Cantero, horticulturist, born in 1805 10. María Peñalver, his first wife 11. Juan José Cantero, born 1806, died 1807 12. Francisco Cantero, born 1808, died 1809 13. Juan Angel Cantero, born 1810, died 1811 14. Pedro José Cantero, born 1811, died 1824 15. Remigia Cantero, born 1813, died 1868 16. Tiburcio Nielfa, her husband, shoemaker, 32 years old in 1843 17. Tiburcia Cantero, born in 1815 18. Domingo Herraiz, her husband, horticulturist, 25 years old in 1843 19. Baldomera Cantero, born in 1818 20. Domingo Martínez, her husband, day laborer, 27 years old in 1843 21. Feliciano Cantero, born in 1820 22. Basilisa Vindel, his wife, 24 years old in 1843 23. Dionisio Alonso Cantero, horticulturist, born in 1820 24. María Soria, his wife, 18 years old in 1843 25. Gil Cantero, landowner, uncle of Remigia Cantero (15), widower, 80 years old in 1843 26. Antonina Cantero, sister of Gil (25) and Juan José (1), single, 64 years old in 1843 27. Ignacio Herraiz, horticulturist, father of Domingo Herraiz (18), 56 years old in 1844 28. María Molina, his wife, 58 years old in 1844 29. Juan Vindel, farmer, widower, 62 years old in 1843, father of Basilisa Vindel (22) 30. José Vindel, his son, farmer, widower, 30 years old in 1843.

Table 6.15. *Household complexity by age of household head*

Age group of household head	Years at risk	(a) Percentage multiple	(b) Percentage extended	Percentage complex (a+b)
Under 30	265	1.5	17.5	19.0
30–39	500	1.6	12.8	14.4
40–49	600	2.7	11.8	14.5
50–59	580	4.7	11.6	16.3
60 and above	375	7.5	12.3	19.8
Total	2,320	3.6	12.3	15.9

Note Based only on households present at the same address for five consecutive years (1843–1847). Age of head based on 1843 listing. The calculations include all families at risk and thus include solitary and no-family households.

difficult not to feel that both this fluidity and the geographic proximity is present, though perhaps to a lesser degree, in the immense majority of Cuenca families.

A simpler, though perhaps just as pertinent, point concerns the life-cycle determinants of household structure in Cuenca. To what extent does the propensity to complexity change with the age of the head? Some years ago Lutz Berkner (1972: 406) analyzed household structure by age of head in order to point out the existence of the stem family in eighteenth-century Austria, despite predominantly simple structures. While the meagre proportions of complex family households in Cuenca suggest that the stem family was a rarity, it seems reasonable to suppose that the life cycle of the head did exert a strong influence on structure.

In order to explore this further, families present continuously between 1843 and 1847 have been used in order to calculate the percentage of years households were multiple, extended or "complex" (a combination of the first two categories).[34] The results confirm the life-cycle influence underlying household structures (Table 6.15). Even though complex households never represented more than 20 per cent of the total, young and old heads were more likely to preside over complex households. While differences are not extreme – indicating that the likelihood of living in a complex house-

[34] The proportions of complex households are slightly higher in Table 6.15 than in Table 6.1 (which is based only on the 1844 listing) owing to the fact that only families present for the entire period are considered. This tends to exclude both smaller and more mobile families as well as single widows and widowers, thus increasing relative complexity.

hold was present at all points of the life cycle – the noticeable concentration in the under 30 and over 60 age groups reveals patterns of household formation and dissolution. Moreover, extended family households are more prevalent among the young, whereas multiple ones increase with age. The explanation for this lies in the nature of the different manifestations of complexity in Cuenca. For younger heads, complexity comes primarily from circulating parents or other kin who were seldom married. Here, for example, the widowed mother or the single niece would be the most common elements of complexity. On the other hand, as has been pointed out earlier, 43 per cent of all multiple family households were the result of temporary co-residence of married children and the possibility of this occurring increased as the parents became old enough to have married children. Where average male age at marriage was approximately 25 years and a woman's child-bearing period was concentrated during the first 15 years of married life, this sort of temporary complexity was most likely to occur when the father was between 50 and 65 years of age.[35] The validity of the exercise I have just gone through is confirmed by the data of Table 6.15, where it is interesting to observe how percentages of multiple households begin to increase in those age groups in which parents were old enough to have married children.

The importance of nuclear families also clearly diminished with the increasing age of the household head. In the 1844 listing of inhabitants, nuclear households occupied 81.3 per cent of the total in the under 30 age group; 77.8 per cent between 30 and 45 years of age; and 73.6 per cent for households headed by persons above 45. Yet this decrease was only partially owing to the above-mentioned increase in complexity, and can be more readily attributed to a marked gain made by solitary households which at younger ages represented 1.3 per cent of all households in 1844, but which increased to 18.0 per cent in households headed by persons above 60. The town abounded with solitary widows and widowers who might spend part of their old age circulating among the homes of their married children, but who were mostly obliged to live by themselves. These percentages are considerably below the 25–35 per cent of solitary households headed by people above 60 in the rural areas of the province during the nineteenth and twentieth centuries (Reher, 1988a: 183). Since life expectancy would seem to have been roughly similar in both rural and urban areas, this pattern was a reflection of a greater tendency among widows and

---

[35] In the early nineteenth century in Cuenca the mean age at first marriage for women was 24.3 years and the mean age at last childbirth was 38.9 years.

widowers to reside in kin households in the town rather than in the countryside.

What then were the probabilities of structural change in Cuenca households? Much of the data presented thus far would seem to suggest that, despite the apparently unchanging proportion of simple households over the long run, the likelihood of living in a complex structure might have been quite high. A more systematic check of these families, however, is necessary if solid conclusions are to be drawn. This analysis only focuses upon transformation in general household structures as defined by Laslett and Hammel (solitary, no-family, nuclear or simple, extended, and multiple) and therefore does not include changes within general categories so prevalent in type 3 households. In other words, the estimates here tend to minimize the importance of structural transformation. The results contained in Table 6.16 confirm my idea that structural change was a common occurrence for most households. Just over 10 per cent changed their basic structure in any given year, the change being largely independent of the age of the head, with the slight exception of those headed by people under 30. If one takes a slightly different approach and measures the propensity to change at least once in 4 years, more than a quarter of all households underwent at least one significant change in structure. These rates of change can be converted into a proxy estimate of structural transformation over a hypothetical 40-year life span of the head (25–64). In so doing it becomes evident that an average household would undergo 4.1 transformations in basic structures over its 40-year existence.[36] These changes were not at all related to births, deaths or the circulation of children since, generally, such events only implied different types of simple households and did not affect the basic structural categories.

Based on my own Cuenca data, the 26 per cent of families whose structure did change between 1843 and 1847, did so 1.6 times over that period. Even though it is impossible to estimate the percentage of households that had consistent structures over the entire life cycle, we can safely assume that it was only a small minority. In other words, the likelihood that a resident of Cuenca would live in a number of different types of household throughout his life was quite high. Moreover, given that most of the transformations shown in Table 6.16 are from

[36] This is done by multiplying the different yearly rates by the number of years in each age group and adding the products, much as a total fertility rate is calculated. Here the yearly rates over the four-year period are assumed constant over the five- or ten-year age groups. This, of course, implies turning period into cohort analysis, a theoretically unsound though frequently used practice among historical demographers.

nuclear to complex and vice versa, and supposing that the percentages shown in Table 6.15 are indicative of life-cycle expectations, then it can be reasonably assumed that a normal household would be complex in structure for as many as six to seven years of its 40-year hypothetical existence.[37] Naturally there were also households and persons with little or no experience in complexity, though they were a minority. If I include in my analysis less general changes in composition and structure resulting from births, deaths and spatial mobility, then levels of fluidity increase sharply, affecting nearly 40 per cent of all Cuenca households in any given year.

This transient nature of household structure adequately reflects the life experience of children who were born into Cuenca families, or of the young married couples starting them. Every three years or so some family member would enter or leave the household. During the early years, these changes would probably be the result of demographic events or the circulation of widowed parents. As the household head aged, this type of movement was replaced by the circulation of children of kin, or of the spouses of his own children, who might temporarily reside in his home immediately after marriage. Only later in life were nuclear and complex households likely to become type 1 (solitaries). A clear-cut developmental cycle is not readily discernible because there is a free mixture of all structures in every age group.

The property transfers so essential to the evolution of peasant households in rural Europe, especially where more complex family forms predominate, are simply nowhere to be found (R. Smith, 1984b). The little real estate involved was normally transferred at the death of either of the parents, and was for the most part located in rural areas. It could only have an indirect, though possibly quite significant, impact on the urban household economy, and less so on its formation, structure and dissolution. It certainly does mean that in most cases the urban family was never completely cut off from the rural world, just as the in- and out-migrational levels mentioned earlier seem to indicate. Within an urban context, though, skills or jobs would be transferred from generation to generation, although such transfers did not take place at any one point in a person's life. Other economic and familial factors strongly conditioned the household, but many of these, especially those not directly tied to demographic events, did not undergo clear-cut life-cycle evolution.

---

[37] This estimate is based on the assumption that practically all households undergo several structural changes (Table 6.16) and that the proportions of complex households shown in Table 6.15 (15.9 per cent) are indicative of life-cycle expectations ($0.159 \times 40 = 6.36$).

Table 6.16. *Propensity to structural change by age of household head*

Age of head	Families	Years at risk (×4)	Changes in structure	Families with at least one change in four years	c/b × 100; annual rate of structural change	d/a × 100; propensity to change at least once in four years
	(a)	(b)	(c)	(d)	(%)	(%)
Under 30	53	212	28	17	13.2	32.1
30–39	100	400	37	23	9.3	23.0
40–49	120	480	49	29	10.2	24.2
50–59	116	464	46	31	9.9	26.7
60 and above	75	300	31	21	10.3	28.0
Total	464	1,856	191	121	10.2	26.1

Note Based only on households present at the same address for five consecutive listings (1843–1847). Age of head based on 1843 listing. Changes in structure *only* include changes in the five general structural categories.

If one changes the analytical perspective and takes a more socio-logical approach based on the individual, one sees that a permeable and mutable household, strictly dependent on its own economic needs and thoroughly integrated into a larger family network, was a fundamental experience for nearly all residents of Cuenca. Since this basic reality was essential to the life experience of even the youngest of children, it had probably long since been considered as normative cultural behavior. While neo-local household formation and nuclear families were evidently central to people's life expectations, they were mediated by a great number of other factors and certainly, in social and economic terms, complemented rather than excluded a larger and more pervasive reality.

Conclusions

Simple household structures, reduced size and neo-local household formation patterns were apparently the norm in eighteenth- and nineteenth-century Cuenca. At least that is what the statistics seem to tell us. Yet by scratching at the surface the deceptive nature of this kind of statement has become evident. Even though the overwhelm-ing majority of people might have lived in households which were simple in structure, it is equally true that over people's life experience they would reside a number of times in extended and multiple households, just as they might well be obliged to live alone if they survived until a fairly old age. Naturally this does not imply the existence of the stem family as a major, or even a minimally sig-nificant, form of social organization within an urban context. However, it certainly does question the true meaning of simple households, especially where they too were but passing forms of co-residence. This line of reasoning could even lead us to question the extent to which the predominance of simple households implied the presence of separate and exclusive household economies or weak kinship ties.

One of the conclusions which inescapably, albeit indirectly, comes from the Cuenca data is that of the existence of a kinship network which transcended individual households. The distance which separ-ated the different households of enlarged families was both dim-inished by their appreciable proximity and bridged by the circulation of kin. In fact, outside the nuclear family, kinship ties could well be conceived as a pool of relationships used on a voluntary basis which acquired both social and economic meaning (Pitt Rivers, 1961: ch. 7). It would be hazardous to affirm that the larger kin group had common economic interests, much as complex families did in other areas of Spain and Europe, though one might suspect that some of this might have existed, especially with commonly owned rural property held by urban families (Hansen, 1977: 44–47, 99; Sieder and Mitterauer, 1983: 341–344).[38] Unfortunately, except for occasional wills, the documentation used speaks very little of this sort of extended family economy. Yet, at the very least, it can be affirmed that, since many co-resident kin were disguised servants, the circulation of kin was an integral part of both the sending and the receiving household economies. Another vital aspect of the extended kinship network was that it could act as a source of assistance to any of its members. While it is clear that not all kin movement was directed to other family households, it is unquestionable that a good deal of it was and, as several examples have borne out, much of it made use of the family network as a type of social welfare system. Conclusive proof of this is not available, but how else, for example, can we explain what at least seems to be the tendency of widowed parents to circulate among the households of their married children?

As a number of historians have pointed out, all family systems in which the nuclear household was the normative ideal ended up imposing considerable difficulties on individuals who, for one reason or another, were not able or did not desire to live alone. This has been called the "nuclear hardship" hypothesis and certainly seems applicable to the situation of Cuenca where nuclear families and neo-local household formation patterns were the norm.[39] Human welfare in Cuenca was provided by a combination of public institutions and family networks. Poor Laws did not exist in Spain, but for cases of extreme need the collectivity played a key role in the care for displaced persons. This care was materialized through certain charitable organizations such as the foundling homes or hospitals and through the distribution of alms to the poor. At least prior to the nineteenth century, these were normally funded by the Church. For the more frequent and less desperate cases of social displacement, however, the kin group was the key welfare institution in Spain. This has been the case in Cuenca where we have seen how a larger kinship network, which transcended nuclear households and seemed to function on a

---

[38] This type of partially shared economy certainly existed in larger family units of the rural areas of the province (Reher, 1988b).

[39] For more on this hypothesis, see R. Smith (1984b: 73; 1988), J. Smith (1984: 439), and Laslett (1988: 153–156).

volitional basis, was a key source of mutual aid and support. The family was an essential element of social cohesion.[40]

The existence of separate households integrated mainly by the immediate family was, nevertheless, an uncontested reality in Cuenca. Here, marriage was the key element in a system in which neo-local household formation patterns prevailed and new households were formed almost invariably by fission. Marriage was the moment in which, at least temporarily, households might become complex in structure, as the newlyweds took up residence in one of the two parental homes. Yet their stay did not usually last long, and these same households once again became simple in structure and small in size as the new couple set up its own residence. Sometimes, however, the opposite dynamic occurred, and the other family members ended up leaving the home. Household complexity was a recurring but temporary reality for the people of Cuenca. In other words, household and family in Cuenca can best be understood within the context of the generalized mobility which took place in and around the town, together with the existence of a larger sense of family. In many ways its reality, at least apparently, had little to do with the stem-family/nuclear-family debate in which inheritance, land and peasant economies played a major role in determining family forms.

This, of course, does not negate the importance of the household economy. Independently of whether a larger family economy may or may not have existed, the autonomous household economy was one of the pillars of the system. Its specific nature, though, determined that it had only a marginal influence on basic household structure. It should be remembered that when family members left the home before marriage, they did not always circulate among other familial households, but, more frequently, found jobs in non-related families as servants or in some other income-producing activity. Both forms of movement were really variants of the imperious need to diversify family economies (Laslett, 1983: 546).

Herein lies the key to an economic understanding of the system, because the need all families had to diversify income was met outside their place of residence. This helps to explain why the structure itself

---

[40] Aged peasants who were interviewed in the province of Cuenca invariably stated that all families felt it their social obligation to care for their widowed parents or orphaned kin, though there were some who refused to give aid. For more on this point, see Reher (1988a: 227–232). Even though there was no legal obligation to help, family members clearly felt strong social pressures to do so. See Laslett (1988: 157).

of co-residence had little or no place-specific meaning. Movement of people into and out of co-residential units was determined by the specific need for their labor. Some families, owing either to their social position or to the nature of their profession, would consistently attract outside labor and thus would not need to send their own labor out (except perhaps to continue studies). Others, such as those of day laborers, would be at the source of the urban labor supply. On this point it is interesting to note that in the professional and administrative sectors, household complexity and the average number of resident kin were considerably higher than in any other social group. Clearly an urban house is not a family farm, even though in each, economic decision-making by families, which ultimately determined the residence patterns of offspring, kin and of the family itself, makes for what Richard Wall (1986) might call "an adaptive family economy" in nineteenth-century Cuenca. Moreover, this reality conditioned the evidently high levels of spatial mobility existing in and around the town of Cuenca, as people were forced to be geographically flexible in order to supplement their family economies as well as to attend to family affairs in their villages of origin.

The data from Cuenca raise a number of additional questions. In the first place, to what extent can these behavior patterns be considered specifically urban? At least presumptively, this would seem to be the case, especially since similar levels of movement have never come to light in rural studies.[41] Yet this mobility transcends the mere circulation of kin, and probably serves as an element of separation for a good number of urban families. In other words, in rural areas, where mobility was conceivably less intense, one might expect the enlarged family networks to be stronger, though, conversely, kin circulation amongst familial households might well be less significant. Moreover, at least theoretically, peasant economies would tend to be more place-specific than in the town. Unfortunately, I have no comparable data from surrounding villages for the same period which might serve to verify some of these hypotheses and so they must remain hypotheses.

Another equally speculative point concerns the role played by the rural world in urban households, kinship networks and family economies. In Cuenca a considerable proportion of kin leaving urban households, did so for a destination outside town, as is suggested by a

[41] Jean Robin (1980: Tables 53 and 54) has found appreciable levels in the Essex village of Elmdon for the mid-nineteenth century. However, the 22–30 per cent levels of in- and out-migration over a ten-year period would not seem comparable to the 14–15 per cent per year in Cuenca.

number of examples given in this chapter as well as by general in- and out-migration rates close to 15 per cent per year. Does this mean that an adequate understanding of family networks and households and their economies, in an urban setting, would necessarily have to include the rural roots of those families? It would certainly seem likely that most of those out-migrant household members who left town were in the process of circulating between the urban world and their rural possessions and households. Further, the great majority of property we see transferred in Cuenca wills is in reality property retained in villages of origin. If this were the normal situation, and I am certainly inclined to believe that it was, then family forms and networks would become considerably more complex, and the family itself would become a major element linking towns to their rural hinterlands. Indeed, perhaps the most important conclusion to be derived from this work is that the study of the pre-industrial household and family is still in its infancy.

7

Mobility and migration in pre-industrial Cuenca

Introduction

One of the least-known yet most visible aspects of the past populations was their mobility. While the great migrations in history have often been extensively analyzed, more local permanent and return migratory patterns have often been neglected or inadequately studied.[1] Traditional analyses often portray a deceptively simple scenario of what we might expect was a dynamic and complex reality. While in Spain this subject has received little or no attention, it cannot automatically be assumed that elsewhere historical research has advanced much further. Despite the existence of noteworthy attempts by European and American scholars, it can safely be assumed that systematic analyses of mobility patterns in pre- and early-industrial societies are singularly lacking.[2]

Due to this situation, the historian is compelled to make use of the empirical and theoretical advances of modern migration research if he is to establish a general framework for understanding migration. Rural–urban migrants have traditionally been seen as responding either to factors "pushing" them from rural areas (unfavorable land tenure, surplus labor supply, population pressure, etc.) or "pulling" them to the towns (higher wages, greater opportunities, etc.). All migration theories emphasize the importance of economic realities and decision-making in the migration process, but often differ as to

---

[1] An important exception here is the work of historians and geographers in countries like Great Britain who have made meaningful advances towards the understanding of migratory patterns within a historical context. See, for example, Lawton (1979, n.d.), Baines (1985) and Poussou (1983).

[2] For examples of innovative analysis of migratory patterns see Akerman and Norberg (1976), Blayo (1970), Corsini (1980), Da Molin (1980), Kertzer and Hogan (1985), Hochstadt (1981), Laslett (1977), and Schofield (1970).

their emphasis on the active more mobile risk-taking migrant or the less mobile passive migrant, or in their macro- or micro-analytical focus.[3] Whatever the emphasis, though, and despite general mention made of the potential importance of counterstream migration, little work has been done on the make-up and consequences of return migration.[4]

Dealing more generally with the phenomenon of migration and its causes, a recent book by Dudley Baines has given strong support to the idea that economic realities determined the timing of migration, but not people's inclination to migrate. He suggests that this propensity was much more the product of information and familial networks, than a response to specific economic conditions (Baines, 1985: 195–212, 246–249). If his ideas are valid, the intensity of return migration would also have to be understood within the context of a world in which migrants and information circulated freely over often great distances. While this framework is well worth exploring in depth, it is unclear as to weather it is applicable to a small, decadent Castilian town where clear-cut centers of attraction, so essential to his analysis, are singularly lacking.

The most visible though certainly not the only consequence of migrations for both historical and contemporary urban areas was the contribution made by net migration to overall urban growth.[5] Apart from moments of political, economic and demographic crisis in which the migratory flow could dry up or even reverse its direction, this kind of population mobility has often been considered permanent and irreversible. In this manner, a more flexible job structure, based often on domestic service or industrial and mercantile activity, ensured that all urban areas would particpate in these flows. Much as occurs nowadays in less developed countries, primate cities would get the lion's share of migration, though smaller towns would also participate, at least modestly, either as permanent destinations themselves, or as links in stage or step migration of unemployed or under-employed peasants from rural areas.[6]

In the final analysis, however, migration determined much of the social make-up of urban areas and was an integral part of the change

[3] For more on the basic typology of migrants, see Findley (1977), Harris and Todaro (1970), and Zuiches (1980: 11–12).

[4] For the subject of return migration, see Margolis (1977: 137), Goldscheider (1971: 52–58), and Baines (1985: 130–142).

[5] For more on this, see Findley (1977: 32–39) and Clarke (1985: 63–72).

[6] Baines has argued convincingly that in the case of England at the end of the nineteenth centry, rural emigration seems to be less important for overall migration levels than urban emigration. This, however, was an exceptional situation, and there is no evidence that anything similar happened in Spain. See Baines (1985: 182–212).

processes affecting not only the society as a whole but the migrant himself. In this light, the fundamental importance of this little-known historical phenomenon cannot be doubted. Thus far in this study I have been able indirectly to identify the key role played by migration for urban population growth, family life, vital behavior, and urban society in times of crisis. It is now time to approach this subject in a systematic manner.

The relative lack of adequate migration studies can be directly attributed to defects in documentation available before the latter part of the nineteenth century. Despite problems inherent in source materials, however, the historian must pose deeper and more probing questions regarding urban mobility which cannot be answered by more traditional means of document analysis. Many straightforward measures of migration such as annual or other period turnover rates of population or information regarding the age, sex, marital status and profession of migrants simply cannot be gleaned from a single listing of inhabitants or a parish register. The role of migrants in urban society, their links to the rural world, the potential importance of return migration, are all questions of the utmost importance which often demand imaginative ideas and the innovative use of existing source material. This chapter is an attempt partially to fill this vacuum in historical scholarship.

The existence of adequate source material and methodology is essential to the success of this analysis. Population registers, which have been so useful for studies of migration in other countries, do not exist in Spain.[7] I have devised alternative approaches to the study of migration based on both parish registers and municipal listings of inhabitants. Of special interest is the existence in Cuenca during the middle years of the nineteenth century of a series of annual listings of inhabitants drawn up by the municipal government.[8] These listings have every appearance of being complete and contain full nominative information as well as age, sex, marital status, occupation, relation to household head and place of origin for practically the entire population. Despite smaller defects such as the lack of surname for some servants, nominative and age variability and possible errors in the declared place of origin, subsequent checks have revealed the documentation to be of excellent quality.

The likelihood that the utilization of listings at five year intervals or

---

[7] For examples of work with population registers, see Hochstadt (1981), van de Walle (1976), and Kertzer and Hogan (1985).
[8] My use of these lists will follow the lines set out some time ago in pioneering studies by Peter Laslett (1977), Laslett and Harrison (1963), and Yves Blayo (1970).

longer, as had been done by other authors, would conceal considerable levels of shorter term mobility, has induced me to make use of the listings annually. Even though this also tends to miss certain kinds of movement, at least it permits a more accurate calculation of yearly rates. Our original methodology followed Y. Blayo's rather closely, though a number of modifications have been introduced.[9] A complete description of this methodology can be found in the Appendix and only a very brief summary will be given here.

The method is based on the identification of all people within their families and the subsequent linkage of individuals over successive years. Once they have been completely identified, those absent or those appearing between one year and the next can be properly considered mobile persons and it is a relatively simple matter to classify them by age group, sex and, at least for household heads, by occupational status. The use of five annual listings (1843–1847) makes it possible to calculate movement over a four-year period. However, in order to minimize random fluctuations most annual rates calculated are the average of four different years. The base population used was either the average between 1844 and 1846 or, in the case of household heads, their occupational distribution in 1844. Most rates are expressed as simple percentages. Finally, the q_x values from a life table drawn up for the city at mid-century have been applied to basic out-migration levels so as not to confuse death with migration. Since deaths are estimated yearly by age groups, this form of calculation is especially problematic for those under five years of age and over 60. Here calculations of out-migration will be little more than rough estimates.

Using the results of this research I can then address a number of issues raised by contemporary migration theory within the context of a small Castilian town midway through the nineteenth century. In- and out-migrational flows will be analyzed in an effort to outline the general characteristics of these patterns as well as the consequences movement had for migrants, the town and the rural areas themselves. My analysis will include the estimation of a number of basic parameters which include annual turnover rates; the age, sex and occupational status and origin of migrants; the importance of return migration; the geographic specificity of marriage markets; the spatial constraints of migration; the generational depth of Cuenca-born children; and intra-urban, sex- and job-specific mobility. Results confirm the mobile nature of urban populations and show that while much of the population was mobile, not all ages and social groups

[9] See, especially, Blayo (1970: 573–582)

Table 7.1   *Annual migration rates in Cuenca, 1844–1847*

Year	Total population	In-migration(%)	Out-migration(%)	Net migration
1844	5,761	15.0	19.0	−4.0
1845	5,719	14.9	15.5	−0.7
1846	5,645	12.9	14.3	−1.3
1847	5,333	11.7	15.7	−4.0
Total		13.7	16.2	−2.5

Note Rates = (in-migrants$_x$ / population$_x$) × 100.
Source Municipal listings of inhabitants, 1843, 1844, 1845, 1846, 1847.

were affected equally. The predominantly or even marginally permanent nature of rural to urban migration will be challenged and a more global view of migration will be proposed whereby it becomes the mechanism which links rural and urban societies and economies to each other.

In- and out-migration in Cuenca

In order to understand the complex and pervasive reality of migration, it is first necessary to evaluate its numerical importance. One of the more generally accepted ideas regarding migration to towns is that it tended to be, by and large, a movement of young people and, apart from some stage migration to other larger urban areas and a trickle of people returning to their villages of origin, it was mostly permanent in nature. This influx of people bolstered often negative urban growth rates and was a major source of labor supply in the town itself. The initial results of this study of Cuenca have obliged me to fundamentally alter many of these ideas.

In Cuenca, as can be seen in Table 7.1 and Figures 7.1 and 7.2, the importance of in-migration was considerable, and it was more than compensated for by out-migration. Well over 10 per cent of the entire urban population entered the town yearly and this rate was equalled and even surpassed by the proportions of out-migrants. Despite the evident decline in the intensity of movement over the four year period, there is no reason to think that these proportions were abnormal. During the decade, the town did not undergo any grave crisis nor was it a moment of economic expansion. It was immersed in the economic stagnation which had characterized it for some time and,

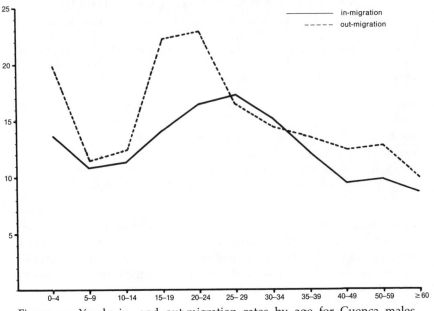

Figure 7.1 Yearly in- and out-migration rates by age for Cuenca males, 1843–1847

in the absence of any elements which might perturb migratory flows, the period under consideration would seem entirely typical. Net migration rates were −2.5 per cent per year and can be more safely attributed to conjunctural factors than to the nature of migration itself.

For males, levels of in-migration were relatively constant until the 35–39 year age group (Table 7.2). While intensity increased between 20 and 29 years of age, the most noteworthy aspect of the data is that from the time of birth until old age, males entered the town at a fairly constant rate. Moreover, while in-migrants were mostly unmarried, proportions single were not as high as might have been expected. A good proportion of them were married, thus suggesting significant levels of movement of entire families. Female in-migration was more intense, younger and more age-specific than male, and reached its peak intensity when girls were between 15 and 24 years of age. Data for both sexes, then, indicate that in-migration was important in all age groups and rarely descended below 9 per cent per year of the total population in any one. It was a flow that, while relatively more intense in young adult ages, could affect any stage of a person's life course. While the age distribution indicates the importance of employment

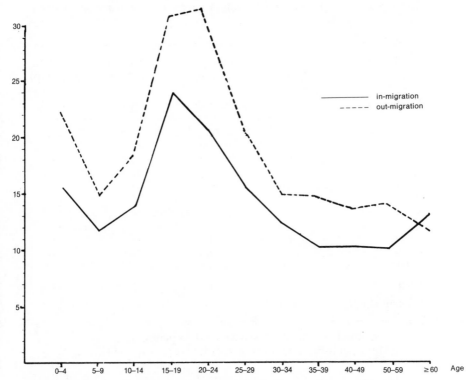

Figure 7.2 Yearly in- and out-migration rates by age for Cuenca females, 1843–1847

and marriage in stimulating migration, it is also clear that an appreciable number of established families participated in this type of movement. The emphasis on young adult age groups as well as the selective participation of families in migrational movements are not surprising and have been documented in numerous studies of contemporary and historical societies.[10] What is considerably more noteworthy is the fact that migration affected all age groups because, whereas the very young might move as members of families, the search for job opportunities or marriage can scarcely be considered as major stimulants of movement among the elderly.[11]

[10] See Akerman and Norberg (1976: 13), Caldwell (1969: 85–86), Kertzer and Hogan (1985: 12), Ringrose (1983: 49–53), and Adams (1969: 529).
[11] Despite the fact that there is a possibility that I have underestimated mortality in higher age groups, thereby increasing rates of out-migration, the high levels of in-migration for these same age groups would suggest that movement was typical of all ages.

Table 7.2   *In-migration and out-migration by age group and sex. Cuenca,*
1844–1847

Age group	Annual in-migration (per cent of age group)		Annual out-migration (per cent of age group)	
	Male	Female	Male	Female
0– 4	13.7	15.4	19.9	22.3
5– 9	10.8	11.8	11.3	14.9
10–14	11.3	13.8	12.4	18.3
15–19	14.1	23.9	22.1	30.7
20–24	16.6	20.1	23.0	31.2
25–29	17.3	15.1	16.5	20.0
30–34	15.2	12.6	14.3	14.8
35–39	12.1	9.9	13.5	14.6
40–49	9.4	9.9	12.4	13.3
50–59	9.7	9.5	12.6	13.6
>60	8.8	13.6	10.0	11.0
Total	12.5	14.9	15.2	19.8
Per cent single	61.4	64.4	61.5	68.8

Note For method of estimation, see text and Appendix 1.
Source Municpal listings of inhabitants, 1843, 1844, 1845, 1846, 1847.

Out-migration from town over the life course was also a characteristic of urban life and always affected at least 10 per cent of any given
age group. For males, however, out-migration appears to have been
far more age-specific than in-migration and was especially strong with
men between 15 and 24 years of age, a fact probably related to
temporary work in rural areas. Despite its continued importance, the
decline in out-migrational intensity after 24 years of age indicates that
age brought a greater stability for men within the town. The age
distribution of female out-migrants, as was the case with in-migrants,
was much younger and more age-specific than was male. Up to 30 per
cent of the female population of the town might leave it annually
between 15 and 24 years of age. The presence of an important
contingent of female servants, together with the role of nuptiality in
stimulating migration, help explain both the age structure and the
intensity of female migration. The relatively greater weight of
migrants among females than among males, a characteristic also
shown in short-distance present-day migrational patterns in Latin

Table 7.3   *In-migration and out-migration in the absence of domestic service,*
by sex and age group

Age group	Annual in-migration (per cent of age group)		Annual out-migration (per cent of age group)	
	Male	Female	Male	Female
0–4	13.7	15.4	19.9	22.3
5–9	10.8	11.8	11.3	14.9
10–14	10.3	11.7	11.4	14.4
15–19	11.3	13.2	16.7	15.2
20–24	13.9	15.0	19.4	17.9
25–29	17.3	13.0	15.6	15.5
30–34	14.9	12.6	13.9	13.6
35–39	11.6	8.4	13.0	13.3
40–49	9.1	9.2	12.1	12.9
50–59	9.1	9.4	12.5	13.0
>60	8.4	13.7	9.7	11.1
Total	11.7	12.2	14.0	15.0
% single	58.2	51.4	57.6	54.8
% single > 20	32.8	19.7	31.1	25.8

America, is a by-product of the importance of female domestic service
in the town.[12]

A major component of Cuenca's population were domestic servants. In 1844 this group made up 8.9 per cent of the total population,
was essentially female (sex ratio = 24) and strongly influenced the
prevailing social make-up of the town.[13] Servants were, perhaps, the
most geographically mobile of all urban groups and could well vitiate
my idea of the nature of migration among other groups. In order to see
in- and out-migration without their influence, the data of table 7.2
have been re-worked so as to exclude all servants both from the
population at large and from the mobile groups themselves. The
results can be found in Table 7.3 and they reveal that servant mobility
affected female migrational patterns considerably, while leaving male
patterns practically intact. In the case of male in-migration, the
differences are hardly worth mentioning except, perhaps, for a small
reduction in the proportions of in-migrants between 15 and 24 years of

---

[12] See, for example, Todaro (1976: 370), and Ringrose (1983: 53).
[13] In Madrid at mid-century, domestic servants made up 11.5 per cent of the entire
population and had a sex ratio of 47.9 (Ringrose, 1983: 57).

Table 7.4   *Age distribution of in- and out-migrant domestic servants*

Age group	In-migrants		Out-migrants	
	Male	Female	Male	Female
10–14	13	5	9	6
15–19	35	47	40	41
20–24	31	30	33	36
25–29	3	9	7	10
30–34	2	2	2	2
35–39	3	2	2	1
40–49	3	3	2	2
50–59	6	1	2	1
>60	3	1	2	1
Total	99	100	99	100
number per year	32	131	45	206
% of total migrants	9.9	29.3	11.4	34.6
% of total servants	32.6	32.5	45.9	51.1
% single	91.9	97.1	94.0	96.8

age. Female age distribution, though, is decisively affected by the elimination of servants. Without them migration mostly ceases to be age-specific, except for the 20–24 age group where the arrival of potential brides or newlyweds can clearly be seen. Otherwise female and male proportions are similar in most age groups and, overall, women no longer display a greater tendency to migrate.

Much of the same holds true for male and female out-migration where the elimination of domestic servants once again alters results significantly. First of all, the age-specific nature of out-migration changes substantially for both sexes. Slight increases in out-migrational intensity at certain ages seem hardly noticeable except for men between 20 and 24 years of age, where figures suggest that this was the key age for men to seek work elsewhere. A comparison with male in-migration, where peak activity occurs in the next age group, might also indicate that young men in their early twenties would leave the town either to seek work or to study, only to return a few years later. While the existence of this sort of return migration is only a possibility, the influence of employment, education and marriage on the migrational trends of both sexes is apparent.

The removal of domestic service also reveals that most other movement was by the ever-married sectors of society. Above the age of 20 and in the absence of servants, between seven and eight in 10 of all migrants who entered or left the town were either married or widowed. Here female migration above the age of 20 seems clearly related to the mobility of their husbands. The movement portrayed differs substanitally from the young and almost universally single job-seeking migrants we might have expected to find.

And what about those servants who influenced the make-up of migrant groups to such an extent? Part of the answer to this question can be found in Table 7.4 where one can see the age distribution of in- and out-migrant servants.[14] The data confirm that migrant servants were almost always single and were very young. People entered the domestic service often as young as 12 or 13 years of age and seldom later than 25. For both sexes, the 15–19 age group was by far the most important, though for women the concentration here was greater. Moreover, almost 100 per cent of all servants were single. The migrational patterns of servants influenced general intensity levels, especially in the case of women where more than 30 per cent of all female migrants were servants. This also explains the changes occurring in the overall female migration picture when female servants are elminated.[15]

The similarities between the in-migration and out-migration patterns of this sector cannot help but attract our attention and point to the transitory nature of domestic service. The fact that every year a high percentage of servants entered or left the city gives weight to the hypothesis that their stay in town was very short. Migration-related turnover for both male and female domestic service was upwards of 30 per cent per year and, if the average between in- and out-migration is calculated, it was appreciably higher. In addition to this, the similar age distribution for both in- and out-migrants as well as their unchanging marital status doubly confirm the highly transitory nature of domestic service. In this way servants streamed into the town at a very young age, stayed there for only a short time, perhaps a year or two or less, later returning to their villages of origin.

14 The size of the samples advised against calculating the proportion of in- and out-migration servants within each age group.
15 The municipal listing of 1847 presents important problems on this count since during that year the number of servant and especially female servant in-migrants drops sharply, and those of out-migrant female servants increases. This change in tendency might well indicate an under-registration of female servants in that listing. Due to this, the percentage of total female servants was also calculated for 1843–1846, thereby excluding the potentially distorting effects of possible servant under-registration in 1847. The results indicate that between 1843 and 1846, female domestic servants represented 34.5 per cent of all female in-migrants and 29.6 per cent of all out-migrants. These results do not fundamentally alter my conclusions.

Domestic service, then, was no more than a temporary source of population gain for the city and should perhaps more aptly be viewed in terms of rural economy and population pressure. In other words, rural youths would only come to the city to work for a short period, save a bit of money which might help bolster the dowries of the girls or their family economies, and return to their places of origin. In-depth interviews with elderly peasants in the province of Cuenca, have confirmed the existence of this practice during the first part of the twentieth century. There is little to suggest that the same dynamic did not exist earlier.[16] It is evident that the permanent servant migrants were a small minority. The return nature of servant movement seems so important, and the stay in the city so brief, that one is inclined to think that frequently female servants came to town with marriage agreements already made at home, and got married immediately upon returning. Unfortunately this last point can be little more than a plausible hypothesis about a reality of which very little is known. Yet it can be safely assumed that such turnover rates point to a situation in which young servants, when they first arrived in town, could scarcely have had any intention whatsoever of remaining in Cuenca in any sort of permanent way.

Whether or not something similar may have occurred with other migrants is not easy to say, though the data at hand suggest that this was generally not the case. Thus, urban migration patterns were, in reality, made up of at least two distinct patterns: a short-term return migration of single youths most often working in domestic service, and another which affected all social sectors and age groups almost equally and could be either short- or long-term. It is impossible to calculate the levels of permanent in-migration which has so often been considered to be typical of urban areas, though one can safely assume that it was but one of the many types of migration affecting the town.

An estimation of the importance of in- and out-migration by occupational status shows that whereas Cuenca as a whole was characterized by considerable mobility independent of occupational category, the groups most likely to move were at the opposite ends of the social scale (Table 7.5). The mobility levels, though, of day laborers on the one hand and public administration, professionals and the wealthy on the other, while far superior to those of other groups, were actually quite different. Both groups moved for economic reasons but the nature of their movement was certainly not the same.[17] Day

---

[16] For more on this, see Reher (1988a: 61–62).

[17] Day laborers represent nearly 80 per cent of the total agricultural sector included on this table.

Table 7.5   *In- and out-migration by economic sector*

Sector	In-migrants		Out-migrants		population (1844)
	n	per cent	n	per cent	
Agriculture[a]	46	10.3	45	10.0	448
Artisan/industry	13	6.2	12	5.7	209
Services	12	7.2	11	6.6	166
Professionals/ administration/ privileged[b]	30	11.2	36	13.4	268
Undeclared	8	13.3	8	13.3	60

Note [a]Day laborers are included in this sector for the table.
[b]The clergy is included in this sector for the table.

The sectorial distribution refers exclusively to household heads.

Table 7.6   *Yearly migrational patterns of male household heads, by age*

Age group	In-migrants	Out-migrants
20–24	8.9	13.3
25–29	19.3	14.9
30–34	12.3	11.7
35–39	12.1	11.2
40–44	7.5	8.1
45–49	7.1	10.6
50–54	6.9	10.1
55–59	7.1	4.7
>60	5.8	6.3
Total	9.4	9.7
Number (per year)	108	112
Per cent single	7.4	7.8

Note Expressed as percentage of each age group.

laborers tended to circulate between Cuenca and its hinterland in search of often temporary or seasonal work. Professionals have traditionally shown a higher propensity to migrate, and Cuenca data merely emphasize the general idea that migration tends to be selective of the more educated.[18] One can also hypothesize that out-migration of professionals was urban directed, thus forming a part of the stage or stepwise migrational patterns so often noted with them; whereas the day laborers probably moved freely between urban and rural areas of the province. Other sectors of the economy had appreciably lower rates of turnover. These differences suggest that the willingness of certain groups to assume the risks inherent in all migration was a function of their specific economic interests and relative place on the social ladder.

The generally high levels of migration suggest that return or cyclical migration was also a common experience for household heads. The fact that peak age groups were not the same simply raises the question as to the normal length of stay in town (Table 7.6). Instead of the one or two year stint which was typical for servants, household heads may have stayed a good deal longer. These patterns were probably quite varied, some heads staying in town for only a short time, probably attending to family business, while others stayed a good deal longer, though they too would end up as return migrants. Finally a certain percentage of these people were true permanent out- or in-migrants.

In Table 7.7 the age structure of household heads migrants is expressed for two key sectors in society, each of which reveals strikingly different behavior patterns.[19] The age structure of professional in-migrants was markedly older and spread over a wider age range than that of day laborers. Out-migration in both cases seems more uniformly distributed over the migrant's productive life. While the samples do not enable us to reach firm conclusions, once again two different patterns of household head migration appear. In the case of the unskilled day laborers, arrival in Cuenca occurred at a relatively young age, though certainly later than for the rest of the in-migrants, and was generally just after marriage. On the other hand, in-migration patterns of professionals and public administration employees were less age-specific, less related to marital status and more spread out over the greater part of the productive life of the migrants. Moreover, the peak age (30–34) indicates that these people arrived in town after completing their professional formation elsewhere, and that their

---

[18] See, for example, Lee (1966), Caldwell (1969), Todaro (1976), and Lawton (n.d.).
[19] Due to the small size of the sample, this has been done as a standard age distribution without considering the population of each age group.

Table 7.7   *Yearly migrational patterns for day laborer and professional household heads, by age*

Age group	In-migrants		Out-migrants	
	Day laborers	Professional/ administrative	Day laborers	Professional/ administrative
20–24	7	3	6	6
25–29	26	15	18	15
30–34	17	22	18	18
35–39	12	13	11	13
40–44	8	16	9	14
45–49	8	7	10	11
50–54	10	8	16	10
55–59	5	3	4	3
>60	7	13	9	9
Total	100	100	101	99
Number	144	119	138	144
% total migrants	33.4	27.6	30.4	30.9
% single	2.1	11.8	2.0	17.2

Note Expressed as percentage of total day laborer (or professional) population.

arrival in town was much less related to nuptiality than that of other sectors.

Most of the people in this sector had received some sort of specialized training which could only be acquired outside the town in places like Madrid. Many of them probably left the city as unwed persons and returned some time after marriage. The patterns evidenced by married professionals probably mirrored those of unmarried children of professionals, though the percentage single was considerably higher than among day laborers. The wider age spread of both in- and out-migrational flows of professionals is not at all surprising, since within this sector economic productivity did not diminish with age. In other words, a doctor, a civil servant or a school teacher would not be nearly as tied to the physical location of his job as would a shoemaker or a shopkeeper. Thus they could move with greater ease. This reality was shared by day laborers, though the location of other employment differed sharply as, naturally, did the stability of their jobs.

Thus far a good deal has been said about the migration dynamics affecting the town of Cuenca. Most noteworthy, perhaps, has been the fact that in-migration was more than counterbalanced by out-migration and migration of a return nature was a major, or the major type of movement affecting the town. Clearly the majority of single young adults coming to town as servants, apprentices, day laborers or in other transitory occupations, did so only for a short time.[20] Some indeed might have stayed on, but they were certainly a minority. Household heads also moved into and out of town with considerable ease. While at least part of their movement was also circulatory in nature, it is unlikely that their sojourns in Cuenca were as brief as those of unmarried migrants. The levels of migration as well as the intensity of return migration I found were surprising because in a small and economically insignificant town like Cuenca I had expected to find a mere trickle of migrants, most of whom would stay and help bolster its faltering population. "Push" or "pull" factors? In reality, both were at work, though the levels of return migration indicate that neither was strong enough to uproot the majority of the people from their rural heritage in any permanent manner. Much of this flow was made up of people whose characteristics were similar to those considered typical of passive, less mobile migrants (kin-related moves, lower occupational status, predominantly female, often temporal moves, affecting all ages, etc.). The professionals, on the other hand, were a clear case of active migrants (Findley, 1977: 16–17).

This multiplicity of movement can only be adequately interpreted if one bears in mind that mid-nineteenth-century Cuenca and its province were still clearly pre-industrial and showed few signs of economic dynamism. Within this context, existing social and economic structures contributed to a situation in which a free exchange of individuals was perceived to be a normal occurrence (Baines, 1985: 146–149). Ultimately, close ties between Cuenca and its hinterland were both cause and consequence of the structures of migration we have seen. Despite its clearly urban nature (less than 15 per cent of the active population was involved in the primary sector), a radical economic and social distinction between Cuenca and its province never arose as it may have done with larger cities. The small size of the town certainly contributed to the strength of these ties

[20] These types of migrant jobs also characterized Madrid's migration, and have led David Ringrose (1983: 34–43, 56–57) to develop the notion of "core" and "peripheral" populations. The abundant presence of more stable and trained migrants in Cuenca, suggests that migration might have fed both the core and the peripheral populations so typical of all urban areas, with the major differences being a question of age, training and intensity of migration.

which were an ever-present conditioning factor of urban life and helped make them multilateral. In other words, not only did Cuenca exercise control over the rural areas by means of political, social, religious and economic links, it was in turn dependent on them for more than merely the supply of basic foodstuffs. A true interrelation between the two worlds existed in which ties of dependence were mutual and where the urban world was an integral part of the rural world, just as "rural" was an essential component of "urban." The exchange of individuals, rural to urban and urban to rural, was the key to this relationship. The concrete economic agent underlying the system was the fact that the natural job market for a young man or woman, whether he or she lived in the town or in the countryside, encompassed both urban and rural areas simultaneously.

This, in turn, was reinforced by the system of land holding and inheritance prevailing in the province itself. Apart from the area to the south of town known as La Mancha where large plots were the norm and which sent relatively few migrants to town, in the majority of the province small plots and extensive land tenure were common. Since inheritance was partible, levels of celibacy low and the population growing, the peasant who could not make a living solely from his own possessions formed an important part of the population and even merited a specific term in Spanish (*pegujalero*) (Reher, 1988a: 69). These people had long since learned to diversify their economic activities with livestock, lumber, resin gathering, work on other people's land and, of course, jobs in town. Land was inherited upon the death of either or both parents, but marriage remained relatively young and household formation ensued shortly thereafter thanks to a certain flexibility in inheritance and the ability of the peasant household to diversify income and housing in the village, in town or both places at once (Reher 1988a: 51–69; 202–216).

It was therefore normal for a number of sons and daughters to live away from the family household at any given time. Their destination was often the town, even though it might be only for a short period of time. Most of these migrants eventually returned to their village of origin, thus completing a cycle which probably took place more than once in a person's lifetime. The return was expected and marriage patterns and family economies probably came to count on it. This mobility clearly existed within a kinship system designed to support movers. Both the kinship system and this type of movement-based income supplementing had probably been happily coexisting for centuries.

Some, however, stayed or would return to Cuenca after marriage.

These people became, so to speak, family beachheads in town and Cuenca became an integral rather than a transitory supplement to family income. This type of permanent movement into town often came about through marriage and family ties and is yet another example of the importance of kinship in underpinning migration.[21] So the circulation would begin again, though this time the migrants were entire families. Some of them, naturally, were permanent migrants but others only resided temporarily in town for more or less lengthy periods.

Where to from Cuenca? With the exception of the professionals who may well have circulated among urban centers on the peninsula, most migrants probably returned to where they had family property. Since the great majority of these people were from the province itself, the distance traveled seldom exceeded, say, 50–75 km, and was often appreciably less. This time the migrants had families in tow. It is clear that the ties between the town and the village were never severed and both were seen by the migrants as complementary aspects of income diversification. The potentially destabilizing effects of large-scale migration, as noted by some authors and disputed by others, is simply nowhere to be found in the town of Cuenca where movement itself had long since become an integral part of the social system (Stephenson, 1979).

The high levels of mobility in and around the town of Cuenca had other implications for nineteenth-century society. We can safely suppose that the intensity of movement tended to lower fertility levels, at least among mobile persons, by means of restricting their nuptiality.[22] The importance of migration for the society as a whole, however, depends on whether or not it also tended to delay migrant nuptiality in rural areas. I do not possess either confirming or contradictory evidence on the matter, but it seems reasonable to suppose that return or cyclical migration had similar effects everywhere. In this manner, migratory movement acted indirectly as a deterrent to population growth. Traditionally, higher urban mortality has been viewed as a major by-product of migration to urban areas. In the case of Cuenca, the reaction of nuptiality in both urban and rural areas might have equal or greater importance in controlling general population growth.[23] The more rapidly the population grew, as was the case in

---

[21] On this subject, see, for example, Hammel (1977).

[22] Earlier age at first marriage was shown to be 1.5 years higher for female in-migrants than for natives of Cuenca.

[23] From a different perspective, however, the theoretical possibility exists whereby rural to urban migration actually stimulated the possibilities of marrying for those

the province as a whole after the latter part of the seventeenth century, the more intensive movement would have become as families hurried to diversify their household economies in order to maintain living standards. Ultimately, of course, the importance of movement in curtailing growth in the province depended on its overall intensity. This, unfortunately, cannot be measured at the present time.

It is also not known whether or not migration led directly, at least among migrants, to lower levels of marital fertility. Though evidence is not conclusive on the matter, lower fertility has been documented for migrants in urban environments who generally had lower fertility than rural nonmigrants, though higher fertility than urban nonmigrants.[24] Unfortunately the effect of short-term migration is generally unknown, though seasonal migration has been shown to depress marital fertility levels.[25] Could this be applicable to temporary absences of household heads in Cuenca? It is impossible to know for sure though the potential importance of human exchanges for the maintenance of some sort of demographic equilibrium in the province should be evident.

Finally, it seems likely that this cyclical movement was an important component of economic and social integration in a province where there was no dominant urban center. Apart from the trade of certain basic food commodities, textiles, lumber and other lesser products, Cuenca played only a marginal role as a market center during the nineteenth century. Nevertheless, the economic links between the city and its province were multiple and were established largely through the exchange of individuals. Not only did short-term migrants distribute "urban" money in rural areas, but the city itself became an integral part of the social and economic world of its hinterland, and vice versa. This human permeability of a small town like Cuenca probably mitigated the alien and hostile nature that cities traditionally conveyed to peasants.

Cuenca migrants and their origins

By now there should be little doubt as to the intensity of migration in and around Cuenca. One of the most important conclusions of our analysis has been the importance of return migratory flows which

urban migrants who, otherwise, would have had no place whatsoever in their overcrowded rural marriage markets.

[24] See Akerman and Norberg (1976), Goldstein and Goldstein (1981), Zarate and Unger de Zarate (1975). In Cuenca, the fertility behavior of migrants has generally followed the above-mentioned patterns (see chapter 3).

[25] On this subject, see, for example, Bongaarts and Potter, 1979, Massey and Mullan, 1984, and Menken, 1979.

were able to offset in-migration completely. Yet not all migrants were going to return to their places of origin, to other parts of the province or elsewhere on the peninsula. Some migrants stayed on and their presence in all types of official urban documents bears witness to this reality.[26] As yet we know little about them. The major purpose of this section will be to clarify many of the social and economic character-istics of people living in Cuenca, many of whom were those who had stayed on in town after earlier migratory moves.

In this section global realities rather than temporal flows will be analyzed and special attention will be paid to the origins of Cuenca migrants and the extent to which social and economic structures prevailing in town reflected the geographical, social and economic constraints to migration. Does the make-up of the urban population at any given time reflect a migration which was specific to a given sex, profession or geographic area? Tackling this subject will lead us once again to the subject of prevailing nuptial patterns, will enable us to estimate the relative importance of stage migration to Cuenca, and will facilitate a multi-generational portrait of the migratory heritage of new-born Cuenca babies. While my use of sources differs substantially from the preceding section, my major purpose of clarifying the basic parameters of migration in Cuenca remains the same. Data for the analysis in this section comes from cross-sectional analysis of munici-pal listings, together with the systematic use of parish registers.

First of all, it is necessary to dispel a number of prevalent misconcep-tions about the nature of migration. Generally it has been thought that only important urban centers were able to attract long-distance migration, and migrants to smaller centers came primarily from local villages. In Cuenca this is not the case at any moment during the entire period studied, as migrants from outside the province always accounted for between 25 and 40 per cent of the total population of resident migrants (Table 7.8).[27] Specifically local migration was cer-

---

[26] At any given moment, anywhere between 50 and 60 per cent of the population was from the town itself. In the case of Madrid in 1850–1851, this proportion was slightly lower (40 per cent) (Ringrose, 1983: 34, 52).

[27] It is important to note that these data are based on parents' names on baptismal records. This has been considered preferable to municipal listings because it affords information from the sixteenth and seventeenth centuries, whereas the listings only provide data about origin between the end of the eighteenth and the middle of the nineteenth century. While marriage records could also have been used, baptisms have been chosen because they reflect actual migration, whereas marriages might only reflect a type of mobility induced by the wedding itself. As might be expected, the major difference between the two data sets is the greater percentage of Cuenca natives on baptismal records. Relevant differences and similarities between marriage-based and baptism-based data will be pointed out when considered of

Table 7.8. *Origin of parents in Cuenca, by distance from Cuenca*

	FATHERS				
Origin	1601–1650	1651–1700	1701–1750	1751–1800	1801–1870
Cuenca	52.8	58.3	52.9	58.9	56.3
<25 km	7.8	7.0	8.5	7.6	6.5
>25 km, <50 km	7.8	13.5	18.5	13.7	9.9
>50 km	3.5	2.8	4.8	7.3	6.9
Adjacent provinces	10.6	9.3	6.4	5.8	6.6
Other provinces	12.3	6.3	7.8	5.2	13.2
Other countries	5.2	2.8	1.1	1.5	0.7
Total	100	100	100	100	100
Number	114	141	850	2,673	3,325

	MOTHERS				
Origin	1601–1650	1651–1700	1701–1750	1751–1800	1801–1870
Cuenca	60.9	58.9	51.5	50.6	51.6
<25 km	12.5	9.4	10.8	13.6	11.0
>25 km, <50 km	6.1	11.2	17.9	18.8	15.9
>50 km	3.0	2.5	6.6	6.4	6.3
Adjacent provinces	9.3	12.9	8.2	7.4	7.5
Other provinces	7.2	5.1	4.5	3.1	6.9
Other countries	1.0	0.0	0.5	0.1	0.8
Total	100	100	100	100	100
Number	97	117	724	2,668	3,357

Note Based on declared place of origin on Baptism registers. After 1750, origin is declared on between 95.5 and 95.9 per cent of all registers. Between 1700–1749, one-third of all registers contain data on origin of parents. Earlier it is fragmentary.

tainly important, especially for women, though it cannot be considered the predominant flow. It is interesting to observe that during the eighteenth century local migration, especially that from villages within 50 km of the town, decreased, as opposed to that from outside the province which increased sharply.[28] This tendency can be seen for

interest. It must be kept in mind that origin at baptism offers a biased sample in favor of fertile couples.

[28] I cannot infer much from the early seventeenth-century data because sample size and possible problems of heterogeneity leave little room for confidence. After 1700 this problem decreases and by 1750 it is quite small.

Table 7.9 Origin of residents in 1844, by economic group, district and distance from Cuenca

Origin	Day laborers	Agriculture	Industry/ artisans	Services	Professional Administration	Servants	
						Male	Female
Cuenca	59	81	71	55	36	37	20
<25 km	10	7	2	4	5	34	17
>25 km, <50 km	13	4	9	8	21	19	31
>50 km	9	5	7	8	8	4	8
Adjacent provinces	5	4	9	15	18	3	22
Other provinces	5	0	3	10	11	3	3
Other countries	0	0	0	1	1	0	0
Total	101	101	101	101	100	100	101
Number	111	105	105	105	106	68	259
Districts							
Sierra	44	25	28	25	19	59	64
Alcarria	26	38	11	10	33	28	19
La Mancha	29	38	61	65	47	13	17
Total	99	101	100	100	99	100	100

Note Data based on declared place of origin for male household heads, except for domestic servants who normally live in other households. Expressed as percentage of all Cuenca residents or, for the districts, as a percentage of all residents coming from those districts.
Source Municipal listing of 1844.

both sexes, though it was more pronounced among men, and was probably the result of the increase in the presence of royal officials and other forms of civil and military employees in Cuenca during that period.[29]

Many of the sex-specific differences which can be observed can be attributed either to the local marriage market or to the economic make-up of different migratory streams. Women were far more likely to be migrants from the local areas than were men, and more fathers than mothers were natives of the town of Cuenca.[30] The observed differences were probably a result of local marriage patterns in which Cuenca-born men sought brides in local villages. Subsequent residence for the couple, though, would be in town. The same is not the case with migrants from the next classified area (>25 km), where after 1750 a clear predominance of women is apparent. As we will see shortly, this area was also the prime sender of female domestic servants to town, some of whom naturally ended up staying on. Long-distance migration (from other provinces) was mostly male and reveals the professions of many of the migrants. After 1750, when there are sizeable samples, nearly 40 per cent of all male migrants came from other provinces, as opposed to less than 27 per cent of females.

Some of the economic constraints on migration can be seen more clearly if we look at the place of origin by profession (Table 7.9). Once again opposite ends of the social spectrum show the greatest propensity to migrate, though the structure of their migration differs substantially. Day laborers were invariably local migrants, and very few of them came from outside the province; the services sector and especially the professionals/administration showed a marked tendency to come from greater distances. In these sectors, almost half of those not born in Cuenca came from outside the province. The highest levels of migration were those among professionals; the lowest belonged to farmers living in town. Both confirm many of the realities seen earlier in this chapter.

[29] These included a wide range of people such as school teachers, lawyers and national and local police. The greater mobility of this social group has already been noted in the preceding section.

[30] The categories of distance from Cuenca have been defined in the following way: any part of a municipality falling within a given distance is included within that category. Thus municipalities falling partially outside the circle are included within it. Distances are calculated by concentric circles and do not represent actual distance traveled between a given municipality and Cuenca. Given the basic shape of the province of Cuenca, to the Northeast of the capital, many of the towns of the Sierra touching on the neighboring province of Teruel actually fall within the 50 km limit. This does not happen in any of the other directions. Thus the category ">50 km" includes practically no villages from the district (*comarca*) of the Sierra.

The province of Cuenca can be divided into three distinct districts known as *comarcas*. Each was characterized by special economic, social, and demographic structures. The "Sierra," the mountainous region to the East and Northeast of town, was a district of widespread access to land, very small farms, appreciable livestock farming, and higher rates of natural demographic growth. The "Alcarria," in the Northwest of the province, was also characterized by widespread landownership, though less so than the Sierra, very small villages, farming based on cereals, wine and olives. Finally, "La Mancha," located in the entire southern part of the province was a district of limited access to property, large farms, fairly large villages and towns, and appreciable proportions of day laborers among the active population. It was also the only district where there was some commercialization of farm products. During the early nineteenth century, the population of La Mancha was nearly twice that of either of the other two districts.[31] The town of Cuenca is situated quite near the confluence of these three districts.

This geographical distribution can also be seen in the migrational tendencies of Cuenca residents. Day laborers generally came from the Sierra. They were the sons of farmers, who came to town in moments of rural population growth to supplement family incomes. They were probably also those involved in much of the return migration already observed. The majority of people in the industrial, services and, to a lesser degree, professional sectors were from La Mancha. In fact, nearly 30 per cent of both the professional or the services sectors were from La Mancha. Once again this is not surprising. La Mancha had long had the most monetized of all the district economies and its active population showed the highest proportions of both sectors (Reher, 1988a: 30–31). For those migrants, going to Cuenca was not considered as temporary a situation as it might have been for people from the Sierra. Distances were greater and those who migrated had professions which demanded specialized training. They were much more likely to stay on than were the unskilled migrants of other areas.

In the twentieth century, Cuenca has always been considered by its own residents as a Sierra town, despite the fact that the Alcarria also touches on its borders and La Mancha is not far away. This has been because the great majority of migrants to town have traditionally come from the Sierra. In the period under study, the presence of *serranos* in town increased substantially, especially for men. By the nineteenth century approximately half of all migrant parents came from the Sierra

---

[31] For a closer analysis of the economic, demographic and social reality of the *comarcas*, see Reher (1988a).

Table 7.10   *Origin of migrant parents, by district and period*

	FATHERS				
Period	Sierra	Alcarria	La Mancha	Total	n
1701–1750	37.9	35.5	26.5	99.9	267
1751–1800	39.6	28.1	32.3	100.0	742
1801–1870	46.1	20.9	33.0	100.0	745
Total	42.1	26.2	31.8	100.1	1754

	MOTHERS				
Period	Sierra	Alcarria	La Mancha	Total	n
1701–1750	48.8	29.4	21.8	100.0	248
1751–1800	56.5	28.8	14.7	100.0	1021
1801–1879	52.4	25.9	21.7	100.0	1096
Total	53.8	27.5	18.7	100.0	2365

Note Based on declared pace of origin in baptismal registers. The data do not include persons from the town of Cuenca or from areas outside the province. See text for further explanations.

(Table 7.10), and this would increase significantly if we controlled for the size of the sending area.[32] The importance within the urban economy of day laborers and of female domestic servants, which has been repeatedly seen throughout this study, is once again apparent. Presumably neither group came to town with the specific intention of staying on permanently, but many of them did and they ended up decisively influencing Cuenca's social make-up. Mountainous areas have always been considered archetypal regions of emigration, and the Cuenca data do nothing to disprove this.

Perhaps the most distinctive migratory patterns were shown by domestic servants. It is often felt that this group was primarily composed of residents of the town itself, or residents of nearby villages who went to town to help supplement family incomes and to save for an up-coming marriage. This, quite simply, was not the case in Cuenca. Very few servants came from the town itself, though this

[32] Controlling for the population of the sending area would only give an approximate estimate of the propensity to migrate to Cuenca of the different districts. Nonetheless, if one standardizes by district population in 1787, the adjusted "total" migration would have 55.9 per cent of male migrants and 65.0 of females coming from the "Sierra," 27.1 and 25.9 per cent from the "Alcarria," and 17.0 and 9.1 per cent from the "La Mancha."

was less true for men than for women (Table 7.9). Most came from the Sierra, and frequently traveled great distances to get to town. While male servants traveled far shorter distances than did females, neither could be considered truly local migrants.[33] In the case of the women, an interesting Sierra-dominated pattern can be observed. As mentioned earlier, due to the geographical characteristics of the province and its districts, as well as to the manner in which we have defined our categories of distance from the town itself, much of the Sierra district lies within the 50 km radius. From a geographical standpoint, however, the mountainous areas of this part of Spain include ample parts of both the provinces of Cuenca and its neighbor, Teruel. The data show that female servants came from the larger Sierra, irrespective of the province. The vast majority of the 22 per cent of female servant in-migrants coming from adjacent provinces, come from the province of Teruel.

Information and familial networks evidently played a more meaningful role in stimulating migration than did distance or clear-cut economic opportunity.[34] Young girls from the Sierra were raised to expect to migrate to Cuenca (or perhaps to the town of Teruel or to some other town) in order to supplement low family incomes. They would travel several days to get to town and, once there, would spend a relatively short time, probably less than three years, serving in a number of different households. Their "route" to town was facilitated by previous migrants from the same family, village or area who had either made contacts in Cuenca, or who now lived there. The frequent coincidence between the place of origin of either the male or female household head and that of servants living in the household suggests that these "routes" were really full-scale migration networks integrated by kin and neighbors in Cuenca and in its surrounding rural areas.

A different perspective of marriage patterns, migration and the ancestry of Cuenca-born children emerges if we combine the place or origin of fathers with that of mothers (or that of brides with that of grooms). Conventional wisdom would suggest that most nuptiality-induced migration involved at least one Cuenca native, and only economically motivated migration might bring couples born and conceivably married elsewhere to Cuenca. In about one-third of all cases, both parents were natives of Cuenca.[35] If one excludes these

---

[33] 54 per cent of the male servant in-migrants came from within 25 km of the town, as opposed to only 21 per cent of the females.

[34] This has been observed by numerous other authors. See, for example, Pérez Díaz (1969), Iriso Napal and Reher (1987: 53–54, 110–111), and Baines (1985).

[35] A major difference between the data set based on baptisms and the one based on marriages is most evident with totally endogamous unions which, as might be

non-migrant couples, the father was from Cuenca in 36 per cent of the cases, and the mother in only 28 per cent. For 24 per cent of all children neither of the parents was a native of town. There is little indication that these levels had changed substantially over the centuries. 25.1 per cent of all couples were non-native between 1563 and 1700, 21.2 per cent between 1701 and 1800; and 25.5 per cent between 1800 and 1870. Much of the movement to Cuenca, then, would seem far more related to economic needs and opportunities than to marriage itself. From the standpoint of children born in Cuenca, a great many of them would be raised in households in which either one or both of their parents were not from the town.

The data in Table 7.11, which are based on marriages taking place in the town of Cuenca, show that there was a marked tendency for young men to marry young women from their villages or areas of origin. In all categories, and even if we exclude marriages of natives of Cuenca, geographically endogamous unions were by far the most important and represented 41.5 per cent of all marriages. This pattern is especially clear in the Table where the only positive residual values are those of cells corresponding to endogamous unions.[36] In other words, urban marriage markets were strongly influenced by the geographical origins of the urban population.[37] The fact that in town people tended to marry others from their own area is a fitting testimony of deeper social and personal links among migrants from a given district than might have been preciously imagined. Once again, the complexity of Cuenca's society comes forcefully to the forefront of this analysis.

It would not be correct to assume, however, that the geographical distribution of marriage patterns was the same for men as it was for women. Fathers were more likely to come from Cuenca than were mothers, though the opposite is true if we base our ideas exclusively on marriages. Evidently, weddings were more likely to be held where the wife lived, but more or less permanent residence tended to be

suspected, were far less important in the marriage sample (22.3 per cent of all marriages) than in the baptismal one (35.2 per cent). The importance of migrant spouses (60 per cent of the grooms and 57 per cent of all brides) is much higher than the levels holding in Seville during the first decades of the nineteenth century (approximately 30 per cent of grooms and 25 per cent of spouses). See Alvarez Santaló (1974: 220–221).

[36] The highly significant chi-squared values are a clear indication that the origin of the husband was not independent from that of his wife.

[37] A part of this pattern in marriages might be attributed to the custom of people coming from local villages to get married in the cathedral. However, the fact that it also existed for people coming from greater distances suggests that a more far-reaching explanation is needed.

Table 7.11 *Origin of bride by origin of groom*

	Cuenca	<25km	<50km	BRIDE >50km	adjacent provinces	Other	Row Total
GROOM							
Cuenca							
1	638	134	217	60	69	24	1,142
2	148.1	−23.4	−45.1	−47.5	−2.9	−29.1	40.0%
3	6.7	−1.9	−2.8	−4.6	−.3	−4.0	
<25km							
1	105	120	69	24	15	9	342
2	−41.7	72.9	−9.5	−8.2	−6.5	−6.9	12.0%
3	−3.4	10.6	−1.1	−1.4	−1.4	−1.7	
<50km							
1	179	80	237	37	20	10	563
2	−62.5	2.4	107.8	−16.0	−15.5	−16.2	19.7%
3	−4.0	.3	9.5	−2.2	−2.6	−3.2	
>50km							
1	93	30	59	108	23	18	331
2	−49.0	−15.6	−17.0	76.8	2.2	2.6	11.6%
3	−4.1	−2.3	−1.9	13.8	.5	.7	

Adjacent
provinces

							Total
Adjacent provinces							
1	73	9	34	12	30	17	175
2	−2.1	−15.1	−6.2	−4.5	19.0	8.9	6.1%
3	−.2	−3.1	−1.0	−1.1	5.7	3.1	
Other							
1	138	21	40	28	23	55	305
2	7.2	−21.0	−30.0	−.7	3.8	40.8	10.7%
3	.6	−3.2	−3.6	−.1	.9	10.8	
Column Total	1,226	394	656	269	180	133	2,858
	42.9%	13.8%	23.0%	9.4%	6.3%	4.7%	100.0%

Cells with expected frequency <5   none

Chi-square	Significance
765.632	.0000

Statistic	Value
Cramer's V	.231
Contingency coefficient	.460

Note 1 = cell count 2 = residual (difference from expected cell count) 3 = standardized residual.
Based on declared district of origin of spouses, ordered by distance from Cuenca.

influenced by where the husband lived. Men from Cuenca were far more likely to marry spouses from neighboring villages than were women, whereas women from Cuenca showed a marked tendency to find their husbands in other provinces. If we exclude all completely endogamous unions, 70 per cent of Cuenca-born grooms married wives from local villages (within 50 km of town), as opposed to only 48 per cent of the brides. On the other hand, once again excluding endogamous unions, 36 per cent of Cuenca-born brides married husbands from other provinces, as opposed to 18 per cent of the Cuenca-born grooms. Since I do not know about migration-induced nuptiality outside Cuenca, I have no ready explanation for this pattern, though the data offer fairly convincing evidence as to its existence.

Did people move from their villages of origin directly to Cuenca, or did they reach the town in stages? If the latter were the case, it would be a good indicator that after their stay in Cuenca these migrants would continue to move up the urban hierarchy, much as the theory of step migration would suggest. The data make an adequate approach to the question of the existence or not of step migrational patterns impossible. I can, however, make very crude estimates of the importance of stepwise progressions towards the town itself. This involves using the places of origin of parents and grandparents, which appear on almost all baptismal registers after the 1760s. In this way, one can visualize the experience of two generations by juxtaposing the origins of the parents with those of the grandparents.[38]

The results contained in Table 7.12 give little indication of the existence of this type of migration, at least between one generation and the next. The most striking aspect of the data is the fact that the area of birth of the parents and that of the grandparents show a strong degree of association. Once again if we exclude parents born in Cuenca, parental and grandparental origin coincided in between 80 and 90 per cent of the cases. This can also be seen in the residuals, in the chi-squared values, and especially in the statistics of association (Cramer's V and the Contingency coefficient) which are understandably much higher than those of Table 7.11. It would seem that normally a family's first clear move outside of these defined areas was precisely to the town itself.[39] There is also very little evidence to

---

[38] An exercise of this nature is subject to severe limitations since only migration toward the town of Cuenca can be controlled and movement within the general categories I have designed goes undetected.

[39] There is very slight evidence that the origin of parents was at times slightly closer to town than was that of the grandparents. This is especially apparent for the "<50 km," ">50 km," and "Other" categories. The differences noted, though, are so slight that they might not indicate the existence of any pattern at all.

suggest that, once there, the next generation returned to the rural areas of the province. Only 4 per cent of grandparents born in Cuenca had parents born outside the town, generally in villages close to Cuenca.[40] They were probably the children of the return migrants who, after a more or less prolonged stay in town, had moved back to their villages of origin. Even though the tendency to move to the town by steps seems not to have been the case for more than a small minority of families, a definite overall trend to move to the city of Cuenca is certainly apparent. Nearly a third of the grandparents not from town had children born in Cuenca. My data do not preclude the possible existence of step migration in which residence in Cuenca was only a middle step. Unfortunately I have no way of estimating a type of movement which could have been important especially among the urban elites such as professionals, administrators, the wealthy, etc.

From a sociological standpoint, one of the most important consequences of the intense migration affecting the town, with the often distant origin of parents and high mobility of certain social groups, was that very few children born in Cuenca could boast of many Cuenca roots at all. In other words, being *conquense* was a relative concept, not just for adult urban residents, nearly half of whom were not even born in the town, but for their children as well. Table 7.13 offers an eloquent testimony of what might be called the depth of people's roots over three generations. It shows that only about 8 per cent of all Cuenca-born children could boast of having both parents and all four grandparents from the town itself, as opposed to the more than 20 per cent who had no roots whatsoever. Apart from these extremes, the most likely situation was to have one parent and one or two grandparents from the town.

Here then is the real picture of the social implications of migration. An important proportion of the families who came to Cuenca were completely new to the town. They had no prior ties, and the move to Cuenca was economically motivated. Though I have not controlled for this, it is possible that these were the migrant families from other provinces who were occupied in provincial and national public administration. School teachers, military personnel, royal officials, and merchants might well be the prototypes of these migrants.[41]

The majority of the migrants, however, must have had some kin in

[40] It is important to remember that in this case (grandparents from Cuenca) our sample is biased in favor of families with strong ties to the town itself. This may well account for the low levels of parents born elsewhere to Cuenca-born grandparents.

[41] Here we can recall the four kin-related households of merchants from far-off Vega de Pas in the province of Santander who lived very close to each other in the parishes of El Salvador and San Esteban during the nineteenth century.

Table 7.12 Origin of parents by origin of grandparents

PARENTS	Cuenca	<25km	GRANDPARENTS <50km	>50km	Adjacent provinces	Other	Row total
Cuenca							
1	6,826	1,168	1,362	424	461	511	10,752
2	2928.0	−374.2	−790.9	−513.6	−541.1	−708.1	54.7%
3	46.9	−9.5	−17.0	−16.8	−17.1	−20.3	
<25km							
1	118	1,520	156	63	39	4	1,900
2	−570.8	1247.5	−224.4	−102.7	−138.1	−211.4	9.7%
3	−21.7	75.6	−11.5	−8.0	−10.4	−14.4	
<50km							
1	79	72	2,306	127	79	40	2,703
2	−900.9	−315.7	1764.8	−108.7	−172.9	−266.5	13.7%
3	−28.8	−16.0	75.9	−7.1	−10.9	−15.2	
>50km							
1	47	39	63	1,034	83	63	1,329
2	−434.8	−151.6	−203.1	918.1	−40.9	−87.7	6.8%
3	−19.8	−11.0	−12.5	85.3	−3.7	−7.1	

							Row total
Adjacent provinces							
1	52	15	29	37	1,120	125	1,378
2	−447.6	−182.7	−246.9	−83.2	991.6	−31.2	7.0%
3	−20.0	−13.0	−14.9	−7.6	87.5	−2.5	
Other							
1	8	7	22	30	51	1,487	1,605
2	−573.9	−223.2	−299.4	−110.0	−98.6	1305.0	8.2%
3	−23.8	−14.7	−16.7	−9.3	−8.1	96.7	
Column total	7,130	2,821	3,938	1,715	1,833	2,230	19,667
	36.3%	14.3%	20.0%	8.7%	9.3%	11.3%	100.0%

Chi-square	Significance	Cells with expected frequency < 5
44586.869	.0000	none

Statistic	Value
Cramer's V	.673
Contingency coefficient	.833

Note 1 = cell count 2 = residual (difference from expected cell count) 3 = standardized residual. Based on declared district of origin of parents and grandparents in Baptisms, ordered by distance from Cuenca. Both sexes combined. The number of cases represents, in fact, a double count of most parents (one for the grandfather, one for the grandmother).

Table 7.13 *The Cuenca roots of Cuenca-born children*

Cuenca-born ancestors				
Parents	Grandparents	1751–1800	1801–1870	Total
0	0	18.1	22.2	20.7
0	1	1.1	1.5	1.4
0	2	0.8	0.6	0.6
0	3	0.0	0.0	0.0
0	4	0.0	0.0	0.0
1	0	7.4	6.6	6.8
1	1	20.2	17.9	18.6
1	2	20.9	16.4	18.0
1	3	1.1	1.2	1.2
1	4	0.1	0.1	0.1
2	0	0.4	1.1	0.9
2	1	4.5	4.2	4.3
2	2	9.9	9.9	9.9
2	3	9.2	9.7	9.6
2	4	6.4	8.7	7.9
	Total	100.1	100.1	100.0
	Number	1,573	3,006	4,579

town already and probably used familial information networks to facilitate their move to Cuenca. This would explain the fact that most children had ancestors from the town. Even those parents and grandparents from other areas, who were linked to *conquenses* by marriage, probably reached the town earlier through their own family or village ties, and only entered the Cuenca marriage market once in the town itself. They are fitting examples of the intensity of flows to and from the town which ended up giving numerous families ties to both the rural and the urban worlds. Their children certainly showed these ties; many probably had grandparents and certainly uncles, aunts, and cousins who still lived in the rural world. They were socialized in an environment in which movement to and from the rural world was perceived to be the norm. As we mentioned earlier, both urban and rural property were bequeathed in most of the Cuenca wills we have read. Even those with multiple roots in Cuenca probably continued to maintain on-going ties with kin and property in rural areas.

This, then, was the network which structured migration to and from the town. Perhaps if Cuenca had been wealthier, or had participated in some kind of significant industrialization, many of the migrants would have been permanent and would have been able and willing to sever their rural roots. This, though, was not the case. Cuenca was only a small town which complemented more than eroded the fundamentally rural nature of the province. It was not a catalyst for change, but a type of security against change. The fact that people were able to use family and village "bridges" to join both worlds in order to supplement peasant family incomes, helped alleviate economic necessity in rural areas. In this manner, the existence of towns like Cuenca tended to contribute to the stability of rural society and thus cannot be considered a force for change in pre-industrial Spain.

And yet more movement: intra-urban mobility patterns

Up until this point, patterns of in- and out-migration have been analyzed for the city as a whole. A careful study of these patterns has made it clear that all sectors of the town were subject to high mobility, though its intensity and the duration of the stay varied according to the age, sex, marital status and profession of the individuals involved. We have also seen a number of the specifically geographic and economic aspects of this migration, often materialized through marriage, family ties or economic opportunities.

Permanent, temporary or return migrational flows, though, were only one aspect of the considerably wider subject of urban mobility. At least in theory, another type of movement existed which could have considerable importance for those who experienced it and for the make-up of urban society as well. Here I am referring to spatial mobility within the town itself. While we can reasonably assume that a certain degree of this sort of mobility did exist, I cannot judge its importance for urban societies, or whether it affected certain social groups more than others, or its age composition, or whether people moved as individuals or as families, or where they went, or the implications of these moves. These questions are intriguing and warrant a closer analysis. The results could well add a completely new dimension to our picture of urban mobility patterns.[42]

---

[42] The method for estimating intra-urban mobility is identical to that used for migrational flows. Only those people "absent" in a given year from a given residence and who were found elsewhere in the town that very year entered into the calculations. It should be noted that this method might tend to slightly underestimate intra-urban mobility, especially when a person moves to another residence close to the original one. In order to minimize this problem, both parish and street names were registered. However, a family which moved to a new residence on the same street

Table 7.14   *Yearly intra-urban changes in residence, for male household heads and economic sector*

Sector	Per cent yearly changes
Agricultural/day laborers	9.8
Artisan/industry	11.0
Services	7.8
Professional/administration/privileged	15.0
Male domestic service	14.3
Female domestic service	18.4

Note Yearly changes are based on the average number of changes between 1844 and 1847. Population in each sector is based on male household heads and on servants in 1844. Servants are not household heads.

The results given in Table 7.14 amply confirm the significance of intra-urban mobility. During any given year over 10 per cent of the entire urban population changed residence within the town. This mobility affected both sexes (though women more than men) and was largely independent of marital status. The percentage single among the mobile groups was practically identical to that in the city as a whole. In other words, this seems to be a general behavior pattern which affected a large and representative part of the town's population. As occurred earlier with the migrational data, the intensity of this mobility diminished over the period studied. Yet nothing indicates that these years were not normal ones and we can safely assume that the rates represent typical on-going levels of intra-urban mobility. Of all economic groups of household heads, the professional sector showed by far the highest levels of mobility. The fact that the privileged groups of Cuenca's society were precisely those most likely to change residence is not surprising and underscores, once again, the dynamic nature of this group which has already come to light not only in Cuenca, but in other studies of migrants as well.

The behavior patterns of servants, the most mobile of all urban groups, shows that their mobility was equal or superior to that of any other group in society. Levels where almost one out of every five servant girls changed residence and job every year are quite startling. The myth of the life-long servant, at least in Cuenca, must be forever

would have gone unnoticed. In any case, any underestimation of mobility is probably slight. See the Appendix for furhter details.

Table 7.15   *Age distribution of intra-urban movers, by sex and for certain economic sectors*

Age group	Males			Females	
	Total	Day laborers	Professional/ administration	Servants	Total
15–19	14	1	3	41	21
20–24	20	10	11	39	25
25–29	19	31	15	11	12
30–34	13	13	19	3	10
35–39	8	13	13	2	5
40–44	9	11	13	1	7
45–49	4	8	6	1	4
50–59	6	6	10	1	8
>60	8	7	10	1	9
Total	101	100	100	100	101
Number	648	144	156	290	1,001

Note The total column includes all males or females in the population, whether or not they were household heads. The sector professional/administration includes the clergy.

banished![43] Not only did female and male servants spend few years in town, but while there they changed residence often. Cases in which the same servants have been found in the same household for more than one year were quite unusual.

In much the same manner as the general migration patterns, intra-urban mobility affected all age groups, though some with more intensity than others (Table 7.15). Males between 20 and 29 years of age and women between 15 and 24 showed the greatest tendency to move. Here too servant mobility and marriage played an important role. First of all, the age distribution of domestic service influenced the overall age structure of their mobility and consequently that of the mobility of the society as a whole. Furthermore, in Cuenca at this time, age at first marriage was 26.9 for men and 24.6 for women, and mostly affected young adults living with their parents. Once married, the prevailing system of household formation induced these couples to

---

[43] It should be noted that our yearly perspective tends to miss moves which take place at shorter intervals. This could be especially important in the case of domestic servants whose stays in one household might well have been considerably shorter.

establish separate residence and so enter the pool of intra-urban movers.

While these reasons help explain the intensity of mobility among certain age groups, they do little to shed light on the high general levels of intra-urban mobility which can be better interpreted in view of the physical and economic availability of rental housing in the town. High degrees of urban movement were closely related to the relative supply of housing, which in turn was dependent on the large numbers of people who arrived in or departed from the town yearly.[44] In a situation where rent control did not exist, the prevailing shortage of housing which tended to push rental prices upwards, was counter-balanced by the great number of dwellings vacated yearly. In this way, the rental housing market was quite dynamic, changing constantly and characterized by sharp price fluctuations. This in turn encouraged people in the town to be on the look-out for more reasonable housing.

The more often people moved, the more they supported this system. Even today elderly Spaniards can remember a situation in which their own families were willing to pick up their belongings, load them on a cart and move, even if it was only across the street, as long as they could find a better rental arrangement. In this way, intra-urban mobility patterns played a key economic role, not only for the owners but for the migrants themselves. The extent of this mobility could not help but become a vital characteristic of urban society where move-ment was a basic part of existence. The prevailing marriage system had always involved mobility by its very nature, yet the age distri-bution of this mobility indicates that it was far more than simply marriage-related, and included circulation of kin among households, entry into domestic service by urban children, as well as movement of servants and families in search of improved economic opportunities. While this interpretation of mobility is difficult to prove completely within a historical context, it is certainly a plausible explanation for the situation of intense movement which existed in Cuenca.

The age distribution of the intra-urban movers varied appreciably according to social group. Once again, sample size restricts my analysis to the household heads of the two most mobile and numerous urban groups of household heads: day laborers and professionals/ administration/privileged. Each showed very different behavior pat-terns (Table 7.15). Peak intra-urban day laborer mobility occurred between 25 and 29 years of age and seems greatly influenced by marriage. The mobility of professionals, however, reveals a far weaker

[44] 83 per cent of the town's residents lived in rental housing. The subject of rental housing and income was discussed in greater depth in chapter 6.

tie to marriage and was spread evenly over most of their life cycle. Apart from the very rich, who probably owned their homes and would generally not move, the relative abundance of rental housing would lead the rest of this group, which included modestly paid civil servants and more wealthy professionals, to utilize their economic position to find housing in the more desirable parts of the upper town. This directional aspect of their mobility will become clear shortly.

Finally, repeated changes of residence characterized the behavior of a certain number of families. It is not uncommon to find a family moving two or three times during the five-year period under consideration. A couple of examples will illustrate this point. Fernando Alonso, concierge by profession and a native of the neighboring province of Teruel, his wife Demetria Rodríguez and their four children, in 1843 and 1844 lived in the parish of San Juan, and in 1845 and 1846 they were in San Gil. By 1847 Alonso was a widower, his eldest son was no longer at home, he had become a bricklayer and the family had moved to the parish of San Martín. Tomás Castro, day laborer from Galicia and married to Dolores Pérez from the province of Cuenca, lived with his wife in the parish of San Juan in 1843 and 1844, in Santa Cruz in 1845 and in Santa María in 1846 and 1847. Finally, Feliciano Cordero, office worker from Madrid, married to María Camarón of Cuenca, lived with his wife, two children, sister and servant in the parish of San Pedro from 1843 to 1845. In 1846 they moved to Santo Domingo and had two more children in tow, only to end up in San Juan the next year. Examples like these are not uncommon and seem to indicate an even more extensive mobility than we might have expected, or at least the existence of hyper-mobile groups in urban society.

The numerical importance of this mobility is now clear, as is its age structure and, at least indirectly, the reasons behind it. Yet my analysis will still not be complete until the spatial dimensions of these transfers have been understood. Where did these mobile individuals move; can discernible patterns be identified? Did they stay in their neighborhoods or change to other parts of town? Was the pattern different if the mobile person was a doctor or a maid, a shopkeeper or a day laborer?

These questions are important and must be clarified if we are to understand mobile behavior patterns more fully. In order to do so, origin–destination tables have been drawn up so as to represent relevant patterns statistically. This required the precise location of people at two different moments and presented few problems since the desired information already existed on the cards made out for

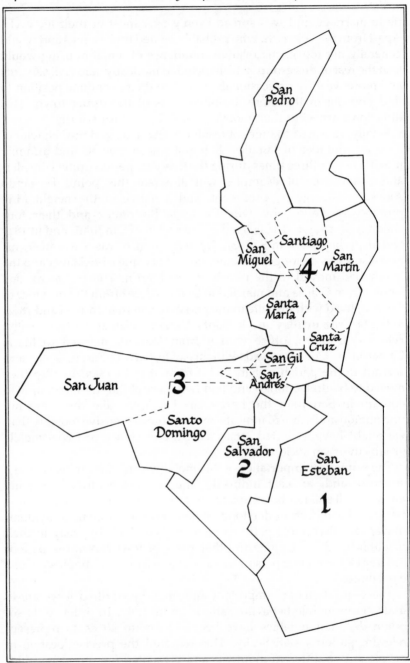

Map 7.1 Division of Cuenca by districts and parishes, *c.* 1850

mobile people. It was also necessary to divide the town up into neighborhoods that would, if possible, be approximately the same size but have different social and geographical characteristics. The number of neighborhoods had to be sufficient to reflect the diversity of this hill town, but not so many as to prevent a clear-cut analysis. Ultimately four districts were rather arbitrarily created. These were the parish of San Esteban (District 1); the parish of El Salvador (District 2); the parishes of San Juan, Santo Domingo, San Andrés and San Gil (District 3); and the parishes of Santa María, Santa Cruz, San Martín, San Miguel, Santiago and San Pedro (District 4) (Map 7.1).

These neighborhoods had approximately the same population and represented clearly distinct sections of town. Districts 1 and 2 were located in the lower part of the city near the Huécar river and were the neighborhoods with the highest concentration of artisans, farmers, day laborers, etc. From a social and geographical standpoint, District 3 was one of transition. The lower end of the parishes of San Juan and Santo Domingo was populated by economically productive classes, much the same as Districts 1 and 2, while the rest was primarily, though not exclusively, a district inhabited by the bourgeoisie and employees of the local administration. This district was located half way between the "lower town" and the "upper town." Finally, District 4 corresponded to the entire upper part of town, had by far the highest economic standing and was where most of the professionals, clergy and other privileged groups resided. At the very top of the parish of San Pedro there was a small neighborhood which was fundamentally agricultural and working-class. However, it only represented a small part of the district's population. While all of these neighborhoods had a distinct social make-up, it would be mistaken to think that they were composed exclusively of this or that social group. In a town such as Cuenca neighborhoods were thoroughly mixed and members of diverse social groups frequently lived side by side. It is only when neighborhoods as a whole are taken into account that clear differences emerge.

One further problem arose when constructing the origin–destination tables. The existence of one-parish districts, I felt, might lead to some degree of under-registration of movement within those districts. Information regarding residence by street helped minimize a problem which, however, is still a real one as can be seen in Table 7.16. Comparative district data suggest that some degree of under-estimation might well exist in the two one-parish districts, though the small discrepancies in district levels might also be explained by differential district mobility. Untimately, any slight underestimation should not fundamentally alter the results.

Table 7.16 *Population and mobility by district*

District	Proportion total population, 1844–1847	Proportion total changes in residence
1	20.1	17.5
2	24.3	22.8
3	25.2	30.2
4	30.3	29.5

Table 7.17 contains several origin–destination cross-tabulations and offers a view of the spatial aspects of intra-urban mobility. In an effort to ensure clarity, my commentary will only touch on its most salient points. The major conclusion which emerges from the data is that this mobility was strongly conditioned by spatial realities. When considering the population as a whole, or by sex, the highest standardized residual normally corresponds to purely local changes in residence.[45] The majority of all intra-urban moves stayed within the district of origin, though some had the adjacent one as a destination. Furthermore, the mobility patterns in Cuenca were not entirely uniform. In the upper part of town where two-thirds of all changes took place within the district, only 6 per cent had District 1 (the lowest part of town) as their destination. As we move down the hill from District 4, this situation changes gradually until Districts 1 and 2 are reached where it was, at least apparently, quite different. As the residuals suggest, between these two neighborhoods there was a clear exchange of people. This indicates that, at least regarding these two districts, the role played by spatial constraints was slightly different, though certainly not negligible. Even though a fair number of District 2 residents moved to District 3, very few moved to District 4; and District 1 sent practically nobody to Districts 3 and 4. Finally District 3, from a social and spatial standpoint, the transition zone of town, despite appreciable intradistrict mobility, did send residents to Districts 2 and 4, but very few to District 1.

In this way Cuenca becomes a town where intra-urban mobility was invariably local, with the exception of the two lower districts where exchanges of people modified what was still a fundamentally local movement. Sex did not change these basic patterns which warrant further explanation. It would seem that for its inhabitants Cuenca was really a number of towns which were only indirectly related. The fact

[45] High chi-squared significance levels and statistics of association also indicate that neighborhood of origin and of destination are not independent.

Table 7.17 *Origin and destination tables for intra-urban moves, by sex and certain social categories*

(a) Day laborers

| | DESTINATION | | | | |
	San Esteban	El Salvador	Middle town	Upper town	Row Total
ORIGIN					
San Esteban					
1	22	20	5	4	51
2	4.1	8.8	−6.3	−6.6	35.2%
3	1.0	2.6	−1.9	−2.0	
El Salvador					
1	24	5	9	1	39
2	10.3	−3.6	.4	−7.1	26.9%
3	2.8	−1.2	.1	−2.5	
Middle town					
1	1	6	16	2	25
2	−7.8	.5	10.5	−3.2	17.2%
3	−2.6	.2	4.5	−1.4	
Upper town					
1	4	1	2	23	30
2	−6.6	−5.6	−4.6	16.8	20.7%
3	−2.0	−2.2	−1.8	6.7	
Column	51	32	32	30	145
Total	35.2%	22.1%	22.1%	20.7%	100.0%

Chi-square	Significance	Cells with expected frequency <5
117.001	.0000	none

Statistic	Value
Cramer's V	.519
Contingency coefficient	.668

Note 1 = cell count 2 = residual (difference from expected cell count) 3 = standardized residual.

Table 7.17 (*cont.*)
(b)   *Industry/artisans*

| | DESTINATION | | | |
	San Esteban	El Salvador	Middle town	Upper town	Row Total
ORIGIN					
San Esteban					
1	3	7	2	1	13
2	1.0	4.5	−3.1	−2.5	14.4%
3	.7	2.9	−1.4	−1.3	
El Salvador					
1	4	3	5	2	14
2	1.8	.4	−.4	−1.7	15.6%
3	1.2	.2	−.2	−.9	
Middle town					
1	7	6	23	1	37
2	1.2	−1.0	8.6	−8.9	41.1%
3	.5	−.4	2.3	−2.8	
Upper town					
1	0	1	5	20	26
2	−4.0	−3.9	−5.1	13.1	28.9%
3	−2.0	−1.8	−1.6	5.0	
Column	14	17	35	24	90
Total	15.6%	18.9%	38.9%	26.7%	100.0%

Chi-square	Significance	Cells with expected frequency <5
62.797	.0000	8 of 16 (50%)

Statistic	Value
Cramer's V	.482
Contingency coefficient	.641

Note 1 = cell count 2 = residual (difference from expected cell count) 3 = standardization residual.

Table 7.17 (*cont.*)

(c)   *Professionals/privileged/public administration*

DESTINATION	San Esteban	El Salvador	Middle town	Upper town	Row Total
ORIGIN					
San Esteban					
1	1	5	3	6	15
2	−.2	2.7	−2.3	−.3	9.6%
3	−.1	1.8	−1.0	−.1	
El Salvador					
1	2	6	10	6	24
2	.2	2.3	1.5	−4.0	15.4%
3	.1	1.2	.5	−1.3	
Middle town					
1	5	12	32	16	65
2	0.0	2.0	9.1	−11.1	41.7%
3	0.0	.6	1.9	−2.1	
Upper town					
1	4	1	10	37	52
2	0.0	−7.0	−8.3	15.3	33.3%
3	0.0	−2.5	−1.9	3.3	
Column Total	12 7.7%	24 15.4%	55 35.3%	65 41.7%	156 100.0%

Chi-square	Significance	Cells with expected frequency <5
36.797	.0000	5 of 16 (31.3%)

Statistic	Value
Cramer's V	.280
Contingency coefficient	.437

Note 1 = cell count 2 = residual (difference from expected cell count) 3 = standardized residual.

Table 7.17 (*cont.*)

(d)   *Female Servants*

	San Esteban	DESTINATION El Salvador	Middle town	Upper town	Row Total
ORIGIN					
San Esteban					
1	3	6	1	6	16
2	1.4	2.2	−3.6	.0	5.4%
3	1.1	1.2	−1.7	.0	
El Salvador					
1	10	27	16	21	74
2	2.4	9.6	−5.4	−6.7	25.2%
3	.9	2.3	−1.2	−1.3	
Middle town					
1	9	15	41	30	95
2	−.7	−7.3	13.5	−5.5	32.3%
3	−.2	−1.5	2.6	−.9	
Upper town					
1	8	21	27	53	109
2	−3.1	−4.6	−4.5	12.2	37.1%
3	− .9	− .9	− .8	1.9	
Column	30	69	85	110	294
Total	10.2%	23.5%	28.9%	37.4%	100.0%

Chi-square	Significance	Cells with expected frequency <5
30.416	.0004	3 of 16 (18.8%)

Statistic	Value
Cramer's V	.186
Contingency coefficient	.306

Note 1 = cell count 2 = residual (difference from expected cell count) 3 = standardized residual.

Table 7.17 (*cont.*)
(e) Males

| | DESTINATION | | | |
	San Esteban	El Salvador	Middle town	Upper town	Row total
ORIGIN					
San Esteban					
1	55	79	21	17	172
2	20.6	42.5	−28.9	−34.2	19.6%
3	3.5	7.0	−4.1	−4.8	
El Salvador					
1	79	39	45	24	187
2	41.6	−.7	−9.2	−31.7	21.3%
3	6.8	−.1	−1.3	−4.2	
Middle town					
1	26	48	145	45	264
2	−26.7	−8.1	68.5	−33.7	30.1%
3	−3.7	−1.1	7.8	−3.8	
Upper town					
1	15	20	43	175	253
2	−35.5	−33.7	−30.4	99.6	28.9%
3	−5.0	−4.6	−3.5	11.5	
Column total	175 20.0%	186 21.2%	254 29.0%	261 29.8%	876 100.0%

Chi-square	Significance	Cells with expected frequency < 5
448.169	.0000	None

Statistic	Value
Cramer's V	.413
Contingency coefficient	.582

Note 1 = cell count 2 = residual (difference from expected cell count) 3 = standardized residual.

Table 7.17 (*cont.*)
(*f*) Females

	San Esteban	DESTINATION El Salvador	Middle town	Upper town	Row total
ORIGIN					
San Esteban					
1	78	80	20	22	200
2	42.7	33.5	−38.5	−37.6	16.2%
3	7.2	4.9	−5.0	−4.9	
El Salvador					
1	88	91	73	38	290
2	36.8	23.6	−11.8	−48.5	23.5
3	5.1	2.9	−1.3	−5.2	
Middle town					
1	30	75	198	71	374
2	−36.1	−12.0	88.6	−40.5	30.3%
3	−4.4	−1.3	8.5	−3.8	
Upper town					
1	22	41	70	237	370
2	−43.4	−45.1	−38.2	126.7	30.0%
3	−5.4	−4.9	−3.7	12.1	
Column total	218 17.7%	287 23.3%	361 29.3%	368 29.8%	1234 100.0%

Chi-square	Significance	Cells with expected frequency < 5
507.242	.0000	None

Statistic	Value
Cramer's V	.370
Contingency coefficient	.540

Note 1 = cell count 2 = residual (difference from expected cell count) 3 = standardized residual.

Table 7.17 (*cont.*)
(g) Total

| | DESTINATION | | | |
	San Esteban	El Salvador	Middle town	Upper town	Row total
ORIGIN					
San Esteban					
1	136	158	41	41	376
2	68.5	61.2	−63.8	−65.8	17.0%
3	8.3	6.2	−6.2	−6.4	
El Salvador					
1	168	130	120	63	481
2	81.6	6.1	−14.1	−73.7	21.7%
3	8.8	.5	−1.2	−6.3	
Middle town					
1	57	121	345	115	638
2	−57.5	−43.3	167.2	−66.3	28.8%
3	−5.4	−3.4	12.5	−4.9	
Upper town					
1	37	162	112	411	722
2	−92.6	−24.0	−89.3	205.8	32.6%
3	−8.1	−1.8	−6.3	14.4	
Column total	398 18.0%	571 25.8%	618 27.9%	630 28.4%	2217 100.0%

Chi-square	Significance	Cells with expected frequency < 5
843.296	.0000	None

Statistic	Value
Cramer's V	.356
Contingency coefficient	.525

Note 1 = cell count 2 = residual (difference from expected cell count) 3 = standardized residual.

that when changing residence most people seemed to ignore the existence of any part of town more than 100 meters or so from where they lived, is a good example of this.

This localism itself was the result of a combination of realities. It is axiomatic in migration theory that information was and is vital for all movement, and people often found out about the possibility of moving to a new residence town by word of mouth, from some friend or neighbor.[46] This itself tended to restrict the geographical scope of the information people received. Moreover the endogamous residence patterns of kin groups in town which we saw in chapter 6, would themselves tend to place limits on people's mobility. Finally, the popular conception of urban space, which led people unconsciously to exclude certain areas as likely places of residence, might well have also played an important role. Whatever the proportional weight of these and other factors might be, there was a *de facto* fragmentation of mobility patterns within the town.

This last point leads to yet another question: why then did the different parts of town reveal at least marginally distinct behavior patterns? Here the social make-up of each district probably played an important role. Both Districts 1 and 2 were predominantly made up of day laborers and artisans and may well have been perceived by their inhabitants as one homogeneous district, clearly separate from the others in town. In this way, the radius of movement would include both as though they were really one, and thus an exchange of residents was a common event. In turn, District 2 was also a kind of middle district which participated fully in exchanges with District 1, but also with parts of District 3, itself partially populated by members of the same social group. Districts 1 and 3, however, had few real exchanges because, ultimately, they shared no common boundaries. In this way, the social group only partially influenced the more general spatial constraints on movement.

In order to delve a bit deeper into the determinants of the spatial aspects of urban mobility, a brief look at behavior patterns of different groups in society might prove useful. In the first place, it is clear that the behavior described for the lower part of town was, in fact, the behavior of day laborers, farmers, artisans and members of the services sector, but not at all typical of professionals. Intra-urban mobility patterns of professionals were less local than those of other social groups.[47] Day laborers and artisans moved freely between

---

[46] See Neuberger, for example, (1977: 470), Morrison (1973), and Ravenstein (1885–1889).

[47] See the statistics of association in Table 7.17 for these groups.

Districts 1 and 2, but rarely reached 3 and 4. On the other hand, professionals showed an ascendant pattern of behavior. Independently of district of residence, the majority of the sector tended towards the upper districts in town and, concretely, District 4. Wherever sample size permits, it becomes evident that other groups showed none of these tendencies. For example, far from showing any upward movement, day laborers either moved laterally (the case of Districts 3 and 4) or in a clearly downward direction (the case of District 2). Nonetheless, continuing with the example of the day laborers, it would be a mistake to overvalue the importance of their social group in these displacements since it also appears that, despite appreciable concentrations of day laborers in District 1 and the upper part of District 4, there was virtually no movement between them.

Evidently, the answer to these questions must ultimately come to grips with the reality that both socio-economic and spatial factors tended to influence the mentality of the people of Cuenca when they set about the business of choosing a new residence. Whereas social group seemed especially important for residents of the lower part of town, space and its conceptualization were vital everywhere. An excellent example of this last point is precisely District 4 in the upper part of town which showed the highest levels of local mobility and, at the same time, from a geographical and social standpoint was also the most heterogeneous and isolated of all the districts.

Let us end by returning once again to the behavior of servants. Of all urban groups, servants showed the least tendency to move within their district of residence. Not only did they make up the most mobile of all sectors, but their intra-urban mobility was also the least local.[48] The data also reveal other noteworthy aspects of female servant mobility. The geographically ascendant nature of their displacements was still more pronounced than it was for professionals. A tendency seems to exist which led servants toward District 4, where most of the domestic service resided, only subsequently to initiate, perhaps, a descent which might end up in District 2. The reality is as follows: maids from District 1 moved preferentially to Districts 2 and 4; those from District 2 moved to 3 or 4; those from District 3 either stayed or moved to District 4; and, once there, a considerable proportion moved to District 3 or 2. Does this mean that while these servants stayed in Cuenca, they circulated from the bottom to the top of town, and then back down again? It would be very risky to answer this question with an unqualified yes and, even if some sort of circulation did exist, it would never be simple or unilateral. What is certainly plausible is that

[48] This can be seen in the cross-tabulation table corresponding to female servants.

in-migrant servants would seldom reach Districts 3 or 4 directly, though sooner or later during their sojourn in the town, they would work there.

Kin often helped either directly or indirectly to bring the servants into town in the first place. Once in town, however, a servant's tenure in a given household was normally quite short. If upwards of 35 per cent of all servants entered or left town in a given year, and another 16–17 per cent changed dwellings every year in town, it is quite difficult to imagine them staying for prolonged periods in any household. These levels of change themselves underscored for all involved the transitory nature of the profession. If the difficulties and misunderstandings which seem universally to affect communication between domestic servants and their employers is added to the general prevailing attitude toward domestic service as a transitory, life-cycle profession, the inclination to frequent change is an understandable reaction. The tendency upward, then, would be a direct product of the concentration of the well-to-do in District 4. Can this hyper-mobile group be considered as "dynamic risk takers"? Hardly. Domestic service was more a life-cycle activity serving a specific economic function, and was left behind once a girl reached marrying age or a man could inherit land or become a day laborer.

Conclusions

By now the extent to which the population was mobile in and around the town of Cuenca has been sufficiently emphasized. While the economic roots of migration and intra-urban mobility can be easily perceived, it is important to remember that they were entirely unrelated to an industrial or even to a growing economy. Other studies have shown that once industrial expansion got under way, there were signs that overall movement of people tended to decrease (Kertzer and Hogan, 1985: 12–18). Here it can be hypothesized that not only might propensity to move decrease with industrialization, but ever greater proportions of those flows would end up being more permanent in nature. Ultimately, though, the intensity of movement, both to and from town as well as within it, speaks for the existence of an economic system based on the dynamic resourcefulness of people who were able to maximize income diversification so as to ensure the maintenance of living standards in the face of on-going rural population growth. The extent to which this system enabled them to survive successfully is a fitting proof of its own durability. Movement was more a solidifying than a disintegrating element of pre-industrial Cuenca.

The human transfers in and around the town ended up involving as much as one quarter of Cuenca's population in any given year. Despite the high levels of mobility found in other studies, none have revealed similar levels to those of the people of Cuenca. This, however, may be the consequence of the methodological focus of each research project rather than of differing historical realities. Intense movement was probably the hallmark of pre-industrial urban society in Europe. Yet an understanding of the complexity of urban society cannot help but make us doubt what might seem implicit in this argument: if up to one quarter of a town's population moved every year, then practically the entire town must become involved sooner or later in those flows. All towns were filled with heterogeneous groups of people which could range from the very wealthy to the very poor, from the very stable to the very transient. In short, any reference to a town, be it industrial or pre-industrial, as some kind of unitary microcosm would seem to be a gross over-simplification. How then can this basic concept of the complexity of urban areas be reconciled with the mobility of the residents of Cuenca?

As has been pointed out in some studies of contemporary migrations, the existence of certain hyper-mobile groups within the town would help explain the intensity of movement as a function of these segments of society, rather than of the population as a whole. In order to test for the existence of these groups in town, I have endeavored to track down frequent movers in order to ascertain their relative importance in the city. The test is based on people selected randomly who were present in the town in 1843. In other words, those selected come from all parishes, all age groups (above 10 years of age) and all social sectors. Since all were present in 1843, a maximum of four possible moves existed for each person which could correspond either to out-migration, in-migration or residence change within the town.

The results can be found in Table 7.18 and reveal the relative importance of mobile and non-mobile sectors in town. Almost half of the sample is made up of people who did not move throughout the period under study. Naturally this does not mean that they were not susceptible to move, but rather that between 1843 and 1847 half of the town's population made up that stable core which we had expected to find (Ringrose, 1983: 35–43). If we pursue the data a bit further, it is also evident that among the mobile population, there are hyper-mobile subsectors. Almost 40 per cent of those who moved at least once in four years, in fact moved more often, and another almost 40 per cent of those moving at least twice, moved more often. More generally it can be affirmed that movement seems to beget movement

Table 7.18   *Propensity to movement in Cuenca, 1843–1847*

		\multicolumn{5}{c}{Total number of moves}		
		0	1	2	3	4	Total	n
	0	47.0	29.3	14.5	6.8	2.3	99.9	557
Minimum	1		55.3	27.5	12.9	4.4	100.1	295
number	2			61.4	28.8	9.8	100.0	132
of moves	3				74.5	25.5	100.0	51
	4					100.0	100.0	13

Note This table estimates the percentage of people within a given category (based on the minimum number of moves) likely to move × number of times during the 1843–1847 period.

in almost one quarter of the town's population. Unfortunately the sample size does not allow me to categorize these groups, though one might suspect that they were mostly composed of servants and other young people who circulated in, out and about town.

The mobile groups were the true floating population in a pre-industrial city like Cuenca and it was they who were most likely to move in times of economic duress. They were a type of barometer which was highly sensitive to economic and demographic conjunctures either in the town or in the surrounding rural areas. They were the ones who would fill the town in times of acute subsistence crisis or leave it when the sources of urban employment dried up, much as probably occurred in the seventeenth century, and they would fill it when industrialization began or leave it in periods of weak rural population growth in which land, jobs and potential spouses might be plentiful in the countryside. Mostly though, they were the ones with their feet in the urban and the rural worlds, making use of both worlds as an integral part of their domestic economies. They were the concrete agents whereby towns were linked to their own hinterlands. In like manner, those people prone to move into and out of the town were probably also those who moved within the town itself, a supposition made reasonable by the fact that movement seems to beget movement in Cuenca. These groups were also those with the restricted nuptiality, oscillating fertility and higher mortality so characteristic of urban areas, as well as the principle source of unskilled labor so essential to urban economies. Once again the city looms before us as an immensely complex reality which historians have yet to fully understand.

8

A culture of mobility

In the course of this book I have attempted to address a number of issues concerning pre-industrial towns and urban behavior patterns. The extent to which these patterns were different from rural ones; whether or not rural, regional or specifically urban factors influenced people's behavior; the nature of the links between towns and their rural hinterlands; towns as agents of change or of stability in early modern European societies; these and other questions have entered into this discussion of pre-industrial urban society. Ultimately I wanted to know just what "urban behavior" entailed. The concrete historical context used for this study has been a small and backward Spanish provincial town, but many of the issues I have looked at have ended up concerning not only Cuenca, but Spain and much of urban Europe as well. My enquiry has entailed the analysis of many different subjects, ranging from urban economic structures to migration patterns. It has been fruitful, not so much for the answers it has provided, but for the questions it has raised.

Resistance to change has proven to be an on-going characteristic of pre-industrial Cuenca. With the exception of the historic reversal of its fortunes during the seventeenth century, most other aspects of its society were marked by their stability. Family structures, basic migratory patterns, economic structures and their spatial distribution in town, reaction to times of dearth and epidemic, demographic patterns, etc. were all basically unchanged, at least between the middle of the seventeenth and the early nineteenth centuries. This is not to say that no evolution at all can be detected, it can, and this has been brought out in the different sections of the book. Yet Cuenca during the middle part of the nineteenth century was fundamentally the same as it had been two centuries earlier. It is highly unlikely that fundamental change could ever have been generated from within early modern urban societies. Exogenous factors, be they political, economic or military in nature, were far more important.

The hypothesis whereby the existence of towns ended up stimulating change in rural social structures and behavior patterns has not received any empirical support at all. On the contrary, for the most part the existence of urban areas has ended up bolstering traditional structures in the countryside. Migration to towns by those people with no place in the rural marriage, job or home market enabled rural societies to maintain traditional modes of behavior long after these had ceased to be demographically or economically feasible. Perennially negative natural growth rates in towns contributed to the maintenance of overall demographic stability in pre-industrial society. The density of urban development was, of course, crucial on this point. Cuenca's influence on its surrounding rural areas was marginal at best, but Madrid's, for example, was not. In both cases, however, towns served as escape valves for imbalances in surrounding rural areas.

In the long run, each needed the other in order to keep traditional society functioning smoothly and the result was that both worlds were closely linked. These ties to the rural hinterland were far stronger in a small town like Cuenca than in other larger urban centers. Ultimately the strength of rural–urban links depended on the type of migration attracted to the town. As we have seen, the growth or not of urban populations, regardless of their size, depended directly on migration. The social make-up of this migration, however, was strictly dependent on the size, and the economic and political importance of the town itself. In Cuenca most migrants streamed into town from the surrounding areas, while some came from outside the confines of the province. Quite a different type of migration emerges if we look at a major city like Madrid. There, migrants arrived from all of the provinces in central Spain, and from more distant points as well.[1] The larger the town, the greater its ability to attract long-distance migrants. This had important consequences for aggregate patterns of urban behavior, especially if we consider that over 60 per cent of Madrid's population and around 45 per cent of Cuenca's were made up of people born elsewhere. Upon arrival in town, and probably for several years, these migrants carried with them their "rural" attitudes towards marriage, fertility, family, social relations and just about every other aspect of urban life. When migrants came from local areas, a town's social structures closely resembled those of its own hinterland, and when they came from afar, similarities were considerably

[1] In 1850 the greatest share of Madrid migrants came from the region of Asturias which is located on the northern coast, some 450 km away (Ringrose, 1983: 52).

more diffuse. The rural links were always there, but they were less place-specific in larger towns.

This is not to say that urban structures and behavior patterns were identical to those in rural areas. All the similarities I have found have been in levels relative to other urban or other rural environments. Regional patterns of behavior existed and included both urban and rural areas. Absolute differences between both worlds, however, were considerable and should not be underestimated. Urban fertility and nuptiality were much lower than in surrounding rural areas, and mortality was higher. Family patterns were generally similar, but differed in many ways mainly affecting the presence of servants and kin, and the age at which children left their parental households. Levels of mobility were far more intense in towns than in the countryside. It would not be difficult to find many more examples of the differences between rural and urban behavior and structures. The Cuenca data have brought this to light and similar results have been found in other studies about rural and urban areas in Spain and elsewhere in Europe. There were also specifically "urban" determinants of behavior, otherwise these differences would not have emerged so clearly.

This obliges me to revise my original idea regarding the static nature of urban society. While it is true that it did practically nothing to stimulate change in rural areas and urban society itself showed little fundamental evolution, for the migrants themselves who came to live in town, urban residence ended up causing profound changes in their entire outlook towards life. When they first arrived in town, they were bearers of basically rural attitudes, but as they stayed on this gradually changed. Their fertility decreased, as did their life expectancy. The organization itself of their family economies could never be the same as in rural areas, and so mobile families were forced to adjust. At least for migrants, urban society tended to alter traditional modes of behavior. Did those who had lived in town and who subsequently returned to their rural origins, as many did, take the urban attitudes they had learned with them? Unfortunately there are no empirical data which might enable us to address this question, though something of this nature probably did occur despite the fact that return migrants eventually reverted to their traditionally "rural" ways of thinking.[2]

For the ideas of return migrants to have an effect on rural society as a whole, there had to be sufficiently high numbers of them to make a

---

[2] Bardet (1989) has hypothesized that the spread of family limitation practices in rural areas around Rouen was in part the work of migrants who returned to the countryside after a more or less prolonged stay in town.

dent in the rural world. This could never have happened in pre-industrial Europe where rural food production placed a ceiling on urban growth and percentages urban were never very high. The case of central Spain between the sixteenth and the nineteenth centuries is eloquent proof of these limits. Even though the backbone of Castile's traditional urban system was broken and Madrid emerged as the single dominant city, the overall density of urban development in the region hardly changed before the beginning of the nineteenth century. Whenever the carrying capacity of agricultural production was surpassed, as it was in central Spain during the late sixteenth century and then again during the latter part of the eighteenth century, all urban growth ceased. This situation changed gradually during the nineteenth century, but by the time levels of urbanization were high enough to have a decisive influence on rural social structures, the nature of migration had changed and return migrants were only a minority. In Spain it was well into the twentieth century before this happened and by then the urban influence over the rural world could be seen more readily in economic activities, government involvement in local life, and cultural manifestations, than in the behavior of return migrants.

People's propensity to move about has emerged as perhaps the single most noteworthy trait of urban populations. Migration levels were extremely intense for people of all ages, sexes and social categories. This pattern was striking in Cuenca, and was quite possibly typical of most pre-industrial urban areas in Europe, regardless of their size or cultural context. Migration was unquestionably the key to the growth or stagnation of urban populations. However, at least in the case of Cuenca, the flow of people into town was balanced by equally strong levels of counterstream migration, often involving people who circulated between the town and its rural hinterland. This type of migration was only part of the overall pattern of movement shown by the people of Cuenca, and was complemented by extremely high levels of displacement within the town itself. The inhabitants of Cuenca shared a common "culture of mobility" which had far-reaching effects on their lives and on the nature of the societies they lived in. People moved to secure jobs, to position themselves in the marriage market, to get better housing arrangements, or for many other reasons. Movement tied household economies and families in town to those in the countryside. More generally, migrants bridged the rural and urban worlds and helped shape social structures in both. The existence of a "culture of mobility" in Cuenca was based on rational decisions made in response to the inescapable need to diversify sources of income. It is evident that mobile persons did not feel great attachment to their place of residence, and perhaps not to their village of origin either. Property and economic assets gave stability, but these were not accessible to everyone, at least not in sufficient quantities.

The kin group played a key role in this entire process. Much of the migration and mobility in Cuenca was a function of family interests and needs, or received the support of kin networks. This was especially true for people who moved about in town or those who circulated between Cuenca and its province. Kin groups often had roots in rural and urban areas and the migration of family members ended up furthering group interests in both of them. Where the kin group had no prior ties to town, sending children there as servants or in other jobs was an essential source of income for the family and for the future wedding of the migrant himself. It was also a source of money in a rural society whose economy was based on subsistence farming and where economic relations until recently were often based on barter rather than on cash.

When a migrant decided to stay on, he and his immediate household became, so to speak, family outposts in town. In this way, migrants and family economies ended up linking both worlds. Nearly every urban migrant whose place of origin was in the province of Cuenca probably maintained on-going ties to kin in his village of origin. These ties provided support for family members in both worlds, and often had very concrete economic implications. Once family outposts had been established in town, they became agents for the migration of other members of the kin group, either directly to kin households or more frequently by helping rural kin find urban jobs. The kin group and the "culture of mobility" were complementary realities and one of the principal ways in which towns were linked to their hinterlands.

The complexity of urban societies has been apparent throughout this study. David Ringrose (1983) attempted to conceptualize urban society with the metaphor of the "core and the periphery," two different and often opposing worlds inside the town itself. The present study has shown that there was no single core or periphery, in either social or spatial terms. The culture of mobility in Cuenca affected every level of society and was so pervasive that it must have been considered by the residents as an altogether mundane phenomenon. Social structures were far more complex, and being a migrant or not was only one of many aspects which conditioned pre-industrial urban life. Despite their fluidity in human terms, however, social structures have proved to be fundamentally stable. The "culture of mobility" can be more readily interpreted in terms of rational choices born of necessity than as an agent of social change. Its widespread existence was one of the key stabilizing elements in a society where economic opportunities were few, change infrequent, and life difficult.

Appendix

The methodology followed in the elaboration of some of the calculations in chapter 6 and especially in chapter 7 is based on an intensive utilization of the municipal listings (*padrones*) dating from the years 1843 through 1847 which are located in the Municipal Archive of Cuenca. As mentioned in the text, these listings are quite complete and contain full nominative information, together with data regarding sex, age, profession, relation to head of household and origin.

Essentially the method is based on the localization of individuals within their households in 1843. A card was filled out for each family in town and contained all pertinent information, including the parish and street of residence. Subsequently the cards were sorted alphabetically within each parish and were given an alphanumerical identifier which itself represented the parish, street, and alphabetical order of the "family" card. In subsequent years, a parish by parish and family by family search was carried out. Once a family was located, new age information was registered. If there were any new members in that household, their pertinent information was written down, along with a "P" (present) in blue ink, and if someone was absent from a given parish, an "A" was written in red ink. When a household disappeared completely, all of its members were given "A"'s; and if a new one appeared, a new family card was filled out and all were given "P"'s. In both cases the cards were put back into the parish file in the correct alphabetical order.

This procedure was carried out for all 12 parishes and for every year until 1847. In this manner, the number of cards for each parish increased from one listing to the next. This was done in order to "catch" returning families and also so that cross-checking could be carried out at a later time in order to detect those households, say, whose heads had changed (marriage, death, etc.) and were thus located elsewhere within the parish file. A number of these "false" cards were, in fact, detected. The next stage consisted of filling out secondary cards for all "P"'s and "A"'s in the file. Each one contained full information about one person as well as the indentifier for his "family" card. A different card was filled out for household heads than for other members, so as to facilitate a classification of movement by economic sector. In all cases, different colors were used for the "P"'s and "A"'s. In total, some 3,000–3,500 family cards were filled out and about 10,000–12,000 individual cards drawn up. These secondary cards, then, represented the true migrants and were ordered alphabetically, independent of place and residence.

Subsequently, all "P"'s and all "A"'s were systematically compared. This was done for all of the cards, whether they were for household heads or other persons. It was carried out for every year and was done to detect not only intra-urban movement, but also movement of heads due to marriage and other reasons. In other words, if a person was single and "absent" in, say, 1846, he might be present, married and a household head in some other parish in the same year. Ultimately, three groups of cards appeared for each year: "P"'s, "A"'s and "matches." These then became the in-migrants, the out-migrants and the intra-urban residence changes respectively. From this point, it was a comparatively simple matter to calculate age and sex distribution, occupational status and even origin–destination for persons for the years 1844–1847. As mentioned in the text, four-year averages were used in order to minimize the effects of random fluctuations. Out-migration due to mortality was estimated from life tables drawn up for Cuenca at mid-century and was deducted from the "A"'s of each year. The denominator used to calculate the rates was the average age distribution in 1844 and 1846 (for age-specific rates) or the sectorial division of Cuenca in the 1844 listing (for household heads and servants).

A small test was carried out to ascertain the degree of under-registration in the municipal listings and to confirm the validity of the method. Since a complete death registration also exists for the same five-year period (1843–1847), if the listings were complete all people found deceased should also be listed as "absent" or as out-migrants in my calculations. The test was based on 279 cases during 1843 and 1844 and included all deceased except for children under 4 years of age and those people whose residence was listed as the Hospital of Santiago. In so doing I endeavored to eliminate those groups most prone to very short-term mobility or high mortality. 82.1 per cent of the deceased were also listed as "absent". Taking into consideration the fact that at least 10 per cent of the town's population entered the town every year and therefore would not necessarily be present on the municipal listing in the year they died, the effective under-registration on the listings would oscillate between 5 and 10 per cent. Therefore the rates of in- and out-migration are possibly overestimated to the same degree.

References

Abrams, P. 1978. "Towns and economic growth: Some theories and problems" in Abrams, P. and Wrigley, E. A. (eds.), *Towns in societies. Essays in Economic History and Historical Sociology*. Cambridge University Press, pp. 9–33.

Abrams, P. and Wrigley, E. A. (eds.) 1978. *Towns in Societies. Essays in Economic History and Historical Sociology*. Cambridge University Press.

Adams, D. W. 1969. "Rural migration and agricultural development in Colombia," *Economic Development and Cultural Change*, 17, 4, 527–539.

Akerman, S. and Norberg, A. 1976. "Employment opportunities, family-building and internal migration in the late nineteenth century: Some Swedish case studies" in Coale, A. J. (ed.), *Economic Factors in Population Growth*. John Wiley and Sons, New York, pp. 453–486.

Alvarez Santaló, L. C. 1974. *La población de Sevilla en el primer tercio del s. XIX*, Seville, Publicaciones de la Diputación Provincial de Sevilla.

1977. "La Casa de Expósitos de Sevilla en el siglo XVII," *Cuadernos de Historia*, 7, 491–532.

1980. *Marginación social y mentalidad en Andalucía occidental: Expósitos en Sevilla (1613–1910)*. Seville, Junta de Andalucía.

Amorim, M. N. S. Bettencourt. 1987. *Guimarâes 1580–1819. Estudo demográfico*. Lisbon, Instituto Nacional de Investigação Científico.

Anderson, M. 1971. *Family Structure in Nineteenth-Century Lancashire*. Cambridge University Press.

1980. *Approaches to the History of the Western Family*. London–New York, Macmillan.

Anes Alvarez, G. 1968. "Los pósitos en la España del siglo XVIII," *Moneda y Crédito*, 105, 39–69.

1969. *Economía e ilustración en la España del siglo XVIII*. Madrid, Ariel.

1970. *Las crisis agrarias en la España moderna*. Madrid, Taurus.

1974. "Antecedentes próximos del motín contra Esquilache," *Moneda y Crédito*, 128, 219–224.

1976. "Crisis de subsistencias y agitación campesina en la España de la Ilustración" in *La cuestión agraria en la España contemporánea (VI Coloquio de Pau)*. Madrid, Edicusa.

Ansón Calvo, M. C. 1977. *Demografía y sociedad urbana en la Zaragoza del siglo XVII. Un estudio con ordenadores*. Zaragoza, Caja de Ahorros de Zaragoza, Aragón y Rioja.

Appleby, A. B. 1973. "Disease or famine? Mortality in Cumberland and Westmorland, 1580–1640," *Economic History Review*, 26, 3, 403–432.

1977. "Famine, mortality and epidemic disease: A comment," *Economic History Review*, 30, 3, 508–512.

1978. *Famine in Tudor and Stuart England*. Stanford University Press.

Arango, J. 1980. "La teoría de la transición demográfica y la experiencia histórica," *Revista Española de Investigaciones Sociológicas*, 10, 169–198.

Arbiol, Fr. Antonio. 1791. *La familia regulada*. Madrid.

Arejula, J. M. 1806. *Breve descripción de la fiebre amarilla padecida en Cádiz y los pueblos comarcanos en 1800, en Medina-Sidonia en 1801, en Málaga en 1803, y esta última plaza y varias otras del reyno en 1804*. Madrid.

Artola, M. 1973. *La burguesía revolucionaria (1808–1974)*. Madrid, Alianza Universidad.

Auerbach, F. 1913. "Das Gesetz der Bevölkerungskonzentration," *Petermanns Geographische Mitteilungen*, 59, 74–76.

Baines, D. 1985. *Migration in a Mature Economy. Emigration and Internal Migration in England and Wales, 1861–1900*. Cambridge University Press.

Barbagli, M. 1984. *Sotto lo stesso tetto. Mutamenti della famiglia in Italia dal XV al XX secolo*. Bologna, Il Mulino.

Bardet, J. P. 1983. *Rouen aux XVIIᵉ et XVIIIᵉ siècles. Les mutations d'un espace social*, 2 vols. Paris, Société d'éditions d'enseignement supérieur.

1989. "Innovators and imitators in the practice of contraception in town and country" in van der Woude, A., De Vries, J., and Hayami, A. (eds.), *Urbanisation in History. A Process of Dynamic Interactions*, Oxford University Press.

Barreiro Mallón, B. 1973. *La jurisdicción de Xallas en el siglo XVIII. Población, sociedat y economía*. Universidad de Santiago de Compostela.

Barrio Gozalo, M. *et al.* 1987. *Historia de Segovia*. Segovia, Caja de Ahorros y Monte de Piedad de Segovia.

Bengtsson, T. 1984. "Harvest fluctuations and demographic response: Southern Sweden, 1751–1859" in Bengtsson, T., Fridlizius, G. and Ohlsson, R. (eds.), *Pre-industrial Population Change*. Stockholm, Almquist and Wiksell, pp. 329–355.

1986. "Comparisons of population cycles and trends in England, France and Sweden 1751–1860," paper given at the *Ninth International Economic History Congress*. Berne.

1989. "Migration, wages and urbanization in Sweden in the nineteenth century," in van der Woude, A., de Vries, J. and Hayami, A. (eds.), *Urbanization in History. A Process of Dynamic Interactions*. Oxford University Press.

Bengtsson, T. and Ohlsson, R. 1985. "Age-specific mortality and short term changes in the standard of living; Sweden, 1751–1859," *European Journal of Population*, 1, 4, 309–326.

Bennassar, B. 1967. *Valladolid au siècle d'or: une ville de Castille et sa campagne au XVIᵉ siècle*. Paris, Mouton.

1968. "Economie et société à Segovie au milieu du XVIᵉ siècle," *Anuario de historia económica y social*, 1, 185–203.

1969. *Recherches sur les grandes épidémies dans le Nord de l'Espagne à la fin du XVIᵉ siècle*. Paris, S. E. V. P. E. N.

Berkner, L. 1972. "The stem family and the development cycle of the peasant household," *American Historical Review*, 77, 2, 398–418.

Bernabeu Mestre, J. and López Piñero, J. M. 1987. "Condicionantes de la mortalidad entre 1800 y 1930: Higiene, salud y medio ambiente," *Boletín de la Asociación de Demografía Histórica*, 5, 2, 70–79.

Blayo, Y. 1970. "La mobilité dans un village de la Brie vers le milieu du xixᵉ siècle," *Population*, 25, 573–605.

Bonfield, L., Smith, R. M. and Wrightson, K. (eds.) 1986. *The World We Have Gained*. Oxford, Blackwell.

Bongaarts, J. and Potter, R. G. 1979. "Fertility effects of seasonal migration and seasonal variation in fecundibility: Test of a useful approximation under more general conditions," *Demography*, 16, 475–480.

Boserup, E. 1981. *Population and Technological Change: A Study of Long-Term Trends*. University of Chicago Press.

Braudel, F. 1966. *La Méditerranée et le monde méditerranéen à l'époque de Philippe II*, 2 vols. Paris, Librairie Armand Colin. Translated as *The Mediterranean and the Mediterranean World in the Age of Philip II* by Siân Reynolds, New York, Harper and Row, 1972.

1981. *The Structures of Everyday Life. Civilization and Capitalism 15th–18th Century*, 2 vols. New York, Harper and Row.

Breschi, M. and Livi Bacci, M. 1986a. "Saison et climat comme contraintes de la survie des enfants. L'expérience italienne au XIXᵉ siècle," *Population*, 41, 1, 9–36.

1986b. "Stagione di nascita e clima come determinanti della mortalità' infantile negli Stati Sardi di Terraferma," *Genus*, 42, 1–2, 87–101.

Brettell, C. 1987. *Men Who Migrate; Women Who Wait. Population and History in a Portuguese Parish*. Princeton University Press.

Brown, A. A. and Neuberger, E. (eds.) 1977. *Internal Migration, a Comparative Perspective*. New York, Academic Press.

Bruneel, C. 1977. *La mortalité dans les campagnes: le Duché de Brabant aux XVIIe et XVIIIe siècles*. Louvain, Editions Nauwelaerts.

Buchan, A. and Mitchell, A. 1875. "On the influence of weather on mortality from different diseases and at different ages," *Journal of the Scottish Meterological Society*, 4, 186–265.

Bustelo García del Real, F. 1973. "La transformación de vecinos en habitantes. El problema del coeficiente," *Estudios Geográficos*, 33, 154–164.

Cabourdin, G. 1981. "Le remariage en France sous l'Ancien Régime (seizième-dixhuitième siècles)" in Dupâquier, J., *et al.* (eds.), *Marriage and Remarriage in Populations of the Past*. London, Academic Press, pp. 273–286.

Cachinero Sánchez, F. 1982. "La evolución de la nupcialidad en España (1887–1975)," *Revista Española de Investigaciones Sociológicas*, 20, 81–99.

Caldwell, J. C. 1969. *African Rural–Urban Migration: The Movement to Ghana's Towns*. New York, Colombia University Press.

1981. "The wealth flows theory of fertility decline" in C. Höhn and R. Mackensen (eds.) *Determinants of Fertility Trends: Theories Re-examined*. Liège, Ordina, pp. 171–188.

1982. *Theory of Fertility Decline*. London.

Callahan, W. J. 1980. *La Santa y Real Hermandad del Refugio y Piedad de Madrid, 1618–1832.* Madrid, C. S. I. C., Instituto de Estudios Madrileños.
Camps Cura, E. 1987. "Industrialización y crecimiento urbano: la formación de la ciudad de Sabadell," *Revista de Historia Económica,* 5, 1, 49–72.
Cantor, M. (ed.) 1979. *American Workingclass Culture.* Greenwood Press, Westport, Connecticut.
Capel Sáez, H. 1974. *Estudios sobre el sistema urbano.* Universidad de Barcelona.
Carbajo Isla, M. F. 1987. *La población de la villa de Madrid (Desde finales del siglo XVI hasta mediados del siglo XIX).* Madrid, Siglo XXI.
Carmona García, J. I. 1976. *Una aportación a la demografía de Sevilla en los siglos XVIII y XIX; las series parroquiales de San Martín (1750–1860).* Seville, Diputación Provincial.
Carpentier, E. 1962. *Une ville devant la peste: Orvieto et la Peste Noire de 1348.* Paris, S. E. V. P. E. N.
Carreras Panchón, A. 1973. "Dos testimonios sobre la epidemia de peste de 1599 en Valladolid," *Asclepio,* 25, 341–357.
Carrillo, J. L. and García Ballester, L. 1977. "Repercusiones sociales de la epidemia de Fiebre Amarilla de Málaga (1803–4): Posturas tradicionales e ilustradas en el estamento eclesiástico," *Asclepio,* 29, 73–100.
Casal Martínez, F. 1951. "Dos epidemias de peste bubónica en Cartagena en el siglo XVII, y una terrible de paludismo en 1785," *Murgetana,* 3, 37–77.
Casey, J. 1979. *The Kingdom of Valencia in the Seventeenth Century.* Cambridge University Press.
  1985. "Spain: A failed transition" in P. Clark (ed.), *The European Crisis of the 1590s: Essays in Comparative History.* London, pp. 209–228.
Casey, J. *et al.* 1987. *La familia en la España mediterránea (siglos XV–XIX).* Barcelona, Editorial Crítica.
Casey, J. and Vincent, B. 1987. "Casa y familia en la Granada del Antiguo Régimen" in Casey, J. *et al., La familia en la España mediterránea (siglos XV–XIX).* Barcelona, Editorial Crítica, pp. 172–211.
Castellanos, J. and Reguero, A. L. 1977. "La peste en la Málaga del siglo XVII (1637): approximación a su historia social," *Asclepio,* 29, 101–118.
Castro, Concepción de. 1987. *El pan de Madrid; El abasto de las ciudades españolas del Antiguo Régimen.* Madrid, Alianza Universidad.
Caxa de Leruela, M. 1631. *Restauración de la antigua abundancia de Espana.* Naples (edn published by the Instituto de Estudios de la Administración Local, with introduction by B. González Alonso, Madrid, 1978).
Chacón Jiménez, F. 1979. *Murcia en la centuria de los quinientos.* Universidad de Murcia, Academia Alfonso X el Sabio.
  1983. "Introducción a la historia de la familia española: el ejemplo de Murcia y Orihuela (siglos XVII–XIX)," *Cuadernos de Historia,* 10, 235–266.
  (ed.) 1987a. *Familia y sociedad en el Mediterráneo occidental. Siglos XV–XIX.* Universidad de Murcia.
  1987b. "Notas para el estudio de la familia en la región de Murcia durante el Antiguo Régimen" in Casey, J. *et al., La familia en la España mediterránea (siglos XV–XIX).* Barcelona, Editorial Crítica, pp. 129–171.
Charbonneau, H. and Larose, A. 1979. *Les grandes mortalités: étude méthodologique des crises démographiques du passé.* Liège, Ordina.
Cho, L. J. 1973. "The own-children approach to fertility estimation: An elaboration," *Proceedings of the IUSSP Conference,* vol. 2. Liège.

Christaller, W. 1966. *Central Places in Southern Germany*. Englewood Cliffs, NJ, Prentice-Hall (first published in Germany in 1933).

Clark, P. (ed.) 1985. *The European Crisis of the 1590s: Essays in Comparative History*. London and Winchester (MA), Allen Unwin.

Clarke, J. 1985. "Patterns of settlement and factors affecting population distribution" in IUSSP, *International Population Conference, Florence*. Florence, vol. 3, pp. 63–72.

Coale, A. J. 1971. "Age patterns of marriage," *Population Studies*, 25, 193–214.

(ed.) 1976. *Economic Factors in Population Growth*. New York, John Wiley and Sons.

1986. "The decline of fertility in Europe since the eighteenth century as a chapter in human demographic history" in Coale, A. J. and Watkins, S. C. (eds.), *The Decline of Fertility in Europe*, Princeton University Press, pp. 1–30.

Coale, Ansley J. and Demeny, P. 1983 (1966). *Regional Model Life Tables and Stable Populations*. New York, Academic Press.

Coale, A. J. and Treadway, R. 1986. "A summary of the changing distribution of overall fertility, marital fertility and the proportion married in the provinces of Europe" in Coale, A. J. and Watkins, S. C. (eds.), *The Decline of Fertility in Europe*, Princeton University Press, pp. 31–181.

Coale, A. J. and Trussell, T. J. 1974. "Model fertility schedules: Variations in the age structure in childbearing in human populations," *Population Index*, 40, 185–258.

Coale, A. J. and Watkins, S. C. (eds.) 1986. *The Decline of Fertility in Europe*, Princeton University Press.

Correas, P. 1988. "Poblaciones españolas de más de 5,000 hatitantes entre los siglos XVII y XIX, *Boletín de la Asociación de Demografía Histórica*, 6, 1, 5–24.

Corsini, C. 1980. "La mobilità delle popolazioni nel settecento: fonti, metodi, problemi" in Società Italiana di demografia Storica, *La popolazione italiana nel settecento*, Editrice Clueb, Bologna, pp. 401–434.

1981. "Why is remarriage a male affair? Some evidence from Tuscan villages during the eighteenth century" in Dupâquier, J. *et al.* (eds.), *Marriage and Remarriage in Populations of the Past*, London, Academic Press, pp. 385–396.

Czap, P., 1983, "A large family: the peasant's greatest wealth: serf households in Mishino, Russia, 1814–1958" in Wall, R. (ed.), *Family Forms in Historic Europe*. Cambridge University Press, pp. 65–104.

Da Molin, G. 1980. "Mobilità dei contadini pugliesi tra fine '600 a primo '800" in Società Italiana di Demografia Storica, *La popolazione italiana nel settecento*, Editrice Clueb, Bologna, pp. 435–476.

Danhieux, L. 1983. "The evolving household: the case of Lampernisse, West Flanders" in Wall, R. (ed.), *Family Forms in Historic Europe*. Cambridge University Press, pp. 409–421.

Danón, J. 1977. "Un brote de fiebre amarilla en el Puerto de Barcelona, en 1803," *Asclepio*, 29, 119–125.

Daunton, M. J. 1978. "Towns and economic growth in eighteenth-century England" in Abrams, P. and Wrigley, E. A. (eds.), *Towns in Societies. Essays in Economic History and Historical Sociology*. Cambridge University Press, pp. 245–277.

Davis, K. 1977. "The effect of outmigration on regions of origin" in Brown,

A. A. and Neuberger, E. (eds.), *Internal Migration, a Comparative Perspective*. New York, Academic Press, pp. 147–166.

Del Panta, L. and Livi Bacci, M. 1977. "Chronologie, intensité et diffusion des crises de mortalité en Italie 1600–1850," *Population*, 32, 1977, 401–446.

de Vries, J. 1984. *European Urbanization, 1500–1800*. Cambridge, MA, Harvard University Press.

1989. "Problems in the measurement, description, and analysis of historical urbanization" in van der Woude, A., de Vries, J. and Hayami, A. (eds.), *Urbanization in History. A Process of Dynamic Interactions*. Oxford University Press.

Díez Nicolás, J. 1972. *Especialización funcional y dominación en la España urbana*. Madrid, Fundación Juan March.

Dobado González, R. 1982. "Salarios y condiciones de trabajo en las minas de Almadén, 1758–1839" in Tedde, P. (ed.), *La economía española al final del Antiguo Régimen, II. Manufacturas*. Madrid, Alianza Editorial, pp. 337–448.

Domínguez Ortiz, A. 1973a. *Las clases privilegiadas en la España del Antiguo Régimen*. Madrid, Ediciones Istmo.

1973b. *Alteraciones andaluzas*. Madrid, Narcea.

1973c. *El Antiguo Régimen: Los Reyes Católicos y los Austrias*. Madrid, Alianza Universidad.

1973d. "Algunos datos sobre médicos rurales en la España del siglo XVIII," *Asclepio*, 25, 317–321.

1976. *Sociedad y estado en el siglo XVIII español*. Barcelona, Ariel.

Domínguez Ortiz, A. and Aguilar Piñal, P. 1976. *El barroco y la ilustración*, vol. 4 of *Historia de Sevilla* directed by F. Morales Padrón, Seville, Publicaciones de la Universidad de Sevilla.

Doré, G. and Davillier, le Baron Ch. 1862–1873. "Voyage en Espagne" published in several issues of *Le tour du monde*. Paris.

Douglass, W. A. 1988a. "Iberian family history," *Journal of Family History*, 13, 1, 1–12.

1988b. "The Basque stem family household: Myth or reality," *Journal of Family History*, 13, 1, 75–90.

Dubert García, I. 1987. *Los comportamientos de la familia urbana en la Galicia del Antiguo Régimen. El ejemplo de Santiago de Compostela en el siglo XVIII*. Universidad de Santiago de Compostela.

Dupâquier, J. 1979a. *La population rurale du Bassin Parisien à l'époque de Louis XIV*. Paris–Lille, Editions de l'Ecole des Hautes études en sciences sociales.

1979b. "L'analyse statistique des crises de mortalité" in Charbonneau, H. and Larose, A., *Les grandes mortalités: étude méthodologique des crises démographiques du passé*. Liège, Ordina, pp. 81–112.

Dupâquier, J. et al. (eds.) 1981. *Marriage and Remarriage in Populations of the Past*. London, Academic Press.

Egido, T. 1973. "La cofradía de San José y los niños expósitos de Valladolid (1540–1757)," *Estudios Josefinos*, 53, 59–74.

1979. "Madrid, 1766: Motines de la Corte y oposición al gobierno," *Cuadernos de Investigación Histórica*, 3, 125–154.

Eiras Roel, A. 1984. "Modèle ou modèles de démographie ancienne? Un résumé comparatif" in *La France d'Ancien Régime: Etudes réunies en l'honneur de Pierre Goubert*. Toulouse, vol. 1, pp. 249–257.

Elliott, J. H. 1977. "Self-perception and decline in early seventeenth-century Spain," *Past and Present*, 74, 41–61.

Estalella, E. and Gubern, E. 1970. "Estructura funcional de las ciudades españolas en 1900," *Estudios Geográficos*, 118, 5–27.

Evans, R. J. 1987. *Death in Hamburg, Society and Politics in the Cholera Years, 1830–1910*. Oxford, The Clarendon Press.

Fauve-Chamoux, A. 1983. "The importance of women in an urban environment: the example of the Rheims household at the beginning of the Industrial Revolution" in Wall, R. (ed.), *Family Forms in Historic Europe*, Cambridge University Press, pp. 475–492.

1984. "Les structures familiales au royaume des familles-souches: Esparros," *Annales, E. S. C.*, pp. 513–528.

Fernández Alvarez, M. 1975. "La demografía de Salamanca en el siglo XVI a través de los fondos parroquiales," *Actas de las Primeras Jornadas de Metodología Aplicada a las Ciencias Históricas*, 3, 281–297.

Fernández García, A. 1979. "Enfermedad y sociedad. La epidemia de cólera de 1865 en Madrid," *Cuadernos de Investigación Histórica*, 3, 155–186.

Fernández de Navarrete, P. 1626. *Conservación de Monarquías y Discursos Políticos sobre la gran Consulta que el Consejo hizo al Señor Rey Don Felipe III* (republished in *Biblioteca de Autores Españoles*, vol. 25, Madrid, 1947).

Fernández de Pinedo, E. 1974. *Crecimiento económico y transformaciones sociales en el País Vasco, 1100–1850*. Madrid, Siglo XXI.

Fernández Ugarte, M. 1988. *Expósitos en Salamanca a comienzos del siglo XVIII*. Ediciones de la Diputación de Salamanca.

Fildes, V. A. 1987. *Breasts, Bottles and Babies. A History of Infant Feeding*. Edinburgh University Press.

Findley, S. 1977. *Planning for Internal Migration: A Review of Issues and Policies in Developing Countries*. U. S. Department of Commerce, Bureau of the Census.

Flinn, M. W. 1974. "The stabilisation of mortality in preindustrial western Europe," *The Journal of European Economic History*, 3, 2, 258–318.

Fontana, J. 1979. *Las crisis del Antiguo Régimen (1808–1833)*, Barcelona, Ediciones Crítica.

Fortea Pérez, J. I. 1980. *Córdoba en el siglo XVI. Las bases demográficas y económicas de una expansión urbana*. Córdoba, Publicaciones del Monte de Piedad y Caja de Ahorros.

Galloway, P. R. 1985. "Annual variations in deaths by age, deaths by cause, prices, and weather in London 1670 to 1830," *Population Studies*, 39, 487–505.

1986a. "Differentials in demographic responses to annual price variations in pre-revolutionary France. A comparison of rich and poor areas in Rouen, 1681 to 1787," *European Journal of Population*, 2, 269–305.

1986b. "Longterm fluctuations in climate and population in the preindustrial era," *Population and Development Review*, 12, 1–24.

1987. "Population, Prices, and Weather in Preindustrial Europe," PhD dissertation, Graduate Group in Demography, University of California, Berkeley.

1988. "Basic patterns in annual variations in fertility, nuptiality, mortality, and prices in pre-industrial Europe," *Population Studies*, 42, 275–302.

1989. "Secular changes in the short-term preventive, positive and temperature checks to population growth in Europe, 1460–1909," paper given at INED symposium on "Reconstruction of past populations and their dynamics." Paris.

García Arenal, M. 1978a. *Inquisición y moriscos. Los procesos del tribunal de Cuenca.* Madrid, Siglo XXI.

1978b. "Los censos de moriscos de 1589 a 1594 establecidos por el tribunal de la Inquisición en Cuenca," *Hispania*, 38, 138, 151–202.

García España, E. with Molinié-Bertrand, A. 1984–86. *Censo de la corona de Castilla, 1591.* vol. 1, *Vecindarios*, vol. 2, *Estudio analítico.* Madrid, Instituto Nacional de Estadística.

García Guerra, D. 1977. "Epidemiología gallega del siglo XVIII; su repercusión sobre el Hospital Real de Santiago," *Asclepio*, 29, 147–167.

García Sanz, A. 1977. *Desarrollo y crisis del Antiguo Régimen en Castilla la Vieja; economía y sociedad en tierras de Segovia, 1500–1814.* Madrid, Akal.

Garden, M. 1970. *Lyon et les lyonnais au XVIIIᵉ siècle.* Paris, Les Belles lettres.

Goldman, P. B. 1979. "Mitos liberales, mentalidades burguesas e historia social en la lucha en pro de los cementerios municipales" in Gil Novales, A. (ed.), *Homenaje a Noël Salomon: Ilustración española e independencia de América.* Universidad Autónoma de Barcelona.

Goldscheider, C. 1971. *Population, Modernization and Social Structure.* Boston, Little Brown and Company.

Goldstein, S. and Goldstein, A. 1981. "The impact of migration on fertility: an 'own children' analysis for Thailand," *Population Studies*, 35, 2, 265–284.

Goldstone, J. 1986. "The demographic revolution in England: A reexamination," *Population Studies*, 49, 5–33.

Gómez Mendoza, A. and Luna Rodrigo, G. 1986. "El desarrollo urbano en España, 1860–1930," *Boletín de la Asociación de Demografía Histórica*, 4, 2, 3–22.

Gómez Redondo, R. 1985. "El descenso de la mortalidad infantil en Madrid, 1900–1970," *Revista Española de Investigaciones Sociológicas*, 32, 101–140.

1987. "La desigualdad espacial ante la muerte infantil en España, 1900–1950," *I Congrés Hispano-Luso-Italià de Demografia Histórica*, pp. 275–285.

González, J. 1960. *El reino de Castilla en la época de Alfonso VIII*, 3 vols. Madrid, Consejo Superior de Investigaciones Científicas.

González, T. 1829. *Censo de población de las provincias y partidos de la Corona de Castilla en el siglo XVI.* Madrid, Imprenta Real.

González de Cellorigo, M. 1732. *Memorial de la política necesaria y útil restauración a la República de España y Estados de ella y del desempeño universal de estos Reynos.* Valladolid.

González Muñoz, M. C. 1974. "Epidemias y enfermedades en Talavera de la Reina (siglos XVI y XVII)," *Hispania*, 126, 149–168.

1975. *La población de Talavera de la Reina (siglos XVI al XX). Estudio sociodemográfico.* Toledo, Instituto de Estudios Toledanos.

Goubert, P. 1960. *Beauvais et le Beauvaisis de 1600 à 1730.* Paris, S. E. V. P. E. N.

1968. *Cent mille provinciaux au XVIIᵉ siècle.* Paris, Flammarion.

Grabill, W. H. and Cho, L. J. 1965. "Methodology for the measurement of current fertility from population data on young children," *Demography*, 2, 50–73.

Granjel, L. S. 1977. "Las epidemias de peste en la España del siglo XVII," *Asclepio*, 29.

Guía del Ministero de la Gobernación del Reino. 1836. Madrid.

Guillamón, J. 1980. *Las reformas de la administración local durante el reinado de Carlos III*. Madrid, Instituto de Administración Local.

Hajnal, J. 1953. "Age at marriage and proportions marrying," *Population Studies*, 7, 2, 111–136.

1965. "European marriage patterns in perspective" in Glass, D. V. and Eversley, D. E. C., *Population in History. Essays in Historical Demography*. London, pp. 101–146.

1982. "Two kinds of preindustrial household formation systems," *Population and Development Review*, 8, 3; also in Wall, R. (ed.), *Family Forms in Historic Europe*. Cambridge University Press, pp. 65–104.

Hamilton, E. J. 1934. *American Treasure and the Price Revolution in Spain, 1501–1650*. Cambridge, MA, Harvard University Press.

1947. *War and Prices in Spain, 1651–1800*. Cambridge, MA, Harvard University Press.

Hammel, E. A. 1985. "Short-term demographic fluctuations in the Croatian military border of Austria, 1830–1847," *European Journal of Population*, 1, 2/3, 265–290.

1977. "The influence of social and geographical mobility on the stability of the kinship system: the Servian case" in Brown, A. A. and Neuberger, E. (eds.), *Internal Migration, a Comparative Perspective*. New York, Academic Press, pp. 401–415.

Hammel, E. and Laslett, P. 1974. "Comparing household structure over time and between cultures," *Comparative Studies in Society and History*, 16, 73–103.

Hansen, E. C. 1977. *Rural Catalonia under the Franco Regime*. Cambridge University Press.

Harevan, T. K. and Vinovskis, M. A. 1978. "Patterns of childbearing in late nineteenth-century America: The determinants of marital fertility in five Massachusetts towns in 1880" in Harevan, T. K. and Vinovskis, M. A. (eds.), *Family and Population in Nineteenth-Century America*. Princeton University Press, pp. 86–125.

Harris, J. R. and Todaro, M. P. 1970. "Migration, unemployment and development: a two sector analysis," *The American Economic Review*, 60, 1, 126–142.

Harvey, A. C. 1981. *The Economic Analysis of Time Series*. Oxford, Philip Allan.

Hauser, Philip. 1902. *Madrid bajo el punto de vista médico-social*, 2 vols, edition of Carmen del Moral. Madrid, Editora Nacional.

Henry, L. 1961. "Some data on natural fertility," *Eugenics Quarterly*, 8, 2, 81–91.

1972. "Fécondité des mariages dans le quart sud-ouest de la France de 1720 à 1829" (suite), *Annales, E. S. C.*, 27, 977–1023.

1978. "Fécondité des mariages dans le quart sud-est de la France de 1670 à 1829," *Population*, 33.

1981. "Le fonctionnement du marché matrimonial" in Dupâquier, J. *et al.* (eds.), *Marriage and Remarriage in Populations of the Past*. London–New York, Academic Press, pp. 191–198.

Henry, L. and Houdaille, J. 1973. "Fécondité des mariages dans le quart nord-ouest de la France de 1670 à 1829," *Population*, 28, 873–924.

1978, 1979. "Célibat et âge au mariage aux XVIIIᵉ et XIXᵉ siècles en France. I. Célibat définitif. II. Age au premier mariage," *Population*, 33, 43–84 and 34, 403–442.

Herr, R. 1958. *The Eighteenth Century Revolution in Spain*. Princeton University Press.

Hochstadt, S. 1981. "Migration and industrialization in Germany, 1815–1977," *Social Science History*, 5, 445–568.

Hohenberg, P. M. and Lees, L. H. 1985. *The Making of Urban Europe 1000–1950*, Cambridge, MA–London, Harvard University Press.

Hollingsworth, T. R. 1979. "A preliminary suggestion for the measurement of mortality crises" in Charbonneau, H. and Larose, A., *Les grandes mortalités: étude méthodologique des crises démographiques du passé*. Liège, Ordina, pp. 21–28.

Hoselitz, B. 1953. "The role of cities in the economic growth of underdeveloped countries," *Journal of Political Economy*, 61, 195–209.

1954. "Generative and parisitic cities," *Economic Development and Cultural Change*, 3, 278–294.

Houdaille, J. 1976. "La fécondité des mariages de 1670 à 1829 dans le quart nord-est de la France," *Annales de Démographie Historique*, 341–391.

Iradiel Murugarren, P. 1974. *Evolución de la industria textil castellana en los siglos XIII–XVI: Factores de desarrollo, organización y costes de la producción manufacturera en Cuenca*. Universidad de Salamanca.

Iriso Napal, P. L. and Reher, D. S. 1987. "La fecundidad y sus determinantes en España, 1887–1920. Un ensayo de interpretación," *Revista Española de Investigaciones Sociológicas*, 39, 45–118.

Jiménez de Gregorio, F. 1980. *La población de la actual provincia de Madrid en el Censo de Floridablanca (1786)*. Madrid, Diputación Provincial.

Jiménez Monteserín, M. 1977. "Los motines de subsistencias de la primavera de 1766 y sus repercusiones en la ciudad de Cuenca," *Revista Cuenca*, 11 and 12.

1983. *Asomarse al pasado. La ciudad de Cuenca en 1773*. Ayuntamiento de Cuenca.

Jiménez Muñoz, J. M. 1974. "Noticia sobre pestes en el reino de Castilla (1478–94)," *Cuadernos de Historia de la Medicina Española*, 13, 347–366.

Johansen, H. C. 1989. "Migration into and out of the Danish city of Odense" in van der Woude, A., de Vries, J., and Hayami, A. (eds.), *Urbanization in History. A Process of Dynamic Interactions*. Oxford University Press.

Kamen, H. 1964. "The decline of Castile: The last crisis," *Economic History Review*, 17, 1, 63–76.

1980. *Spain in the Later Seventeenth Century (1665–1700)*. London–New York, Longman.

Kertzer, D. L. 1984. *Family Life in Central Italy, 1800–1910: Sharecropping, Wage Labor and Coresidence*. New Brunswick, NJ, Rutyers University Press.

Kertzer, D. I. and Brettell, C. 1987. "Advances in Italian and Iberian family history," *Journal of Family History*, 12, 1–3, 87–121.

Kertzer, D. I. and Hogan, D. P. 1985. "On the move: migration in an Italian community, 1865–1921," *Social Science History*, 9, 1–24.

Klein, J. 1920. *The Mesta: A Study in Spanish Economic History, 1273–1836*. Cambridge, MA, Harvard University Press.

Knodel, J. E. 1974. *The Decline of Fertility in Germany, 1871–1939*. Princeton University Press.

Lachiver, M. 1969. *La population de Meulan de XVIIIe au XIXe siècles*. Paris, S. E. V. P. E. N.

Lanza García, R. 1988. *Población y familia campesina en el Antiguo Régimen. Liébana, siglos XVI–XIX*. Santander, Universidad de Cantabria.

Lapeyre, H. 1959. *Géographie de l'Espagne morisque*. Paris, S. E. V. P. E. N.

Larquié, C. 1974. "Quartiers et paroisses urbaines. L'exemple de Madrid au xvii siècle," *Annales de Démographie Historique*, 165–195.

1978. "Une approche quantitative de la pauvreté: les madrilènes et la mort au xvii siècle," *Annales de Démographie Historique*, 175–196.

Larruga, E. 1787. *Memorias políticas y económicas sobre frutos, comercio, fábricas y minas de España*. Madrid.

Laslett, P. 1977. *Family Life and Illicit Love in Earlier Generations*. Cambridge University Press.

1893. "Family and household as work group and as kin group" in Wall, R. (ed.), *Family Forms in Historic Europe*. Cambridge University Press, pp. 513–563.

1983b. *The World We Have Lost – Further Explored*. London, Methuen.

1987. "The character of familial history, its limitations and the conditions for its proper pursuit," *Journal of Family History*, 12, 1–2, 263–285.

1988. "Family, kinship and collectivity as systems of support in pre-industrial Europe: a consideration of the 'nuclear-hardship' hypothesis," *Continuity and Change*, 3, 2, 153–176.

Laslett, P. and Harrison, J. 1963. "Clayworth and Cogenhoe" in Bell, H. E. and Ollard, R. L. (eds.), *Historical Essays, 1600–1750, Presented to David Ogg*. New York, Barnes and Noble.

Laslett, P. and Wall, R. 1972. *Household and Family in Past Time*. Cambridge University Press.

Lawton, R. 1979. "Mobility in nineteenth-century British cities," *The Geographical Journal*, 145, 206–224.

n.d. "Population mobility and urbanisation: nineteenth-century British experience" in Lee, W. R. and Lawton, R. (eds.), *Comparative Urban Population Development in Western Europe c. 1750–1920*.

Leasure, J. W. 1963. "Factors involved in the decline of fertility in Spain, 1900–1950," *Population Studies*, 16, 3, 271–285.

Lebrun, F. 1980. "Les crises démographiques en France aux xviie et xviiie siècles," *Annales, E. S. C.*, 35, 2, 205–234.

Lee, E. S. 1966. "A theory of migration," *Demography*, 3, 47–57.

Lee, R. D. 1981. "Short-term variation: vital rates, prices and weather" in Wrigley, E. A. and Schofield, R. S., *The Population History of England 1541–1871. A Reconstruction*. Cambridge, MA, Harvard University Press, pp. 356–401.

1987. "Population dynamics of humans and other animals," *Demography*, 24, 2, 443–465.

Lee, W. R. and Lawton, R. (eds.) n.d. *Comparative Urban Population Development in Western Europe c. 1750–1920*.

Le Flem, J. P. 1976. "La cultura de un arbitrista en el siglo xvii: el ejemplo de Caxa de Leruela," *Moneda y Crédito*, 136, 29–37.

Le Roy Ladurie, E. 1969. "L'aménorrhée de famine (xviie–xxe siècles),"
Annales, E. S. C., 24, 6, 1589–1601.
Le Roy Ladurie, E. and Goy, J. 1982. *Tithe and Agrarian History from the
Fourteenth to the Nineteenth Centuries. An Essay in Comparative History.*
Cambridge University Press, and Paris, Editions de la Maison des
Sciences de L'Homme.
Lesthaeghe, R. J. 1980. "On the social control of reproduction," *Population and
Development Review*, 6, 4, 527–548.
Lévy-Vroelant, C. 1988. "Fragilité de la famille urbaine au XIXe siècle:
itinéraires versaillais de 1830 à 1880," *Population*, 43, 4, 639–659.
Lisón-Tolosana, C. 1966. *Belmonte de los Caballeros: A Sociological Study of a
Spanish Town.* Oxford, Clarendon Press.
Livi Bacci, M. 1968. "Fertility and nuptiality changes in Spain from the late 18th
to the early 20th century," *Population Studies*, 22, 1, 83–102, and 2, 211–234.
   1977. *A History of Italian Fertility during the Last Two Centuries.* Princeton
University Press.
   1978. *La société italienne devant les crises de mortalité.* Florence, Dipartimento
statistico.
   1981. "On the frequency of remarriage in nineteenth-century Italy: methods
and results" in Dupâquier, J. *et al.* (eds.), *Marriage and Remarriage in
Populations of the Past*, London, Academic Press, pp. 347–362.
   1983. "The nutrition–mortality link in past times: A comment," *Journal of
Interdisciplinary History*, 14, 2, 293–299.
   1986. "Social group forerunners of fertility control in Europe" in Coale, A. J.
and Watkins, S. C., *The Decline of Fertility in Europe.* Princeton University
Press, pp. 182–200.
   1987. *Popolazione e alimentazione. Saggio sulla storia demografica europea.*
Bologna, Il Mulino.
   1988. "La Península Ibérica e Italia en vísperas de la transición demográfica"
in Pérez Moreda, V. and Reher, D. S., *Demografía Histórica en España.*
Madrid, Ediciones El Arquero, pp. 138–178.
Llopis Angelán, E. 1982. "Las explotaciones trashumantes en el siglo xviii y
primer tercio del XIX: la cabaña del Monasterio de Guadalupe, 1709–1835"
in Anes, G. (ed.), *La economía española al final del Antiguo Régimen, I.
Agricultura.* Madrid, Alianza Editorial, pp. 1–101.
López, Mateo. 1787 (1949–1953). *Memorias históricas de Cuenca y su obispado,
Cuenca* (published by A. González Palencia [ed.]), 2 vols. Madrid, Consejo
Superior de Investigaciones Científicas.
López Alonso, C. 1986. *La pobreza en la España medieval: estudio histórico-social.*
Madrid, Ministerio de Trabajo y Seguridad Social.
López Yepes, J. 1971. *Historia de los Montes de Piedad en España. El Monte de
Piedad en Madrid en el siglo XVIII.* Madrid, Confederación Española de
Cajas de Ahorro.
López-Salazar Pérez, J. 1976. "Evolución demográfica de la Mancha en el siglo
xviii," *Hispania*, 133, 233–299.
Lotka, A. J. 1941. "The law of urban concentration," *Science*, 94.
Luna Rodrigo, G. 1988. "La población urbana en España, 1860–1930," *Boletín
de la Asociación de Demografía Histórica*, 6, 1, 25–68.
Malefakis, E. 1970. *Agrarian Reform and Peasant Revolution in Spain. Origins of the
Civil War.* Ann Arbor, University of Michigan Press.

Malthus, T. R. 1798. *An Essay on the Principle of Population*. London. Reprinted for the Royal Economic Society (1926).
McKeown, T. 1976. *The Modern Rise of Population*. New York, Academic Press.
McNeill, W. 1976. *Plagues and Peoples*. New York, Anchor Press.
  1984. "Migration in historical perspective," *Population and Development Review*, 10, 1, 1–18.
Marcos Martín, A. 1978. *Auge y declive de un núcleo mercantil y financiero de Castilla la Vieja. Evolución demográfica de Medina del Campo durante los siglos XVI y XVII*. Universidad de Valladolid.
  1978. "El sistema hospitalerio de Medina del Campo en el siglo XVI," *Cuadernos de Investigación Histórica*, 2, 341–362.
  1985. *Economía y sociedad; pobreza en Castilla: Palencia, 1500–1814*. Palencia, Diputación Provincial.
Margolis, J. 1977. "Internal migration: measurement and models" in Brown, A. A. and Neuberger, E. (eds.), *Internal Migration, a Comparative Perspective*. New York, Academic Press, pp. 135–144.
Martín Galán, M. 1981. "Fuentes y métodos para el estudio de la demografía histórica castellana durante la Edad Moderna," *Hispania*, 41, 1–231.
  1985. "Nuevos datos sobre un viejo problema: el coeficiente de conversión de vecinos en habitantes," *Revista Internacional de Sociología*, 43, 4, 593–633.
Martín Rodríguez, M. 1984. *Pensamiento económico español sobre la población. De Soto a Matanegui*. Madrid, Ediciones Pirámide.
Martínez Carrión, J. M. 1988. "Peasant household formation and the organization of rural labor in the Valley of the Segura during the nineteenth century," *Journal of Family History*, 13, 1, 91–110.
Martínez de Mata, F. 1650–1660. "Memoriales y discursos, 1650–1660," republished by *Moneda y Crédito*, 1971, Madrid.
Mártir Rizo, J. P. 1629. *Historia de la muy noble y leal ciudad de Cuenca*. Madrid. Facsimile edition published in 1974 by Ediciones El Albir, Barcelona.
Martz, L. 1983. *Poverty and Welfare in Habsburg Spain. The Example of Toledo*. Cambridge University Press.
Martz, L. and Porres Martín-Cleto, J. 1974. *Toledo y los toledanos en 1561*. Toledo, Diputación Provincial.
Marcílio, M. L. 1981. "Mariage et remariage dans le Brésil traditionnel: lois, intensité, calendrier" in Dupâquier, J. *et al.* (eds.), *Marriage and Remarriage in Populations of the Past*. London, Academic Press, pp. 363–374.
Massey, D. S. and Mullan, B. P. 1984. "A demonstration of the effect of seasonal migration on fertility," *Demography*, 21, 4, 501–517.
Mauleón Isla, M. 1961. *La población de Bilbao en el siglo XVIII*. Universidad de Valladolid.
Maza Zorilla, E. 1978. "Villalón de Campos y la peste de 1599," *Cuadernos de Investigación Histórica*, 2, 363–386.
Melón y Ruiz de Gordejuela, A. 1966. "Areas metropolitanas de España según el vigente censo de población," *Estudios Geográficos*, 104.
Menken, J. A. 1979. "Seasonal migration and seasonal variation in fecundability: effects on birth rates and birth intervals," *Demography*, 16, 103–120.
Meuvret, J. 1946. "Les crises de subsistances et la démographie de la France d'Ancien Régime," *Population*, 1, 643–650.
Molinié-Bertrand, A. 1976–1984. *Atlas de la population du Royaume de Castile en*

1591. *Etude cartographique. Commentaire de l'Atlas de la population du royaume de Castille en 1591*, 2 vols. Caen.

1985. *Au siècle d'or. L'Espagne et ses hommes. La population du Royaume du Castile au XVIᵉ siècle*. Paris, Economica.

Moll Blanes, I. 1987. "La estructura familiar del campesinado de Mallorca, 1824–1827" in Casey, J. *et al.*, *La familia en la España mediterránea (siglos XV–XIX)*. Barcelona, Editorial Crítica, pp. 212–257.

Moll Blanes, I. Segura i Mas, A., and Suau Puig, J. 1983. *Cronología de las crises demogràfiques mallorquines*. Palma de Mallorca, Institut d'Estudis Balearics.

Mols, R. 1954–1956. *Introduction à la démographie historique des villes d'Europe du XIVᵉ au XVIIIᵉ siècle*, 3 vols. Publications Universitaires de Louvain.

Moncada, Sancho de. 1619. *Restauración política de España*. Madrid (edition published by the Instituto de Estudios Fiscales in 1974).

Montemayor, J. 1987. "La red urbana en Castilla la Neuva en los siglos xvi y xvii," *Brocar*, 13, 141–153.

Morrison, P. A. 1973. "Theoretical issues in the design of population mobility models," *Environment and Behavior*, 5, 125–134.

Muñoz y Soliva, T. 1860. *Noticias de los ilmos señores obispos que han regido la diócesis de Cuenca aumentadas con los sucesos más notables acaecidos en sus pontificados*. Cuenca, Imprenta de Francisco Gómez e hijo.

1866. *Historia de la Ciudad de Cuenca y del territorio de su provincia y obispado, desde los tiempos primitivos hasta la edad presente*. Cuenca, Imprenta de El Eco.

Nadal i Oller, J. 1963. "Les grandes mortalités des années 1793 à 1812: Effets à long terme sur la démographie catalane," *Actes du Colloque International de Démographie Historique*. Liège, pp. 409–421.

1984. *La población española (siglos XVI a XX)*. Barcelona, Editorial Ariel.

1988. "La población española durante los siglos xvi, xvii y xviii. Un balance a escala regional" in Pérez Moreda, V. and Reher, D. S., *Demografía Histórica en España*. Madrid, Ediciones El Arquero, pp. 39–54.

Nadal i Oller, J. and Sáez, A. 1972. "La fécondité à Sant Joan de Palomós (Catalogne) de 1700 à 1859," *Annales de Démographie Historique*, 105–113.

Nalle, S. 1981. "Desde el olvido a la fama: El culto a San Julián en los siglos xvi y xvii," *Almud*, 2, 149–166.

Neuberger, E. 1977. "Internal migration: a comparative systematic view" in Brown, A. A. and Neuberger, E. (eds.), *Internal Migration, a Comparative Perspective*. New York, Academic Press, pp. 463–479.

Palop Ramos, J. M. 1977. *Hambre y lucha antifeudal. Las crisis de subsistencias en Valencia (siglo XVIII)*. Madrid, Siglo xxi.

Pérez Aparicio, C. (ed.) 1988. *Estudis sobre la població del país valencià*, 2 vols. Valencia, Edicions Alfons El Magnànim.

Pérez Díaz, V. 1969. *Emigración y sociedad en la tierra de Campos. Estudio de un proceso migratorio y un proceso de cambio social*. Madrid, Escuela Nacional de Administración Pública.

Pérez García, J. M. 1979. *Un modelo de sociedad rural del Antiguo Régimen en la Galicia costera: la península de Salnés*. Universidad de Santiago de Compostela.

1988. "La familia campesina en la Huerta de Valencia durante el siglo xviii," *Boletín de la Asociación de Demografía Histórica*, 6, 2, 5–28.

Pérez García, J. M. and Ardit Lucas, M. 1988. "Bases del crecimiento de la población valenciana en la edad moderna" in Pérez Aparicio, C. (ed.), *Estudis sobre la població del país valencià*, 2 vols. Valencia, Edicions Alfons El Magnànim, vol. 1, pp. 199–228.

Pérez Moreda, V. 1980. *Las crisis de mortalidad en la España interior, siglos XVI–XIX*. Madrid, Siglo xxi.

1982. "El paludismo en España a fines del siglo xviii: la epidemia de 1786," *Asclepio*, 34, 336–360.

1985a. "La evolución demográfica española en el siglo xix (1797–1830): Tendencias generales y contrastes regionales" in SIDES (ed.), *L'evoluzione demografica dell'Italia nel secolo XIX*. Bologna.

1985b. "La modernización demográfica de España" in Sánchez Albornoz, N. (ed.), *La modernización económica de España*. Madrid, Alianza Editorial, pp. 25–62.

1985c. "Consum deficitari, fam i crisis demogràfiques a l'Espanya dels segles xvi–xix," *Estudis d'Història Agrària*, 5, 7–24.

1986. "Matrimonio y familia. Algunas consideraciones sobre el modelo matrimonial español en la Edad Moderna," *Boletín de la Asociación de Demografía Histórica*, 4, 1, 3–51.

1988a. "La población española" in Artola, M. (ed.), *Enciclopedia de Historia de España*, vol. 1: *Economía. Sociedad*. Madrid, Alianza Editorial, pp. 345–431.

1988b. "Hambre, mortalidad y crecimiento demográfico en las poblaciones de la Europa preindustrial," *Revista de Historia Económica*, 6, 3, pp. 709–735.

1988c. "Respuestas demográficas ante la coyuntura económica en la España rural del Antiguo Régimen," *Boletín de la Asociación de Demografía Histórica*, 6, 3, pp. 81–118.

Pérez Moreda, V. and Reher, D. S. 1985. "Demographic mechanisms and long-term swings in population in Europe, 1200–1850," *IUSSP International Population Conference, Florence*, 3, pp. 313–129.

(eds.) 1988. *Demografía histórica en España*. Madrid, Ediciones El Arquero.

Pérez Picazo, M. T. 1981. "El modelo demográfico y económico del secano murciano durante el siglo xix: un ejemplo de estructuras estables," *Hispania*, 41, 149, 563–582.

Perpiñá Grau, R. 1954. *Corología: teoría estructural y estructurante de la población de España, 1900–1950*. Madrid, C. S. I. C.

Perrenoud, A. 1979. *La population de Genève, XVIᵉ–XIXᵉ siècles*. Geneva, A. Jullien.

Peset, J. L. *et al.* 1977a. "Los médicos y la peste de Valencia de 1647–8," *Asclepio*, 29, 217–242.

1977b. "Gobierno y poder político en la peste de Valencia de 1647–8," *Asclepio*, 29, 243–263.

Peset, J. L. and Carvalho, J. A. 1972. "Hambre y enfermedad en Salamanca. Estudio de la repercusión de la crisis de subsistencia de 1803–1805 en Salamanca," *Asclepio*, 24, 225–266.

Peset, J. L. Mancebo, P., and Peset, M. 1971. "Temores y defensa de España frente a la peste de Marsella de 1720," *Asclepio*, 23, 131–189.

Peset, J. L. and Peset, M. 1972. *Muerte en España (política y sociedad entre la peste y el cólera)*. Madrid, Seminarios y Ediciones.

1978. "Epidemias y sociedad en la España del Antiguo Régimen," *Estudios de Historia Social*, 4, 7–28.

1968. "Salarios de Médicos, cirujanos y médico-cirujanos rurales en España durante la primera mitad del siglo xix," *Asclepio*, 20, 235–245.

Peyron, J. F. 1783. *Nouveau voyage en Espagne fait en 1777 et 1778*, 2 vols. London, Chez P. Elmsly.

Philips, C. R. 1979. *Ciudad Real 1500–1700. Growth, Crisis, and Readjustment in the Spanish Economy*. Cambridge, MA, Harvard University Press.

1987. "Time and duration: A model for the economy of early modern Spain," *American Historical Review*, 92, 3, 531–562.

Pindyck, R. S. and Rubinfeld, D. L. 1981. *Econometric Models and Economic Forecasts*. New York, McGraw Hill.

Pineda, Juan de. 1589. *Diálogos familiares de la agricultura cristiana*. Salamanca.

Pitt Rivers, J. A. 1961. *The People of the Sierra*. London, Weidenfeld and Nicolson.

Pla Alberola, P. J. 1987. "Familia y matrimonio en la Valencia moderna. Apuntes para su estudio" in Casey, J. et al., *La familia en la España mediterránea (siglos XV–XIS)*. Barcelona, Editorial Crítica, pp. 94–128.

Ponz, A. 1789. *Viage de España en que se da noticia de las cosas mas apreciables, y dignas de saberse, que hay en ella*. 18 vols. Madrid, viuda de Ibarra, Hijos y Compañía; facsimile edition by Ediciones Atlas, Madrid, 1972.

Post, J. D. 1976. "Famine, mortality and epidemic disease in the process of modernization," *Economic History Review*, 2nd series, 39, 14–37.

1977. *The Last Great Subsistence Crisis in the Western World*. Baltimore and London, The Johns Hopkins University Press.

1985. *Food Shortage, Climatic Variability, and Epidemic Disease in Preindustrial Europe. The Mortality Peak of the Early 1740s*. Ithaca and London, Cornell University Press.

Poussou, J. P. 1983. *Bordeaux et le sud-ouest au XVIIIᵉ siècle; croissance économique et attraction urbaine*. Paris, Editions de l'Ecole des Hautes Études en Sciences Sociales.

Poza Martín, M. C. 1985. "Nupcialidad y fecundidad en Valle de Tabladillo entre 1787 y 1860. Una nota de investigación," *Boletín de la Asociación de Demografía Histórica*, 3, 2, 32–50.

Quadrado, J. M. and Fuente, V. de la. 1853–1885 (1978). *Guadalajara y Cuenca*. Barcelona, Ediciones Al Albir.

Ravenstein, E. G. 1885–1889. "The laws of migration," *Journal of the Royal Statistical Society*, 48 (June 1885), 167–227; 52 (June 1889), 241–301.

Reher, D. S. 1980. "La crisis de 1804 y sus repercusiones demográficas: Cuenca (1775–1825)," *Moneda y Crédito*, 154, 35–72.

1983. "Historia demográfica y social de la ciudad de Cuenca en la edad moderna," Doctoral dissertation defended at the Facultad de Historia, Universidad Complutense de Madrid.

1986. "Desarrollo urbano y evolución de la población: España 1787–1930," *Revista de Historia Económica*, 4, 1, 39–66.

1987. "Old issues and new perspectives: household and family within an urban context in nineteenth-century Spain," *Continuity and Change*, 2 (1), 103–143.

1988a. *Familia, población y sociedad en la provincia de Cuenca. 1700–1970*. Madrid, Centro de Investigaciones Sociológicas – Siglo xxi.

1988b. "Household and family on the Castilian Meseta: The province of Cuenca from 1750 to 1970," *Journal of Family History*, 13, 1, 000–000.

1989a. "Urbanization and demographic behavior in Spain, 1860–1930" in van der Woude, A., de Vries, J., and Hayami, A. (eds.), *Urbanization in History. A Process of Dynamic Interactions*. Oxford University Press.

1989b. "Population and economy in eighteenth-century Mexico: An analysis of short-term fluctuations," Paper given at the Conference on the Population History of Latin America, organized by the International Union for the Scientific Study of Population (IUSSP), Ouro Preto, Brazil.

Reher, D. S. and Sanz, C. 1982. "Un archivo histórico en ordenador: vaciado, estructuración y validación de la información," *Revista Internacional de Sociología*, 41, 7–26.

Reisman, L. 1964. *The Urban Process: Cities in Industrial Societies*. New York, Free Press.

Richards, T. 1983. "Weather, nutrition, and the economy: Short-run fluctuations in births, deaths and marriages, France 1740–1909," *Demography*, 20, 2, 197–212.

Riera, Juan. 1977. "Noticias de una epidemia segoviana de viruela (1740–41)," *Asclepio*, 39, 310–315.

Riera, J. and Jiménez Muñoz, J. M. 1977. "El doctor Rossell y los temores en España por la peste de Milán (1629–1631)," *Asclepio*, 29, 283–295.

Ringrose, D. R. 1970. *Transportation and Economic Stagnation in Spain, 1750–1850*. Durham, Duke University Press.

1983. *Madrid and the Spanish Economy, 1560–1850*. Berkeley, University of California Press.

1988. "Poder y beneficio. Urbanización y cambio en la historia," *Revista de Historia Económica*, 6, 2, 375–396.

Robin, J. 1980. *Elmdon: Continuity and Change in a Northwest Essex Village, 1861–1964*. Cambridge University Press.

Rodríguez, L. 1973a. "El motín de Madrid de 1766," *Revista de Occidente*, 121, 29–49.

1973b. "Los motines de 1766 en provincias," *Revista de Occidente*, 122, 183–207.

Rodríguez Cancho, M. 1981. *La villa de Cáceres en el siglo XVIII (Demografía y sociedad)*. Cáceres, Caja de Ahorros.

Rodríguez Galdo, M. J. 1977. "Hambre y enfermedad en Galicia a mediados del siglo XIX," *Asclepio*, 29, 331–342.

Rodríguez Sánchez, A. 1977. *Cáceres: Población y comportamientos demográficos en el siglo XVI*. Cáceres, Aula de Cultura de la Caja de Ahorros y Monte de Piedad de Cáceres.

Rowland, R. 1987a. "Nupcialidade, familia, mediterraneo," *Boletín de la Asociación de Demografía Histórica*, 5, 3, 41–63.

1987b. "Mortalidad, movimientos migratorios y edad de acceso al matrimonio en la Península Ibérica," *Boletín de la Asociación de Demografía Histórica*, 5, 3, 41–63.

1988. "Sistemas matrimoniales en la Península Ibérica (siglos XVI–XIX): una perspectiva regional" in Pérez Moreda, V. and Reher, D. S., *Demografía Histórica en España*. Madrid, Ediciones El Arquero, 72–137.

Ruiz Martín, F. 1967. "La población española al comienzo de los tiempos modernos," *Cuadernos de Historia*. Anexos de la revista *Hispania*, 1, 189–207.

1970. "La Banca en España hasta 1782" in *El Banco de España. Una historia económica*. Madrid, Banco de España.

Saavedra Fajardo, D. 1640. *Idea de un Príncipe Político Cristiano* (republished by Editorial Aguilar in *Obras Completas*, with introduction and notes by A. González Palencia, Madrid, 1946).

Salas Auséns, J. A. 1981. *La población en Barbastro en los siglos XVI y XVII*. Zaragoza, Institución "Fernando el Católico."

Sanz Sampelayo, J. 1980. *Granada en el siglo XVIII*. Granada, Diputación Provincial.

1982. "Estudio de la población de Granada en el primer tercio del siglo xix (1808–1833). Desarrollo cuantitativo, movimientos migratorios y estructura socio-profesional" in Eiras Roel, A. (ed.), *Actas del III Coloquio de Metodología Histórica Aplicada*. Santiago de Compostela.

Sarrialh, J. 1954. *L'Espagne eclairée de la seconde moitié du XVIIIe siècle*. Paris, Impr. nationale.

Schmidtbauer, P. 1983. "The changing household: Austrian household structure from the seventeenth to the early twentieth century" in Wall, R. (ed.), *Family Forms in Historic Europe*. Cambridge University Press, pp. 347–407.

Schofield, R. S. 1970. "Age specific mobility in an eighteenth century rural English parish," *Annales de Démographie Historique*, 261–273.

1985. "The impact of scarcity and plenty on population change in England, 1541–1871" in Rotberg, R. I. and Rabb, T. K. (eds.), *Hunger and History, the Impact of Changing Food Production and Consumption Patterns on Society*. Cambridge University Press, pp. 67–93.

1989. "Family structure, demographic behaviour and economic growth" in Walter J. and Schofield, R., (eds.), *Famine, disease and social order in early modern society*, Cambridge University Press, pp. 279–304.

Schultz, T. P. 1986. "Short-term changes in economic and demographic variables: Comparisons of preindustrial English and Swedish time series using alternative statistical frameworks," paper presented at the *Ninth International Economic History Conference*. Berne, Switzerland.

Segalen, M. 1977. "The family cycle and household structure: five generations in a French village," *Journal of Family History*, 223–236.

Sharlin, A. 1978. "Natural decrease in early modern cities: a reconsideration,"*Past and Present*, 79, 126–138.

1986. "Urban–rural differences in fertility in Europe during the demographic transition" in Coale, Ansley, J. and Watkins, Susan Cotts, *The Decline of Fertility in Europe*. Princeton University Press, pp. 234–260.

Sieder, R., and Mitterauer, M. 1983. "The reconstruction of the family life course: theoretical problems and empirical results" in Wall, R. (ed.), *Family Forms in Historic Europe*. Cambridge University Press, pp. 309–405.

Sjoberg, G. 1960. *The Preindustrial City*. New York, Free Press.

Smith, C. A. 1982. "Modern and premodern urban primacy," *Comparative Urban Research*, 11, 79–96.

1989. "Types of city-size distributions: a comparative analysis" in van der Woude, A., de Vries, J., and Hayami, A. (eds.), *Urbanization in History. A Process of Dynamic Interactions*. Oxford University Press.

Smith, J. E. 1981. "How first marriage and remarriage markets mediate the effects of declining mortality on fertility" in Dupâquier, J. *et al.* (eds.), *Marriage and Remarriage in Populations of the Past*. London–New York, Academic Press, pp. 229–246.

1984. "Widowhood and ageing in traditional English society," *Ageing and Society*, 4.

Smith, R. M. 1981a. "Fertility, economy and household formation in England over three centuries," *Population and Development Review*, 7, 4, 595–622.

1981b. "The people of Tuscany and their families in the fifteenth century: medieval or Mediterranean?", *Journal of Family History*, 6, 1, 107–128.

1983. "Hypothèses sur la nuptialité en Angleterre aux xiiie–xive siècles," *Annales, E. S. C.*, 1, 107–136.

(ed.) 1984a. *Land Kinship and Life Cycle*. Cambridge University Press.

1984b. "Some issues concerning families and their property in rural England 1250–1800" in Smith, R. M. (ed.), *Land Kinship and Life Cycle*. Cambridge University Press, pp. 1–73.

1988. "Welfare and management of demographic uncertainty" in Keynes, M., Coleman, D., and Dimsdale, N. (eds.), *The Political Economy of Health and Welfare*. New York, Macmillan Press, pp. 108–135.

Soler Serratosa, J., 1985. "Demografía y sociedad en Castilla la Neuva durante el Antiguo Régimen: la villa de Los Molinos, 1620–1730," *Revista Española de Investigaciones Sociológicas*, 32, 141–192.

Soubeyroux, J. 1978. "Paupérisme et rapports sociaux à Madrid au XVIIIème siècle," Dissertation presented at the University of Montpellier, Paris, Diffusion Librairie Honoré Champion.

Stephenson, C. 1979. "A gathering of strangers? Mobility, social structure, and political participation in the formation of nineteenth-century American workingclass culture" in Cantor, M. (ed.), *American Working-class Culture*. Westport, Connecticut, Greenwood Press, pp. 31–60.

Stouffer, S. A. 1962. *Social Research to Test Ideas*. New York, The Free Press of Glencoe.

Thomas, R. N. and Hunter, J. M. (eds.) 1980. *Internal Migration Systems in the Developing World; with Special Reference to Latin America*. Boston, G. K. Hall & Co.

Todaro, M. 1976. "Rural–urban migration, unemployment and job probabilities: recent theoretical and empirical research" in Coale, A. J. (ed.), *Economic Factors in Population Growth*. New York, John Wiley and Sons, pp. 367–385.

Troitiño Vinuesa, M. A. 1982. "La epidemia colérica de 1885 en Cuenca," *Revista Olcades*, 9, 135–151.

1984. *Cuenca; Evolución y crisis de una vieja ciudad castellana*. Madrid, Universidad Complutense.

United Nations. 1983. *Manual X. Indirect Techniques for Demographic Estimation*. New York.

Valero Lobo, A. 1984. "Edad media de acceso al matrimonio en España. Siglos xvi–xix," *Boletín de la Asociación de Demografía Histórica*, 2, 2, 39–48.

Vilar, P. 1962. *La Catalogne dans l'Espagne moderne*, 3 vols. Paris.

1965. "Quelques problèmes de démographie historique en Catalogne et en Espagne," *Annales de Démographie Historique*, 11–30.

1972. "El motín de Esquilache y las crisis del Antiguo Régimen," *Revista de Occidente*, 107, 199–249.

Villalba, J. de. 1802. *Epidemiología española, o historia cronológica de las pestes, contagios, epidemias y epizootias que han acaecido en España desde la venida de los cartagineses hasta el año 1801*. Madrid.

Vincent, B. 1969. "Les pestes dans le royaume de Grenade aux XVIᵉ et XVIIᵉ siècles," *Annales, E. S. C.,* 6.
  1976. "La peste atlántica de 1596–1602," *Asclepio,* 28, 5–25.
  1977. "Las epidemias en Andalucía durante el siglo XVI", *Asclepio,* 29, 351–358.
Wall, R. 1978. "On the age at leaving home," *Journal of Family History,* 3, 2, 181–202.
  (ed.), 1983a. *Family Forms in Historic Europe.* Cambridge University Press.
  1983b. "Introduction" in Wall, R. (ed.), *Family Forms in Historic Europe.* Cambridge University Press, pp. 1–65.
  1986. "Work, welfare and the family: an illustration of the adaptive family economy" in Bonfield, L., Smith, R. M., and Wrightson, K. (eds.), *The World We Have Gained,* Oxford, Blackwell, pp. 261–294.
Walle, E. van de. 1976. "Household dynamics in a Belgian village. 1847–1866," *Journal of Family History,* 1, 80–94.
  1978. "Alone in Europe: the French fertility decline until 1850" in Tilly, Charles (ed.), *Historical Studies in Changing Fertility.* Princeton University Press, pp. 257–288.
Walter, J. and Schofield, R. 1989. "Famine, disease and crisis mortality in Early Modern society" in Walter, J. and Schofield, R. S. (eds.), *Famine, disease and social order in early modern society.* Cambridge University Press, pp. 1–74.
Watkins, S. C. 1981. "Regional patterns of nuptiality in Europe, 1870–1960," *Population Studies,* 32, 2, 199–215.
Weir, D. 1984a. "Rather never than late: Celibacy and age at marriage in English cohort fertility," *Journal of Family History,* 9, 4, 340–354.
  1984b. "Life under pressure: France and England, 1680–1870," *Journal of Economic History,* 44, 1, 27–47.
Weisser, M. 1973. "The decline of Castile revisited: The case of Toledo," *Journal of European Economic History,* 2, 615–640.
Wilcox, P. 1982. "Marriage, mobility and domestic service in Victorian Cambridge," *Local Population Studies,* 29, 19–34.
Wilson, C. 1984. "Natural fertility in pre-industrial England, 1600–1799," *Population Studies,* 38, 2, 225–240.
World Health Organization. 1948. *Manual of the International Statistical Classification of Diseases, Injuries and Causes of Death,* 2 vols. New York.
Woude, A. van der. 1982. "Population developments in the northern Netherlands (1500–1800) and the validity of the 'urban graveyard' effect," *Annales de démographie historique,* 55–75.
Woude, A. van der, de Vries, J., and Hayami, A. (eds.) 1989. *Urbanization in History. A Process of Dynamic Interactions.* Oxford University Press.
  1989b. "Introduction: the hierarchies, provisionment and demographic patterns of cities" in van der Woude, A., de Vries, J., and Hayami, A. (eds.), *Urbanization in History. A Process of Dynamic Interactions.* Oxford University Press.
Wrigley, E. A. 1967. "A simple model of London's importance in changing English society and economy 1650–1750," *Past and Present,* 37, 44–70.
  1978. "Parasite or stimulus: The town in a pre-industrial economy" in Abrams, P. and Wrigley, E. A. (eds.), *Towns in Societies. Essays in Economic History and Historical Sociology.* Cambridge University Press, pp. 295–309.

1981. "Population history in the 1980s," *The Journal of Interdisciplinary History*, 12, 207–226.

1985. "The fall of marital fertility in nineteenth-century France: Exemplar or exception?" (Parts 1 and 2), *European Journal of Population*, 1, 31–60, 141–177.

1985. "Urban growth and agricultural change: England and the Continent in the Early Modern Period," *Journal of Interdisciplinary History*, 15, 683–728.

1987. *People, Cities and Wealth*. Oxford, Basil Blackwell.

1989. "Brake or accelerator? Urban growth and population growth before the industrial revolution" in Van der Woude, A., De Vries, J., and Hayami, A. (eds.), *Urbanization in History. A Process of Dynamic Interactions*. Oxford University Press.

Wrigley, E. A. and Schofield, R. 1981. *The Population History of England, 1541–1871; A Reconstruction*, London, E. Arnold.

1983. "English population history from family reconstitution: Summary results, 1600–1799," *Population Studies*, 37, 2, 157–184.

Yun Casalilla, B. 1980. *Crisis de subsistencias y conflictividad social en Córdoba a principios del siglo XVI*. Córdoba, Diputación Provincial.

Zarate, A. and Unger de Zarate, A. 1975. "On the reconciliation of research findings of migrant–nonmigrant fertility differentials in urban areas," *International Migration Review*, 9, 2, 115–156.

Zipf, G. K. 1949. "The P_1P_2/D hypothesis: On the intercity movement of persons," *American Sociological Review*, 11, 677–686.

Zubiri Vidal, F. and Zubiri de Salinas, R. 1981. *Epidemias de peste y cólera morbo-asiática en Aragón: Zaragoza, 1652 y 1685; Caspe, 1834; Alcañiz y Jaca, 1885*. Zaragoza, C. S. I. C.

Zuiches, J. J. 1980. "Migration methods and models: a demographic perspective" in Thomas, R. N. and Hunter, J. M. (eds.), *Internal Migration Systems in the Developing World; With Special Reference to Latin America*. Boston, G. K. Hall & Co.

Index